MW00938527

THROUGH
THE
RED DOOR

THROUGH THE RED DOOR

The Eternal Season of Coach Clink and the Division II Chico State Wildcats

Carson Medley

Copyright © 2018 Carson Medley
All rights reserved.
ISBN: 1979933286
ISBN-13: 9781979933285
Library of Congress Control Number: 2017918346
CreateSpace Independent Publishing Platform
North Charleston, South Carolina

Dedication

To everyone who pursues their dream and works to hone his or her craft,
day in and day out, behind closed doors.

"A man who views the world the same at fifty as he did at twenty has wasted thirty years of his life."

—Muhammad Ali

Table of Contents

PART II:

STARTING LINE UP

PART III:

PRESEASON

PART IV:

THE SEASON

PART V:

POSTSEASON

Acknowledgements

I WOULD LIKE TO THANK Coach Greg Clink for allowing me to become a Division II basketball tourist and follow him around for the last three years and putting up with my chasing him around with a pen, Moleskin, legal pad, my blue book, recorder, and camera. Coach Lucas Gabriel and Coach Justin Blake taught me a lot about the game of basketball, and they provided much of the material for this book by getting beneath the crawl space of a college basketball team, on their hands and knees with a flashlight, doing the jobs that no one else wants to do. I would not have material for a book were it not for the 2015-2016 Chico State Wildcats men's basketball players that grace the pages of this book. A book only scratches the surface of the work ethic, courage, endurance, integrity, and the brotherhood that these young men displayed throughout my time with them. I thank them for allowing me to enter their space—to walk through the Red Door with them on Friday and Saturday nights—and I thank them for making me feel like a part of the team. I am also grateful for the insight that Coach Chris Cobb, Coach Jay Flores, and Coach Gus Argenal provided about the program they helped build. A big shout out to former Chico State basketball players Jake Lovisolo, Amir Carraway, Sean Park, Terrence Pellum, Chris Sharp, Rashad Parker, Damario Sims, Jon Baird, Robert Ash, and Roderick Hawkins for the gathering at Coach Clink's house a few years ago that launched the first sentence of this project. Thank you to Courtney Gray for allowing me to interrupt her busy Saturday morning jewelry business at Famers Market as I looked for an inside scoop, and lots of high fives to the Clink boys—Justin, Tyler, and Ryan for all their smiles and keen interest in my writing process.

I am grateful to Athletic Director Anita Barker for her support of the project. I also don't know where this book would be without the help of my favorite sports writer, Chico State Sports Information Director Luke Reid. His rich, detailed, and creative stories provided much of the historical backstory of the Chico State basketball program as presented in this book. Luke's writing filled in the gaps for all those moments in Chico State basketball history that helped me understand and present to you the what, where, when, and why components of Coach Clink's program, while Coach Clink gave me the how part. Together, Coach Clink and Luke Reid were the Michael Jordan and Scottie Pippen of the book. Mike Baca played a huge role by feeding my imagination on those nights when I couldn't travel with the team. Mike is a repository of Chico State athletics knowledge, and I had the pleasure of sitting behind him for all the home games. I always knew I had a writing moment whenever Baca would raise his arms and his chair at the scorer's table would roll back and almost crush my foot.

Thank you Rory Miller for handing me stat sheets at every game. I would like to express my gratitude to Chico State Hall of Famer and team manager Tommy Wigton for providing me with his insight and the long view of Chico State basketball—having served under Coach Puck Smith (when Coach Clink was a player) and now under Coach Clink. Tommy, you inspire me. Art Cox, thanks for the sandwich advice. Noon Cats, I love y'all, miss playing with you, and the last line of the book marks the official retirement of Mississippi Flash.

I would like to thank Lee Litvin and Ricky Delgado-Martinez, the team managers, who were my sidekicks in the locker room and in the tunnel by the Red Door; it is the unsung deeds of these young men—along with the Black Shirts, and you know who you are—that serve as a pulse to the book. I would like to thank Tom Spock, the athletic trainer, for filling me in on his world. I knew nothing about collegiate athletic training prior to meeting him. I would like to thank the fans for inspiring me to continue with this project when I thought I could not push any harder. Every writer needs an audience, and the entire time I was composing the book you were in my mind's eye. David Day, my spiritual mentor, filled my soul with sweetness and light for almost three year during the struggle to write this book. I might still be combing line through line with a metal detector, stuck on my 23rd draft, were it not for Gina Ursini, the night owl, throwing on her jersey late in the second half to help edit the book, give it shape, and pick up the pieces. I would like to thank both sets of my Chico family. Thank you Dan and Sue Wagner (Acker-Backers) for introducing me to Chico State basketball and bringing me to witness that three-second play by Robert Duncan, then just a freshman, that planted the seed for this book. I would also like to thank Anne Yates and Patrick Proctor for bending their ear for these last three years as I went on and on about my project; they also helped out almost every other weekend with my children during the last three years as I was not only writing this book but also working toward my doctorate. I would like to thank my father for letting me join my first YMCA basketball team when money was tight, my mother for always telling me I would be the next Larry Bird, and my grandmother for giving me a Larry Bird basketball every Christmas for as long as I can remember.

Finally, I would like to thank the three most important people in my life—my wife, Julia, son, Holden, and daughter, Beatrix. I apologize to you three for cutting short our Friday and Saturday nights so I could pursue this book dream, but now that it's complete, we can all go to the home games together. You know I love basketball, but basketball is a distant second to the love I have for all you. You are *my* Red Door.

—Carson Medley

Forewords

Fall 2017

I KNOW THE WORLD THAT Carson Medley portrays in *Through the Red Door*, a world where head coaches drive players to the games in cramped rental vans. A world where the coaching staff take turns doing coin-operated laundry when on the road. A world where head coaches play exhibition games against Division I schools to raise money to pay their staff, and a world where head coaches and assistant coaches are like a revolving door as the picayune wages they are paid necessitates looking for a place where the grass is greener. However, money aside, the grass *is* greener in the world of Coach Greg Clink as Medley reveals. How do I know this? Well, I have seen a lot of college basketball in the last thirty-something years. I have been a college basketball gypsy and traveled many paths.

Some may remember me as the young UCLA basketball head coach with the slicked back hair who, in 1996 at the tender age of 32, took the reins of the Bruins program. After 12 years (1991-2003) coaching at UCLA, I traded my whistle for a microphone and transitioned to ESPN/ABC as a college basketball analyst. After seven enjoyable years at the Disney Corporation, learning the sports television business as a college basketball analyst, I chose to return to the sidelines for a second tour of duty as the head coach at St. John's University. My marching orders were to return a once-storied program that had fallen on hard times back to the top of the Big East. We got the Johnnies back into the NCAA tournament in 2011. I was sidelined from coaching during the 2011-2012 season as I recovered from my cancer treatments, a battle well chronicled by the media. My father passed in 2013, and after leading the Johnnies to the postseason four times in five years, including two NIT appearances (2013, 2014) and two NCAA tournaments (2011, 2015), I was let go by St. John's and replaced by Chris Mullin in March 2015. In spite of some unforeseen circumstances and challenges, my time coaching exceptional young men at St. John's made for a most rewarding experience in the Big Apple. Most recently, I have been back in the broadcast booth covering college hoops for Fox Sports and the Pac-12 Network during the college basketball season and CBS/Turner at March Madness time. But long before this journey began, I was just a kid who loved the game of basketball. I would eventually walk the same path as Chico State Coach Greg Clink as a Division II college basketball player with marginal talent, riding the pine yet aspiring to coach.

My love affair with basketball began in my earlier years at lower levels, playing on teams at Ross Grammar School, Sir Francis Drake High School, San Francisco State University, and Chapman College. I was fortunate during my formative years as a basketball player in junior high, high school, and college to have coaches who imparted helpful knowledge: Dan Morena, George Lewis, Pete Hayward, Lyle Damon, and Kevin Wilson. All these coaches were mentors who instilled confidence and provided vital life lessons through the sport of basketball; they were teachers that helped inspire my pursuit of coaching as a vocation. Coach Clink's journey was not that much different than mine, one of many reasons why Medley's *Through the Red Door* resonates with me.

Coach Clink and I took parallel roads to break into coaching. The only real difference is that I went the Division I route, and Coach Clink took the Division II route. Coach Clink received sound advice from one of his mentors: write to the coaches whom you respect, and see if they will let you learn the craft from them. Clink adhered to the advice, eventually landing with Coach Bob Williams, who took the young, aspiring coach under his wing.

Clink took notes, filled up as many pages of legal pad paper as he could, and asked endless questions.

In a similar fashion to Clink, as a student at Chapman College with aspirations of becoming a coach, I, too, began writing letters to some of the best basketball teachers in the game and asked for career advice. I was pleasantly surprised to receive responses from some of the most respected names in the business: Bob Knight, Gene Keady, Mike Krzyzewski, Tim Grgurich, Bud Presley, Mike Legarza, and Mike Dunlap. Indiana University head coach Bob Knight and Purdue head coach Gene Keady were especially helpful. After a period of corresponding with Coach Knight and Coach Keady, they granted me the opportunity to visit their respective basketball programs to sit in and observe practices, video sessions, and team meetings over a four-week period during the 1987-1988 season. My experience at Indiana University and Purdue University was essentially a crash-course on college coaching, my maiden voyage into the world of what it takes to become a college basketball coach.

Coincidentally, Coach Clink did the same thing. When he was young and starting out, he would spend the month of July in Newport Beach sleeping on the couch of his friend Tim Cleary, who was at the time an assistant at UC Irvine. While Bob Williams first opened the door to the coaching profession for Coach Clink, it was Gene Keady in 1988 who first opened the door for me. Coach Keady—who by the time he retired had taken the Boilermakers to the NCAA tournament 18 times —hired me as a graduate assistant at Purdue University. After working for the Boilermakers from 1988-1991, UCLA head coach Jim Harrick provided me with the opportunity of a lifetime. In 1991, he asked me to come back out to the West Coast and join his UCLA staff.

See, what a lot of people might not have known at the time (1996) was that UCLA didn't just throw me the keys and ask the kid to start driving the Bruins bus. I started out at the bottom and slowly worked my way up—not unlike Coach Clink and the assistants present within the pages of *Through the Red Door*. Coach Harrick hired me as an entry-level assistant coach. I then moved up the ranks to third assistant, to second assistant, and finally to first assistant in 1996. Shortly before the start of the 1996-97 season, in a twist of fate, Jim Harrick was fired by UCLA just one campaign removed from having won the 1995 NCAA Championship—the first since 1975 and the only title not won by Bruins Coach John Wooden. When Coach Harrick was dismissed, UCLA administrators elevated me to interim head coach before commencing a national search for a permanent replacement. Just a few months later in February of that 1996-97 season with our team sitting atop the Pac-10 Conference standings, the UCLA brass ceased the national search and lifted my "interim" tag, announcing me as the Bruins permanent head coach. As Medley will describe in his book about how Coach Clink learned life-changing lessons from Coach Puck Smith and Coach Bob Williams, one of the aspects I treasure most from my 12 years coaching at UCLA was the time spent learning from John Wooden. Coach Wooden's life teachings were informative, enlightening, and inspiring.

I first met the author Carson Medley when the Chico State Wildcats played the University of Arizona in an exhibition game on November 8, 2015. Just prior to our Pac-12 Network broadcast, Medley introduced himself and spoke to me briefly about a book he was writing. Spending most of the past 30 years in Los Angeles and New York, I've been around quite a few people "writing a book." Something about Medley struck me as authentic, original, and informed—texting me throughout the game with details on all the different players, particularly one player named Robert Duncan who he claimed was the "Pistol Pete of Division II" basketball. I was impressed with the skill, chemistry, and grit on display by the Wildcats. At the conclusion of the game, Medley introduced me to some of the young Chico State players. The few moments shared with the players reminded of me of my time as a Division II basketball player.

Medley resurfaced a few years later by reaching out through email. He shared that he had completed his book, and asked if I would consider writing a foreword. He believed because of my particular experiences in basketball that I would appreciate and understand the essence of his book. Not long after I moved back to San Francisco from Manhattan, I invited Medley down for a visit. We met at a local haunt and talked more in-depth about his book. He brought twenty or so photographs that he had taken during the season. The photos reminded me of the kind of photographs Edward Hopper would have taken if photography rather than painting had been his medium, and his subject of choice was basketball rather than capturing places where interesting lighting brought forth haunting beauty. Medley's photographs were of stark lockers; players grooming in the training room before an ESPN 3 appearance; scuffed, banged up walls where the players view film; a makeshift college band I could only imagine was playing a bad rendition of some Journey song; Coach Clink and his staff meeting during the half in a room filled with outdated workout equipment; and coaches on their hands and knees scrubbing their players' sweat off the floor. Medley also brought to our meeting the two books he said served as both the models and the bookends for the book he wanted to write: *The Courting of Marcus Dupree* by Willie Morris and John Feinstein's *A Season on the Brink*. "But what I really aimed to do," he told me, "was write the *Friday Night Lights* version of college basketball."

Medley has done just that. If you yearn for the days of college basketball when it was local, intimate, pure, and the uniforms were without corporate logos on them, this is the book for you. The student-athletes that Medley depicts often work part-time jobs in addition to their full-time job as student-athletes. This is a world where an assistant coach works for free and bartends at Round Table Pizza at night while also trying to finish his undergraduate degree. It is a book that serves as a reality check for all college basketball players, particularly those in Division I programs who might take for granted what a privilege it is to ride on a luxury bus or fly to games let alone have an academic advisor that travels with the team.

Through the Red Door is also important for anyone who wants to become a leader. Medley shows the 'rags to riches' story of how Coach Clink turned an underfunded, struggling basketball program into an elite Division II program. More importantly, the great majority of student-athletes that play for Coach Clink leave the university with a college degree. As that wonderful banged-up Red Door on the cover of the book metaphorically portrays, the young men in this book both literally and figuratively move through the door and go beyond. Medley told me he wanted to write a book that transcended basketball. He has done it. Basketball is just a way into the story. The reader learns how Coach Clink built his program by establishing a culture that amplifies the value of work, cohesion, family, and integrity. Coach Clink instills the timeless fundamentals of life that translate to any aspect of life—whether it's a class room or corporate conference room—and assists his players in sharpening their leadership traits.

None of the players you will read about in this book will play in the NBA. Some might go on to have successful careers playing professionally overseas, but you will not have an opportunity to see them play on television. As Medley writes early in the book, "These Division II players are a lot more like you and me." Reading this book for me triggered memories that captured the most refreshing and compelling aspects of life in Division II basketball. It's the purity of small college athletics that resonates most. This book is about as feel-good and earnest in content as it gets; there's not even profanity in it.

Finally, in my 12 years at UCLA, Coach Wooden shared so many helpful lessons that resonated in profound ways. Here are just a few: *Being humble in victory and gracious in defeat; The most powerful form of teaching is rooted in one's actions and deeds—leading by example; The best thing we can do for those we love is to not do for them what they are capable of doing for themselves; Never mistake activity for achievement.* These are just a few pearls of wisdom Coach Wooden shared with me over the years. I still have yellow notepads and his handwritten letters full of his teachings, adages, observations, and quotes. He was a unique human being. I think you will find that Coach Clink's leadership style and his relationships with his current and former players will provide similar inspiration and helpful lessons. I imagine that for many of his players, Coach Clink is their John Wooden.

I am thankful someone has finally written a book that shines a light on this unseen side of college basketball. There is not simply one shining moment here but hundreds of pages worth.

—**Coach Steve Lavin**
Former UCLA and St. John's head men's basketball coach
Basketball Analyst, Fox Sports and Pac -12 Network

Fall 2017

I congratulate Carson Medley for writing a highly successful book that gets it right. *Through the Red Door* presents a great understanding of both the players, the coach, and the world of Division II basketball. The book accomplishes a triple threat. I found myself rooting for the Chico State players, rooting for Coach Clink, and rooting for Medley the writer. I know the stomping grounds and the characters Medley writes about in this sensational book. More than twenty years ago, Greg Clink—when he was in his second year as a graduate assistant at Chico State—wrote a letter to me while I was the head coach at UC Davis. Greg said he had a lot of respect for me and my program and wanted to learn how we do what we do. Later that winter we were coming up to Chico State for a conference game. I approached Greg before the game and invited him down to Davis to have lunch and talk. After we finished lunch, I offered Greg a job.

Fast forward twenty-years. I am not surprised by the success Greg is having at Chico State. What did surprise me, though, when reading this book was the agony Greg feels during games. When Greg was my assistant, I knew him as off-season Greg. When we were in Santa Barbara, he was always body surfing, running on the beach, and enjoying the sunshine. I loved his youthfulness, his energy, his infectious smile, and his positive attitude. He was always a breath of fresh air. He was also a hard-working, diligent, selfless assistant who was above all a student of the game. The only thing that ever irritated me about Greg was my inability to keep him on staff. I lost him twice—once at UC Davis and then again at UC Santa

Barbara. I understood, though, because in this business young assistants have to keep moving if they want to make it. I know that Greg loves coaching and being around the players, but I had no idea that he feels so much pressure during games, and I didn't know the kind of self-induced stress he places upon himself to be great and his wish that games could be more enjoyable. Medley really gets beneath the skin and explores the soul of regular-season Greg and reveals a different side of him.

Greg learned from one of the best. No, I'm not talking about me but the legendary Puck Smith whom Greg played for and would later work under before coming to join my staff at UC Davis and then UC Santa Barbara. When I was at UC Davis and we were in Chico State's league (back then the NCAC), Coach Puck Smith and his Wildcats were the gold standard. I knew Puck well and respected him not only as a basketball coach but also as a man. Puck embodied what I believe it means to be a man. He served with the Long Range Reconnaissance Patrol/Rangers during the one of the bloodiest years in Vietnam, 1968, and was awarded the Bronze Star Medal and Army Commendation Medal for valor. Puck came home and started teaching and coaching. Puck coached at many levels before he got to Chico State in 1987 where he coached for 21 seasons, along the way becoming NCAC Coach of the Year three times, winning four NCAC championships, and taking five of his teams to the NCAA tournament.

So, you wonder from whom the man Medley so accurately portrays in his book received his formal education in coaching, character, leadership, and the development of young men? Although Medley gives me a lot of credit in his book for helping Clink create the culture of success at Chico State, it all started with Puck. And I see a lot of Puck in Greg—the latter whom I met when he was barely 25 years old—now a man in full.

What I have enjoyed most about *Through the Red Door* is the portrayal of the purity that still exists within basketball, a decency that still exists in Division I, Division II, and Division III but often gets tarnished by the scandals in Division I college basketball. *Through the Red Door* has many similarities and reads a lot like John Feinstein's classic *A Season on the Brink* with one glaring difference: Greg Clink is not a tyrant like Bobby Knight. You will not find any chairs being thrown or players being cursed out or shamed in front of their peers throughout these pages. In fact, you won't even find any foul language. But what you will find in this book is a story about one of the good guys in college basketball, and a story about how this coach built a team around a culture grounded in good guys. Chico State has now become the team to beat in not only the CCAA but also the country. Still, even though the team might have a bullseye on their back, it's hard to root against them and their coach.

Through the Red Door would make for a good read and lesson in any coach's syllabus. Although the book covers Division II basketball, with the exception of the Wildcats playing an exhibition game against the University of Arizona, it's the Division I players and coaches who might benefit most from the book. I say this because Medley's book shows the other side of college basketball, one far removed from the bright lights and cameras and *Sports Illustrated* covers and *ESPN* highlight reels and *Bleacher Report* blogs. In these pages, you will find a world not uncommon to many Division II schools where coaches drive team vans and help wash the uniforms and serve as academic advisors to their students and a whole bunch of other tasks. Shoot, in this world, one of Coach Clink's assistants even has to work as a bartender at a pizza joint just to make ends meet—yet this team, just last year, made it to the Elite Eight in the NCAA tournament. Ultimately, the players and the coaches in this book are doing more with less.

Who cares, you still might ask, about Division II basketball players? I'll tell you who cares. Right after we won the Division II National Championship at UC Davis in 1998—going 31-2 without any scholarship players—I was invited to the NCAA Division I Final Four along with the Division III National Championship coach Bo Ryan (who would later coach the Wisconsin Badgers to two straight Final Fours in a row and a National Championship game in 2015) of Wisconsin-Platteville. I was seated at the dais in an interview with Coach Dean Smith of the Tar Heels to my left, and Coach Bo Ryan and Coach Roy Williams to my right. One might think the conversation would have been all about the Tar Heel stars Antwan Jamison and Vince Carter. However, the attention turned to my Division II player, senior Dante Ross. Coach Smith, who had been the in-studio analyst during the game, kept saying during the game broadcast: "What I want to know is how in the world a Division II school got a player like Dante Ross?" I was blown away.

Division II basketball has a lot of players of the Dante Ross caliber. People just don't get to see them because a handful of Division I schools capture most of the media glory. I'll tell you this: In my 19 seasons coaching at UC Santa Barbara in the Big West, I've never seen basketball bodies like the ones I've seen at Division II schools like Kentucky Wesleyan and Virginia Union University. Contrary to what many might think, the level of play at this level exceeds expectations.

The players in this book aren't in the limelight. They are hard-working student-athletes trying their best to balance academics and basketball and walk away in four to five years with a college degree. It doesn't happen all the time, but NBA rosters often do have Division II players—many you've probably heard of: Darrell Armstrong, Manute Bol, George Gervin, Phil Jackson, Caldwell Jones, Jerome Kersey, Rick Mahorn, Earl Monroe, Charles Oakley, Ben Wallace, Dennis Rodman, and Caldwell Jones. The reality is that regardless of the division, not many college basketball players will ever make it into the NBA. Even fewer will become stars. However, all college basketball players have a chance to make it in life. I think this is one of the most important messages in *Through the Red Door*, and one of the most important lessons Greg is teaching at Chico State. There are lots or red doors we enter in life, whether it's a Red Door leading into a gym or a red door leading into the classroom where you teach or the office where you work or the red door that leads you into the house where your family awaits. And as Greg tells his players before they walk through the Red Door that leads them into Acker gym: "Take as much time as you need, but when you walk through that Red Door, you better be ready to get after it."

I hope every educator and coach, whether you're teaching and coaching third graders or high school students or college students, will take this journey with Coach Clink and his Wildcats. I also hope every kid with a dream, and every parent with a dream for their kid, will take this journey with Coach Clink and his Wildcats. The book should be required reading for young coaches so they can see the consistency of Greg's approach and how he handles the business of coaching. And I hope that all those out there who believe that sports don't matter, and who believe that there's no such thing as a student-athlete, will take this journey with Coach Clink and his Wildcats.

So, if you're tired of the diaper dandies and the one-and-done sensations and the scandals turn off the television, get off the internet, and pick up a copy of *Through the Red Door* and be transported back into a world where the game you love still exists. Go to the high school, the community college, or the Division II campus near you and just enjoy basketball for the sake of basketball.

—**Coach Bob Williams**
NCAA Division II National Championship
and Former UC Santa Barbara head coach for 19 years

Fall 2017

Every Tuesday and Thursday at noon there is a group of middle-aged men that get together and play pick-up basketball in Shurmer Gym here on the campus of Chico State University. Shurmer Gym is down the hall from our basketball office. The players that gather call themselves the Noon Cats. For the first few years of my career here, I would poke my head in and say hello. The basketball played here twice a week is some of the worst played basketball in the world, but by a group of the greatest guys around. The group consists of vice presidents, athletic department staff, professors, WREC staff, academic advisors, directors, IT tech staff, deans, etc. One day about four years ago I stuck my head in and they needed an extra player, so I stayed and played. Since that time, I have been a regular in the Tuesday and Thursday Noon Cats game. I have loved every minute of it.

One day during the spring of 2015 I got an email from one of the players in the game, Carson Medley. He sent me a note telling me he wanted to talk to me about a project. I had gotten to know Carson a little bit, but really had no idea what job he performed on campus. All I knew was that he was a writer of some sort. I thought he was probably working on some type of sports piece and wanted input. So we decided we would sit down and chat after the next pick-up game. So I show up that Tuesday, and as I walk in he hands me an envelope and tells me to sit down and read it that afternoon and get back to him.

The envelope contained a proposal for a book that he wanted to write about our basketball program. It detailed his thoughts on our team. He gave me a sample of his writing. After reading the proposal it was obvious Carson could write. I liked the idea of a book being written about our program and Division II basketball. There are a lot of books that have been written about college basketball, but not many, if any, about a Division II program. My only reservation was that I wasn't sure I wanted a writer following us around all season. I wasn't sure that I wanted someone sitting behind the scenes during meetings, film sessions, team meals, and practices documenting everything we said and did.

Carson Medley plays basketball like he lives his life. If I were going to use one word to describe his game, and his life, it would be passion. The man is passionate about everything he does. During the noon pick-up games, he is the first guy to dive on the floor. He mixes it up with the dean of the criminal justice department and pumps his fist in the air after a game winner. He also leads the game in rebounds. Most of the time they come off his own missed shots, but he has a knack for shooting the ball and knowing exactly where it will come off the rim.

It was his passion for this project that ultimately made me decide to let him into our inner circle. Carson sat in the shadows for a year and followed us. He and I conducted several interviews over the course of the year. These were some of the greatest moments because it allowed me to reflect on past years and talk about the former players that gave themselves to the program. Carson sat in on team meetings, film sessions, traveled with us at times, and was a fixture on the sidelines at our practices. What I was once apprehensive about turned into a great experience for us all. We did not tell him what to write in the book. What you are about to read is his account of the 2015-16 basketball season and all of the euphoria and heartbreak that went into it.

—**Greg Clink**
Head Men's Basketball Coach
Chico State Wildcats

Preface

MOST OF BASKETBALL, LIKE LIFE, is about imperfection. This book is mainly about imperfection. The coach, the players, the writer, and the season reveals the pattern of imperfection, the revision, the "do it again" that Coach Clink echoes throughout practice until perfection is finally within grasp. This book is about those fleeting moments of perfection, the ephemeral moment of bliss upon catching the snowflake only to have it instantly melt in your hand. Even though we know the snowflake will melt within a second, we continue our pursuit of it.

I believe Nick Carraway from *The Great Gatsby* said it best: "There are only the pursued, the pursuing, the busy, and the tired." This book is about the pursuing types, the grinders, the basketball players and coaches, the writers—all of us who have the courage and stamina to chase and pursue a dream that will probably not come true yet pursue the dream anyway. It's the air we breathe, and to not pursue our dreams would be to die. Just like the coaches and the team and the season(s) you are about to read about pursued perfection, so, too, did I. I wanted to write a flawless book where the narrative flowed seamlessly, each metaphor was original, each game had you on the edge of your seat, the syntax sizzled, and there were no punctuation gaffes or typos. I believe the image on the cover of the book best represents the chronicling of the journey you are about to take—all the blemishes from the weather-beaten book bag to the old leather ball to the stack of beat up books and to the dented, fingerprint-smudged Red Door itself. A professional photographer did not take the photograph on the book cover, but the Sports Information Director, Luke Reid, a character (and fellow writer) within the book.

If I were to have produced a flawless book, well, that would have been false advertising, wouldn't it? I imagine there will be commas out of place, names possibly misspelled, facts misconstrued, and tangential moments irrelevant to the story. I warn you ahead of time. However, the organic, imperfect nature of writing—the constant revision and pursuit of perfection—is what I love about both writing and basketball. Sport, after all, is unscripted drama. So, too, is the writing process.

A writer, though, not unlike a coach can only do so much with the time he has and within the rules and limits of the game. The writer not unlike a coach tries to maximize the talent he or she has, and both the writer and the coach strive to write the perfect sentence or perfect the jump stop, and capture an original metaphor or draw up and execute the perfect play, or make the right substitution or manage the clock down to the last second.

I tried to write this book in a way that would be timeless. I hope that fifty years from now the book—the season—will still be relevant. As long as there is the game of college basketball, as long as there is a Red Door that generations of young men can walk through and go beyond, the book will persist.

Prologue

Thou still unravish'd bride of quietness,
Thou foster-child of silence and slow time, Sylvan
historian, who canst thus express
A flowery tale more sweetly than our rhyme: What
leaf-fring'd legend haunts about thy shape
Of deities or mortals, or of both,
In Tempe or the dales of Arcady?
What men or gods are these? What maidens loth?
What mad pursuit? What struggle to escape?
What pipes and timbrels? What wild ecstasy?

—John Keats, Ode on a Grecian Urn

Chico State University head men's Division II basketball coach Greg Clink, 44, lives in a regular neighborhood—regular meaning that it's a lot more like the kind of neighborhood that most people in this country live in; the men and women, the fathers and mothers, who get up and go to work every day to support their families. The house, the neighborhood, everything down to the Chevy Silverado that Clink drives symbolizes the basketball teams that he has assembled, the team culture that he has created, a reminder that a Division II coach and Division II student-athletes are a lot more like the rest of us: lifetime grinders.

SATURDAY, APRIL 11

I park across the street from a house where in the driveway stands a humble basketball goal with a ramp attached to the rim that rolls the ball back out to the shooter. Two barefoot kids walk down the sidewalk. One of the boys is carrying a basketball. I roll down the car window.

"Can you tell me where Coach Clink lives?" The two young boys give each other a confused look.

"Right there," the taller boy says, pointing to the house. "He's my dad."

I get out and ring the doorbell. "Come on in," a husky voice bellows. Lining the entry wall are at least a dozen basketball shoes, shoes so long and wide that they look like cross-country skis. These are the shoes of Clink's former players. Big shoes to fill. Clink is in the kitchen slicing and stacking salami and cheese. An ice chest of beer sits sweating outside on the patio. Former players have gathered at Clink's house today because he asked them to—a Who's Who of Chico State basketball under the Clink era have gathered together on a warm Saturday afternoon in April to talk about their experiences in front of some writer whom they've never met.

Some of the former players gathered here were stars. Some hardly played at all. Some of the players gathered here were recruited and coached by Puck

Smith—who spent 21 years at Chico State as the head coach before Clink took over. Others knew only Coach Clink. But the players gathered here are all part of the Clink spectrum, a timeline that stretches from the 2008-2009 season when the Wildcats went 8-19 to the 2014-2015 season when the Wildcats went 22-8 and won the California Collegiate Conference (CCAA).

The former guards huddle comfortably like brothers on the sofa. They've been inside the Clink home before, some on many occasions. This is not just a reunion of a basketball team (some of the men here never even played together), but a reunion of family. Clink serves the food and the players dig in. Jake Lovisolo, Rashad Parker, and Amir Carraway begin to argue about the best recruiting class which segues into an argument about the best backcourt. Clink takes a seat. His youngest son, Ryan, 9, is fired up and wide-eyed about having all the guys here. Ryan proudly wears the 2015 CCAA Champion T-shirt that his father handed out at the recent spring banquet. Clink whispers directions into Ryan's ear, pointing to various players, telling the young boy what to bring them. His other two sons, 11-year-old twins Tyler and Justin, wander in and out of the room. The players joke around with the young Clink kids. They have watched these boys grow up. A cat slinks back and forth and rubs against my legs. The cat pauses and looks up at Clink with condescending eyes. Clink returns the gaze. A stare down ensues. The cat and Clink seem to have an agreement: leave me alone, and I'll leave you alone. I would hate to be that cat in February, when Clink is in the thick of things.

Although the young men remain buffed and in shape, the former Chico State Wildcats look more like recreational league Saturday morning basketball players with college degrees who have joined the ranks of the Monday through Friday 9-to-5 world and gone on to become the stars of the office noon ball game. All but Jay Flores (wearing a blue polo shirt) and Jon Baird (a button up shirt) wear tank tops and have big-time muscular arms and broad shoulders and bowling ball sized deltoids. Damario Sims has cut his dread locks and has a buzzed head—major reversal and recognition from his playing days. Robert Ash could pass for an Abercrombie & Fitch model rather than the Lincoln High School basketball coach. Amir Carraway has the smile of a Hollywood actor, and when he's done playing ball overseas might consider a career in broadcasting. Sean Park wears recreational basketball clothes; he doesn't look nearly as cutthroat and menacing as he did when he wore his Chico State uniform, that taut pale skin that hardly saw the light of day, a gym rat in dire need of a Vitamin D supplement. Clink looks like he might be an older brother rather their former coach.

Ash and Hawkins talk about the early Clink years—the rebuilding years when a CCAA championship seemed miles down the road, if at all. Hawkins has a big personality and seems to be the big brother of the group. He was recruited by and played for Puck Smith for one season. He recalls when Clink was interviewing for the head coach position. "There were five guys that came in and talked to us. Coach was talking to us then all of a sudden he ripped his dress shirt off. Underneath he was wearing a T-shirt from a 1994 CCAA championship. I thought he was crazy. But he explained it to us. He told us he was on that team. Said he wanted the guys to know how much pride he had experienced as a Chico State basketball player and wanted every player in the room to have the same feeling when they left Chico State. And you know what? By the fourth year Coach Clink was here, we got our own CCAA championship shirts."

Chatter floods Clink's house. The living room sounds like a locker room. Coach Clink's wife Courtney—a local artist (jewelry maker) with a huge following—walks in. Everything stops. She says hello to everyone. Every player stands to greet her. She goes around the room for a good five minutes and hugs each player. The players are not hugging her in return because it's the thing they're supposed to do—be nice to the coach's wife. The hugs are authentic. Love drives those hugs. There's a lot of respect here, the kind of respect that's earned, respect that comes from someone being kind and nonjudgmental and accepting to young men for whom the world might not have previously offered such a courtesy.

Courtney takes a seat in the back with her sons. She listens intently as the young men in the room turn reflective. They're no longer trading basketball stories and reliving memories from seasons past: the conversations have turned inward, an exercise in introspection that might shock those whom doubt the emotional depth of high-level athletes. All this talk of the past has allowed them to pause and see just how far they've come from their days when only winning games and going to class mattered. They're now grown men with college degrees and real life responsibilities, young men who will one day have their own families. These young men are blessed to have realized one of the most important lessons in life: Nobody has gotten where they are without the help of someone else. And this someone else is their surrogate father, a man who at one point in their lives was an Old Testament coach/father figure and now a New Testament mentor and father. Yes, he could hurl lightning bolts and cast fire in one breath while yawning the light of grace and faith in the next.

That man is Greg Clink.

Memory—the most potent of elixirs—has turned the basketball reunion into the kind of loving reflection of their time under Clink that one would expect to hear at the funeral of a loved one. Only Clink is in the room, a man in his prime, far from pushing daisies.

I ask a Jake Lovisolo what made playing for Clink so special. "It's what Coach Clink does off the court," Lovisolo says. This young man who barely played at all in his basketball career was hands down, according to every player present, the most inspirational player. Clink will later tell me that Lovisolo set the standard that every player in the program must live up to. He was not only a stellar student but a genuine leader. He was always the first one through the Red Door leading into Acker Gym and the last one to go back through it—a pattern that started day one of his redshirt freshman year. "Coach Clink is influential and impactful," Lovisolo continues. "I can call him up about anything." Lovisolo wipes tears from his eyes. Damario Sims speaks next. He will soon start training to become a correctional officer with the Santa Clara County Sheriff's Department. He has returned home to his 510 roots to try and help others who were once like him, to help others in the way that Clink helped him. "I'm from West Oakland. All my friends were either dead or in jail when I got to Chico State. Coach showed me a different way of life here. We still text each other all the time. He calls me Little Homie. I call him Big Homie. He lets me be myself. Everything he ever told me about life is true."

Jon Baird, who with his soft beard and thoughtful way of speaking makes it hard to believe he was once a great ballplayer, thanks coach for giving him a second chance. Clink allowed Baird back on the team after he had been previously declared academically ineligible. Clink gave him a second chance to prove himself, and he did. "Coach is about pride and appreciation," Baird says. "You always have to wear your Chico State gear in the gym. When you put that jersey on and walk through the Red Door, it's about pride. Yeah, Coach Clink gave me a second chance. A new beginning."

Jay Flores, another former player who looks more like a leisurely golfer than a one-time MVP of the CCAA, says of Clink: "He changed my life. He even introduced me to my future wife. I plan on having Coach marry us." Hawkins, the most talkative and straight shooter of the bunch, booms in. "He's the first guy I called when I got arrested." This is no punchline. Nobody laughs. "Coach is selfless and genuine," Hawkins says. "He puts his players first and makes us better men. This relationship with 12-15 men lasts longer than four seasons. It's for life."

Carraway, never at a loss for words, grows quiet when his turn to speak arrives. He fights back tears. "It's not just that he's a father figure, but it's how he embraces life." He wipes a tear from his eye and looks around at everyone. "Look at us. We're all successful men now."

Sean Park, who looks (and played) as if he had never cried a day in his life, swallows tears. "None of us are going to the NBA," Carraway continues. "Coach prepared us to succeed in life after basketball." Park finally jumps in: "Coach is about loyalty. Give Coach Clink four years, and he'll do whatever is in his power he can do for you for the rest of your life." Ash—the most seemingly edgy and outwardly hard member of the group—turns emotional: "Coach Clink gives you friendship for life. If you go longer than a couple of months without contacting him, he'll get in touch. He texts us all the time. Never longer than three weeks goes by without hearing from him."

The room has grown still. Terrence Pellum, whom I thought had been dozing the entire time with a bottle of beer between his legs, comes to. He tries to speak, but this big man is fighting to catch his breath. He has been listening the entire time. Tears stream down his face. This starts a chain reaction. The room becomes awash in tears. "Coach Clink—I love him. He's always there for us. I didn't have a dad. Coach Clink was like my father. I never had that. He taught me to be selfless." Pellum lowers his head into his large hands, his broad shoulders bouncing up and down.

Hawkins stands up and shuffles over to him. In a matter of seconds, four other former players have embraced him and wrapped their arms around him. Pellum, despite growing up without a father, now has both a father and brothers for life.

If only the legion of people who claim that sports don't matter could be here to witness these shared emotions from young men who had once performed athletically (while also academically and earning a college degree) as most of us can only dream of performing. I, too, have often wondered if sports matter, burned out by the one-and-done nature of collegiate sports today—athletes playing for the name on the back of their jersey rather than the team name on the front. But hearing these stories renews my faith in the infinite positive moral and ethical possibilities of sport. Sports, I'm reminded, have the ability to transcend the game and break down the institutional barriers that keep so many young men and young women from realizing and ever reaching their potential. Sport—unlike higher education—does not exclude on the basis of social or cultural capital but prefers to exchange in the currency of aspirational capital, a currency that overflows in the coffers of Clink's players.

Clink's sons watch in awe. They're too young to fully comprehend the approbations directed toward their father. These kinds of feelings and emotions, these kinds of memories, for now will be packed away in the young subconscious of the Clink boys, ready for retrieval when needed, the vignettes of our life that resurface as we one day recall and write the autobiographies of our lives—works that inevitably always go back to the fathers. It would be unfair and certainly unrealistic to expect the young Clink brothers, the young sons, to understand and grasp the weight of this moment until much later in their lives. Only when Coach Clink has retired and along comes a new young coach to step in and fill the big footprints that he has left on the program, same as he stepped in when filling the big footprints that Puck Smith left, and only when the Clink boys have their own children, will this memory reach its apex and fully emerge. There's a reason young boys look up to their fathers, and there's a reason that the disappointment young boys can have in their fathers weighs so heavily, cuts to the bone, rips the heart asunder. But I doubt there'll be long-term disappointment for the Clink boys. This particular moment in time will trump any of the times down the line when the father might seem to stumble, to falter, as we fathers always do, and no longer remain infallible in the eyes of his offspring and perhaps cast temporary shame into their eyes. The Clink boys, though, will always have this moment, one that has already become an indelible memory. The way those boys looked at their father when Terrence Pellum broke down crying must have bewildered them. How can a man be a father to so many? These are the moments in life that create future leaders, when young men can look to older men and see the application of leadership theories unfold right before their eyes—the perfect interchange of theory and practice. Maybe this is how leaders are made and not necessarily born. Certainly, it is a privilege and advantage to be the sons of a man so respected and loved, but at the same time it cannot be easy.

Even though Clink doesn't push his young sons into things, the standards the boys have seen set by their father on other young men must set his biological sons' imaginary standards high as the heavens. A constant theme in the biographies of great men and women reveal the story of the strong father who did not rule by an iron fist but ruled by example and gentleness. Excellence became a habit, the standard, and winning just became something that was expected—the reason why losses hurt so much more for those whom are accustomed to winning.

To what great heights, then, will the Clink boys soar? To what great further heights will their father soar? To what great heights will Clink's current basketball sons soar—a team loaded with talented freshmen and sophomores who might not yet peak for another three seasons?

For now, there is only the 2015-2016 season. And it's only April.

The start of next season is six months away.

For everyone but Coach Clink.

PART I

Reason Behind The Season

CHAPTER 1

3:43 A.M.

FOR PLAYERS A SEASON BEGINS and a season ends. Then there's all that stuff in between called the off-season. Some players go home and work a summer job. Some players hang around in town and play pick-up ball and work on their strength and conditioning. Coaches, though, at the collegiate level don't have an off-season. Nor do they have a beginning and an ending. Time is continuous. For Coach Greg Clink it's always 3:43 a.m. He wakes up at 3:43 a.m. several times a week during both during the off-season and the regular season. Only one thing can get his mind off basketball: 30-minute sitcoms. Clink loves them. He grew up watching them. *Frasier* is his favorite. It calms his mind. He wakes up, goes out to the couch, and finds *Frasier*

on Netflix. He reclines and closes his eyes and listens to the episodes. "I've seen them all multiple times. I just picture the scenes in my head. Thirty minutes later I'm back to sleep." Clink calls *Frasier* his TV therapist—the only way to relax his mind, get it off basketball, so he can fall back to sleep.

Clink will wake up at 3:43 a.m. on March 14, 2015, less than 12 hours after his young Wildcats have been bounced from the NCAA Division II tournament by California Baptist University, 67-61. However, *Frasier* will not calm his thoughts: *What will I do next year without Jordan Semple? How do I replace the school's career record holder in rebounds (927), blocked shots (153), double-doubles (22,) and games played (126)? He ranked third in steals (139) and sixth in scoring with 1,300 career points. How in the world do I replace that?* But in the midst of his early morning haze, Clink remembers that teams, not players, win championships. And he has one whale of a team coming back. Robert Duncan, only a sophomore, had just been named All-West Region. His talented freshmen foursome will all be sophomores. Christopher Magalotti (Magz), a senior, might finally live up to his 6-foot-11 potential. Drew Kitchens and Tanner Giddings will be seniors. Trevor Priest will be a junior. And all five of those talented redshirt freshmen will be ready to start their four years of eligibility. Clink turns off *Frasier*. He staggers back to bed, falls asleep, visons of cutting down the net after winning the 2016 CCAA regular season championship dancing through his head.

Clink does not blend in well on campus. He looks too young and athletic to be a professor, a little too old to be a student, and way too happy to be an administrator. Possibly an older graduate student switching careers, but upon first meeting him one would not think college basketball coach. The same could be said of many coaches. I think of the late Rick Majerus with his tight-fitting sweaters (and how he lived in a hotel while coaching the Runnin' Utes because he liked the mint the housekeeper put on his pillow each night) and swollen torso. Clink doesn't have the multi-millionaire real estate tycoon slick demeanor of a Rick Pitino, nor the aging handsome gangster looks of a John Calipari. He is not pretty like Reggie Theus, and he's not the George Clooney of college basketball like Jay Wright. Clink is handsome in a rugged, boyish way. It's hard to imagine a guy like him ever getting old. He has the kind of charm and character that a university wants and should promote. He has a winning smile, but the kind of smile that almost seems embarrassed by the greatness, the drive that lives within him. It's also a smile that disappears the second he walks through the Red Door and steps on to the floor of Acker Gym. He has a humble demeanor and acts appreciative for the opportunity he's been given to coach, and he possesses the ultimate basketball voice—gravely and a tad strained. He's a genuinely nice guy, authentic to the bone, and he can work a booster table like none other. But despite his charisma, don't get into the ring and challenge Clink to go toe-to-toe. He'll fight you to the end.

Clink is also in excellent physical shape. He's still young enough to get out and play physical and competitive basketball. On most Tuesdays and Thursdays, he comes out to Shurmer Gym—right down the hall from his office—to play lunch hour ball with an eclectic group of men in their late 30s, 40s, and 50s: we call ourselves the Noon Cats. The men are professors, staff, administrators—all walks of campus life. Clink gets a kick out of running with us old dudes playing a young man's game. The Noon Cats don't discriminate based on ability. If you can hustle for fifty minutes, you're in. Our style of ball is a lot like organic chemistry for students thinking of becoming a doctor; just as organic chemistry is a weed-out class for pre-med students, ball with the Noon Cats is weed-out hour for the middle-age male "athlete." Men who work on campus hear rumors about this group of older men who bang each other up two days a week. Men show up to play—men who underestimate the level of competitiveness we old dudes exude. Most new men who show up only play once or twice and retreat back to their Nautilus machines, indoor track, and swimming pool. Injuries often occur. The old dudes smash and mix it up. Fight for loose balls. Teeth get knocked out. Knees get blown out. Fingers busted. Lips split. More pulled hamstrings than pulled pork down in Dixie on the Fourth of July. Elbows to all body parts—sharp, dirty, John Stockton type of elbows that often draw blood. Players get scratched. Ankles get twisted. Skulls get cracked. Blue and Yellow pinnies stained from sweat, blood, and higher education frustration.

This is basketball's version of *Fight Club*.

The old dudes get knocked down. They get back up. They play hard until 12:50 p.m.

Clink sprints up and down the court. He brings a quiet intensity to the lunch hour game, almost a suppressed competitive spirit clawing to get out and win. He raises the level of play. An old dude once apologized for diving for so many loose balls and his erratic play. Clink looked him dead in the eye: "That's something you can't turn on and off. Don't apologize for it."

Watching Clink play a lunch hour game is a privileged glimpse into the mind of the brilliant coach putting his theories into practice—an opportunity to watch him engage in what academics calls praxis. Clink plays error-free basketball. If he makes a bad pass or takes an errant shot, he yells at himself. It makes him furious. Here in Shurmer Gym playing with these old dudes Clink can experiment and practice the fundamental skills he must pass on to his players. His passes are crisp—always two-handed (the coach in him cannot resist telling one of the old dudes to stray from the one-handed pass). He shoots a jumper with the form of a man doing squats: balanced, back straight, butt out. He doesn't take a bad shot, and he usually takes the high percentage shot beneath the basket. He gets knocked down to the ground like the rest of the old dudes, usually by the intimidating physical force of the Director of the Recreation Center who often confuses basketball with rugby. If the clumsiness of the old dudes frustrates Clink (three men filling one lane on the break; ball handler dribbling to the basket with his head down, four men on him, and clangs the ball off the rim; balls constantly kicked out of bounds; no boxing out; pitching a tent and starting a campfire in the paint; no defense; the constant water breaks; and many other holy violations of the game), he doesn't let them know. Sure, sometimes the coach in him comes out, but he's often just competing with himself.

Clink gets fired-up when the old dudes do something right, and he's quick to lavish praise. He always sprints up and down the court. He has an old habit from his Puck Smith (the legendary Chico State coach and mentor whom Clink replaced) days of touching the sideline with his foot when running down on offense. When Clink shows up to a lunchtime game, every old dude puts his game face on. It's as if all the old dudes have been transported back in time and are trying to make the high school basketball team. The play rises when Clink is around. The play also sinks when he's absent. The old dudes don't play nearly as hard. The game is downright ugly, a beautiful disaster, yet a love letter to the game of basketball.

CHAPTER 2

The Letter

No man is an island, entire of itself; every man is
a piece of the continent, a part of the main.

— JOHN DONNE, NO MAN IS AN ISLAND - MEDITATION XVII

GREAT LEADERS MUST HAVE VISION. Not only can they "see" their goal in their mind's eye, but they make it happen. Basketball players call this "court vision." The great player sees everything on the court not only during a play but before the play unfolds. His head is never down but always up. He sees everything, a soothsayer of the hardwood. Coaches must also have this vision. Clink is a man who believes in vision. He has a vision for everything he and his team does from basketball to academics to scouting to weights. "I know in my head what I want it all to look like then I go about turning that vision into reality by explaining it and demanding it," Clink says. However, before he formulates his vision, Clink says he asks a series of important questions so he can create a plan of action to make the vision a reality.

Clink's questions cover the entire court: How are we going to make that vision a reality?

How do we want to play? What type of offense will we run? How will we defend? In what areas will we recruit? How will we run our academic system to ensure our student-athletes excel in the classroom? How will we fundraise? Clink says, "We go down the line thinking and getting excited about all of our goals and plans for our organization. We think about the championships we're striving for. We envision what it'll be like cutting down the nets after we win a conference championship on our home court. It's these types of thoughts that drive our vision and make us excited to continue to expand our vision."

Clink makes stakeholders out of everyone associated with the team, gets them all thinking about these goals off the court—to visualize how they'll unfold. "We think of all the things we're going to accomplish, and all of the time and effort and commitment that it'll take to make this vision a reality. This all comes down to the people you allow to be a part of your organization. The people you invite into your circle will either make or break you."

Clink was never a star basketball player, but he was a good player. "When I was a kid we didn't have all the personal trainers like guys do today. My high school coach, Jim Green, gave me a video tape my junior year. It was Steve Alford's *50 Minute All-American Workout*. It was Alford (former Indiana University star and, at the time of publication, current UCLA head coach) doing and explaining how he went about working out in the gym every day. I watched the video over and over, did the workout religiously. To this day I still go into the gym by myself and do a version of the workout. It's a great conditioner."

Clink played basketball at Gavilan Community College from 1989-1991. He transferred to Chico State and played under Wildcats coaching legend Puck Smith. It was here that Clink got the first taste of victory at the collegiate level. Clink was part of three Chico State conference titles (1992-1994) and experienced the NCAA Championship Tournament West Regional in 1992-1993. His senior year he was voted Most Inspirational Player. He graduated from Chico State in 1994 with a degree in physical education. He entered graduate school at Chico State where he worked towards a teaching credential and a master's degree in physical education. During this time, he served as an assistant coach under Coach Smith for the 1994-1995 and 1995-1996 seasons.

Enter Clink's never-ending season as no longer the player Clink, but Coach Clink. And like all young coaches who want to someday be a head coach, he had to leave his comfort zone and go out and get experience.

Long before the days of social media networking, Clink networked the old school way. Clink was working Russ Critchfield's (current Butte College's men's basketball head coach) basketball camp at Palma High School in Salinas, California. "Coach Critchfield gave me the names of 18 college coaches he knew," Clink says. "He told me to send each one of these coaches a letter and resume."

In Clink's second year as a graduate assistant at Chico State, he sent out his resume and cover letter to every coach he knew or thought he could get to know. He particularly wanted to get to know the UC Davis head coach, Bob Williams. "I had always been intrigued by the program at Davis," Clink says. As a Chico State player, he had played against UC Davis. Clink respected how hard the Aggies always fought, and how the fight paid off in a lot of scrappy wins. "They did it with smart, tough players who were unselfish," Clink says. "They dove on the floor for loose balls, took charges, and shared the ball on offense. They never blinked an eye at an official and always responded well to coaching. They were winners. I knew their leadership was as good as it got. Bob Williams had all the answers. And I had all the questions."

So Clink wrote to Williams. "I told Coach Williams that I would love to get any feedback from him on how to pursue a career in college coaching. I was hungry." A couple months went by and Clink didn't hear back. "You have to remember, this is before email and texting. I checked my mailbox—the one you have to physically open up—every day."

That January, UC Davis was coming up to Chico for a conference game. Before the game, Coach Williams approached Clink. "I got your letter," Coach Williams said. "Come down to Davis after the season. We can grab lunch and talk." It is often said that April is the cruelest month, but for Clink it would be the kindest. He went down and met Coach Williams for lunch at Café Italia in Davis. "We mainly just talked about making contacts," Clink says. "We just chatted."

Clink was only 25 years old. His world was opening up. Still, the young coach knew better than to get his hopes up. "I was fired up," Clink says. "But I was also looking at it realistically. I was having lunch with a coach I admired and respected. I wasn't expecting anything."

Williams not only picked up the tab that day, but he offered Clink a staff position at Davis. "I was blown away. Not only was I going to get to learn from one of the best, but I was going to get paid for it. $5,000 for the year. I felt like I'd won the lottery. Shoot, I had. I went back to Chico to talk it over with Coach Smith. He gave me a hug and said go for it. I accepted the job the next day."

Williams would be the perfect professor for Clink, and Clink was the perfect student for Williams. Williams was born in 1953. Clink was born in 1971. The 18-year difference was just right. Both Williams and Clink were entrenched in and had grown up around California basketball. Clink grew up in the golden age of basketball: Larry Bird, Magic Johnson, and Michael Jordan. He would see the inception of the three-point line and what it could do for little schools like Providence and small kids like Billy Donovan. He would see the rise of Duke, the fall of UNLV, and the heartbreak of the Fab Five. Williams, on the other hand, grew up in a time when basketball was at a crossroads, a sport still overshadowed by football and baseball. Williams had paid his coaching dues working at every level. He started as an assistant coach at San Lorenzo Valley High School in 1975-1976. From 1976-1978 he was the JV Coach at Santa Cruz High School. He would spend 1978-1979 working the bench as an assistant at Cabrillo Community College. From 1979-1980, he was the head coach at Lincoln High School in San Jose. He would finally stop at Menlo College for five years from 1983-1988. He then bounced down to Pepperdine to work as an assistant, then spent the next eight seasons from 1990-1998 at UC Davis.

Clink arrived at his new job with lots of questions. And like all good teachers, Williams relished the questions and usually had answers. "I would ask him questions all the time about different parts of the program, and how this worked and how that worked," Clink says. "How did he get the players to buy in? How did he get them to go to class and take their education seriously? Why did the players work so hard in the weight room? Why were they so coachable? Why did everyone seem to put the program ahead of themselves?"

Williams had a simple answer each time. "Get the right people on board," Clink says. "The day I started working for Bob Williams was the day my basketball world changed. The culture that he had built in his six years there was amazing. He got the student-athletes to buy in. They believed in the philosophy of the program, and they operated on a level I didn't expect. They went to class. They got in the gym on their own and cared about their development. They were coachable. They were tough and committed. The program hummed like a well-oiled machine."

Clink admits that what he didn't understand at the time was that it wasn't always like this at UC Davis. "I was seeing the by-product of Coach Williams's vision: effort, toughness, unselfishness, and passion." During that year under the wing of Williams, Clink was learning the method and process to building an elite program. "I learned that if you want to truly lead, you have to find people willing to follow you through the storm of building a program long before the sun starts shining again. Coach Williams taught me that you must find people who want to be a part of something special and will buy into doing the hard things for the chance at being great."

The Aggies would finish the year at 20-9 and win the Northern California Athletic Conference championship and advance to the NCAA Championship Tournament. At the end of the great season, though, Clink would have to move on. "I was lucky to have been an assistant coach for him that year. Little did I know that my real education on culture-building would come during the next basketball season."

Clink would spend the 1997-98 season in his first head coaching role at Gavilan Community College in Gilroy, California—fitting since this is where his own collegiate basketball career began. "This was a miserable job, but probably the best learning experience of my life. I had to do everything from coaching to pulling out the bleachers before games, finding score keepers, washing uniforms, and a ton of other things you would never imagine a head coach would have to do. But it taught me how to be organized and get things done."

This would begin an early pattern in Clink's life where he seemed to always return home, not unlike Odysseus, a walking, living, breathing, working example of the prisoner in Plato's Allegory of the Cave who must go back into the cave and return home upon after experiencing enlightenment and educate others to become *truly* enlightened. Clink showed up in the Garlic Capital of the World with a clear mission: "I went there to try and resurrect a floundering junior college basketball program. I learned a lot those in those nine months." Clink, then 26, credits that year as the head coach at Gavilan College for teaching him how to become organized and efficient. "At a job like that it's not just about coaching basketball. It's about mentoring young men, many of whom are on the tipping point of their lives. I had a variety of characters that year that could be a book in itself." During that year Clink says that he tried to implement the things that he learned at UC Davis. "I would talk about character, unselfishness, passion, and commitment. I felt like I made some headway in turning around the culture of the program, but what I had gotten started was quickly left behind after that spring when I got my next coaching offer."

During those nine months at Gavilan College, Coach Williams and his UC Davis Aggies were on the road to winning the NCAA Division II National Championship. The culture was at its peak and reaping the benefits. "The truly amazing thing about UC Davis winning the national championship," Clink says, "was that they did it without any scholarship players. If you would've lined up the UC Davis players with the ones from Kentucky Wesleyan, their opponents in the national championship game that day, you would have bet all your money on Kentucky Wesleyan. But because of the level of buy-in there was to the team culture, the Aggies did that day what no one thought they could do. It was amazing."

Shortly after the national championship, Coach Williams accepted the job of head coach at UC Santa Barbara (UCSB). One can only imagine the excitement the 43-year-old must have felt when he was offered the position. The UC Santa Barbara men's basketball program was in peril, and the university was searching for a coach who would come in and resurrect a once-proud basketball team. "I went down to UCSB and met with Coach Williams," Clink says. "He talked about what he was about to embark on and how challenging it was going to be. I told him I wanted in. I wanted to be a part of this building process. He offered me an assistant position. I was down there a few days later ready to start my new job. I was only 26."

Clink would follow Coach Williams that spring of 1998-1999 to the sunny central coast paradise of the UC Santa Barbara campus. UCSB would have a respectable season that year going 15-13. They would win the Big West Conference West Division Championship. Clink would remain on the UCSB bench for the 1999-2000 campaign. They would finish second in the division.

It was here at UCSB that Clink would receive an education in putting "people first." He tells it like this: "Right from the start Coach Williams went on a mission to find out who in the program was worth keeping and who had to go. He had to find out if there was anyone currently in the program who was ready to step up and lead and who would follow him through the fire he was about to start." Williams had several methods for finding the right men—most of which came from the daily testing of their commitment level. "Who was committed to getting better?" Clink continues. "Who was committed to going to class? Who was committed to being coachable? Who was committed to winning?"

Clink says it took no time at all to figure out that not every member of the program was on board and ready to help fulfill the vision that Williams had for the program. "We had to take away scholarships in this first three weeks," he said. "The next step in the 'people first' process, once we had established who was on board, was to go out and recruit people who would buy into the vision."

Clink believes this was the area of culture-building where Williams most excelled. "He didn't need All-Americans to win. Sure, he needed really good basketball players, but he needed them to be student-athletes that wanted something real and special. The type of people who will surrender their hearts and souls to the team. People who will see the future of the program without knowing what that future held in store for them."

Clink says it was a challenge to find these kinds of personalities. "We needed givers, but givers are rare in the world of college basketball. Coach Williams did a great job of finding those people and convincing them that they could help build something special and that the experience would be rewarding for them personally."

Clink says that the first season at UCSB was one of the most difficult but rewarding seasons of his coaching career. "We lost our first eight games, four by one possession. The people we had assembled were far from perfect. A lot of personnel changes needed to be made for the following year to get more of the right people on board. But the culture had started to change," Clink says. "Coach Williams coached culture more than he coached basketball. He coached habits in the gym. He coached communication. He coached the importance of getting a college education. He had the vision in his head of what he wanted the program to look like long term, and he had a plan of how to turn that vision into a reality."

Clink reflects again on the losing streak. "But Coach Williams never once wavered from his mission. It wasn't about winning games that year. Certainly, we all wanted to win, but it was about establishing a culture and building for the future."

Clink notes Williams's good fortune in having a staff of assistant coaches who understood his vision. "I'd seen the finished product two years earlier when I worked for him at UC Davis." Jon Wheeler, Clink says, one of the other UCSB assistants, had gotten his start with Coach Williams at UC Davis. He had been a big part of the building process. "Wheeler understood what the vision looked like. Meanwhile, Marty Wilson—another assistant on the staff—knew Coach Williams well; he had played for Coach Williams when he was an assistant at Pepperdine University."

The 2000-2001 season offered Clink a unique opportunity: go back to UC Davis as an assistant coach and help them transition from Division II to Division I. At UC·Davis, Clink would be in charge of recruiting, scouting, and player development. Two years with Williams had laid the foundation for the change that Clink would be able to offer. "I learned more in the two years I was with Coach Williams about culture-building than any other time in my career. It was like going to school all over again, only this time I was into the coursework. I learned that you can try and do all of the right things as a leader, but if you don't have the right people following you then it's not going to work, no matter how hard you try. You have to assemble a team of people that'll buy into the vision. People that want to give themselves to something special and be a part of something bigger than themselves." Clink would spend the next eight years at UC Davis before coming home.

Many are called but few are chosen. In April 2008, after paying the quintessential dues that all the great ones undoubtedly pay, Clink was both called and chosen. It had been eight years since he'd earned his MA in physical education at Chico State and turned in his Master's thesis to the Office of Graduate Studies. The thesis was titled "A Guide to Teaching Wing Play in Basketball." In his Acknowledgements, he wrote:

> *I would also like to thank my basketball coach and one of my mentors Puck Smith. Coach Smith was a great teacher of the game of basketball while I was a player for him, but he taught me more than basketball. He taught me about life. As a player he pushed and tested me and brought out characteristics in me that I never knew I had. The education I received from Coach Smith goes far deeper than any skill or fundamental that one can learn on a basketball court. I hope*

*that someday I have as much of an impact on one of my players as he
had on me.*

Coach Puck Smith had turned Chico State into a conference powerhouse
during the early 90s. Puck won four conference championships in a row
from 1991-1994 and made it to the NCAA tournament three times. "He
did it like Coach Williams did at UC Davis and UC Santa Barbara—good
people who bought in," Clink says. "Their coaching styles and basketball
philosophies were different, but they both understood that to sustain the
success long-term they needed great people willing to be led."

By 2008, the landscape of Chico State Basketball had changed since the
days when Clink played in the early 90s. The Northern California Athletic
Conference, which was a non-scholarship conference, had dismantled in
1998. Chico State had joined the California Collegiate Athletics Association
(CCAA). The CCAA was, and still is, regarded as one of the best Division
II conferences in the country.

"Chico State was asked to compete with schools that offered full scholarships while we had little to give," Clink says of the change. "Consequently,
our program struggled for years." The week leading up to Puck Smith's last
game—the 2007-2008 season—Puck called Clink and said he was going to
retire after the last home game against Dominguez Hills. Clink came up to
the game and sat in the stands with Kele Fitzhugh (the Shasta College coach
and assistant at Chico State when Clink played there). Clink knew he was
going to apply for the job. It was his dream job. He was intrigued that the
financial situation of the basketball program was improving.

"Scholarship dollars were being put into place," Clink says. "I felt that
if that continued to improve, then the program had a chance to be really
successful." Clink recalls his job interview, noting that he talked a lot about
culture and how to build it. "I talked extensively about the type of student-
athlete I would recruit. Of course I talked about talent and the type of athlete we would need to win, but I talked a lot more about the type of person
we needed to win. We needed student-athletes who cared about getting

their degrees. Student-athletes that cared about winning and wanted to be great as a team as well as individually."

Clink was consumed with getting the job for more than two months. He started working with a graphic designer at UC Davis to put together a book of his philosophies and plans for how he was going to build the basketball program. "I spent about $1,000 getting this thing made for me to give to the people I interviewed with on campus. I typed out any possible question that I thought I might get asked and then I would go and write answers to each of the questions. I came up with around 150 potential questions. There was nothing that the interview committee could ask me that I didn't have an answer for."

His wife Courtney put him through mock interviews at night when their young children had gone to sleep. She would grill him on every question. They had even driven up to Chico and started looking at neighborhoods, envisioning their lives here. Clink interviewed and thought it went great. "I remember driving back to Davis after the interview and calling Gus Argenal and telling him I thought I was going to get it. A couple weeks passed and I hadn't heard back. I was worried someone else got the job."

Clink was back home where he grew up in Morgan Hill, California, when he got the call in May from Anita Barker, the Athletic Director, that would change his life. "It was special. I went down to my friend Mike Torres's house in Gilroy to play cards. Mike was one of my roommates at Chico State. We were sitting around his living room with all of my close childhood friends and my brother—five of whom went to Chico State with me—when Anita called me. I went out into Mike's front yard and talked to her. She offered me the job and told me to take a day or two to think about it. I told her I didn't need a day or two. I accepted it right then and there. I walked back in and my friends all just stared at me because they knew I was waiting for the call. They all obviously wanted me to get the job. I just said, 'I got it.' It was an emotional deal for all of us because they were happy for me, but Chico State means so much to them, too."

Years later Clink still revels in that day. "I was fortunate to be offered the job. Chico State was always a dream job for me. Partly because I loved my experience at Chico State as a student-athlete, but more importantly because I knew in my heart that it was a program where I could do it my way." He knew at Chico State he could attract good high school students. "That was important because I wanted guys that I could coach and lead for four years. I knew we could get the right people on board and build the program for long-term success." The truth really is stranger than fiction. What a homecoming. Clink was now a head coach.

CHAPTER 3

Hiring Gus

THE FIRST THING CLINK DID as the head coach at Chico State was to hire an assistant coach he knew would share his vision. He wanted someone that would not only help him recruit student-athletes with great character and to help make the team great, but someone who would also help hold everyone accountable for that vision. He was fortunate to hire a former player he had coached while an assistant coach at UC Davis, Gus Argenal. When Clink was an assistant coach at UC Davis during the summer of 1997, he went down to Diablo Valley College to watch high school summer league games.

He was particularly interested in the De La Salle High School team. Frank Alloco, one of the best basketball coaches in the country, had just been hired at De La Salle. He had been at Northgate High School and had just won a state championship. Clink was impressed with what he saw. "He was coaching the players how to run back on to the floor after a time out," Clink says. "You don't see that often. Then he'd teach the kids how to look at him when he was talking to them during a time out. He was teaching them about culture."

Gus Argenal immediately caught Clink's eye. Clink could tell the kid was coachable and had bought into the system. "From the first time I saw Gus play as a high school sophomore at De La Salle High School, I knew he was my kind of guy," Clink says. "I was sitting in the bleachers at Diablo Valley College in the summer of 1997 watching high school summer league games when I saw this 5-foot-11 point guard diving all over the floor, running in and out of timeouts, finding the open man, and looking his coach in the eye every time he was given instructions. He was exactly the type of guy you build a program with. He was a winner and someone that wanted to be led and wanted to be great."

After the game, Clink went up to Alloco and introduced himself. "Can you tell me a little more about number 10?"

"That's Gus Argenal," Alloco said. "He's only a sophomore." Clink thought for sure by the way Argenal played and acted on the court he was a senior.

Two years later Clink—who had spent the last couple of years as an assistant coach at UC Santa Barbara—was in the Bay Area to be the best man in the wedding of a former Chico State teammate. On the day of the wedding, Clink and the groom went to a health club to play open gym basketball. All the players were in their late 20s and 30s—all but this one high school kid. In between games the kid was shooting around. Clink, eyes always open for talent, had been impressed with the kid's play. He went up and asked him if he played around here.

"Yeah," the kid said. "I just finished the season at De La Salle."

"What are you doing next year?" Clink asked.

"I got a scholarship to play for UC Davis," Argenal replied.

Clink didn't realize this was the same kid he had watched two years earlier. The spring after his second year at UC Santa Barbara, Clink got the head assistant position at UC Davis. His first day on the job he walks into the open gym with the second assistant, Kevin Nosek. One player stuck out more than the others. "It was the way he played—how hard he played."

It clicked. Clink realized this was the same guy he'd seen a year earlier at the open gym, the same guy he'd seen two years earlier in the summer league game at Diablo Valley College. "All three times I watched Gus play I was immediately drawn to him. He played hard. He was scrappy." Clink coached him for the next four years. They developed a great player-coach relationship. The day of Argenal's senior game, Clink gave a speech to the team after the shoot around. "I told them I wanted to talk about my favorite college basketball player." He told them the story of Argenal and how he'd seen him on three different occasions, and how each time his game was inspiring. Clink said both he and Argenal were in tears. "We went on that night to beat San Bernardino who was ranked 8th in the country."

When Clink and Argenal first came to town, Chico State put them up in the Diamond Hotel—the most charming and historic hotel in downtown, a place that immediately transports you back to the 1920s—for two weeks. "When our two weeks were up, we were moved to the Vagabond Inn. It lived up to its name." Clink says it was the time of his life. "We would go out to dinner and then come back to the Vagabond, smoke cheap cigars, sit by the dirty pool, and phone recruits all night. We were desperate. We wanted to win so badly."

From day one on the job, Clink and Argenal were on a mission to get the right people on board. First, though, they had to figure out their office space. "Gus and I threw out six trashcans of stuff from the office," Clink says. "There were all these old files. I had everything taken out. Then it dawned on me. We didn't have a desk to work on. Se we had two of those little school desks that you see in the public schools from back in the day.

That's where we made all our calls, did all our recruiting for a few weeks." He pauses to laugh, shakes his head. "We did this the same exact way I had seen it done 10 years earlier at UC Santa Barbara with Coach Williams," Clink says. During Clink's first year at Chico State, most of his coaching duties had nothing to do with putting a ball through a hoop. "I had to coach how we dressed. How we talked. How we treated each other. Where the players sat in class. How we communicated with teachers. How we conducted ourselves when we travelled. We made some poor personnel choices that first year. I had to dismiss two student-athletes during the middle of that first season. One for plagiarizing a paper and another for not getting good enough grades after the first semester."

Clink immediately got rid of guys who were dead weight. He replaced them with the type of guys who would buy into his vision. "I truly believe that whether you're taking over a new organization or trying to improve the one you currently lead, it's not about what you do. It's about who you're doing it with. For us it wasn't about the X's and O's. It was about the people we could find to represent those X's and O's. I'll say it over and over again. A leader must have the right people on board to help execute their vision. People first will be the most important part of the process in making your culture great."

In less than two weeks, the two young coaches got rid of seven players who either were ineligible or refused to go to class. "There were losers in the program," Clink says. "Guys that didn't care about winning and had no idea what it took to be great." He replaced them with six young men who laid the foundation for the program. "When I accepted the job here at Chico State," Clink says, "my main recruiting objective was to find the most competitive student-athletes around. I wanted winners in and out of the classroom."

Clink then signed one of the Bay Area's best players. He signed three other high school seniors, and added two community college transfers. One of his best moves, to this day, was helping point guard Jay Flores transfer from Sonoma State to Chico State. His first recruiting class as an NCAA head coach was a success.

Clink says he loves coaching college basketball because it's one of the few jobs where you get to choose the people to let on board. "Most high school coaches have to coach whoever shows up. That makes it so much harder to build a great culture. Often times you're trying to lead people that don't believe in what you're doing." The next step was to put together a recruiting class of eight student-athletes that he believed would be the future of the program. "They weren't all great basketball players, but they were all guys that we thought would help us build the culture of the program," Clink says. "We made a couple of mistakes, but for the most part we got it right."

Six of those players would make it on Clink's office wall. Clink has plaques of every student-athlete that has ever completed eligibility and graduated hanging on his wall. All six of these first Clink recruits earned their degrees. "I credit all six of them for being instrumental in the great culture that we have today."

CHAPTER 4

Couch Surfing

CLINK AND HIS STAFF TRY and out-recruit all the other schools they compete against. The goal is simple: recruit a student-athlete harder than anyone else. "Recruiting is always changing and evolving," Clink says. "When I was an assistant at UC Davis, email became the way to recruit. Then text messaging. Then Facebook and now Twitter. There's always a new avenue for communicating with recruits. We use all of them and are always on the cutting edge with how we recruit, but we still do a lot of our recruiting through the good old fashioned US Postal Service."

Clink and his staff still buy stamps. "We try and get something in the mail to our top recruits every day," he says. "We want them seeing something from us constantly. We want our recruits to have gotten more notes, mail, and texts from us than any other school."

When Clink was an assistant coach at UC Santa Barbara, he worked with Marty Wilson, the current head coach at Pepperdine. Wilson was yet another coach who mentored Clink. Clink says that Wilson played a major role in the recruiting strategy he uses today. "Marty was very organized. He had a system of how he got information out to the recruits. And it was always personalized." Wilson, Clink says, had a talent for talking to the recruits on the phone. He excelled at building relationships with them. "Marty spent time everyday writing personalized notes to all of the recruits. That's something most coaches do, but he took it to another level."

Wilson involved Clink in recruiting. Clink was the third assistant at UCSB. Back then, the third assistant was not allowed to recruit off campus. However, Wilson found ways to get Clink involved.

"He would give me a list of guys to call. He was having me help him put together mail outs. When we had recruits on campus for visits, he would make sure to have me involved with the whole trip. This allowed me to see how it was done."

Wilson, like all the best coaches, was also influential off the court. "He not only taught me a lot about what it was to be a great assistant coach, but I watched him with his family," Clink says. "I remember back when his kids were little and I'd watch how he fathered them. He's a great dad and was very disciplined and loving with his kids. He would have them around all the time, and I would watch him do things with his kids and think about how I would do that someday if I ever had kids." Clink left UCSB to take the head assistant position at UC Davis because he would be in charge of recruiting. "UC Davis was Division II at the time. It gave me a chance to do what Marty was doing at UCSB. I was aggressive. I sent daily notes to our top recruits, bi-weekly mail outs, etc."

Ryan Moore was the first high-profile recruit that Clink helped sign. Clink had seen Moore play at the Double Pump Camp during the summer between his junior and senior year in the beginning of July. He followed him all over southern California for the rest of the summer, and spent about 10 months recruiting him.

Clink also learned a lot about recruiting from head coach Gary Stewart at UC Davis back in the early 2000s. "Even though he was the head coach, he recruited like an assistant. No one on staff called more guys, wrote more notes than him. And when we brought recruits to campus he was involved in every aspect of the visit. He was also very creative in things we did with recruits on campus. We would bring the guys in the arena at night, and we would have a big presentation with the kid's name being announced in the starting lineup. Things like that."

Clink would spend the month of July in Newport Beach sleeping on his friend Tim Cleary's couch when Cleary was an assistant at UC Irvine. "We were graduate assistants at Chico State together. We became great friends. We were in each other's weddings." So Clink spent the month of July on his pal's couch. "I'd hit all of the exposure camps and tournaments and in between those tournaments find summer league games in Los Angeles to watch. I was trying to find as many guys as possible to add to our recruiting list."

Most of the Chico State's recruiting efforts are in the Bay Area and Sacramento regions. "These are the two areas where we can drive to catch a high school game and be back that night," Clink says. Highway 99 has become as familiar as the neighborhood streets he grew up riding his bicycle on. He is a regular at the Starbucks in Gridley. "Chico is a hard place to recruit from, not to, because of our location. I like to see our recruits play in person and these two areas give us the best access to do that."

Clink spends mid-June to the end of July (Division II recruiting time) watching high school team camps, summer games, and AAU teams play. "We're trying to find as many players that are going into their senior year that we can recruit. We're evaluating guys we've heard about and seen as underclassmen. We're also trying to find new guys to add to our list during this time. We spend time in Southern California watching AAU games from morning until night."

At Chico State, Clink is always recruiting guys that are also being recruited by Division I schools. "We can't beat a DI school on a guy, but I always feel like if we're recruiting a guy that's 'getting interest' from low major DI schools, then we're probably on the right guy." Clink is quick to clarify what he means. "When I say that we'll never beat a DI school on a guy, I mean that all of these players have a dream of playing DI basketball. They see all of the big time teams playing on TV and watch the NCAA tournament. They have this idea in their heads that all DI basketball is like what they see on TV. This is far from the truth."

Clink points out that players don't realize that Division I is not what they see during March Madness. He says, "The mistake is made when a player takes a DI scholarship, or a walk-on position, over a great DII offer. They assume that DI is better. Then they get there and realize they made a decision based on the level and not the program."

Clink believes the culture of the Chico State program is as good as any in the country. "I tell recruits that I'll put our culture and the experience they'll get at Chico State against any program in the country. That includes DI schools. We put just as much into what we do as the big time schools you see on TV. We feel just as good, celebrate just as much if not more, when we win a conference championship as anyone else does." In a way, Clink (and most coaches in the CCAA) has to be the Billy Beane of college basketball. Like Beane, Clink must field a competitive team with a budget that doesn't match his competitors. "That's what we do here. It's what many of the coaches in the CCAA do. I have a pool of scholarship money that I need to manage between the guys on our team. I need to calculate how much I need to spend in order to sign someone. We package our basketball scholarship money with state and federal aid that some of our student-athletes qualify for."

At the Division I level, 13 full scholarships must be provided. The only exceptions are the Ivy League and Patriot League. At the Division II level, only the equivalent of 10 full scholarships can be provided, and only a couple of schools in the CCAA provide all 10: Chico State is not one of them.

"At Chico State we don't have the equivalent of 10 full scholarships," Clink says. "Everyone is at a different level, though. I take the money we have in our scholarship pool and spread it out the best way I can to field a competitive team. Just like a general manager for a pro team does with a budget and salary cap."

Clink explains that in the CCAA, everyone is at a different level in terms of the amount of scholarship money they have to offer. "No one is the same. One of the biggest learning curves I've had is how to manage the scholarship money. I've had to learn how to calculate how much money to offer a student-athlete without breaking the budget and still being able to sign the recruit."

Clink says that every now and then he comes in too low and misses. "That doesn't bother me. One of the reasons we've been so good is because we're smart and calculated with our money. We've streamlined this process. We make very few mistakes now."

Clink says his assistants always want him to spend more than needed to sign guys. "They've put so much time and energy into recruiting a guy. They don't want to miss on signing a guy because there's not enough money." Clink laughs. "If we signed the players for what my assistants suggested, we'd only have six players." He says his assistants don't always understand how smart they must be about their budget. "I include them in the budget process so they can learn how to manage money."

Clink compares it to an NBA team's salary cap. "I have to field the most competitive team possible and still stay under the salary cap. I try and raise each guy's scholarship as he becomes an upper classman." He sighs. "I've been able to do this with almost every guy that's worn a Chico State jersey in recent years."

When Clink and his staff are out evaluating guys in the summer or during their high school seasons, they are looking for guys that have a good skill set, athleticism, etc. Depending on the player's position, there are certain physical characteristics Clink looks for. "At our level we never get a complete player. There's always something missing. Maybe a kid is a big-time shooter, but lacks foot speed. Maybe we find a point guard that can shoot, pass, dribble, and run a team, but is undersize. Or we might get a 6-foot-10 physical specimen that has limited footwork in the post. A guy that we can see enormous potential in, but that we know we need to work with in order to get him good. Once we've identified the guys that can play, we start to do our homework on all of the other stuff that goes into 'finding the right person' to get on board. The first thing we do when we get back to campus in August and September is to start to call the registrar's office at the kid's high school and get unofficial transcripts. We evaluate all those transcripts to see who we can and can't get into Chico State. That eliminates a lot of the guys from the list."

Clink or his assistant will then call the player's high school and AAU coaches and ask about the recruit's character. "We want a good player. We want someone who wants to be great. We want winners with great work ethic and great attitudes."

Clink tries to get the student-athletes up to campus in the fall for visits so the team can be around the potential player and get to know him. "Sometimes we stop recruiting really good players because they don't have the type of personalities or characteristics that we want to be around."

I wonder if this is why Clink has not left Chico State for a bigger school, a Division I opportunity. Here at Chico State he can recruit a young man because of his character and talent, while so many other schools pick players solely based on talent.

CHAPTER 5

Rebuilding

CLINK WAS STARTING TO REVIVE a basketball program that had once been great and was now struggling. He brought youth, vibrancy, and a hunger that had been cultivated in the last decade of his coaching experience, a pedagogy that had been developed by real life experience and great mentors. He had an insatiable thirst that could only be slaked by winning the CCAA conference. He immediately installed a gritty, fast-paced style of play: The team would reflect his own character and drive.

November 3, 2008, marked Clink's debut in an exhibition game against two-time National Champion (1955, 1956) Division I University of San Francisco Dons. While Clink could not have been happy with his team offensively—they shot a measly 24 percent from the field— the Wildcats showed an aggressive style of play that mimicked the coach's personality. They would also get to the free throw line 39 times and force USF into 26 turnovers. Clink almost pulled off an upset in his first regular season game as head coach against Division I Seattle University, but would fall 61-58. Close usually only counts in horseshoes and hand grenades, but for Clink the loss was a huge victory. The previous year, the Redhawks had scored 95 points against the Wildcats. This time around they were held to 19 at the half. The Clink Era had officially started. He would get his first win as the head coach of Chico State on November 28, 2008, against University of Colorado-Colorado Springs.

Clink's first season was long and must have been painful for a man accustomed to winning. It was a season of close games, a season of close losses. At one point the Wildcats had lost six straight. By Valentine's Day, 2009, they had lost 12 games overall. A pattern of losing second-half leads set in. The Wildcats finished the year at 8-19 overall and 5-15 in conference. While on paper Clink's first season might appear a flop, it was actually a success. "If you judged us only on wins and losses that first year you would have called the season a failure, but that's not how I looked at it. I knew that first year was going to be hard. It wasn't about winning and losing. It was about establishing the culture of the program and the way we were going to do that was by getting the right people on board. That's what we did."

The 2009-2010 season opened at No. 12 ranked University of California Golden Bears. Clink must have felt euphoric when he looked up at the scoreboard that Thursday night in Haas Pavilion and saw the score tied at 9-9. The Wildcats would lose the exhibition 84-42, but he felt proud with Flores's efforts: In only 16 minutes of play, the transfer guard had four points, three assists, two rebounds, and a steal. Flores would not commit a turnover.

That's a Clink rule. No turnovers.

A couple weeks' shy of Christmas, Clink had led the Wildcats to their best start in twenty years at 4-1. Not only that, but the fans were returning. The once empty Acker had life again, and more than 1,100 students had packed the student section for the Pacific Union contest. The wins kept coming. By December 17, the Wildcats at 6-1 were off to their best start since the 1944-1945 season. They were also winning on the road. At one point they had sealed six victories away from Acker. Streaks end, and the Wildcats soon went on a 0-6 skid away from home. By February 6, they had dropped below .500 in the CCAA. They would finish the season with an impressive 16-13 record. Not bad considering two years' prior the Wildcats were last in the CCAA at 3-17.

The highlights of the 2010-2011 season mainly came off the court. The Wildcats would finish the season at .505. Clink was rebuilding. It would take time to create a winning culture, but it happened a lot faster than anyone had expected. Clink signed 6-foot-10 post player Christopher Magalotti. He signed 6-foot-5 guard Drew Kitchens, the 2011 San Diego

Section Division I Player of the Year and Cal-Hi Sports Division I All-State Teams selection.

The 2011-2012 preseason coaches poll had picked the Wildcats to finish seventh in the CCAA. Clink's team responded with a chip on their shoulder. Clink would take the Wildcats up to Arcata and beat Humboldt State for the first time since 1998. By December 1, the Wildcats would be in tie for first place with a 14-4 overall record, and 8-4 in the CCAA. They'd never been in first place that late in the season since joining the CCAA in 1998.

The Wildcats were also winning in the classroom. Jay Flores, the star point guard for the last three years and the catalyst to the revival of Chico State basketball, had just received the Capital One Academic All-West Region award for his high caliber of work in the classroom and on the hardwood. His academic drive was infectious. The Wildcats started off the Spring 2012 semester with the University Foundation Board of Governors Award for Academic Excellence. This award was presented because they had earned the highest GPA of all men's programs in the Chico State athletic department during the 2010-2011 academic year. "I'm more proud of that than anything. That's the banner I'd like to see hanging in Acker," says Clink.

By February 18, Coach Clink had the Wildcats at 20-6 overall and 14-6 in the CCAA. Five days later, the Wildcats would clinch their first ever CCAA title—not bad for a team picked to finish seventh. The Wildcats would make it to the CCAA Championship Tournament final, but fall short to their nemesis, Humboldt State University. They would face the number four seed Lumberjacks again as the number five seed in the opening round. The Chico State Wildcats dominated the with a final score of 75-68. The last time the Wildcats won an NCAA Championship tournament game was in 1958. The season would end in the next round. They would lose to the No. 12 ranked Western Washington University Vikings, 74-65. The Wildcats shot just 36% and turned the ball over 15 times.

What a change a year—and a CCAA regular season title—makes. The 2012-2013 season had the Wildcats picked to finish first. They would play an early exhibition game against the No. 12 University of Arizona Wildcats at the McKale Center in Tucson. They might have made a game of it, but they missed 11 of 19 free throws and committed 17 turnovers. The Wildcats would get back on track, start winning, and make it back to their third CCAA Championship tournament game again. But they would fall to Cal Poly Pomona, 78-64. The Wildcats would not get the automatic berth into the NCAA tournament. At 19-10, they didn't even know if they would get a bid. Further, they had not finished first but third in the CCAA. The Wildcats would make the tournament as a number seven seed and would face Cal Poly Pomona again—a rival that was growing each year.

Cal Poly Pomona was coming off a great season at 27-2. They had swept Chico State in the regular-season series. They also had one of the best defenses in the nation only allowing 55.8 points per game. By late afternoon on Friday, March 15, 2013, in Bellingham, Washington, five seniors would walk off the court wearing the Chico State uniform for the last time. Cal Poly Pomona would again get the best of Chico State, beating them for the fourth time that season, 69-61.

Clink's Wildcats had not lived up to their own expectations. The four losses to the same team, the early exit from the tournament, would make for yet another long "off-season" for Clink. His thought at 3:43 that morning: "*How* am I going to replace five seniors?" The Wildcats now had expectations. Clink could only say the season was interesting. "For the first time in my Chico State career, and for the first time in the players' careers, we had expectations. There was pressure being picked to finish first. I think we were ranked nationally in the preseason that year, too. None of us knew how to handle this."

The disappointing season didn't keep Clink from signing the young man who would eventually become one of the greatest Wildcats in history. Over the summer, Clink landed Robert Duncan, a 6-foot-3 guard who'd spent the last year at the United States Air Force Academy Preparatory

School in Colorado Springs, Colorado. As a senior at Granite Bay High School, Duncan had averaged 20 points per game. Clink knew he was getting something special in Duncan, but probably didn't know how good.

CHAPTER 6

Coach Cobb

COACH CHRIS COBB IS A 28-year-old version of Coach Clink. They even sound alike. When I phoned him in his office in Missoula, Montana, where he serves as an assistant for the Division I University of Montana Grizzlies, he answered with the same, deep, scratchy, no-nonsense voice that Clink has: "Montana basketball."

Coach Cobb, at the time of this book, is singing for his supper in Missoula. Chico and Missoula have many similarities, none more striking than that they're both college towns, and they're both college towns that make recruiting a challenge because of their location. Coach Cobb is finishing up what he calls the most stressful time of the year: recruiting. "Yeah, up here it's like recruiting in Chico. You have to really travel to see a player. It's not like when you live in the Bay Area and drive all around and see kids on a daily basis. It's more of a commitment to see a player here. You have to be organized."

I've heard rumors and stories about the toughness of Coach Cobb. Every player I've talked to "loves" Coach Cobb. Although only 5-foot-7, I am told by several people who know him that he was one heck of a high school basketball player. He played college ball at Menlo College. He claims not to be basketball obsessed, and that he's able to put it in perspective. Somehow, I don't quite believe him. "Greg is a good role model," he tells me. "He has a good balance, a good perspective. He has a life outside of this world. A lot of guys turn coaching into a 12-month job."

Case in point: I've been tailing Clink since last March. I've not seen him take a month, let alone a day, off. I know he went camping for a weekend, but something tells me he was still fielding basketball related texts. Everyone wants something from Clink. That is the cross he bears.

Coach Cobb's aggressive recruiting style is now Chico State basketball lore. A young man of 28 does not find himself in the position he is in without an insatiable hunger, a tapeworm in his stomach that only eats victory. "I like to win the right way," he says. I ask him what is right way to win. "Winning," he says.

Coach Cobb says he owes everything to the Chico State Wildcats basketball program. "I got to Chico State through Gus." All roads in the Clink story seem to lead through Gus Argenal. "After I played at Menlo, I got into coaching. I started out at San Francisco State University." He admits he had no idea what coaching entailed. "I knew Gus from my Bay Area connections. He played at De La Salle. I played at Bishop O'Dowd. We kept running into each other on the road. One night he told me that Greg was looking for someone. I got lucky. I got on the staff with Coach Clink and Coach Argenal."

When I ask Coach Cobb what the best thing about coaching is, he parrots Clink: "Picking the guys you want to work with. It's the coolest thing. See, coaching, I found, has little to do with X's and O's. It's so much more than that. Picking guys that fit into the culture." He pauses. "Greg taught me this. I didn't think that way before."

Coach Cobb says that coming up with plays is only about 20 percent of what he does at this level. "Here's the thing about Greg, and the thing that helped me recruit such good players. It's what I would tell a player's parents. Coach Clink is a really good basketball coach. He's a great leader. But he's an even better person." He thanks Clink for also teaching him how to be a professional. "He sets the tone for everyone from top to bottom, bottom to top. He genuinely loves his guys. You know, there's around 700 transfers each year at the DI level. Guys never transfer out of his program."

Coach Cobb talks affectionately of the players who have come and gone—guys like Rashad Parker and Amir Carraway—and displays equal affection for the guys who are still here. I ask him to confirm the Giddings story. "Yeah, we recruited Giddings out of high school. I like to recruit some guys just because I don't think they're going to last where they're going." He had a feeling that Fresno State wouldn't work out for Giddings. "I knew we weren't going to get him right away. I also knew that if it didn't work out at Fresno State, he'd come back around. I made three or four calls to him when I found out he was leaving."

Coach Cobb says one of the amazing things about the Chico State program is that once a guy leaves, there's another guy who steps right in to fill the role. "Greg's program is like what the Oakland A's have done," referring to the Athletics' GM Billy Beane and his storied approach to recruiting a winning team. "They go out and find the guys for the best value and piece all the parts together. When Jay Flores left, Rashad Parker stepped in. That's how we pushed through and won the conference. That's how we won the West Regional."

Coach Cobb was instrumental in bringing Isaiah Ellis to Chico State. Although this story has been told from Clink's perspective, Coach Cobb adds to both the story and what I predict will be the legend of Isaiah Ellis. Coach Cobb had seen Ellis play in the summer. He told Argenal about him. Argenal agreed that he thought Ellis could be great. Coach Cobb started calling Ellis. He wasn't receptive. "Normally, when we get a response like we got from Isaiah, we let him go." Coach Cobb wasn't ready to let go. He was heading down to the Sacramento area to do some recruiting. Antelope High School, where Ellis went to high school, was off the highway. "I popped in and watched a practice." Cobb had asked around and heard that Ellis wasn't good in social situations. "I saw a different side of him in practice. I got a vision about him. He was smiling all the time and goofing around with his teammates. But when I talked to him, I could tell he was uncomfortable."

Coach Cobb went to see him play two weeks later. He asked a random mother in the stands which player she liked best. "Oh, I love Isaiah. He's such a jokester. The sweetest young man. All the kids love him. He comes over to our house all the time."

Coach Cobb tried to convince Clink that Ellis would be a good fit. Clink wasn't buying it. He had been to a game and watched Ellis. Clink, as he told me earlier, saw Ellis sitting on the bench and horsing around. He had rolled up a program and was pretending that it was a microphone. "We went and watched him in one of his first games his senior year at the Gridley tournament. He got into foul trouble in the first half and sat on the bench pretending to interview one of his teammates. Cobb made me go watch him again in the playoffs at the end of his senior year. I told Cobb I was only going because I trusted him. I called him at half time and told Cobb we needed to get Isaiah."

Ellis came to visit in the spring. He was disinterested. Clink was ready to cut bait. Coach Cobb was not yet ready to reel in the line. "So I was driving to the Bay Area to see this tournament that Isaiah had told me he wasn't going to play in," Coach Cobb says. "He said he had hurt his ankle or something. Sure enough, I'm sitting in the stands watching, and who comes out on the floor?"

Coach Cobb couldn't resist sending him a text: "Hey Isaiah that was a fast ankle rehab." He said Ellis also saw him in the stands. "That following Monday morning Ellis called and said 'I'm ready.' Ellis committed to Chico State. Coach Cobb says that if Ellis were playing in his league, the Big Sky, he'd be an All-Conference player.

Coach Cobb reflects on Magz. "I got really close to him. Really spent a lot of time helping him transition from high school to college." He laughs. "That kid was always talking to a different girl. He always had a different haircut." I mention to him that Magz might have a Dennis Rodman transformation this year. "What do you mean?" Coach Cobb asks. I mention that he wants to dye his hair a different color before each game, and possibly grow a dirty moustache. I can almost hear him falling out of his chair from Chico to Missoula he's laughing so hard. "We'll see how long Greg lets that one last." I have a feeling that if Magz can produce the way the Worm (Dennis Rodman) did, Clink won't care. Coach Cobb remembers fondly the courting of Robert Duncan. "We were on a bus. I got a message on Facebook from him. I spent the next six months talking with him."

Coach Cobb laughs when I tell him that Silverstrom might just be the most confident person I've ever met. "He sure is. I'd heard about Corey from a lot of people. He played at Bullard, and Bullard plays a really crazy style of basketball. It's weird. Up and down, up and down. Dribble drive stuff." He went down and saw Silverstrom play in the Gridley Invitational. Gridley is a small town that you pass through on Highway 99 South when driving to Sacramento. I call it the town with the really fancy "hubcap shop." Actually, there are a few hubcap shops—or rim shops as I have often been corrected—on the street corners in Gridley. "It's a great tournament," Coach Cobb says. "Six or seven of the best high school teams in Northern California always play in it."

Coach Cobb watched Silverstrom play that night. He was impressed. "I went back. I wanted to see how he would perform against Jabari Bird." Bird, who at the time of this book is now a star at Cal and future NBA player, was also a McDonald's All American (Bird would score 9 points and have 3 assists in the contest) the year he went up against Silverstrom. "Silverstrom was the best player on the floor. He took it to Bird. I recruited him hard. He also comes from a great family. I even went and saw him play on senior night."

When Silverstrom made his visit to Chico State, he had a bad visit. "He played with the guys and just wasn't any good. We still took him." Coach Cobb says that his first year on campus, Silverstrom wasn't impressive. "He was mentally soft. He was adjusting, though. He wasn't healthy, either. But when he healed and started to adjust, man, he was good. He just needed time to learn the culture." Coach Cobb says that guys are able to make the tough transition because Clink gives players the independence they need to find their way. "Oh, but he still holds them accountable to the standards of the program."

The conversation shifts to Jalen McFerren. "I just talked to him a few days ago. Over the summer, we met and had coffee." Cobb's parents live in Castro Valley, and McFerren went to Castro Valley High School. "McFerren is the figurehead of that program." He mentions how the future Hall of Fame NFL player Charles Woodson played in last Sunday's game (at the time of this book) despite a bad shoulder injury. "That's something Jalen would do. When Jalen's hurt, he pushes through. He's a good ball player, but he's an even better person. People will be talking about Jalen McFerren for a long time. He's a winner. That's what the program is about. People, not just players, who are winners." Coach Cobb thinks that McFerren will be the key to everything that happens in the next couple of seasons. "He's the guy that will hold everyone else accountable. He will make the players and the team better because of who he is. I can't wait to see what does his senior year."

Robert Duncan comes up. "He's the perfect example of what this program can do for a kid." He says Duncan was a mess when he got to Chico State. "Now he's excelling." He says that Duncan had a dark side when he got here. "He was hard to coach. He didn't want to be held accountable. Then the light bulb went off. He knew we cared about him. Yeah, the great year that Rob had actually started the spring before."

Coach Cobb compares the Chico State program—without the infractions and allegations of cheating—to how USC football was running under Pete Carrol. "He'd sign one of the top running backs in the country and put him at number seven on the depth chart." He says this is what's happening at Chico State. "I think competition is the greatest. It brings out the best in everyone. Take Trevor Priest for example. He's a good player. He's a great person. Well-rounded. Great socially. Everybody knows him, but the social atmosphere of a place like Chico can swallow you up. It's hard to balance. He has not excelled on the court yet, but he has as a teammate. The way Greg's culture works, if you don't work hard, you get passed up. If Rob doesn't get it done, Nate will. If Drew doesn't get it done, someone else will."

I've heard Coach Cobb say the word "relationships" several times in our discussion. "Out here, at this level, in the DI world, it's more like a business. I miss the relationships that a place like Chico State lets you form. I don't think what Greg has created at Chico State could be done at any other place in the country to tell you the truth." He adds that Chico is a place that forces young men to be social—to get to know people well. "To form relationships. I forged a lot of strong bonds and relationships in my four years there. Four years. Wow." He accredits the special relationships to being in a unique position as a coach where he could serve in a big brother/little brother capacity. "I'm young enough. They still respected me, though."

I start to wonder if Coach Cobb knows something that I don't. In our conversation, he has almost said "As long as Greg is there" as much as he mentioned "relationships." For at least the fifth time, Cobb says, "As long as Greg is there, they have a chance to win big every year." I ask him if he thinks Clink is going anywhere. No pause. Immediate response. "I don't see Greg ever leaving. Why would he?"

When I first began writing this book, I was obsessed with the question: Why is Clink still here? That question really no longer interests me. Clink has it figured out. California, at the time of this book, might be brown from one of the worst droughts in history, but the grass over in Acker is vibrant green. "He loves it there," Cobb says. "Chico State is engrained in him. I don't think there's any other place in the country where he can do what he can do at Chico State."

Part of Coach Cobb's confidence that Clink will stay is because he believes a National Championship is around the corner. "At some point, he's going to win it all."

Coach Cobb says that when Clink took the job, and while Cobb was coaching at SF State, he told his father that Chico State would win a National Championship within five years. "They beat us up. The bench was rowdy. They out rebounded us by 21 or something. They were good. And I knew they were going to be great." He says this greatness is a consequence of Clink's drive. "No one is more driven to win than Coach Clink. And no one puts more pressure on himself to win than Coach Clink. No coach I've ever seen gets more excited after a win."

I ask Coach Cobb to tell me a little bit about his favorite Chico State memory. Silence permeates permeates the phone for a good minute. He occasionally smacks his lips or utters an "hmm" just to let me know he's still there, but I can tell he's plumbing the depths of his memory, flipping fast through the drawers in his mind that must hold hundreds of grand memories.

"I'll tell you a story that is the epitome of Greg. Yeah, it's my favorite memory." He tells the story of the game two years ago when the coaching staff (he is careful not to single out Coach Clink) blew it at the end of an important game against UC San Diego. "We had done a poor job of preparing guys for the end of close games," Coach Cobb says. "We just called a bunch of bad plays. One after another. We had a bad out of bounds play. We fouled when we shouldn't have. We just didn't communicate. And we got beat at the buzzer." Cobb recalls this as the lowest moment during his four years at Chico State. "It was awful. At home. Embarrassing. I felt that the team's faith in us was wavering. I felt so bad for Greg." He says that Clink quietly slipped out of the office, and that he could tell his head coach was down. "I drove over to his house. We stayed up until past 1:30 in the morning just talking. We knew what awaited us the next night." The following night, they were playing No. 11 San Bernardino. "We were in a bad spot. It was a must-win situation."

Coach Cobb says that the next day, Clink went on the air with Mike Baca for his radio show. "Greg said right away that he screwed up against San Diego. He took all the blame. He addressed the players the same way." Coach Cobb said Clink stood in front of all these young men who, despite being great kids, were still college basketball players with big egos. "Coach Clink was at his most vulnerable. He told them he was down. He said he screwed up. He opened up his heart to the guys. He said to 16 young men: 'Pick me up. I need you to pick me up just like I need Rashad to pick Amir up and Amir to pick Sean up.' It was 100 percent from the heart. We went out there and beat a team that had a lot more talent than us." Clink's Wildcats won in overtime 86-82. The rest of the season was a wild run that would send them to South Carolina to play in the Elite Eight." He pauses to clear his throat.

"Yeah, that's the epitome of Greg."

Coach Cobb realizes how lucky he is to have come this far at only age 28. "I owe everything to that program. Whether it's Anita Barker or Coach Fogel or Greg. Chico State had a profound effect on me. I was able to be real when I recruited. I could honestly look a mother in the eye and tell her that her son would truly be cared for here. I could tell parents and grandparents that their son would graduate with a college degree."

I ask the generic question of where he wants to be in five years.

"Five years? This is a hard profession to forecast. But I want to run my own program. I want to run a program filled with people that I want to be around every day."

Until that day comes, Coach Cobb is in Missoula. While Clink and his team of underdogs are preparing for the University of Arizona, Coach Cobb will be getting his team ready to play the underdog Whitworth. Coach Cobb might be in a different world now—a world where he has to go on the road and play powerhouse like Gonzaga, Washington, and Kansas—but he'll still be checking in with Clink and the Wildcats every Friday and Saturday night this winter.

CHAPTER 7

Leadership

Anyone who has ever played for Clink has fought for him. His players march through walls of fire for him.

One also gets the impression they would die for him, too. Clink—as a basketball coach—is rare, a working example of the theoretical academic study of leadership. Clink and his team are a microcosm of leadership that can translate to any macrocosm. His gym, his office, his camps, his clinics, his banquets, are all laboratories for the study of leadership. At the time of writing this book, I have also been working toward my doctorate in educational leadership. I have read dozens of books and a least one hundred journal articles regarding leadership theory. I have found myself constantly making the following comments in the margins: *This is what Clink does.* In the last two years, I have written at least 10 research papers about different components of leadership based on my participant observations (I am a qualitative researcher) of his practices. I will soon be writing my dissertation about how redshirting positively affects the identity, social, emotional, academic, and athletic development of his freshmen student-athletes and helps them become incorporated into the university as they undergo the difficult transition from high school to college. Clink's teaching, his coaching, is Confucian. To study his pedagogy is to examine the concept of leadership as a pedagogy grounded in morality. There's nothing theoretical about the way he teaches and coaches. Everything is grounded in reality, preparation for the here and now whenever the here and now comes. It's genuine. I've seen the consistency. And I have studies his leadership not as a basketball fan, but from an academic lens.

Walk into the self-help section, or the business section, of any bookstore in this country. The shelves are flooded with books on leadership. These books are filled with one example after another of leaders and the lives of these great leaders. But what about *leadership*? Why does there have to be one specific leader? If a leader assigns roles to those whom follow him, can't the follower also become a leader? Maybe not *the* leader but *a* leader?

Clink is not heroic, and he's not demonic. His audience is small. He's not nationally famous and probably rendered unimportant outside of the North State, maybe even Chico. He's not elitist. He has humble roots. It's impossible to romanticize what Clink does because he can't be cast as the heroic figure in the murky background of the powerless, unmotivated, insipid masses. He chooses who he works with. He picks the assistant coaches, the players, the team managers. His leadership engages his followers. No one is alienated or powerless. The players are not inert. Everyone is engaged. If not, well, then they're no longer a part of the team.

The *team*.

The team is the umbilical cord to Clink's leadership and the collective purpose of winning as students and basketball players and later in life outside of Chico State.

Clink is a transformational leader. He causes change in individuals. His players improve as basketball players, but more importantly they improve as individuals. They turn into young men during their four to five years with Clink. They leave Chico State with degrees, and they enter the world prepared to succeed. Clink's end goal of each basketball season is to become CCAA Conference Champion and National Champion, but the end goal of the season—the end goal of their eligibility as a Chico State basketball player—is to become a better man.

The same can be said of his assistant coaches. Clink mentors them. If they commit to their role and execute Clink's game plan, they move up and on in the coaching world; this has happened with every one of his assistants. How does Clink do this? His leadership is genuine and authentic. Being genuine and authentic motivates his followers. There are no gimmicks, no Kevin Costner playing a coach making some earth shattering half-time speech. The team's identity matches Clink's identity. It's the one consistent pattern in the student-athlete's inconsistent world. The older players serve as mentors to the younger players, and the baton of the team mission is passed down from older players to younger players.

The organization has a collective identity yet made up of unique individuals. Clink serves as a role model to all the players. The older players serve as role models to the younger players, year in and year out. The players are inspired. The players are challenged. The players are charged with being accountable for their actions, and this accountability leads to a greater ownership of their individual efforts that branch out to the entire team and thus make it collective. Finally, Clink's assigning of a role to each player allows the player to better grasp and embrace his strengths and weaknesses. And Clink knows each player's strength and weakness which helps him get the team to perform at the highest level and squeeze the most talent he can from each individual.

Clink knows basketball is just a game. He's not in a situation where he has to win or walk. Unlike so many coaches in the Division I world, Clink doesn't live in fear of losing his job. This lets him be person-centered with his players, to see them for the students, the individuals, they are rather than just basketball players whom he must use to keep his job and maybe even get a better job. Being a Division II coach has allowed Clink to rethink and implement his changing perceptions and unchanging values and adapt to a new wave of player each year. No two players, and no two humans, are identical. He's able to meet and exceed the expectations of his administration, and he can keep raising the aspirations of his players. There's no winner take all mentality, and it's not a world of "give and take" with his players and his university.

Clink's personality and his character and his values are on full-display in each practice and each game for the world to see, whether it's the President of the university or the custodian who cleans the President's office. He does not have to hide who he is, and he does not have to broadcast a phony vision to his fans and boosters and bosses. Clink has changed the culture. Ask him if you can walk through the Red Door and see for yourself. What you may see, and what you might learn, could also help you create a positive cultural shift in your organization.

Clink doesn't have to think more than three seconds when I ask him how to define leadership. "It's the consistent example of the behavior you want, you expect, you demand your people to follow." He points out that he must always practice what he preaches. "You have to always be on time. You have to always put forth your best effort. Consistency. A lot of coaches stress character and punctuality on their players, but they themselves don't live up to it. I've seen it."

Clink himself would be out of character to name any specific coaches. "Oh, yeah. I've seen it. A lot."

Clink also believes a good leader must enforce consequences for not acting in accordance with the rules. "I do this a lot by making defense our main priority. Every man is accountable. We run drills until we get it right. And if a player doesn't want to follow the rules, his playing time suffers."

Clink believes that a good leader must have mastered his or her communication skills. "You have to know your audience," he says. "I know that with the 5 to 7-year-olds at basketball camp I have to speak slowly and clearly. I also have to watch the duration of my speech. How I talk to the 13-year-olds at camp is totally different than how I talk to the 7-year-olds."

Clink believes one either is or is not a leader. "I think anyone can develop leadership skills if they work at it, but I really believe you either have it or you don't. It's hard to get some guys to lead. It's just not in their nature. And it makes sense that it's this way. Not everyone can be the leader. If everyone had leadership potential, things would be chaotic. The world needs followers, too."

How, I ask, does a leader emerge from a group of Alpha males on a competitive basketball team? "They were all Alpha males in a little pond before they got to Chico State," Clink says. "Then they all get thrown into the bullring together. By week three, the leader emerges. If there is one. Sometimes teams really don't have a dominate leader. When that happens I lead differently." And Clink has never appointed a player captain.

Clink's motivation as the overall team leader is simple: "I want to be the best. When I was a player in elementary, junior high, and high school, I knew I was good. I knew I was better than most of the guys around me." By the time he got to college, though, Clink says he no longer felt good enough. "I often felt inferior as a player. Growing up in the Bay Area, and going to open gyms, I was always playing with guys who were great. The best talent around. I was always trying to improve. But what happened is that that I was always second guessing myself." As a head coach, though, Clink says he feels differently: "I view myself differently now than when I was a player. Now I know I'm a really good coach."

Clink doesn't say this to be arrogant, but because he's confident that he is in fact one of the best coaches in Division II basketball. His record—not just in the win and loss column but the persistence and graduation rates of his players—supports this claim. "Last year was supposed to be a rebuilding year. We ended up winning the CCAA."

Clink doesn't relax once the season starts. He'll tell you that the man you see now, in July, is a far cry from the man you'll see in October. "Everyone we play gets my full-attention. I prepare for Arizona the same way I prepare for Pacific Union and the same way I prepare for Pomona."

Clink, despite his instincts to always throw the first punch and go for the jugular, doesn't have a Machiavellian streak in him. "I'd much rather be loved than feared. I don't want my guys to follow me because they're scared. I want my guys to follow me because they know I value them." Clink doesn't want to be around losers. "Losers don't care. Losers are selfish. Losers are unproductive." The young men that Clink brings into his fold are nowhere close to being losers. They are the kind of young college men that shine a positive light on masculinity and male behavior in the current climate of what has been called "toxic masculinity."

Clink knows that a program is much more than winning the conference and getting into the NCAA tournament. Winning for him involves the big picture. "My job is to show these young men what they're capable of doing. How great they can be. I bring out characteristics that reside within them that they didn't even know they had. I get them to reach and exceed their potential—that's what Puck Smith did for me."

Clink recalls a time during Amir Carraway's freshman year when the young player was running sprints and asked to stop and go to the training room. "He said his knees were hurting. He didn't know how to play through pain. But we pushed him. He played through the pain and he was never the same player again. He started to see what he could become if he put his heart and mind into it—if he just committed."

Clink says Rashad Parker, one of the greatest players in Chico State history, had unlimited potential. He wasn't tapping into it, though, so Clink had to find a way to squeeze the potential out of him. After Parker's sophomore season, Clink brought him in for his end of the year exit meeting. "I asked him what his plans were for that summer," Clink says. "Rashad shrugged his shoulders and said he was going back to his dad's house in Castro Valley. Rashad always went back home for the summer. I thought he sat around and didn't do much. And until that point in his career he hadn't played much." Clink wanted that to change. "He came into my office, and I had $17,142 written on the white board. I asked him what his summer plans were." Parker shrugged his shoulders. "I pointed to the number and asked him what he thought that was. He shrugged again, said he didn't know. I told him that's what we were paying him in scholarship dollars to go home to his dad's house and sit on his dad's couch all summer. I told him he had a choice to make. He could go back to Castro Valley for the summer and I would give him his scholarship for one more year, but if he came back and wasn't any better and didn't play as a junior it was going to be his last year. But I told him that if he stayed in Chico for the summer and I saw him in the gym and weight room all summer working to get better, I'd give him his scholarship for the next two years whether he played a minute or not. I just wanted to see him work at it."

Clink says Parker came back into the office the next day and said he was going to stay in Chico. "He worked his butt off all summer and ended up not only playing, but being a two-time All- CCAA player for us. It just goes to show you what dedication and hard work can do for you. In order to have something great, you have to risk losing it all. It paid off. Always does."

Clink attributes a lot of his success as a leader to being stubborn. "Yeah, I'm bullheaded. I want things done my way. I believe, I know, that what I'm doing is the best way. It all goes way back to when I was a basketball player. I don't have to second-guess anymore. I know that whatever direction I take my team in is the best way. And the beauty is that I get to do it my way." Clink says that leaders also have to be willing to not be liked. "I'll admit that I care what people think about me. But it doesn't matter if you like me or not. I just want to be respected." He notes that a good leader also cannot be afraid of confrontation. "Coach Gabriel is a good example. He does it a little differently, though. He's like a big brother to Isaiah Ellis, but if Isaiah Ellis does something wrong, he lets him know right away."

Clink says that when he was hired, the Athletic Director Anita Barker—not only among a handful of female athletic directors in the country (in 2015, out of the 313 athletic directors in Division I sports, only 37 were women; in 2012 only 18.4 % of athletic directors in Division II were women) but also the best (just look at the championships and graduation rates of the athletic teams Chico State fields)—asked if Clink would win more games than he would lose. He surpassed her expectations. "Seriously, though, I knew we could compete. I was always confident in my ability to coach."

Clink has another drive. "I have a fear of losing. Even the year we were 28-5, when we won our 14th game I was delighted that we were over .500. Winning and losing are really fragile to me. The worst feeling is thinking about it. That's why I always wake up 3:43 a.m. and can't go back to sleep unless I watch an old rerun of *Frasier.*"

CHAPTER 8

The Wall

HEAD COACH GREG CLINK'S OFFICE—WHICH he shares with his two assistant coaches—is sparse with no unnecessary parts. A few nice chairs. A lap top computer. No clutter. A big flat screen TV for reviewing film. A drawing board with magnets numbered 1-5. The NCAA West Regional trophy with an old net hanging on it. However, his office walls are covered with plaques of former basketball players who have gone through their four years of athletic eligibility and graduated since he took over the program in 2008. The only way a player gets on the wall is if he graduates. And most of his student-athletes do indeed graduate.

Clink leans back in his chair. "See that guy," he says. "That's Chris Sharp. Let me tell you a story about him. The season ended and I told the team I'd be having exit interviews with them in the next week or so. So the next night I'm in Sacramento scouting a player (Robert Duncan). I get a text from Chris Sharp asking me if we can go to lunch the next day. So the next day we meet downtown for lunch. I thought he was going to let me have it," Clink says. "I rode him pretty hard for two years. We engaged in small talk and then Chris starts talking about what a great experience he had playing for Chico State, and how much all of the brotherhood he experienced meant to him. Chris was on the Maderos Scholarship. Scholarships attached to names are endowed. The donors give $10,000 to a scholarship fund. The money the athletes receive is a percentage of the interest from the $10,000. Chris knew how the scholarship worked. He had asked me about it before."

Clink says they finished lunch and Sharp slid an envelope over to him. "I opened it. Inside was a check for $10,000. He said, 'I want you to create a scholarship under my name.' His father died when Chris was 12, and he still had some money left over from the trust. He could have gone on some crazy trip or bought a car, but he wanted to give back to the program. He said he wouldn't have graduated from college without basketball."

Clink points to another plaque. "See that guy? That's Zach Graves. He's down in Hollywood acting now." He points to a few more players. "These are the guys who built the program. Most of them never won the CCAA Championship. We went 8-19 and 14-13 with most of these guys, but we could not have won down the line without them."

Clink has a great view from his office window. Magz, ducking beneath a branch, walks by and waves. Acker is steps away. Like a church, the priest's office is around the corner from the cathedral. Clink looks at his watch. "Time to go," he says. "Practice."

April 30 and the players are practicing as if it's October 15 rather than a month away from summer break. The players run each drill station with precision. NCAA rules stipulate that players can only meet eight hours per week during the off-season, and that they must drill and cannot be on the court with a ball in their hand for more than two hours. Beneath one goal the wings go one-on-one. Silverstrom and Duncan are playing as if their lives depend on it. Under the center basket, Clink has a blue cushion that looks like a seat he ripped out of a bass fishing boat. He smashes it against the big men when they pivot in the post and go up for a layup. On the other end of the court, guards are working on ball handling drills.

North State coaching legend Jerry Cleek has come to watch the Wildcats practice today. He has a yellow number two pencil behind his ear. He has a full head of white, wavy windblown hair. He no longer stands straight but a little stooped. A penny could roll perfectly from his neck down his rounded back. He has a goatee. He has piercing, knowledgeable eyes—the scrutinizing squint of a coach who has spent a lifetime assessing the skills of young basketball players. Coch Cleek rubs his chin. "That player, number 5, is going to be great." He smacks his lips and points to Robert Duncan. Coach Cleek watches Duncan with a faint smile. "I'm 72. Seen a lot of great players. He might be one of the best I've ever seen. And I've been coaching since 1965."

Cleek marvels at how fast Duncan slaps the ball from his right to his left hand and back again, how in doing so he toys with the defender, teases him. He points down to Isaiah Ellis under the basket. "And I really like that kid. He's special. Maybe *he'll* be the best ever." He continues to rub his chin. "Yep, that number 5 might be the best I've ever seen."

CHAPTER 9

Recruiting the Future

NOBODY WOULD KNOW UNTIL A season later the true talent and genius of
Robert Duncan. Did Clink see in Duncan flashes of the Pistol Pete po-
tential when Mavarich played college ball at LSU? Would Duncan be a
Division II Pistol Pete? How would a Pistol Pete fit into Clink's culture?

If it were not for Robert Duncan, I doubt the story of this coach and
this team would have ever been told—at least by me. I am a self-professed
basketball snob. I like to consider myself an arbiter of good taste when it
comes to hoops, not because I was or am a great player but because it's the
thing in life that's been with me the longest. Friends, jobs, dogs, houses,
zip codes, have all come and gone. But basketball has always been there for

me; the basketball court is a place where I will always have a permanent residence.

I'm not so much a snob of the collective team game but of the individual game. To this day, I have a hard time keeping up with the fast-paced frenetic movement of basketball. Too much happens too fast when watching two good teams go at it. My eyes can't keep up with all the action, so I key in on a few isolated plays and watch the individual. I imagine a lot of fans do that. I imagine most of us miss at least one-tenth of the action—action that happens with the nine other guys who don't have the ball: that's where the action takes place.

The one-tenth of the action I saw one night in my first Division II basketball game was enough to inspire me to spent three years writing a book.

It was a cold January night in 2014. I had not been out of the house, other than to go to work, in what felt like years. It actually had been about a year. I was a new dad (and a scared, older dad at 41). My son Holden was only one and a half years old. I never liked to leave him and his mother. But I knew Chico State was playing a team from Los Angeles. I figured a team from Los Angeles had to be good, right? We had only recently moved to Chico. Before my wife and I moved here, the only thing I knew of the town was that the brewery that brewed my favorite beer was located in this college town. That wasn't necessarily enough of a pull to leave the Pollyanna paradise of Cal Poly and San Luis Obispo, but add two sets of grandparents and a newborn, and that was enough to punch the ticket. So my father-in-law, a long-time physician in town who supports any and all things Chico-sports related, invited me along to the game. I jumped at the opportunity. I'd never seen a Division II basketball game, let alone the Chico State Wildcats.

I was blown away that night by the caliber of play. We beat the daylights out of this team from Los Angeles. I was confused. Who was this Chico State coach in the suit crouching on the sidelines? From far away, he looked a little like Billy Donavan before Billy Donovan started looking older and like the middle-age NBA basketball coach he has become. Even though the Wildcats were winning by 30 points, the head coach still had this intense, pained look on his face as if he'd put his children's entire college savings on the color black at the roulette table. The coach finally started clearing the bench.

This has always been my favorite moment in sports. As a kid, and now as an adult, I could never understand, and would get mad, when the coach—whether it was football, baseball, or basketball—would not put in the "grunts" and let them get a little playing time in when it was an unquestionable blow out. I was pleased that this coach put a few guys in.

One player particularly impressed me. When he entered the game, he had the excitement in his eyes of a little kid at Christmas. I could tell that he had a lot to prove in a short amount of time.

I watched him as he inbounded the ball close to our seats. I looked at my roster. Number 5. Robert Duncan. He looked like a church ball player to me. Maybe a middling track athlete. He had the wiry body of a runner, wiry but with lean muscles and not a jot of fat. He looked hungry, kind of like the scrawny, sinewy, tough-muscled rats I'd recently seen in the back alleys of Shanghai. He threw the ball in. He didn't step on to the court after that. He flew. I could tell by what he did *without* the ball that this kid could play. I watched him intently during those final minutes of garbage time. I would not see him again until a year later when he surprised everyone and became an overnight star and Chico State basketball fan household name.

Robert Duncan was yet another Division I player who had landed at Division II Chico State. The only difference between him and the big-time stars at the Division I level was about three inches and 35 pounds. Clink had recruited Duncan out of high school. He saw Duncan play in Anaheim with his Amateur Athlete Union (AAU) team the summer before his senior year. "I followed him around to every one of his games," Clink says. "He was my favorite player that summer."

Clink tried to sign Duncan his senior year. "He came up for a visit with his grandfather, who also happens to be retired Army. We had a great visit. Gus and I were driving in my car going down Ivy Street during the afternoon of the visit. Rob and his grandfather were in the car behind us. We hit the corner of Ivy and West Second and there was a party going on in the front yard of this house. Girls in bikinis. Guys in board shorts. Red cups and kegs. Beer pong. Kiddie pool on the lawn with a bunch of guys wearing hats made out of the cardboard from a case of beer. I looked in the rear view mirror. Rob's face was lit up. His grandfather, though, was frowning. He had a stern, disapproving look on his face. I looked over at Gus and said, 'We just lost Robert Duncan.' And we had." Duncan's grandfather made him go to the Air Force Academy Preparatory School. "The next spring," Clink says, "I get a Facebook message from Rob saying hello. I knew at that moment he was coming to Chico State. I told Coach Cobb—my assistant who had replaced Gus—to stop setting up visits for any other wings until we got Rob here."

The success of the 2013-2014 campaign would lure more Division I talent to Chico State. Clink signed 6-foot-5 guard Corey Silverstrom from Bullard High School in Clovis. Silverstrom was the Fresno Bee's Co-Player of the Year for the 2012-2013 season. He had won the tournament MVP at the Gridley Invitational, the premier tournament in Northern California. Silverstrom had helped lead Bullard to the state regional finals in 2012. He was a First Team selection on the Cal-Hi Sports All-State Division I team. He was also on the All-State Elite Squad's third team—a list of the top 30 players in the state. The kid could score and distribute. He turned down Division I offers to come and play for Clink. Silverstrom knew the word on the street was out: The CCAA was one of the toughest conferences in Division II. Silverstrom would redshirt.

Clink also signed Tyler Harris who, like Robert Duncan, had spent the last season at the Air Force Academy Preparatory School. Harris had spent four varsity years at the private Bakersfield Christian High School before signing with the Air Force Academy Preparatory School. He had become the high school's all-time leading scorer, averaging 25 points and 10 rebounds a game his senior year. He was also named an ESPN IV All-State "Next 10" player. Clink liked Harris because he was a guard who could nail the three. He excelled at coming off ball screens. He was smart. He handled the ball well. He was long. He would redshirt as well.

Clink then signed the 6-foot-7 forward Isaiah Ellis from Antelope High School in the Sacramento area. Ellis was a find. Already at a substantial height, he would grow and get even stronger. He had the potential to be a big-time collegiate power forward. He looked like a young James Worthy. He was a 220-pound post who had both defending and shot-blocking skills. He had range. He could work the paint. Clink was also impressed with his ball handling skills, and believed that his shooting skills would stretch the floor. He had the potential to surpass George Maderos as the best overall player in Chico State history.

Coach Cobb and Clink went and watched Ellis play in the Gridley tournament his senior year. He got in foul trouble early and sat on the bench for most of the first half. Clink was unimpressed with what he saw. "I sat there and watched him take a rolled up program and mock interview one of his teammates on the bench. He was totally not engaged with the game. I started giving Coach Cobb a hard time, told him I'd never coach this guy." Clink put the name Isaiah Ellis in the hopper. So the season went by, and Coach Cobb kept nagging Clink to go back and watch Isaiah Ellis again. "I kept blowing him off and telling him there was no way I was going to recruit this guy. So finally I agreed to go watch one of Isaiah's playoff games. I took my son Tyler with me. I told Cobb that I was only going so he would stop riding me about it. At halftime I called Cobb and told him that we had to sign Isaiah. He was that good." Ellis would redshirt.

CHAPTER 10

(530)

CLINK DOESN'T HAVE TO DO "living room jobs" when he recruits. He rarely makes an in-house visit. "I bring recruits here," Clink says. "I let the campus and its surroundings do the talking."

One of the first stops Clink makes with his recruits is the pool at the campus WREC center. From March until June the pool looks like a scene from an MTV Spring Break special. The smell of coconut suntan lotion intermingled with that familiar summer scent of grilled meat from an afternoon barbecue across the street wafts in the air, and the sound of student laughter is soon drowned out by the roar of a passing train. Once the train passes, the sound of splashing water and lively chatter picks up again.

Chico is one of the last true college towns in California. The university is able to recruit the best and brightest young professors because the town remains affordable. Unlike most college towns in California, the prices— the real estate—in Chico is reasonable. Staff and faculty can buy a home here and have a life. Artists can afford to live here, and galleries are throughout the town. Students can afford rent without having to work two jobs, take out huge loans, or financially strap their parents.

The 530 area code is a place where people live and raise children, a community where people lay roots and live and die. It has not sold its soul like so many other California towns have to wealthy Southern or Northern Californians looking for a place to exploit. Chico is a place where those who were raised here will eventually go out into the world but often return home. The writer Thomas Wolfe proclaimed "You can never go home again."

But Chico proves that wrong. People *do* come home again. Clink might not have been reared here, but he did *grow up* here. He did his undergraduate work here. He played college basketball here. He did his graduate work here. He broke into his coaching career here. How fitting that he would come back to raise his family here.

Chico State offers first-rate academics for students but without the academic stress and anxiety found at other California schools. High school students don't have to academically break themselves trying to get into Chico State. Chico State students don't have to forgo a social life and spend every free minute in the library to get out of Chico State. And most alumni would give anything to come back and do it all over again.

The campus blends into town. Students live in houses across the street—literally steps—from the university. Couches, swimming pools, and ping pong tables decorate the lawns. Young men are scattered throughout the streets playing catch with baseballs and footballs, fetch being played with dogs. Young women in bikinis catch rays on the rooftops of their houses, dash in and out of the sprinkler. Laughter is everywhere. Music blares from the houses. Young men and women play volleyball in front yards. Every house seems to have a grill fired up.

Chico State has worked hard to shed the party school image associated with being named Playboy's first Number One Party School back in 1987. While Clink does not champion the drunken revelry aspect of partying, he does see the positive benefits from being in a college town that realizes the importance of mixing fun with academics. "When we recruit and parents are on campus, the 'party school' question always comes up," he says. "I talk about how most of the students live within walking distance of campus, and how this is one of the biggest college towns in the country—one of the last true college towns in California. I talk about how the university in recent years has changed the 'party' climate, but unfortunately that reputation will never go away. I also talk about how social the students are, and learning to be social is why Chico State students get jobs when they graduate because they know how to talk and deal with people."

Chico was originally a mining camp. Were it not for Chico State University, Sierra Nevada Brewery, and Aaron Rodgers, most people outside of the 530 would never have heard of the town. When my wife told me she was from Chico, I asked: "Isn't there a big penitentiary there?" She quickly corrected me: "That's Chino, and it's in San Bernardino."

Chico is considered rural yet not small (86,000 and growing). Despite the large number of people living here, the feeling of a small town exists. A short drive out of Chico and it becomes clear that the town really is in the middle of nowhere. But it is *somewhere*. Chico is nestled between two national forests, the gateway to Mount Shasta, Lassen Volcanic National Park, and Lake Tahoe—all about a three-hour drive away. San Francisco is also a three-hour drive away, and Sacramento just a ninety-minute drive. Bidwell Park is the major draw to Chico. For someone who is not a California native, or someone who has spent his or her entire life confined to a California city, it's hard to believe that Chico is in California. Bidwell Park represents one of the largest municipal green areas in the country.

Chico is the perfect summer town. Sycamore Pool is a throwback. A portion of Big Chico Creek is cemented into the shape of a large swimming pool where the creek runs through. It's free to swim here. People picnic and grill all summer long in a big grass area by the pool. Lifeguards perch high in chairs at various spots around the pool. The water stays cold, the creek always storming through. Despite the drought of the last four years, the small dam traps the creek water, even when the creek is dry. Kids young and old splash here all summer long. Caper Acres, where generations of Chicoans grew up playing and now take their kids to frolic, is right around the corner. Bidwell Park has swimming hole after swimming hole: Alligator Hole; Diversion Dam; Salmon Hole; and Brown's Hole—all reachable along the Yahi Trail. The town is also a runner's and mountain biker's paradise.

When Clink was in high school, he visited some friends that were freshmen at Chico State. "I fell in love with the place. I remember riding my bike through Bidwell Park and through campus. It was beautiful." Clink notes that he was not much of a student in high school. "Going to community college was my only option. But during my two years at community college, I knew I wanted to go to Chico State." He followed the course outline at his community college to make sure he took all the right classes that would transfer to Chico State. "I loved going to school here. I had friends from my hometown that I lived with, but made many more. It was so much fun to be able to walk out of our apartment and step across the railroad tracks onto campus. We would walk across campus to downtown. Everyone that lived in our apartment complex was a student. It was a magical time in my life. And it seems like a blur. It went by so fast. I stayed after I graduated and got my teaching credential at Chico State. Then I stayed another year and got my master's degree. I didn't want to leave."

Yes, people live here. People go away. People come back to start their own families. People come back to die here. Chico is a place with roots. It is a place to be *from* and a place to come back to and *live*. Chico has a nice balance of redneck meat-eating culture with a mix of summer of love throwbacks. It has Schubert's, a shop that has been making ice cream since the 1950s. The town is teeming with art galleries. It is one of the last affordable bohemian—if not the only—towns in California. Hunting and fishing are a big deal here. So is lacrosse. So is birding. So is just about everything. Winters are mild. February brings Chico snow when the almond trees blossom. Summers are hot. Spring is short. Fall brings an East Coast feeling as the leaves change colors. There's one good thing of everything: one great used bookstore, one great independent theater, one great Indian restaurant, and so on. The people here are proud. Every third person one sees walking through town is either sporting Sierra Nevada Brewery or Chico State gear. Even though this is Raiders and 49ers country, one sees almost as many Green Bay Packers hoodies to support the town's favorite son, Aaron Rodgers. Almond and walnut and olive trees thrive here. There's always the possibility of a party lingering in the air. The Esplanade, with its big trees and old homes flanking both sides, has a striking similarity to St. Charles Avenue in New Orleans—the only thing missing is the trolley and Mardi Gras beads hanging down from the trees like tinsel. Downtown

Chico smells like stale beer and grilled meat; blasts of air conditioning pouring out from stores as one passes on hot summer days.

The town is divided by streets and avenues. The avenues running north-northwest to south-southeast toward campus are generally named after trees. They spell the word Chico: Chestnut, Hazel, Ivy, Cherry, and Orange streets. The streets are south of the campus and run downtown. The avenues are north of campus and run to the Esplanade. For a town of only 86,000 there are a lot of parks—22 total.

Chico, mainly in the summer when the temperature daily flirts with 100 degrees and the students have fled, has the feeling of an old Southern river town. The Sacramento River is close by and brings out a river culture of free-spirited river rats. Tubing down the Sacramento River is one of the students' favorite activities. Locals and students often get their first sunburn of the year (Memorial Day), and their last sunburn of summer (Labor Day), on the Sacramento River. In the fall, fishermen and fisherwomen go up and down the Sacramento River catching monster-sized salmon. The actor Errol Flynn spent time in Chico while filming the 1938 classic *Robin Hood* in Bidwell Park. The writer Raymond Carver once studied and taught at Chico State. Chico is the almond capital of California. A familiar Chico sound from spring to fall is the hum of the sprint cars from the Silver Dollar Race track. The university makes Chico the hub of culture. There are two major public high schools (no private high school) that hate each other about as much as Cal and Stanford, or the Dodgers and Giants, hate each other. Butte Community College is a sports powerhouse. That is where Aaron Rodgers played. By now, most sports fans know his story about how he wasn't even the player that Cal's head coach Jeff Tedford had come to Butte to recruit. Chico is that kind of town. Rodgers can still be found in town during the off-season. His father has a chiropractic business here. Even though the Raiders and the 49ers are so close, Green Bay Packers flags still fly on Sundays.

Chico and the surrounding towns are the perfect breeding grounds for athletes. Long, hot, lazy summer days and long nights with lots of open space to play in. The perfect boring venue for the imagination to grow, those long days and gaps between early June and late August filled in with sports. Chico is the kind of town where young boys and young girls learn how to skip rocks— learn the motion of throwing—in the creeks or ponds or lakes. Friday night football is a big deal. The local newspaper and the news station make local sports front and center. College (even Chico State) and professional sports often take a smaller front page column or get pushed to the back pages to make way for stories about high school teams and athletes.

Chico State men's and women's basketball helps stave off the boredom and malaise of winter on Friday and Saturday nights. It really is the only game in town. Fans don't have to fight parking when they come out. Downtown restaurants and bars are an easy walk to campus. The community needs basketball. Basketball needs the community. Clink uses this as a selling point when recruiting. "I talk about how the players are recognized in town. They're like celebrities. They walk into a restaurant and people know who they are. I also let them know while this is a perk, it's also a responsibility. The players must be careful about how they talk and how they act. I let them know that there's always someone watching. A booster, a kid who comes to the games. This is another reason why we only recruit great guys."

Baseball rules spring and summer in Chico. When fall dawns in Chico, there's no football ·team to root for. The university got rid of the program in 1997 citing insurance costs being too high. The students root for their college and pro teams, and they await the start of basketball season. October 15 is never that far away. And if baseball in Chico measures the rhythm of summer, then Chico State basketball monitors the quickening heartbeat of winter.

CHAPTER 11

Greatest Game in Chico State History

CLINK AND HIS SQUAD WOULD receive an early Christmas present, one they had earned. The National Association of Basketball coaches poll had them ranked as the No. 21 team in the country. This was only the fifth time in the program's 98-year history that the Wildcats had been in the top 25. At 7-1 they were off to their best start since the 1942-1943 season. The Wildcats were on a 17-game home winning streak—they had not lost at home since December 6, 2012—when Cal State Monterey Bay came to town. When their nemesis Cal Poly Pomona came to Acker the next night, the Wildcats were defeated. The Broncos won the game in the final seconds on a three-point play, 67-64.

The Wildcats recovered quickly and started winning again. Clink was now on the brink of winning his 100th game. It would happen on February 21 at Cal State Monterey in the Kelp Bed. The Wildcats would beat the Otters, 87-80. Clink had become the first Chico State coach in his history to win 100 games in his first six seasons. Clink laughs when recalling that night. "After the Monterey game we all went to Denny's. One of the players had his phone out and looked up the article about the game on our web site. They saw it was my 100th win. They all came over to shake my hand and say congratulations. Amir Carraway was the last one in line. He shook my hand and with his big smile said: 'You're welcome!' It was great. I will never forget that."

Clink did not have time to rest on his laurels, though. February was a short month. March would bring a new season, and with that new season a chance to avenge Cal Poly Pomona. The Wildcats would beat the Broncos after six straight losses to make the CCAA Championship finals for the third season in a row. And for the third straight season in a row, he would not be able to hang that blue banner in Acker.

This time the Cal State Stanislaus Warriors would deny the Wildcats the CCAA tournament championship. They also handed the Wildcats one of their worst losses of the season, 82-70. This was not the kind of loss a coach wanted heading into the NCAA tournament, particularly when his team was out-rebounded 40-21 like the Wildcats had been. Still, Clink was proud of the regular season. They were 22-7 and still hot, only losing twice in the past 10 games. Further, before this drumming, their six losses were by a combined 14 points.

The Wildcats would earn the number four seed in the NCAA West Regional. They would take on number five seed Cal Baptist. Clink had four seniors who'd been had already been on this tournament journey twice in a row. The Wildcats would rebound from their CCAA Championship final loss and beat Cal Baptist, 77-71. The Wildcats advanced.

The Wildcats would get a second round win over host and number one seed Cal State San Bernardino. They would pound them by 20. They'd next get another shot against Cal State Stanislaus. The Wildcats still had blood in their spit from the beating they'd taken in their last encounter. The winner would move on to the Elite Eight at the Ford Center in Evansville, Indiana. Clink knew the way to beat the Warriors this time around: defense and rebounding. They trailed the Warriors 74-61 with 2:48 remaining. What followed was one of the most amazing comebacks in Division II history. If this were the NCAA Division I tournament, clips of these final minutes would take up a good portion of the *One Shining Moment* music video played at the end of each March Madness.

The magic started hours before tipoff as the Wildcats were waiting for the shoot around. Clink was pacing around the gym. He caught sight of a ladder propped up on the wall just under the basket. He had a vision. He brought the team over to look at the ladder and said: "Tonight, after we win this thing, we're going to take that ladder and cut that net down." He then looked down at the other end of the court. "And you see that net? Once we cut this net down, we're going to take the ladder down to the other end of the court and cut that net down, too."

At halftime, Clink's prophecy was not going as envisioned. The Wildcats had been outplayed and were down by a lot. In addition to their poor play, the Wildcats were crying to the refs and not handling the adversity. Clink looked around at the five seniors. "Let's go play the way we're capable of playing. If this is the last time we're all going to be together, let's go out the right way. Don't look at the scoreboard until there's two minutes left on the clock. You got it? Only *then* will we take a look at the clock. Until then, let's just play."

The Wildcats scored 20 points in the final 2:34.

Everyone had stepped up.

All eyes were now on the clock and scoreboard. It was go time.

It came down to Jordan Semple stealing an inbounds pass near midcourt. Getting fouled with 3.9 seconds left and down one point. Missing the one-and-one free throw. Carraway snatching the rebound. Putting up a floater. Getting fouled. Making two free throws. A desperate Warriors Hail Mary from the other end of the court. The ball hitting the iron and bouncing away.

The Wildcats rushing the court.

A trip to the Elite Eight was sealed. It took Clink six years to get here. It took Michael Jordan seven years to win an NBA title. These kinds of things take time.

Clink summed it up in the post-game interview with Mike Baca: "I can't wrap my head around what just happened. I just want to say how proud I am of these guys, win or lose." He had taken Chico State from being in the basement of the CCAA to now being truly elite. With proven success also comes a change in perception. Clink was starting to see his dreams come true. He was now fielding questions from reporters other than the hometown sports beat writers for the local *Enterprise-Recorder*. Coach Clink had arrived.

"We've evolved," he said in the post-game interview. "Our goals have changed drastically. At the beginning it was about academics and getting our culture right. Three years ago it was about competing for a conference championship. Now, being in the Western Regional is an expectation."

For the players, the dream season would end on March 26th against South Carolina-Aiken in the Elite Eight. The 85-70 loss would not change the fact that this had been the greatest season in Chico State basketball history. In a 99-year basketball history, this was the first Chico State team to win the West Region title and advance to the Elite Eight.

Clink would wake up at 3:43 that morning and wonder how in the world he was going to win the CCAA next year without his five seniors—the five kids (Carraway, Parker, Park, Estrada, and Appel) that he had recruited as teenagers and helped mold into young men. His program now had expectations. His thoughts immediately turned to next season. Clink turned on the television, and as he settled into *Frasier*, he remembered that he had three more seniors: Rosaroso, Barton, and Semple. He would also be returning seven letter winners from a team that went 25-8. And all those talented redshirt freshmen would be ready to play. With this thought, he turned off *Frasier*, stumbled back to bed, and drifted off to sleep. But Clink always sleeps with one eye open.

Little did he know that Robert Duncan, who had only played in nine games that season and averaged 1.9 minutes a game (1.9 minutes that was enough to inspire the book you have in your hand), was about to become a star.

CHAPTER 12

Second Time's a Charm

THE 2014-2015 SEASON WOULD BE the 100th season of play in Chico State basketball history. Clink wanted it to be special. He also wanted to make sure there would not be any more 41-20 rebounding deficits like there had been in the CCAA tournament championship game last season. Clink needed to bring in a big man with experience who could crash the boards, bang underneath, and help bring his freshman Isaiah Ellis along. He found this man in 6-foot-11 Tanner Giddings.

Giddings would transfer from Fresno State where he had averaged 14 minutes a game, two points, 1.9 rebounds, and had 21 blocked shots. He was also a good student, named two-time Academic All-Mountain West honoree at Fresno State. He had also received the team's Most Improved Player as a freshman and the Service Award his sophomore year. Giddings, despite his size, his smarts, and his talent, was not being used efficiently by the Bulldogs. Here was a kid who had starred at Windsor High School near Santa Rosa. Giddings had set the school's career scoring record with 1,307 points. He was the league's MVP and All-Empire Athlete of the Year after averaging 16 points and 10 rebounds per game as a senior. He had led Windsor to a 28-7 record and the second round of the CIF Division II state playoffs. Clink, not one to take transfers, would give Giddings a chance.

Clink also needed to sign some future players to play alongside Ellis and Silverstrom. The Wildcats' conference success and postseason resume had put Chico State on the radar. Once again, Clink would bring in a talented recruiting class. He signed Nate Ambrosini of Fortuna Union High

School in Humboldt County. Ambrosini had averaged 21 points, seven rebounds, and three assists per game. He shot 50% from the field and 55% from the 3-point line. He was also voted the Humboldt-Del Norte League Most Valuable Player. He was a two-time All-League pick, team captain, and a Eureka Times Standard All-Star. Ambrosini would redshirt. Clink also signed Keith Datu, a 6-foot-7 wingman from Saint Joseph's High School in Santa Maria. Datu had averaged 19.3 points a game, 9.5 rebounds, and 2.3 blocks per game his senior year. He was a First Team All-CIF Southern Section 4A selection and two-time First Team All-Pac 7 pick. He also played AAU with the Nor Cal Wildcats. Datu would redshirt. Clink also signed Marvin Timothy from the familiar recruiting grounds of Franklin High School (where Carraway and Rosaroso had gone to school) in Elk Grove, California. Timothy, at 6-foot-6, would bring strength and size to the front line.

According to NorCalPreps.com, he was also Northern California's 39th ranked prospect. He had averaged eight points, nine rebounds, and two blocked shots per game. Timothy would redshirt. Clink signed Joseph Lynch from up the road in Redding. A 5-foot-11 guard from Liberty Christian High School, Lynch had led his team to three state North Section titles—two that were in Acker Gym. He had scored 1,437 points in his career. He was a First Team All-Northern Section and won MVP of the 5-Star League. He finished his high school career by scoring a record 38 points in the Lions All-Star Game. Lynch would redshirt.

Finally, Clink signed the young man whom he knew would have to replace Rosaroso at the end of the season, and the young man whom he imagined could lead the Wildcats to a National Championship. Clink knew who he wanted and got him: Jalen McFerren, 5-foot-10, who was not only ranked among the NorCalPreps.com as a top 22 prospect but was also an excellent student. McFerren had averaged 15.6 points and four assists a game at Castro Valley High School. He was a two-time All-Hayward Athletic League Selection. Clink liked the kid's quickness—his bounce. Despite his small frame, McFerren had an instinct for rebounding. He could get to the ball fast and start the break. He was a player who thrived in the transition game. He could score and facilitate. And he would play right away—a rarity in Clink's program. Clink did not redshirt McFerren. Surely, Clink must have seen a future when McFerren, Silverstrom, and Ellis would cut down not one and not two but three nets by the time their senior year of 2017-2018 was complete. By not redshirting McFerren, Clink was relying on both his instincts and the manifestation of a vision.

These student-athletes that Clink recruited and redshirted had all been stars in high school. Imagine the identity strain they would encounter not being able to play an official game until at least sixteen months later. But the talented-redshirted-freshmen practice had worked for Clink so far, and he wasn't about to change the recipe. McFerren would be the exception to the rule.

Enter the season that is the prelude to the season this book covers. The season that, yet again, had wildly exceeded the realistic expectations of a team that had lost five seniors—two of whom were now playing professionally (Carraway was off to Germany to play for Rasta Vechta in the ProA League; Park would sign with the Worcester Wolves of the British Basketball League).

From an outsider's perspective that had followed the 2013-2014 season, the 2014-2015 season would be a mystery. Barton and Rosaroso had been major contributors to last year's Elite Eight run, and Semple was a season away from becoming one of the best Chico State players in history. Magalotti had played but sparingly at 6 minutes per game. Kitchens only played 12 minutes a game. If anything, this season would give the younger players and freshmen experience. McFerren would be the rare true freshman and back up Rosaroso. Duncan and Priest had only played in nine games the previous year. Duncan averaged 3.2 minutes and 1.3 points per game, while Priest would average 4.8 minutes and 0.9 points. Ellis, Silverstrom, and Harris were redshirt freshmen. Ambrosini, Datu, Lynch, and Timothy would be redshirted.

The 2014-2015 season began with the rise of an unexpected star. Clink must have known Duncan would be good, but did he have any idea the kid would be this good? Robert Duncan made the most of his first two college starts. Now a sophomore, he won the Most Valuable Player honors at the 14th Annual Sonoma State Ron Logsdon Basketball Classic by averaging 15.5 points on 60% shooting (12-of-20). He also pulled down 2.5 rebounds, 1.5 assists, and one steal per game. Duncan showed flashes of brilliance. Sometimes it was like watching old highlights of Pistol Pete. The kid knew how to create shots, and for a young man that had played less than 29 minutes total the previous year, he was teeming with confidence. Also, against Alaska-Anchorage the freshmen were playing like juniors. McFerren, Harris, Ellis, and Silverstrom combined for 25 points on 9-of-17 shooting (4-of-8 from 3), 16 rebounds, two assists, and one turnover. They were playing Clink-style ball.

The Wildcats were also winning on the road. They went down to Cal Poly Pomona and beat them 51-50. That would be nine consecutive CCAA road games the Wildcats had won. Not bad considering four freshmen were getting significant minutes and playing major roles in the victories. Duncan was getting better each game. He was scoring down the stretch. He was getting rebounds when they were most needed. Semple was producing one stellar balanced game after another—points, rebounds, steals, and blocked shots. By January 24, the Wildcats were in a three-way tie for first place. Ellis's year spent preparing as a redshirt was paying off. He was coming off a 14-point game against Cal State East Bay. Kitchens and Giddings were stepping up when needed. Acker was getting packed. 1,173 fans showed up for the 64-59 win against Cal State L.A. The Wildcats had now won six in a row.

Duncan would lead the Wildcats to their seventh win in a row with 23 points on a mere 11 shots. He was 8-for-11 from the field, 1-of-2 from downtown, and 6-of-7 from the line. He won two straight CCAA Player of the Week awards. Against UC San Diego and Cal Poly Pomona, Duncan had 19 points in each game. He shot 67% (14-for-21) from the field and averaged 19.4 points, 4.5 assists, 4 rebounds, and 1.5 steals per game. The winning streak was at nine with their victory over Cal Poly Pomona. The Wildcats were in sole possession of first place.

On February 28, 2015, the Wildcats would beat Cal State East Bay 87-61 to win the CCAA Championship for the second time in their 100-season history, and on the night that they celebrated that history by honoring many of the greatest athletes and coaches in Chico State athletics history. Jay Flores, who played an important role in Clink's past and the success of the program, and now an assistant coach at East Bay, was among those honored. So was George Maderos, the greatest athlete in the school's history.

Clink was beaming. The Wildcats had been picked to finish fourth in the CCAA, quite an honor since they had lost four starting seniors and 70% of their scoring from the team that had made the Elite Eight team last year. The Wildcats had won 14 of their last 15. Led by Rosaroso, Semple, and Barton—who had won more post-season games and gone further in the tournament than any senior class yet—and ignited by Duncan (he would match his career high 23 points; the Wildcats beat Cal State Stanislaus 72-60 in the second round of the CCAA tournament).

The Wildcats would reach their fourth consecutive CCAA Tournament Championship game, but the fourth try would not be a charm. Cal Poly Pomona would make the Wildcats wait another year to try and win the title. The good news was that Duncan and Kitchens were All-Tournament selections. Duncan had averaged 20 points a game while Kitchens had averaged 11 points.

The season for the players would come to an end on March 13. Cal Baptist, the team Chico State had beaten a year ago in round one of the NCAA tournament, would get revenge, 67-61 win. For a team that was picked to finish fourth, the Wildcats season was a success. They had fulfilled the major goals Clink set at the beginning of the season: Winning the CCAA Conference and reaching the NCAA West Regional. Next year would be good. Clink had the pieces. Granted, the pieces were young, but they would soon mature. The future was doggone bright.

3:43 a.m. dawned and Clink shot up out of bed. He had had a good dream. He was standing on a ladder and cutting down a net. He didn't need *Frasier* tonight. He plopped his head back down on the pillow and fell back asleep.

PART II

Starting Line Up

CHAPTER 13

The Glass Jewelry Maker

THE MORE I GET TO know the "Greg" side of Coach Clink, the more it makes sense to me that he would have married an artist who specializes in making handmade glass jewelry. Courtney Gray had moved to Morgan Hill and started going to Gavilan Community College in 1995. Clink was not yet there—he was coaching at UC Davis. Courtney started hanging out with a group of guys who turned out to be Clink's best friends. They told her that a friend who coached at Davis was coming into town for a Super Bowl party. Courtney was fired up to meet the Davis coach; she was planning to transfer there.

"So I was there at the party, right, and I see him through the window walking into the house," she says. "He walked into the room and, yes, he was gorgeous, but there was something significant about him. He really stood out."

Courtney had to leave the party early that night to go work her shift at Applebee's. "I walked in and told my friends I worked with that I just met a guy. I told them he was mine—done." And then, Courtney tells me, she asked him out. Courtney and Greg dated long distance while he was at Davis and she was studying at Gavilan. "The week I moved to UC Davis, Greg moved here because he got the head coaching job at Gavilan. The first three years of our relationship was long-distance."

Courtney knew nothing about basketball. "My dad didn't follow sports at all. We would go to my uncle's for Thanksgiving. Football would always be on. And I just remember thinking to myself: Why are we watching this?" Courtney had no interest. I ask her if she ever talks to Greg about basketball. She smiles and shakes her head. "He's not a talker, and he doesn't like to talk about work. When he gets home, he doesn't want to talk about it. The only aspect of his work that we talk about are the business aspects. He will ask me for advice when he needs to talk to a player about something he might be struggling with, but we never talk about the actual basketball side of what his players are doing. Greg is just not a talker. Sometimes when he's on the road we don't even talk. That's just how we are. We have the best relationship, and it gets better each day. But do we talk about basketball?" She smiles and shakes her head again.

Greg and Courtney dated for five years before they got married. When Clink got the job at UC Santa Barbara, Courtney stayed behind at UC Davis to finish college. "I didn't want to move down to Santa Barbara, because I knew once I moved to him that was it. Greg's career took precedence. I didn't want to have a career. I wanted to be a mom. So after I graduated from Davis, I stayed in Northern California and got a job at Hewlett-Packard. It wasn't for me. I also really missed Greg. Seven months later I was down in Santa Barbara."

In Mississippi, where I'm from, a coach's wife often struggles with her identity outside of being, well, a coach's wife. Perhaps this has changed since I left the South, but, sadly, the way that I have always viewed the wife of a coach has been colored by those experiences. Courtney, however, does not fit that role.

So I ask: How does it feel when someone calls you "the coach's wife?"

"I love it," she says. "This summer we were at Jay Flores's wedding. Actually, Greg got a one-day license online so he could officiate the marriage of Jay and Molly. So we're driving home the next day, and I'm an emotional wreck. I told Greg how lucky I felt to be a part of all this. I get to go to all these wonderful games and build lifetime relationships with these players and their families. The players graduate from the program and then the relationship takes on a different dynamic. We get to be Instagram friends or a former player will text me if they need something. If Greg were out of town, and a former player was passing through town, I'd ask him to stop by the house to see me and the boys. I feel so grateful to be a part of all this."

Courtney does acknowledge the misunderstanding and stereotypes that coaches wives encounter. "I hate it when someone feels sorry for me because Greg isn't around. No, the worse thing is when they say I'm a coach's widow. I'm thinking, come on, people. He might be gone for three days. It's going to be okay. And when he's gone, I get to watch what I want to watch on TV. It's great—I love it. Look, we are both very lucky that we each have a job that we are intense and passionate about."

Courtney is a glass artist. She specializes in fused glass, separate pieces of glass together in a kiln and fused at around 1400 degrees. She uses a technique called slumping. "This is when you melt glass dishes and wall sconces over ceramic and stainless steel molds to create shape. It's all done in the glass kiln." Her business—grayc glass—has a huge online presence and focuses on custom handmade fused glass lighting, jewelry, and art. She also has a stand at the Chico Certified Farmers Market every Saturday, and I've never passed her booth without there being a swarm of women around. She makes everything: bridal jewelry, cuff bracelets, earrings, necklaces, nightlights, ocean inspired glass, rings, and wall sconces.

Courtney's art career started back when she and Greg were dating long distance. She was at UC Davis, and when she wasn't working at night or going to school in the day, Courtney says she was bored out of her mind. "I started doing pottery in the ceramics center at Davis. Not long after, I saw a class about making glass bowls. I've always loved glass ashtrays. Whenever I'm in an antique store, it's the glass ashtrays for some reason that always get my attention. So my mom and I took a glass class together. I loved it. I wanted to buy a kiln." Courtney had no intention of every turning this newfound passion into a business. She bought a large kiln when she and Greg started living together in Davis. She had the kiln in their small second floor apartment. "It took Greg and the other assistant Kevin Nosek to help us get that thing up the stairs. I started making things out of that apartment, but it wasn't until we had kids that I started making the nightlights and that's when the business started taking off."

One of Courtney's nightlights—an owl—was the first item my wife and I purchased when we moved to town. Little did I know when changing my newborn's diapers in the wee hours that the light guiding me would be the nightlight created by the wife of the coach whom I would follow for a year: The metaphors here are endless.

The nightlights—not being the coach's wife who sells nightlights— put Courtney's art on the map. I figured being the wife of the successful basketball coach in a small town might help draw women to her wildly popular booth at the Chico Certified Farmers Market. "Most people don't know I'm the coach's wife," she says. Clink, though, isn't too common of a name, and Coach Clink is a town celebrity. "My last name is Gray. I kept it." I give her a confused look. She starts laughing. "I think it's important to keep your own identity. I certainly wanted to keep mine." I ask her where her motivation comes from. "I want to be successful. If I don't get up every morning and do some research or work on my blog or work in my studio, I'm not going to get paid. Greg can spend the summers watching high school players to recruit and he'll still get paid. Not me. If I don't get up and produce, I'm not going to get a paycheck."

Courtney Gray is no coach's widow.

"It's funny, you know, because boosters will come up to me and ask me what I think about the new 6-foot-7 recruit, and what do I think about him? People will sometimes fish for information. But I don't know. I have three kids and my own business. If Greg wants to talk about the recruit, I'll talk about it with him. Otherwise it's not my business." I ask her how the sensibility of the artist and the sensibility of the coach come together. Once again, I have applied an incorrect stereotype. "A lot of the players always ask me how I deal with Coach Clink's intensity, and I just laugh because, believe it or not, I'm way more intense than Greg. He's intense with his job, but when he gets home he's relaxed. I'm intense about everything. Yes, I'm an artist, but I'm more of a businesswoman than an artist."

Still, though, I wonder how the relationship between two intense people works. I have never seen this relaxed side of Clink—I just know him professionally. Ten minutes into a conversation with Courtney and I feel the same intensity. "You know how a lot of couples talk about being yin and yang and how their differences complement each other? Well, we're not like that. We're lucky because we're on the same page about almost everything. I almost don't even need to check-in with him about making decisions because we have such similar beliefs." Courtney revisits the question about being identified as a coach's wife. "I think if you're a coach's wife, you have to understand that there are parts of the year when your husband gets really busy. It's the same thing if you're the wife of an accountant. During those first four months of the year, the accountant's wife needs to have her own life and know what you signed up for. Figure it out."

Courtney loves being self-reliant and that she and Greg have independent lives. "Right now, Greg and the three boys are down at his mom's house in Morgan Hill. He's coaching a camp there. When he gets off, he goes and plays golf with his childhood friends. We might talk three times this week. I love him. I know he loves me. But do what you want to do. He knows I'm here running my business. I'll clean the baseboards this afternoon. Tonight I'm going out to play Bunco."

I can't help but wonder why the Clink family has not left Chico for other job offers.

"We love it here," she says. "You know, when he first took the job, I thought that after maybe five or six years we might go somewhere else. But we love it. Greg's not even close to being finished with what he set out to accomplish at Chico State. Our kids are happy here. My business is really taking off."

I ask Courtney who Greg was all those years ago when she first met him—the young basketball coach walking into a Super Bowl party carrying a platter of appetizers his mother made—compared to the man he is today.

"He's the same person," she says. "He's so simple. He's the same person. What you see is what you get. He does have a lot more on his shoulders now, and he has a lot of stress he has to deal with. He's just always been confident—that 26-year-old kid who walks into a football party carrying his mom's appetizers and getting flak from his buddies."

Courtney relies a lot her on intuition. "I just get these strong feelings about things, and they usually turn out right. I remember when Greg came home and told me that Puck Smith was retiring. I had this feeling that Greg would get the job. I knew in my heart." Courtney says when she and Greg were dating, she'd never been to Chico. "We were young, right, and he brought me up to Chico. He told me this is where he wanted to coach. This is where he wanted to live and raise his kids." She says when Greg told her about the job opening, she started getting their house ready to sell. "Before we even knew that Anita was going to interview him, we drove up to Chico for the day and drove around looking at houses and trying to find the perfect neighborhood. After we put the kids to bed, Greg and I would practice interviewing for hours. I also videotaped him. We would come up with all these questions he thought he might be asked. I would critique him, particularly little nervous habits he had when he talked. We'd often finish at 10 p.m. and then I'd have to go out and work at the kiln."

When he got the job offer their house was sold nine days later. "We were ready to go," she said. I ask Courtney if her family gets any kind of special treatment when they go out and about in town.

Again, my background experience guides the question. Down in Dixie, if you're the college basketball coach and winning, the red carpet gets rolled out. "No, none of that. Every now and then someone offers to buy Greg's breakfast, but nothing more than that. I do get to fly under the radar a lot because of my last name, and between his profession and my business, we know a lot of people in town. There have been a few times when I've been friends with someone for years, and they never even know that Greg is my husband. They find out and are totally surprised." Courtney says she looks forward to the start of a new season just as much as she looks forward to the season ending. I ask her about February—the high-water mark of Greg's season—imagining that his stress must crossover into her world. "February is really busy for my business. It's Valentine's Day." That would have never dawned on me. She's busy fulfilling gift orders in February. I love knowing what I don't know. I can't help but wonder if Greg, or the man I refer to as Clink throughout this book, ever relaxes. "I guess you've never met summertime Greg," she says.

"But does he do anything, you know, that might be considered corny-dad things?" I ask. She smiles. "He sings and plays the guitar. He's really good at it. But the person that's really good is my son Tyler. We go camping and sit around the campfire and sing—very cheesy but hilarious." Even though in the midst of relaxing and having fun, Courtney says Greg gets intense. "He takes playing the guitar and singing so seriously. He always asks me to give him feedback on how he sounds. He has a playlist he follows and everything. He's intense about it, but he loves it. This is how he has fun. And he makes me sing. If I don't he gets upset. We'll have friends over and the next thing I know he's busted out the guitar."

This is a side of Clink I didn't know existed. I ask her why he never talks about these things.

"To who?" she says. "He's a really private guy. You know, one of the greatest aspects of this program is that players who go through the program and think of Greg as this really intense guy eventually get to see the other side of him. But it's not until they've finished playing and graduated that Greg reveals this other side of his personality."

As I drive home from the their house, I'm still not convinced that Clink has this fun-loving, corny Greg side to him. Later that night I get a text from Courtney with a video attached. It's Clink playing the guitar (wearing a Hawaiian shirt even!) with his son Tyler as the family sits around a swimming pool.

CHAPTER 14

Division II Sushi Chefs in Training

GETTING A HEAD COACHING POSITION is not unlike becoming a master sushi chef in Japan. An aspiring sushi chef doesn't start making sushi right away. Nor does an aspiring college basketball coach instantly land a head coaching position. The sushi master behind the counter at a quality sushi restaurant does more than just make sushi. He also makes his customers feel special. The skilled sushi master observes the eating habits of his customers. He will make softer pieces for those who eat with their fingers, and firmer pieces for chopstick-users: A piece should never fall apart when dipped in soy sauce. The master sushi chef must also have mastered the art of communication.

A sushi master's day—just like the day of a head basketball coach—begins before sunrise and ends long after the sun has set. Similar to the head basketball coach, the road to becoming a master sushi chef is arduous. Only those who have diligence and patience will succeed. Breaking into the business starts with an apprenticeship. The master sushi chef starts as a busboy. Long days of cleaning bathrooms, mopping floors, and sharpening knives humble him right away. After a few years doing this, he moves up to *shikomi* (food preparation). Here he learns to be detailed and meticulous. The student learns by observing. There are no guides or instructors.

Becoming a head coach is similar. That's the road that Coach Justin Blake is traveling on right now.

Coach Blake, 28, struggles with school. He's still working toward his BA degree. When he's not coaching or going to school, he works as a bartender at Round Table Pizza. "I try to schedule as many shifts as I can before the season starts." Nevertheless, despite his woes with formal education, Clink praises Coach Blake for his other intelligence. "He hates school, but he loves, and I mean *loves*, basketball. He can't manage his time. He goes home and instead of doing his homework he sits and watches basketball coaching videos on his computer for hours on end. I tell you, though, he has one of the best basketball minds of anyone I've ever met. He has the ability to watch during our games and see what's happening. I get caught up in subbing and running plays and don't always see the little technical things going on, but he sees them. He's often the guy I go to after the game to talk about the game and what happened. He doesn't get emotional about the game too often, and he can analyze really well. Coach Blake hates school so much that he can't even tell you what year he's in.

"I'm a senior," he says. "I think."

Coach Blake has taken an unorthodox road to break into the coaching world. He was not a high school basketball star. He lost interest in playing when he was 15. "Girls and cars became more important." When he graduated from high school, he had no clue what he wanted to do. "All my friends left for college. I enrolled in CSU East Bay. I hated it. I dropped out." Coach Blake regrets not going away for college. He also started regretting not having tried harder with basketball. He got a job at an Italian restaurant in his hometown. When he wasn't working, he was reading about basketball, and when he wasn't reading about basketball, he was watching basketball DVDs. "I didn't know enough technical stuff," he said. "I read every book on X's and O's that I could get my hands on. I also started collecting DVDs. I had more than 60 of them." He strokes his goatee. "Yeah, being an assistant coach, it's all about mercenary work. I would not leave this position if the next position didn't have a similar environment." He seems to live in a basketball reverie. He eats, sleeps, and drinks basketball. His mind drifts.

"Jake Lovisolo is the Mt. Rushmore of this program," he says. "The Chico State basketball program changes people lives. We're close knit, tight. It all comes back to Coach Clink creating the team culture. The program will be successful no matter what as long as Coach Clink is here."

When Coach Blake first got into coaching, the first thing he did was to let go of his selfishness. "In high school I played ball only for myself." His high school coach later gave him a chance to come back and work as his assistant. He then got a job coaching in the Catholic Youth Organization— the St. Raymond sixth grade team in Dublin, California. "We only lost one game," he says. "I kind of cheated, though. We trapped a lot. We used 1-3-1 zones." The next year he coached seventh graders. "We lost a game. It killed me. The team that beat us denied us on the wing. I think that's when the obsession started. I had to find ways to get better. I was always looking for a solution. How to counter the opponent."

The next step for Coach Blake was getting involved with summer camps. He got hooked up with the Bay Area's Triple Threat Academy, the first basketball academy in the Bay Area to offer daily skill training. "I started teaching and working as many camps as I could, and teaching as many classes as I could. I taught small group sessions. I would do these on weekends and weeknights."

Coaching is about relationships. The Triple Threat camp introduced Coach Blake to a lot of players and coaches. He worked with Orlando Johnson, Theo Robertson, and Brandon Johnson. He also got to know Lou Richie, the head coach at Oakland's Bishop O'Dowd High School, who had just won the state championship. "Ivan Rabb came to the camp. There was all kinds of talent." Coach Blake met Coach Cobb at the camp. "I remember seeing him (Cobb) play in high school. I remember looking at him and thinking this guy can't play. He's too small. But he was tough as nails. Shoot the lights out of the three." Coach Blake and Coach Cobb talked a lot during camp. "He told me I should come up to Chico State and help out." Coach Blake set up a meeting with Clink. "I became the team manager." He was in charge of setting-up practice. "That's the hardest." He would get there a half an hour early. Mop the floor. Get the balls out. Get the gear out. Get out the pads. Set-up the cones. Rebound. Keep time. Keep score. Refill the water. Get the players water. Film all the home games.

Coach Blake volunteered his time. There was no pay. But his paycheck came in the experience he was getting. He was learning how to become a leader. "I think I'm a lot like Coach Clink. He reads about basketball a lot. He never stops trying to learn. He always does what it takes to get better. And he's not so much into the technical stuff as he is about building relationships. "I've learned so much getting to know Coach Clink and from his leadership style and how he makes decisions. Coach Clink is whatever he needs to be at the time. It's how he communicates, brings in players, and talks to them."

Coach Blake had never experienced what it felt like to win until he came to Chico State. "The only winning I'd ever done was at the youth level. You know, when I was a little kid. Winning feels awesome." However, he's quick to note that it's not just about winning. This has become a cliché in sports, but Coach Blake is sincere. The eyes don't lie. "It really is more about the relationships. Things are different here. High school basketball is usually about being selfish. Here we share." Coach Blake says the way things are done at Chico State is different. This is something that comes up time and time again when I ask those associated with the program about Clink and his teams. "It's our culture. It's all so real. So transparent. So honest. No excuses."

Coach Blake says he would like to someday be a Division II head coach. "I'd also be fine being a high school coach."

For many students, basketball is what keeps them in school. That holds true even for college students. "I know I need that piece of paper," Coach Blake says about getting his degree. "I just want to get through." Coach Blake, though, is working on his PhD in basketball, and the success of the 2015-2016 season will be his dissertation.

Each day for Coach Blake is a grind. He's a student/coach/worker. "I get up early and go to bed late." He starts his day by meeting players around 7 a.m. for a workout. He'll then go to class then stop in at the office. All three coaches share the space. "I'll check-in and do whatever needs to be done. I make calls. If a player comes in and wants to go practice or workout, I do that. I might scout. I'm always preparing and making a list of things to discuss with Coach Clink." Coach Blake then goes to study hall from 1:30-2:45 p.m., then it's off to practice. And after that it's a night class at Chico State. And after that it's off to work at Round Table Pizza. "I never tell people I'm an assistant coach," he says. "I mean, I have a lot of pride but it's not the only thing I do. Besides, they'd never believe me." Basketball is always on Coach Blake's mind. "When I'm bored, I look at basketball websites and look for basketball DVDs."

If Coach Blake is the brain, then Coach Gabriel is the mentor.

It's particularly hard to juggle being both a student and an athlete. It's even harder, and rarer, to succeed in both categories. A college basketball coach at the Division II level has a set of responsibilities that include recruiting and student-athlete evaluation, recruiting updates and mailings, assisting in campus visits for recruits, all film exchange for pregame, regular game and postseason, opponent scouting, game plan development, on the floor coaching, practice plan organization, promotion of all youth camps and clinics, supervision and daily leadership of youth camps and clinics, film breakdown and editing, assisting in organization of strength and conditioning, individual skill development during offseason, and group skill development during season. Plus, there's a substantial amount of time that assistant coaches spend on the road both with the team and on their own recruiting and evaluating. And then there's the academic piece. One would think that a position with this much responsibility would pay a livable salary, but it doesn't. Clink's assistants always leave for financial reasons. He knows it's only a matter of time.

"I don't know what I'll do without Lucas," he says, in reference to Coach Lucas Gabriel. "But I said that about Chris Cobb and Gus Argenal, too."

The great coach is an educator, a professor. His players are students. He hands them a syllabus, and each practice they have a lesson plan. The students' grades are monitored in a box score, not just for the coaching staff to assess and evaluate but the performance open to scrutiny from the public. Practice is studying for the big tests in the CCAA that come every Friday and Saturday night. Clink teaches his players, his students, how to keep winning after they take off their Chico State jerseys. He's able to evaluate the talent and skills, the strengths and weaknesses, of each player and maximize their potential by establishing roles for them. Clink could not do this without his assistant Coach Gabriel; together, they are wedded to the idea of student-athlete.

One of Clink's first orders of business and goals when he got to Chico State in 2008 was to improve the men's basketball academic standing. He had inherited a team that needed to improve its academic standing in the entire athletic department. Anita Barker, Athletic Director, hired Coach Clink to not only turn the team around in the win/lose category, but to improve the academics of players. In the fall of 2008, when Clink and his staff officially took over the basketball program, the team's cumulative

GPA was 2.1. Furthermore, six players were deemed ineligible to participate in any of the games because they had GPAs below 2.0.

When Coach Clink arrived, he immediately met with one of the leading experts in the field of supporting at-risk student-athletes (who taught
at the university), Dr. Kathleen Gabriel. Dr. Gabriel taught Coach Clink
how to set-up an academic program for at-risk students. Coach Clink also
hired Dr. Gabriel's son, the earlier mentioned Lucas Gabriel, to become the
graduate assistant coach. Coach Gabriel at the time was working toward his
MA in education.

Coach Clink set a goal to win the award for the highest GPA in the
athletic department. He wasted no time punishing players for violating
the culture of strong academics he was instituting, expunging one of the
most talented players on the roster for plagiarizing. He also charged Coach
Gabriel with rebuilding the academic program that had been freefalling for
some time. Coach Gabriel put into practice an academic system based on
the research he had conducted for his MA thesis in education regarding the
special academic services needed to support Division II basketball players:
*Design, Implementation, and Effects of Academic Coaching on Men's College
Basketball Players at a Northern California University.*

Coach Clink, working in tandem with the academic program Coach
Gabriel was creating, put his foot down. Every player had to give his best
effort in the classroom. Cheating or short cuts of any kind would not be
tolerated. Every student-athlete would stay in close communication with
the coaching staff by having weekly meetings with their assigned academic
coach. Coach Gabriel's system consisted of a student-athlete program com-
prised of tutoring, class monitoring, frequent meetings with players and professors, and any other additional support that players needed. The academic
support program would also require a high standard of not only effort but
strict monitoring of the student-athletes' progress by the coaching staff.

The first step in Coach Gabriel's study program was to give all the
players an academic binder. They also completed a Weekly Schedule form,
and they had to write in all of their standing appointments. Each player

was assigned an assistant coach who would closely monitor their academic progress. Coach Gabriel was assigned the most "at risk." He had an accountability plan; progress reports and self-evaluations; contact with advisors, counselors, and professors.; helping players utilize campus resources, workshops, tutoring, and guest speakers; study hall four times a week; and there were random class checks.

It was all paying off. At the end of the first year of the implementation of the academic support program, the men's basketball team cumulative GPA rose to 2.7. At the end of year two, the men's basketball cumulative team GPA improved again to a 2.84. Furthermore, all of the student-athletes remained academically eligible. By year three Clink reached his academic goal: The basketball team won the award with an overall 3.2 GPA. In the last two years (at the time of this book), eight out of ten student-athletes who completed their four-year eligibility have graduated. The two players who did not graduate went on to play professional basketball overseas. If the men's basketball team continues this pattern, the projected graduation rate will be above 80%. To put this in perspective, the freshmen four-year graduation rate at Chico State (2017) is 26%, and the six-year graduation rate is 64%. Meanwhile, Sacramento State (2017) has a 9% four-year graduation rate, and the six-year graduation rate is 46%, the same graduation rate as Division II student-athlete basketball players.

Clink will not hesitate to punish a player for violating the culture of strong academics that has been created. Coach Gabriel says that a professor once turned in a player for plagiarizing. "The player was one of the most talented players to ever wear a Chico State jersey" Clink took away the player's scholarship and kicked him off the team midseason. "We only won three more games the rest of the season." On another occasion, a star player received an 'F' in Nutrition class. Clink lost it. He looked at Coach Gabriel and said, "Lucas, get in your car right now and go out and find me a new wing. I'm not going to have someone on this team who can't pass *Nutrition!*" Clink told the player that if he didn't get a B when he retook the course, he was done. The player went on to earn a B+.

Coach Gabriel enjoys sitting down and helping students with their schoolwork. He spends a lot of time working with the most at-risk student-athletes. "My first season here, I would show up at Damario's dorm room at least 10 times during the season and work with him on various assignments," he says. Coach Gabriel would also walk Damario over to office hours with his professors. "Then one day he told me, 'Coach, I can do this on my own now.' And he did."

Coach Gabriel is not all work and no play. He connects with the players. He feels a close connection to Robert Duncan just as he did with Damario Sims. "We like the same kind of music—Eminem, Naz, Jay-Z, Lil' Wayne." Coach Gabriel emulates the kind of student that he wants his players to be, on and off the court. "You have to embrace the things that aren't as fun." Coach Gabriel says that after his first season as a graduate assistant, he went in and talked to Clink. "I asked him how I could get better."

Clink told Coach Gabriel that he had a good grasp of the time commitment involved with coaching. That wasn't a problem. "I mean, he pretty much told me that I could be a star among stars—maybe not that exactly, but he said something like that in a positive Coach Clink kind of way—but only on one condition. He said that I had to excel at the things that I didn't enjoy as much."

Clink had given Coach Gabriel two big spring assignments. He wanted Coach Gabriel to put together a highlight tape for the postseason banquet, and he wanted him to go into the elementary schools to run clinics and promote the summer basketball camp. "Coach Clink told me straight up that he was worried. He knew I'd be great at the highlight reel because I eat that kind of stuff up, but he was worried that I wouldn't have the passion and enthusiasm to get kids into the summer camp. Coach Clink told me that once I put the same effort into things like summer camp, only then would I become great."

Summer camp recruiting is now one of Coach Gabriel's biggest strengths. "I've already got 60 kids signed up for June and 40 kids for July, but I won't be satisfied until I get 90 kids for June and 100 in July."

Coach Gabriel has since reached and surpassed his goal.

CHAPTER 15

Redshirt Experience

JUSTIN BRIGGS, THE 6-FOOT-10 REDSHIRT freshman, entered Chico State at 17 years old. He would not turn 18 until a few weeks before the official start of practice on October 15. However, despite his age, Briggs should have no problems adjusting to Clink's regimented practices and off the court discipline. Both his parents were in the Air Force. Briggs was born in Okinawa, Japan, and came to California when he was around two. Even though his parents were in the military, Briggs says they had different roles in his upbringing.

"My mom was the one who kept everything organized and structured," he says. "She kept me on task and made sure I studied. My sister was super smart and got amazing grades in high school, so my mom wanted me to meet those academic standards. My dad was the one who was more laid back. He always gave me options and never pushed in any one direction. It was a great balance." Briggs will be the second one in his immediate family to attend college. His sister was the first. She recently graduated from UC Santa Barbara.

Briggs was a late bloomer to the world of basketball, late as in he started hooping in the fourth grade (most of the players in this book were exposed to the game, if not already playing, by the time they were knee high). Briggs says he was always a couple of inches taller than the other kids in his class, but would really start to grow in middle-school when he grew to be at least six inches taller than his classmates. It was also around this time that his competitive nature emerged. "I hate to lose. Challenge me and I will try and win every time." He says this comes from (yet another) the sibling rivalry he had with his sister—five years older. "I was always following in her footsteps, and I wanted to one-up her."

Chico State was not the only school that courted Briggs. "When I was playing AAU ball, Air Force, Weber State, Sacramento State, Northern Arizona, University of the Pacific, CSU East Bay, and CSU Los Angeles recruited me. I had a verbal offer from CSU Northridge."

Briggs says that when he was in high school, he knew he wasn't as developed as he needed to be. "I wasn't even allowed to play with the guys when I came to visit on my recruiting trip to Chico State because my physical had never been cleared. I just sat there on the sidelines with my mom and watched the guys practice."

Briggs's role as spectator rather than player worked in Chico State's favor. "It really helped to just watch. I could tell the coaches cared about player development. Everything was on hands on. The coaches separated the players according to their position, and there was a coach at each station who worked with players to develop specific skills. After the workout, we went to the weight room. We stayed long enough for me to feel the energy that was in there and the attention the coaches gave players."

Briggs was not sold on Chico State by the coaches alone, but by the way the players greeted him. "Yeah, when I came up for that spring practice, all the players walked up and introduced themselves to me. They told me how excited they were to see me play. Robert Duncan said he was bummed he wouldn't get to see me dunk on Isaiah. I felt welcomed. Yeah, they all greeted me with open arms. No other school I visited made me feel like that."

I'm curious to find out which NBA big man Briggs models his game after. "I'm mesmerized by players with handles, players like Jamal Crawford. Big men," he says, laughing, "bore me. They're just not as interesting and entertaining."

Briggs went through seven weeks of workouts before he found out that he would redshirt on October 15. "We had an evaluation meeting. I was told to ask any questions that I wanted. I was disappointed when I found out. I know that Coach Clink redshirts almost every player. So it was an expected disappointment." I ask Briggs if it will bother him when the team goes off to play big teams like Arizona or during the regular season when his team plays away games. "My roommate is a redshirt. We'll watch the games." He says it's actually a great experience. "It's almost like watching a scouting video and figuring out how I need to improve. What went wrong. What I'll need to do next year when I play."

People associated with Chico State basketball refer to Briggs in the future tense. "Next year he's going to be great. Next year he's going to be a star. In four years, he might be known as the greatest player in Chico State history." However, this "star identity" is all new to Briggs. "In high school, I wasn't a star. I didn't play varsity for four years like a lot of really good guys. I just worked my way up. I kept developing and getting better each year. People never came up to me and said: 'Oh, Justin, we saw you go crazy last night.' My teachers and the students at my school never really acknowledged me as a basketball player."

Briggs was academically focused in high school. Basketball was not his only identity. When he walked on to the Chico State campus, he knew right away that his role was not simply a basketball player but a student-athlete. "This goes back to high school. I knew that I had to balance these two. I was academically ready. I had my major—business—chosen before I even got here."

Briggs almost seems too poised to be a redshirt freshman. I can't help but wonder if redshirting has contributed to this. "Redshirting has really helped me with my time-management for sure. The first few months of school are overwhelming. All the classes are hard and we also have to practice. As I get further into the redshirt year, I'm starting to discover that the weeks are getting easier. You start thinking things are easier, but really you're just doing the same thing you've been doing the whole time. You just get better at managing it. When I first got here, yeah, I was overwhelmed, but now I've figured it out."

Briggs says when he was in high school, he hardly ever lifted weights. But when he got here, all of that changed. He and Vinnie Saffin—his roommate and the other redshirt freshman (Saffin had to leave Chico State after his first semester to return home because his mother got sick.)—would always lift weights together. Saffin, one of my favorite players to watch in practice for his toughness (he always seems to have a black eye and recently got dinged hard from a Magz screen) and intelligence (we once had a twenty-minute conversation about the physics of the putting the proper spin and rotation on a basketball). The loss of Saffin hurt Briggs. The two redshirt freshmen had gotten close. Thankfully, the older players took good care of Briggs and put him under their wing. The lone redshirt freshman and Coach Blake are in the weight room every day after practice. "I can see the changes in my development. It's hard, though. Every day right after practice I have to get a second wind and go to the weight room." Briggs says a lot of his motivation comes from the others around him being so strong. "Magz is a lot stronger than me. I can play and use my skills and touch to get the ball in, but he uses his body to push me. He's always moving me around when I try to guard him. Every time he bullies me in the post, I'm fired up to get back in the weight room."

It must be strange for the newly-minted 18-year-old to know that next year he will step into the role that the fifth year Senior Magz—a grown man—will be vacating. "This redshirt year allows me to watch him and learn from him in practice and out practice. I use the good and the bad to help my own development. It's a mentorship."

I ask Briggs if he has any culture shock coming to Chico from his hometown of West Sacramento. "Where I grew up, I wouldn't just get up and walk to the store. Here everything is close, a community. I was always used to commuting to school, but here I walk to class. I walk everywhere. It's also great living so close to the basketball court. I can go there anytime. That's really helping with my development. I'm right here on campus, and so is the gym."

I ask Briggs about the social trappings of being a young and social student-athlete on a campus known for having a good time. "I look up to all the older guys. I watch their behavior when they go out. I see what they do and build upon their ladder, follow in their footsteps, and then I'll branch off and create my own path. I follow the lead of guys like Jalen, Magz, and Rob."

Briggs says the way Clink has structured his practices with a daily practice sheet of everything the players will address that day has translated into his academics. "Nothing is up to chance. Nothing is random. It's all planned. Everything is laid out before the players even walk through the Red Door. Before you go through the Red Door, you have to take a deep breath and get ready to play. Coach Clink tells us all the time not to go through the Red Door unless we're dialed in and ready to play. He tells us he'd rather we stand out in the hall and stretch, mess around, get it all out. He says you can come to practice two minutes late if you have to, but get it out in the hallway and be ready to get after it when you walk through the Red Door. I enter the classroom the same way."

Briggs says that when he walks back through the Red Door to go back to the lockers, he takes another deep breath. "I take that deep breath because I'm glad to get out of that environment," he says with a huge grin. "I know I can tone it down when I get to class. But what I'm learning and doing out there on the court in practice all transfers into what I'm doing in the classroom." Briggs says he feels relieved when he leaves practice. I'm glad he says that. I'm just the writer, and I feel like *I've* aged a few years after practice—they're that intense. "Clink searches for 100 percent perfection in everything we do. When I get to the classroom, I also expect everything I do to be 100 percent perfection. That's what he drills into us. When I do group work in class, just like when we do group work on the court, I try and bring out the best in everyone around me."

I ask Briggs the million-dollar question: When do you have time to be a college student? "It's all about setting up your schedule. I know which days are busy, and which days are my study and homework times." Briggs also has a meal plan. "Yep, I make all my food for the next day. When I have a break in between classes, I don't want to waste time cooking. I'd rather have it ready to go in a container and heat it up."

And something tells me that next year, after this redshirt season is in the past and Briggs is no longer spoken of in the future but present tense, he, too, like the meals he prepares, will be ready to heat up.

CHAPTER 16

Hometown Hero

EVERY STORY HAS A BEGINNING, a middle, and an end. Every story also has a hero. What, though, makes this hero? The hero must overcome a great source of conflict. He must stare down into the abyss and be dragged through the depths of hell. After facing and defeating foe after foe, after conquering obstacle after obstacle, the hero saves the day and wins the prize.

Sometimes it's just a matter of the hero coming home and signing a letter of intent to play basketball at his hometown college.

Enter Jesse Holmes. The return of Holmes symbolizes all that is uniquely great about sports. And every now and then, sports—the greatest unscripted drama of all—falls into the three-act structure of the drama that rigidly adheres to the 12 steps of what Joseph Campbell (whose theory George Lucas used to create *Star Wars*) deemed the Hero's Journey. Holmes is a hometown hero. He only graduated from Chico High School in 2013, but he's already a legend, beloved by teachers, students, and the entire Chico sports community. Clink wanted him to play basketball at Chico State. Holmes chose to play football at Air Force instead. Not long after, though, Holmes's world would come crashing down.

His older brother Casey, just a couple years ahead of Jesse in high school, graduated from Chico High School in 2011 and joined the Marines in May 2012. Casey Holmes would soon become Private First Class Casey Holmes. He was assigned to the 3rd Battalion, 3rd Marine Regiment at Marine Corps Base Hawaii. On the night of March 11, 2013, at 10:55 p.m., Casey was directed by his platoon leader to dig a "fighting hole" in a remote area of the sprawling Twentynine Palms facility. The shallow foxholes were interspersed among a unit of amphibious assault vehicles taking part in the same exercise. Close to 11 p.m., a pair of Marine bulldozers approached the encampment. Casey was in a sleeping bag in the fighting hole. The lead bulldozer stopped on top of Holmes and crushed him to death. The death was ruled a "traffic accident."

Casey's final words before he died were about Chico. A Marine lying next to Casey said that they were looking up at the stars, just relaxing. "Casey said something about how many stars there were above and how he missed California sunsets, and how I needed to visit him in Chico and meet his family and friends," the Marine said. "I remember asking Casey something but don't remember what and noticed he was already asleep. Next thing I know I woke up to bright lights and dust in the air."

Clink was aggressive in his pursuit of Jesse Holmes, but he also understood and took into consideration Holmes's desire to play collegiate football. Holmes had put in the hard work and turned out the prep numbers worthy of a Division I football opportunity. Holmes was a good basketball player, but he was a star wide receiver for Chico High—a legitimate potential big-time football star. He was the Northern Section's all-time receiving yards' record-holder. He finished his three-year varsity career with 189 catches and 3,436 receiving yards, the most for any Northern Section player. He also scored 39 touchdowns. The record was 41. He ranked seventh in California for yardage.

How could Holmes turn down the opportunity, particularly when it was for the U.S. Air Force Academy? He opted for the Division I Mountain West Conference football rather than Division II CCAA basketball.

Air Force, though, was not a throwing team and known for having a run-heavy offense. The season prior to Holmes's arrival, the Falcons only threw the ball 151 times for a measly 1,334 yards. Meanwhile, they rushed the ball 804 times for more than 4,000 yards. Nevertheless, getting his degree while also playing a sport he loved was one of Holmes's big dreams. He was a legitimate two-sport star for the Chico High Panthers. He led the section in points per game for the basketball team and led them to the state playoffs twice. Chico State was not the only basketball team that courted Holmes: Pepperdine, Oregon State, and Boise State all gave him preferred walk-on opportunities. However, when he went on a visit to Colorado Springs, his decision was made. The high level of both education and athletic competition was the fruition of Holmes's dream. He wanted to prove that he could compete on the gridiron at a Division I school.

The decision to stay home and play for the hometown basketball team and a coach he trusted, or leave and play for the glory of a famous Division I football school, tugged at the heart of Holmes. He could either play college basketball four blocks away from where his Chico High Panthers had played, or he could travel to Colorado Springs and enter the Saturday night lights of football and catch passes on national television. Not only that, but his entire football experience had consisted of home games on the home field of his football rival, Pleasant Valley. Chico High did not even have its own grid iron. "Basketball's always been my first love, so it's special to me," Holmes says. "With Chico State, it was definitely hard. It's my hometown. The coaches are all good guys, and I really like them and what they're doing and how they're developing. It's a special place and it was hard to turn down."

Life is a sum of all your choices.

It has been said that the road to hell is often paved with good intentions. The full-circle journey of Jesse Holmes started out with the best of intentions, but what he thought might be heaven had turned into a nightmare of unknown proportions. Some subscribe to the philosophy that things happen for a reason. This is the only way to put tragedy in perspective and move forward. Holmes had to leave Chico so that he could come home. This is a tale that stretches back to Odysseus. Odysseus, like Holmes, is a hometown cultural hero. Odysseus was gone for ten years. Holmes only two. But two years in the life of an 18-to-20-year-old is much longer than it seems. In Holmes's case it must have seemed like a lifetime. Holmes, after taking off for Colorado Springs, never would've thought that one day he'd trade in the football cleats for high tops, get the chance to wear a Chico State jersey, and play in the gym just down the street from the gym where he starred in high school.

Basketball is unpredictable. A lot can happen in 40 minutes—a lot can happen fast. Same thing with life.

Holmes realized right away that Air Force might not have been the best choice. "I knew pretty fast it wasn't the right fit. I was calling my mom all the time. All the what-if thoughts ran through my mind. What if I would've just stayed in Chico and played basketball for Coach Clink? I was homesick. I would look up YouTube videos of Bidwell Park. I missed Chico." And when Holmes's older brother died, Jesse said it was strange waking up and putting on the Air Force uniform every day. "I knew he'd want me to do it, though."

Nevertheless, Holmes made the decision to return home. He planned to play football at the powerhouse Butte College, but suffered an injury. Part of his rehabilitation was doing yoga with Rex Stromness, the Chico

State basketball team's yoga instructor. "He asked me if I had any desire to play ball at Chico State," Holmes says. "Yeah, I told him. I went to a lot of basketball games that season. For the first time in my life, I was a spectator. I loved the atmosphere at Acker. I could really see myself wearing a Chico State jersey. Not only that, but making an impact and helping the team. But I felt guilty for turning Chico State down."

Stromness casually mentioned to Clink one day that Holmes was back in town and said he wanted to play basketball for Chico State. Clink had no idea Holmes was back in town, but told Stromness to have Holmes get in touch with him.

"I met with Coach Clink," Holmes says. He told me what I needed to do. He said I needed to first contact my football coach and let him know my intentions. And here I am." Holmes pauses and smiles. "This is the first summer in ten years that I haven't been getting ready for football." He shakes his head and laughs. "I don't even know how to lift for basketball."

CHAPTER 17

Something's Cooking

DREW KITCHENS DOESN'T LOOK LIKE a basketball player. He looks like any other college student dressed in a T-shirt and flip-flops. He has a slight paunch—the kind that weekend athletes with a penchant for beer often carry. It's hard to believe that this laid-back San Diego senior is an assassin with the highest basketball IQ on the team. "I hate to lose more than I love to win," he says.

Like all of Clink's players, Kitchens came to Chico State with a chip on his shoulder. "My dream had always been to play DI. I wasn't really recruited, though."

Kitchens's assistant coach at La Costa Canyon, Brian Falustich, had played two years at Chico State under Puck Smith. Falustich's teammate, Tim Haley, had been one of Clink's assistants. Falustich called up and Haley and told him about Kitchens. "Tim kept hounding me on the phone," Kitchens says.

Kitchens and his mother came to visit Chico State. He had never actually met Haley in person until his recruiting visit. "I loved him right away."

Kitchens went through some one-on-one drills with Damario Sims. "Damario was so vocal. I'd never seen anything like it before."

Kitchens had a tough decision to make. Either stay at home and play for UCSD, or move ten-hours away and play for Chico State. "Coach Clink was real up front with me. He put the heat on. He said I was their number one guy, but he needed a fast decision. My mom and I weighed the pros and cons the entire way home. When we got home, I called Coach Clink and committed." He was 18 then. Today he is 22.

Kitchens has been around basketball his entire life. "I've been playing since I could first walk. My dad introduced me to the game. I loved the up and down. The pace. I loved the Lakers. Kobe was my hero."

He would come straight home from school and shoot for hours. He had a lot of baby fat, and then, the summer between his sixth grade year and seventh grade year, he shot up. "I grew six inches." His redshirt freshman year was tough. "I was in culture shock," he says. He soon adjusted, and he also started getting spot minutes during his first year playing, some 16 months after stepping on to campus as a redshirt freshman. Kitchens has a lot of confidence, but unlike many athletes, his confidence does not come off as arrogant. This, along with his physique, makes him a deceptive player. "People never had to tell me I was good. I already knew. I'm confident, and my confidence comes from repetition. Just another shot." He says that when walks on to the court, a calmness comes over him. "All the struggles I've been through help me deal with whatever situation I'll face. I realize that nothing is perfect. I just go out there and do my job. And have fun." Kitchens gained a lot of confidence when Clink started him last season. "I don't mind coming off the bench, but there's something about starting. It's the ultimate green light to go out and just have fun."

Kitchens knows he has a big role to fill this year. He will be one of only three seniors. He also knows that he has the greatest basketball intelligence on the team. "Just growing up and watching basketball all the time and playing it all the time has given me this feel for the game." He also attributes his understanding of the game to having had great coaches. "They all instilled the fundamentals. My youth coaches for the Mavericks, my AAU team in the 5th, 6th, and 7th grade, drilled skills into me. They taught me the different nuances to the game. I've done the fundamentals the right way for so many years that now all I do is react." Kitchens admits he is not the most athletic guy, so he has no choice *but to* rely on his basketball intelligence. "I have to always be thinking when I'm out there." After four years in the program, he also knows Clink's program inside out.

Kitchens knows that if he wants to play, he has to abide by Clink's style of play. "He's a defensive guy. He wants to know how hard you're going to guard. When you come off the bench, you have to focus on what you can control, and defense is something you can control. You have to focus on defense and rebounding. You have to be positive."

Kitchens is the kind of basketball player whose best efforts will never show up in the box score. "When I come in off the bench, I get the movement going. I will catch the ball at the top of the key. Fake a shot. Pass to the corner and move."

Kitchens is the consummate team player. "I'd rather go 0-of-10 from the field and win then 5-of-10 and lose." He knows there will be a lot of pressure on him to lead this year, but he looks forward to it. "I'm ready. I've waited. Now it's my turn. I'm personable. I can talk to others. I've been doing things the right way since I got here. I'm not going to be selfish, and if something needs to be said to a player, I will say it to him."

Kitchens says his biggest goal over summer is to stay healthy and get in good condition. "I'm working on my ball handling, too, and I have to make 300 shots a day. I make 100 from 18 feet. I make 100 from the 3-point line. And 100 from the NBA 3-point line." He is also in summer school.

He smiles. "Yeah, I'm taking Magic, Witchcraft, and Religion online and a multicultural class." He pauses. His eyes brighten again as he switches the conversation from school to basketball. "Athletes at this level, you know, we don't get a lot of help. It's a job playing basketball. Coach Clink owns us from the middle of October until April. We're students and always working on our craft—basketball."

His personal goal for the season is to make first team all-league. My selfish goal is for Kitchens to stay academically eligible and not succumb to the social trappings of being not only a senior but the big man on campus—he is wildly popular. Kitchens also says he wants the Division II trifecta. He is hungry to win the league championship, the West Regional, and the NCAA championship. "We just have to get hot at the right time." He, like so many others, notes that the Wildcats are unlike any other team in the league. "A lot of teams don't hang out together, but we do. We're a family. We go out together. We go to battle together. Not a lot of programs have this feeling of togetherness."

Kitchens says that Clink is a man's man. "I heard that he doesn't use shaving cream when he shaves and he uses cold water and a really cheap rusty old disposable blade." He also remarks on Clink's strength. "He gets out there and lifts with us. He's one of the strongest guys I've ever been around." Kitchens also believes that Clink will be at Chico State for a long time. "He's found his niche. Here he can get guys who buy into his program. Guys that come here feel lucky to play. It's a winning culture. People step into their roles. He has a system that works. You buy into it. It keeps working. It's consistent. And at 54, I think he'll be the same coach as he is now. On game day, he's so zoned in. He gets consumed by it. On game day it's no nonsense."

CHAPTER 18

Gladiator

CHRISTOPHER MAGALOTTI, KNOWN AS MAGZ, looks like a Roman warrior. A gladiator. He should. He is Roman. His father was born in Rome. He also looks like a model. He should. His mother was a model. "My mom was a model living in Madrid," Magz tells me. "She met my father in a nightclub. You know how the rest of the story goes," he says with a laugh. "My dad was 20. My mom was 29."

If Magz were from a city, surely he would've been discovered by a talent agent and had his head shots sent off to every agency in Manhattan. He is from Stockton, California, though. Books about boxers are from Stockton (*Fat City*), not fashion models. Stockton is a rough and tough spot. It doesn't look like what most people outside of California envision California to look like. That's why so many movies have been filmed in Stockton. In the movies, Stockton's waterways have pretended to be the Mississippi Delta, and the farmland that surrounds Stockton has served as a fill-in for the American plains and the Midwest. And Magz is pretending to be a basketball player. Maybe pretending is not the right word, but if he were three inches shorter it's doubtful he would have picked up the sport. And if he were three inches taller, he'd probably be in the NBA.

Magz is walking proof that being a tall Roman soldier who plays competitive college basketball is both a blessing and a curse. The more I get to know Magz, and the more I study his basketball career, the more it seems like his physical gifts will serve him much better in the outside world, the world of business (he is a business major) than in the athletic world. He came to Chico State with great expectations, a physical specimen of 6-foot-10 and 250 pounds. He can run like a gazelle. He towers over everyone else. He's muscular. He's beautiful, but a tough kind of beautiful, not a pretty-boy beautiful.

Expectations have followed Magz with each season. His junior year was supposed to be a breakout year. He started the season, but by the end of the season in March he had only averaged 10.8 minutes a game, 2.2 points, and 1.8 rebounds. He had to play behind Jordan Barton, but Jordan Barton is gone. This season there are no expectations placed on Magz's wide, heaping shoulders. Ellis and Giddings will take that burden off his shoulders. The only one who expects anything from Magz is Magz. He's a senior. He knows this is his last year of basketball. He's going to enjoy every second of it. He's going to have a break-out season.

Magz is going to have a Platonic Conception kind of season.

Magz is finally going to unleash the villain inside that he has waited four seasons to unleash.

Magz is well aware that he's a crowd favorite. When he comes into the game, it's like Superman taking off his cape. Not so much that he's a hero, but that he's the hero everyone wants him to be. He can't be a hero on the bench, and he hasn't yet become a hero on the floor. But the longer he's out on the floor, the greater are his chances of becoming Superman. What people don't understand, though, is that Magz is a villain. "You either die a hero or you live long enough to see yourself become a villain," he tells me. He says it's nerve-racking knowing that when Clink puts him in he has to produce right away or he gets pulled out. He won't have that pressure this year with the absence of Jordan Barton.

Magz brings instant energy and chatter to the court. He's always talking when on defense. He's the most vocal player on this year's team. "If I only get two minutes, it's going to be the most treacherous two minutes." Magz never thought, though, that he would have to fight for two minutes. He had been recruited by his hometown's college, the University of the Pacific. "I wanted out of Stockton." He wanted to play at UC Davis. "I didn't have the grades." When he got to Chico, Jake Lovisolo became his mentor. "We'd all go out and a lot of the other guys were partying and doing their thing. But me and Jake just hung out in the corner and played video games." He and Lovisolo still keep in touch.

Up until a couple of years ago, Magz would spend a month every summer in Rome. He went to kindergarten in Rome, and has lived in Madrid and different parts of Mexico. His family moved to Redwood City, California, then back to Rome, then back to Mexico, where his father played professional soccer, and then to Madrid for another year and a half where his mother modeled. Then it was back to Redwood City. "When we came back from Spain, my dad got a job in Redwood City as a janitor at an auto broker. Not long after, one of the auto brokers quit. My dad was asked if he wanted to do it." His father excelled at the job. The family moved to Stockton for a better opportunity. "Stockton is a tough place," Magz says. "A lot of the kids I graduated with have gotten killed."

Magz lives with Robert Duncan and Tyler Harris. Drew Kitchens and Trevor Priest are his next door neighbors. "Kitchens and Priest," he says with a shy smile. "Trouble." He says that living with Duncan has made him a better player. "I'll be sitting on the couch watching TV. He'll turn it off and say we're going to the gym." Magz says that Duncan has a relentless work ethic. "He had a full-time job this summer moving furniture. He would haul stuff all day from 8-5. When he came home, we'd go lift weights. Then we'd go the gym and take shots, play one-on-one, all night. He's making me a much better player."

Magz, like all the players, thinks that Isaiah Ellis will go down as one of the all-time greats. "He'll end up setting the record for charges," he says. "I roughed Isaiah up his sophomore year in high school. I was a senior. We met in the Section Championship Division II game. I blocked his first two shots."

I ask Magz what it's like being his size. Does he mind knowing that when he enters a room, he's the first one everyone sees—well, not necessarily sees—but gawks at. "It doesn't bother me," he says. "A lot of tall people don't like it, but I kind of do. What bothers me is when people treat me like an oddity. When I go out, someone always comes up to me and makes some kind of comment like 'How's the weather up there?' I also don't like when people call me a giant. I'm not a giant."

Magz says that his growth was steady, not over one summer like it happened to so many other tall people. "I grew gradually about two and a half inches every year. This started when I was in the sixth grade." Magz had no idea he would be so tall. Unlike all of the other Chico State players, the game of basketball came to him late. He didn't grow up watching the sport like so many of his teammates. "The first NBA games I ever watched was when the Lakers and the Celtics played each other in the NBA finals back in 2010 or something." He was drawn to soccer early on, his father's sport. I wondered why he didn't play football. I imagined that coaches would've been all over him. "My father wouldn't let me play football." He started playing basketball in high school. "The only reason I even played in high school was because my coach came up and asked if I'd play. I didn't have basketball shoes or anything."

Magz recalls the first time he stepped on a court.

"One of my teammates kept licking his fingers and spitting into his palm and then wiping off the bottom of his shoes. I didn't know what he was doing." He admits that he didn't give basketball his all. "I didn't take it seriously until my senior year. We had a lot of younger guys. I knew I had to step up and become a leader. We went 21-10. In the playoffs, I caught fire. I averaged nine blocks a game."

Magz's basketball career has come full circle, similar to that of Kitchens. Both young men had to become leaders their senior year in high school and guide the younger players. The same will happen this year. "To be honest, I'm not ready to be a leader. I get down on myself a lot. I get frustrated from the pressure of having to perform fast. But I think I can do it. We have a quiet team. I'm one of the loudest." Even though Magz didn't get a lot of playing time last season, his presence was felt from the bench.

Magz knows that this year his team needs him. He knows that Clink will call on him more. He doesn't care if he starts, though. He just wants to play more than he has in the past. "I want 15 minutes a game." He says he'll do whatever it takes to get those 15 minutes. He knows this means cooling his hot head. He is known as being a gentle big man off the court, but on the court a switch inside of him turns on. "Everything makes me angry. I'm the biggest hot head out there. I don't have any friends on the court. Nobody wants to go up against me. And I set the best screens in the league. I love setting them for Rob and Drew."

The talk of setting screens gets him excited. As a senior, maybe he has finally realized the damage that he can do with his body. Magz loves Chico. He hasn't even graduated yet and he already misses the town. "I love it here. I'll miss all my teammates. I haven't cherished my experiences enough." He's been working harder this summer than ever before. "I've gotten better offensively. I used to be a liability on offense. I didn't have a jump shot. I've got one now. Coach doesn't know. I'm going to surprise him on the first day of practice." Magz says he's spending two hours a day practicing his moves. "Wait until Coach sees my left handed hook." He has also been working on his stamina. He knows that'll keep him on the floor. "I'm going to have the best motor on the team. I'm running in cleats on the grass. Doing 100 meter springs. Jumping hurdles." After he graduates this spring, Magz plans to move to Italy. He hopes to make a professional Italian team. He believes his dual citizenship will help him land a spot. "As long as my body holds up, I know I can do it. But if it doesn't work out, no big deal."

Magz says he doesn't live for basketball like the other guys do. He laughs a little. "To be honest, I don't even really like the game. It's not something I die for. I just want to do something after college and after basketball that I really enjoy." He says that he doesn't have the fire. "Amir had it. Tyler has it. Jalen has it. Not me."

The young man is also symbolic of how international the game has become. His father is Italian and Spanish. His mother is African American, Native American, Italian, and Caucasian. As a student, he fits the bill of what educators call an at-risk/first-generation student. He has never used his status, though, to get scholarships. "Scholarships like that exist?" he says, bewildered. Basketball has been the way he has paid for school. He laughs when I mention his GPA. "I think it's the lowest on the team. Somewhere around a 2.3." That's still impressive. He will earn a degree. The first one in his family to accomplish this.

Magz plans to let loose this year. He will forge an identity other than the big guy who still hasn't developed. "I'm going to grow a nasty moustache just like Steve Adams of the Oklahoma City Thunder." That's not the only change he'll make. He's also been studying Dennis Rodman. "I'm going to dye my hair different colors before each game just like he did. I'm also going to play like him." He insists that his team needs a dark guy, the league villain. He'd be the man. Clink, though, would never let a player do this. Magz will just have to keep this a fantasy. The Platonic Conception will have to be played in his mind only.

Like all the other players, Magz has his share of Clink stories and rumors. "You know that scar on his cheek? I heard he got it in a bar fight." He laughs when he talks about how Clink always has coffee in his hand. "He doesn't sleep, either. The guy's intense. He shaves with cold water and no shaving cream." He laughs even harder when he tells the story of how each year Clink will come unraveled in a practice and kick the ball in the stands. "The guy is so intense, but I love him. I really do."

CHAPTER 19

Can't Stop Me

COREY SILVERSTROM MIGHT JUST BE the most confident person I've ever met. "I'm going to play in the NBA."

"I'm going to be the best wing in the country."

"I showed up to my first ever *Call of Duty* tournament and left the second best player in the world."

"We're going to win the conference. We're going to win the conference tournament. And we're going to win the National Championship. Why not?"

After listening to Silverstrom talk, I get the feeling that he really believes everything he says. If so, he's right: Why not? I'm waiting for him to start talking in the third person, but he's not arrogant.

Just confident.

And 20 years old.

Silverstrom started playing ball when he was in the second grade. His brother, nine years older, was always playing basketball. "I went to all of his high school games. I thank him for putting the ball in my hands."

Silverstrom, same as most of the Wildcats, was overlooked in the DI recruiting process. He went on a visit to Pepperdine. He got a late phone call from Seattle University. "But I had already committed to Chico State. I didn't want to back out. That's not my style." He said that Chico State felt like the perfect fit. "I liked the culture of the program and the people I met. I also really liked the people who weren't part of the program"

Silverstrom was a big star in his hometown. He was frequently in the paper and on the news. "People back home knew me," he says. "People here don't know what I can do."

I can tell this bothers him. I expect him at any second to say "But they will." Only Silverstrom's not arrogant. Like I said, he's just confident. And 20.

"Playing here has been humbling. I had a big chip on my shoulder coming in, too. I've played against a lot of great players, you know."

Here it comes: "I'm a great player."

Only he doesn't outright say it.

But I can tell he's thinking it.

A game like the one against the University of Arizona is the kind of challenge Silverstrom dreams about. He knows the kind of attention it will bring if he and his team can beat them. "Gabe York doesn't worry me." No, York, one of the Arizona stars, doesn't worry Silverstrom, but Silverstrom has waited for the chance to get even with York since he was in the eighth grade. "It was the summer before ninth grade for me. We were playing Orange Lutheran High School in an AAU game. There was the kid that kept dunking the ball during the pregame warm up. He was really showing off. Everybody was talking him up. I was the seventh man for my team, but I was hot that game. Scored 18. On the last play of the game, coach drew up a play for me. I couldn't believe it. Anyway, York stole the ball from me. I'm sure he forgot later that night. But I still haven't forgotten it."

Those that hate losing as much as Silverstrom forget the wins long before they forget the losses. "I hate losing. Absolutely hate it. I'd cry in high school when we lost." He says he always believed in himself and his abilities. "Arizona will put their shoes on the same way that way we do. There's nothing we can't do. Listen, I believe that when I get the ball coming off a screen, I can't be stopped. This feeling takes over. I guess it's called being in the zone or something."

Silverstrom also has a bone to pick with another Arizona star: Elliot Pitts. "My AAU assistant coach knew the University of Arizona coach Sean Miller. Coach Miller came to two of my games. Elliot Pitts was on the other team. They picked him, even though I scored 30."

Silverstrom believes he has the perfect starting line-up for the National Championship game. "McFerren at the one. Rob at the two. Me at the three. Isaiah at the four. Giddings at the five. Who's going to stop that? The sky is the limit for us. Jalen knows what Rob and I can do with the ball. He can guide us, push us."

Silverstrom can't let go of the loss against Cal Baptist last March. "It was a blur. Frustrating. I was timid out there."

Silverstrom worked hard over the summer. He went home to Fresno and played all the time. "I worked on staying lower. Worked on my shot. My ball handling. Played against a lot of really great players. Constant workouts." He says he patterns his game after Steve Nash. "I live to make the ridiculous pass like he does. Growing up, I was the guy that had to score all the time so I didn't work on my passing that much. Not until now."

When Silverstrom leaves my office, I'm a little depressed. He reminds me of how I used to feel, and how I wish I still felt. To be young and confident and an elite athlete with the genuine feeling that anything really is possible. My own reality, even though it's a great reality filled with blessings, is that my knees hurt, my hips ache, and my hair is turning white and thinning and that I have responsibilities and, well, I'm no longer young. It takes me five days to recover after playing basketball for 50 minutes once or twice a week, and that a guy my age might want to think about swimming or playing golf or doubles tennis instead. Yet, my sadness soon lifts because I can live vicariously through Silverstrom.

That, after all, is why I and so many other millions of fans love sports. Why we love basketball—because we desire and hold in reverence those things we cannot have or do.

I can only imagine what Silverstrom will be like when he is 44.

CHAPTER 20

(510) Rebel

JALEN McFERREN SHOWS UP TO my office breathing hard. He has just ran from Acker where he challenged Coach Gabriel to a shoot-off and finally won. That's no easy feat. It's one thing for a 5-foot-10 point guard to beat a worn-out tired father of a new born and assistant coach (even if the coach did play collegiate basketball) in a game of one-on-one. But a shoot-off is a different game. It favors the experienced shooter. Coach Gabriel has been putting up shots in gyms from the Alan Fieldhouse in Kansas to the McKale Center in Arizona and a lot of other gyms and playgrounds across the country since McFerren was in diapers.

Clink almost always redshirts freshmen. Jalen McFerren was an exception. He's that good. McFerren has had since last March to grow up. After the Chico State Wildcats stepped off the court against Cal Baptist, Mike Rosaroso handed the keys over to the freshman. On October the 15th, McFerren will put the keys in the ignition and start the car. Those freshman days are over. He has a new role. He's the sophomore starting guard, the floor leader.

McFerren was born in the same Oakland house that his father was born in. Unfortunately, he would not be raised here. His parents divorced when McFerren was two. That's when he started bouncing back and forth from Oakland and San Leandro. "I moved ten times in high school," he says. One would never it know it now, but as a boy McFerren had a lot of anger. "I was always getting in trouble in school. I was suspended 26 times in the fifth grade."

Things would change for McFerren when he reached middle school. "My fifth grade teacher told me I wasn't going to make much out of my life. She said I wasn't going to be anybody." By the eighth grade, McFerren was a 3.8 student. He would also meet his best friend DJ Clayton, who at the time of this interview was playing basketball for the Western Kentucky Hilltoppers. "That's when it all started with the Oakland Rebels." McFerren would play for the legendary Bay Area coaches Raymond Young and Phil Taylor. "They were father figures. I was lucky. I had my real dad. He's always been in my life. And then I had these two men who were like my other two dads. I grew up under them. They helped me mature and become a man." McFerren's parents were no longer together. However, they both remained positive role models in his life. "Even though my mom and dad moved me around a lot, we always stayed in nice houses. It was always a good environment. I'm still close with both of them. I call my mom every day."

The Oakland Rebels Youth Basketball Club is a Bay Area basketball institution. The Rebels are a non-profit organization founded in 1987 with the intent of helping kids develop successful academic and social skills. It's a privilege and an honor to be an Oakland Rebel, but that privilege and honor—no matter how talented the kid is—gets taken away if the players don't maintain a high GPA.

A lot of great players have gone through the program, most recently (and notably) Damian Lillard. Lillard was the number 6 pick in the 2012 draft. He had played with the Oakland Rebels since he was in the third grade. I ask McFerren about this. He smiles. "The guys on the team give me a hard time, say I have a man crush on Damian." I ask him if it's true. He laughs. "The Chico State team shoes this year are the Damian Lillard shoes." Yes, he definitely has a man crush, and rightfully so. If I'm being honest I've had a man crush on Lindsey Hunter—who I played with in high school and who went on to be the handpicked successor to Isaiah Thomas, win three NBA titles, and forge a 17-year career in the NBA—for 26 years. I get it. The crush will inevitably follow me to my grave. That's the way it works when someone in your small tribe, someone from your small village, makes it big. "My time with the Rebels taught me to be poised and let go of all that rage and anger that I felt about my parents being divorced," McFerren says.

For a college sophomore who is only 19 years old, McFerren has spent a lot of time reflecting on his past and how he once behaved. He's not shy about telling me how this has shaped the young man and leader he is today. "I used to think I didn't have to listen. All I wanted to do was play basketball. I was pretty good. I won't deny it. The other kids didn't want to play with me. I'd let them do all the scoring so they would."

Perhaps here was the point guard's first educational moment at his position. How do you get other players to like you?

Get them the ball and let them score.

McFerren was four when he first picked up a ball. His brother was three years older. He had to play up to his older brother's level. When he was in the seventh grade, he started running track. He met Nate Moore who convinced him to do it. Moore, two inches smaller than McFerren, is running track at the University of Oregon at the time this interview takes place. In high school, Moore was the nation's top high school horizontal jumper in his senior year at Castro High School, the same school Mcferren attended. McFerren reluctantly went out for the track and field team. At his first meet, he qualified in the 100 meter and 200 meter junior Olympic trials.

McFerren accredits his speed to always having to play with bigger guys. This all started when he was knee-high. "We'd be out playing flag football in the streets. I had to evade the bigger, older kids and outrun them. And it didn't feel good to get tackled on the concrete."

McFerren committed to Chico State by his senior year. Coach Cobb, now at Montana State, recruited him aggressively. He took it hard when Coach Cobb later left Chico State for a DI job at the University of Montana. "I was really bummed. He's been one of my favorite coaches." Coach Cobb and McFerren still hold the line. "I just helped him recruit and sign an Oakland Rebel," McFerren says, smiling.

At McFerren's first game against Pacific Union last year, his mother arranged a surprise visit. "She rented a couple of vans and brought up 30 family members. I have a huge family support system." He recalls that game, smiling. I think the smile is going to jump off his face. "First time I was wearing a Chico State jersey and touched the ball, I went in for a finger roll and scored."

One would think that the leadership role McFerren is stepping into would create pressure. "Tell you the truth, I feel less pressure now. Now I'm in a comfortable position. I had lots of ups and downs last year." He says he learned a lot of from his freshman campaign. "Consistency. I learned that I can't take a day, a minute, not even a second off. I changed my diet. I get at least eight hours of sleep a night. I make sure I eat three solid meals a day." He says he has also learned the importance of getting his mental frame set. "Breathing. I breathe easier now. Really pay attention to it."

McFerren's fast-paced style of play is a world apart from the more contained play of Mike Rosaroso, the senior McFerren played behind last year. Rosaroso's game was conservative and a no thrills style of play. McFerren's game is flashy and fast. The difference between the two players is like watching the *Wizard of Oz* in black and white (Rosaroso) without sound, then watching it in color (McFerren) with surround sound. "Mike was always poised and calm. I learned a lot from him. How he carried himself on and off the court."

The competitive spirit doesn't care, though, if a person is a freshman and inexperienced or a senior and experienced. McFerren didn't like sitting on the bench. "It was the first time I've ever had to play behind someone. I really thought I was going to start last year. Mike played it safe. Me, I would come in and try to pick up the tempo. Run and gun." He looks down. Surely he must hear Clink's voice in the back of his head. He looks up. "But I have to take better care of the ball."

I ask McFerren which Wildcat he likes playing with the most. This question always puts Clink's players in an awkward situation. To be honest would seem like going against the team culture. To lie would be to go against the morals and ethics the team culture is built on. "Me and Rob really connect," he finally says. This is good news for Clink. Every Wildcat I have interviewed has said the same thing. "I really look up to Rob. He's mature and polished. He's been through a lot of struggles and overcame them, learned from them. When we were doing all the 7 a.m. workouts last year, he really pushed me.

He pushed me to another level I didn't think I could get to."

One of the things that impresses me most about McFerren's game is his rebounding ability. The young man has an uncanny way of knowing exactly where the ball will land. I've seen this ability with a lot of players who started off as poor shooters—poor shooters who spent hours playing by themselves and rebounding their own missed shots. McFerren admits to having once been an average shooter. About rebounding McFerren says, "I see the way the ball is released and the way it goes up. I see the angle. I know where it's going to bounce and land. I get there and then it's off to the races." McFerren's shot has improved. He says he struggled with it during high school, but once he got to Chico State, Coach Gabriel eased his struggle. "My mechanics weren't all that great. He changed how I guide my hand." McFerren will still miss, but more importantly, the players on the other team will still miss. That he means he can get the rebound and be off and running. "A point guard who can rebound and fly down the court with Rob to the left and Isaiah to the right presents a huge challenge for the other team. Corey can push it and create. Tanner is a pick and pop guy.

I anticipate and know where the ball's coming. This gets me in trouble a lot of times. I get going so fast. I have to tell myself to slow down." McFerren notes that he'll play with more rhythm and balance this year. "I'm dancing out there," he says. "It's a chess game, and I'm dancing."

McFerren says that's another thing he's learned most from last year is to not dwell on things. He recalls a game against Cal Poly Pomona last year when he struggled. "I had four turnovers in five minutes. They pressed me. My confidence went way down. Thankfully, we won. I got my confidence back." He says that now, if he misses an assignment, he's able to move on. "Actually, I started to learn this when I played for the Oakland Rebels."

McFerren credits a lot of his ability to bounce back from mental lapses from the confidence that Clink instills in him. "Most of my former teammates from Castro High and the Oakland Rebels are now playing at DI schools. I keep in touch. None of them can relate to their coaches. But me and all the other players here relate to Coach Clink and he relates to us." McFerren attributes this to the way Clink approaches his players and motivates them. "He has the right intentions. He wants the best for you. That's how we all feel." McFerren says that although Clink is intense, he can also appreciate a joke. "I joke a lot with him. I'll pop into his office and say 'What's up, Clinkmeister?' He accepts me for who I am." McFerren says he finds comfort in this. "Coach foams at the mouth during his pregame speeches. He cares."

McFerren, like all the returning players, still feels the burn of their season-ending loss in the first round of the tournament to Cal Baptist last season. "Losing the CCAA tournament in overtime hurt. But losing to Cal Baptist in the NCAA was horrible. The season was over. I had to look into the eyes of the three seniors and see their pain. They didn't know what was next in their lives. I just wanted to say I was sorry."

Part of McFerren's success derives from an authentic desire to get better. He says he's always established good relationships with his coaches by asking them what he can do to get better and become a better team leader. "I texted Clink a few time over the summer. I'd ask him what I should be working on to get better. I would have texted him a lot more, but I know he's busy with three kids and all." McFerren, however, doesn't just want to get better. "I want to be great."

McFerren considers what he does on the basketball court as performance. He's an actor, a dancer, an entertainer. "It's performance art. Only I'm not performing on my own. I've got family alongside me." McFerren says when he's out there, he's dancing with the ball. He also has a prayer ritual during the National Anthem. He's been saying the same prayer at tip-off for as long as he can remember. That helps him stay focused, help him with the performance he's about to put on.

McFerren knows what his teammates can and can't do. "Corey, you just have to trust him. Give him the keys to the car and let him drive. He likes isolation plays. He creates. He's good with the run and gun." He calls Isaiah Ellis a "motor" and says he's never seen a player with so much stamina. "I call him 'The Motor' because he's that little kid who goes outside and plays for three hours straight and never takes a water break. He never gets tired." McFerren is also impressed with the jumper Ellis has added to his game during the summer. "He's already hard to guard, but now it makes it even more difficult to guard him. If he starts scoring from the outside, now the big men on the other team have to get moving. This opens up all kinds of opportunities."

McFerren also knows Giddings must get involved. "He's got the sweetest jump shot. Magz sets the best screens in the league. Nate is poised and unselfish. I've always got Nate in the back of my head when I'm driving." He calls Duncan the alpha dog on the team. What, then, does he think of himself? "I'm the pit bull. Verbally, physically. I hate losing. Particularly when I lose the wrong way. A missed opportunity means no sleep for me."

McFerren believes this season will be one to remember. "We'll be back to back CCAA champs. We'll win the CCAA tournament. And we're going to win at least three games in the NCAA tournament."

I think back to a recent conversation I had earlier with a player when I asked him about the upcoming season. He shook his head in wonder and said: "Jalen. People just don't understand how good he really is."

People soon will.

There's a reason why Clink didn't redshirt him last year. Clink always has a reason.

This will be a season of reasons.

CHAPTER 21

Leftie Turncoat

NATE AMBROSINI'S DECISION TO PLAY college basketball at Chico State could not have been easy. Many kids who grew up playing basketball in or close to a college town dream of playing college basketball in their backyard institution someday. Nate Ambrosini might have been reared a Lumberjack and honed that smooth left-handed shot in Humboldt State territory, but Ambrosini now bleeds crimson and has come of age as a Wildcat.

Ambrosini hails from Fortuna, California, about a half-an-hour drive from Arcata where Humboldt State is located. Ambrosini, who would be a three-star athlete until high school when he wisely settled on basketball, started hooping when he was six. Ambrosini is an only child. Both his parents—Chris and Deedra—grew up in Eureka. They were high school sweethearts. His father has lived in Humboldt his entire life. "I grew up in the perfect family setting," Ambrosini says. "My parents supported everything I wanted to do. They taught me to be the man I am today. They taught me to respect other people—love the people you surround yourself with—and to just go out there and enjoy my life."

I mention to Ambrosini that so many of the players I have interviewed got their competitive edge from sibling rivalries. "It got it from my dad," he says. "My dad was kind of like a big brother to me." Ambrosini says that he outgrew the jungle gym in his backyard, so his father ripped it out and created a three-point basketball court. "My dad and I would shoot every night until it got dark. When it got dark, we turned on the light and shot some more. My dad pushed me to be the best I could be. We battled playing one-on-one when I started middle-school. I would always come into the house angry after he beat me and tell my mom he was cheating, and she'd be the mediator."

Once Ambrosini grew and became quicker and stronger, his father actually became the rebounder. "I'd shoot for a couple of hours and he'd just rebound." Ambrosini recalls the first time he ever beat his father in a game of one-on-one. "When I was around twelve, I really wanted a quad (four-wheeler). My dad and I made a bet. If I beat him in a game to five, he said he'd get me one. It was an all-out battle. He said if I lost, there would be no second chance. My mom was out in the yard watching us go at it. It took forever to get those five points. We kept fouling each other. But I wanted that quad."

Ambrosini would get the quad. He beat his father that day. Ambrosini might have excelled at an indoor sport, but he was always outside. A true Northern California kid, he grew up in a culture that celebrated the outdoors, where a lot of time was spent riding quads and shooting BB and pellet guns. "The rule was whatever you shot in the woods or caught from the river, you had to eat it."

I still can't figure out why Ambrosini would want to play at Chico State rather than in the town so steeped in Ambrosini blood. "Humboldt State was late at recruiting me, but they did heavily recruit me. I went on a visit to the school, and they came and watched me play in a couple of AAU tournaments in Las Vegas and Los Angeles. Maybe the head coach just assumed I would choose Humboldt State since I'm from the area. I knew Humboldt State wanted me. The head coach even said he thought I might go down as one of the greats in Humboldt State history. Chico State, on the other hand, was always sending me handwritten letters. They showed a genuine interest in me and made me feel wanted. I thought Humboldt State would have done the same thing. But what really made the difference was the coaching staff and the players. When I came to visit Chico State, the players not only knew my name but they also knew the names of my parents. They put in a lot of effort. I just really fell in love with the coaching and the area and everything about Chico State."

Ambrosini would choose Chico State even though his parents are Humboldt State boosters, and even though his father is part owner of a hotel near the university and gets free season tickets every year, and even though Ambrosini grew up wearing HSU—as he calls it—jerseys. Ambrosini puts the decision in perspective: "Growing up there, I pretty much experienced everything I could in Humboldt. I wanted to get out of the area and have other experiences and see something new. My parents were 100% supportive, whether I wanted to go to school on the East Coast or whether it was going to school at Chico State. They said it was up to me, and they would work with whatever I chose."

Ambrosini also has a healthy perspective on his role in the game of basketball. "I love basketball and it's my passion, but for me it's a tool. It has put me in a position to be successful. I just love the game, always have. I love the feeling of practice and working out and afterwards feeling like you got better. It's a sense of self-accomplishment." Basketball accomplishments, however, are only half of the story. "My father has always drilled into my head the importance of academics. Going to class, doing the homework, turning work in on time, and getting the best grades you can translates into the real world." He sees what he does on the court similar to what he does in the classroom. "I work as hard in the classroom as I do in practice. I'm used to this. In high school I was an AP student and always made the honor roll."

All great student-athletes are competitive in their sport. But not all great student-athletes are also as competitive in their school work. Ambrosini places an equal emphasis on both. "My motivation comes from pride and proving to people who you are—living up to your name." He seems to have a switch he turns on before he enters the competitive playing field, be it the classroom or the court. He says it's the same for both. "Regarding basketball, I turn on the switch way before the game. I turn it on before warmups, when we're in the locker room. I start to focus on what I need to do to help my team win and achieve our goals. The greatest motivator is winning. Winning is something bigger than who you are. It's winning for your coach and your teammates and the name that's across your chest. On day one, Coach Clink drills into us that culture is the most important thing we have here, something that sets us apart from every other program in the nation. We really have a brotherhood and a family."

CHAPTER 22

The Motor

RUMOR HAS IT THAT WHEN head coach David Odom of Wake Forest went down to the U.S. Virgin Islands to watch this high school player he'd heard so much about from the great Miami Heat NBA player Alonzo Mournin, he went to a playground where a pick-up game was taking place. He sat down on the ground next to a player who'd lost the previous game and was sitting this one out, the sweat still pouring down his face, and Coach Odom asked the player: "Which one of those guys out there is Tim Duncan?"

"He's not out there," said the player.

"Where is he?"

"He's right here."

Tim Duncan is the best power forward that ever played the game. He's also probably the most boring. Ask most young college basketball players to name their favorite NBA player, and not many will name Timothy Theodore Duncan—despite a 19-year NBA career with the San Antonio Spurs, two time NBA MVP, three-time NBA finals MVP, NBA All-Star Game MVP, NBA Rookie of the Year, 15-time NBA All-Star, and an NBA championship ring for each finger on his shooting hand.

Chico State sophomore power-forward Isaiah Ellis doesn't hesitate when I ask him to name his favorite player.

"Tim Duncan," he says.

He senses my confusion.

"He's quiet," Ellis says. 'He's quiet and lets his play do the talking." He pauses. "Like me."

It all makes sense now. Since I have been following the team, Ellis has been the hardest for me to get to know. He has always smiled and responded when I've talked to him, but, like the coach he plays for, what you see is what you get. Ask a question and he'll give you a short answer without explanation. He is not prone to hyperbole. On the surface, Isaiah Ellis seems to be a yes-no guy. However, once you earn his trust and he opens up, a different side comes out. He is introverted and thoughtful. If you want extroversion and hyperbole from Isaiah Ellis, you will have to go and watch him play basketball.

Still, I'm intrigued by his interest in Tim Duncan. I think claiming him as your favorite basketball player is akin to the tennis player claiming Pete Sampras as his tennis hero, or the political science undergraduate citing Harry Truman as his favorite politician—all quiet, unassuming champions. "The first memory I have about basketball comes from one of those small little hoops you get as a kid," Ellis says. "It was always my sister, my cousin, and me with a little rubber basketball trying to make our shots. We'd have the television on with an NBA game in the background. The Spurs and Tim Duncan were always on. My mom even has a video of me trying to do that little Tim Duncan shimmy off the glass. It all started then."

I'm surprised that Ellis, only two or three at the time, remembers Duncan. Then again I remember watching Rod Carew laying down a left-handed bunt back in 1974 (when I was only three) and practicing that in the mirror. Turns out Ellis is a lot closer to being Duncan, though, than I ever was to being like Carew.

"Yeah," Ellis continues, "the Spurs were always the team I looked up to. I even wore 21 back in the day—before I became 44 here—because of Tim Duncan. I've tried to model my life on and off the court by Tim Duncan. He's a humble guy and knows what he can do on and off the court. Just look at the way he retired. He kind of just walked away."

When I've asked the other Chico State players about the most aggressive and competitive player on the team (what Clink calls a "pit bull") most of them have named Ellis. At least five players have called him "The Motor," marveling over the indefatigable energy he exhibits in practice and games.

I ask him where this comes from.

"Growing up with my sister," he says.

Turns out Ellis has a twin sister.

"She was born ten minutes before me. She reminds me of it all the time. We love each other now."

"Now?" I ask.

He smiles. "You asked me where my aggression level and competitive spirit comes from. Well, it's my sister." Ellis's sister, Tyler, at the time of this book, is a starting basketball player at New Mexico State, a fierce rebounder and scorer like her "younger" twin brother. "It wasn't until high school when I hit my growth spurt that I finally caught up and passed her." Like so many of the players I have profiled, it was the sibling rivalry that created the thick skin, tough demeanor, and competitive edge of Clink's players. "She was always bullying me. My mom said she used to teeth on my head. Yeah, she would use my head as a teething toy. We took Tae Kwan Do as kids and she would come home and show our cousin, who also grew up with us, different moves. She kicked him in the mouth and he bled like crazy. She was always aggressive. We used to have wrestling matches in the house."

Just as Ellis has chosen Tim Duncan to model his game off the court, it seems that his twin sister Tyler has served as the model—by nature rather than nurture—of Ellis's game on the court. I've seen Ellis wrestle many a Chico State player to the ground in practice for a rebound. "I wouldn't get my first wrestling win against her until my junior year of high school. My mom would be there watching television and let us go at it until we'd hear her say: '1…2…3…Okay, it's done.' And it was. I got tired of always being bullied. I had to learn how to fight back against her."

I've met LaShawndra, the mother of Isaiah and Tyler, before. So, too, have the fans at Acker. She might be the loudest fan in the building. I once walked out to the parking lot with her after a game. She broke down the game with almost equal precision as Coach Clink. She had an evaluation of every player, the good and the bad, and it became immediate that she was no "bleacher mom." Sure, she could cheer and wave a foam #1 finger, but she also has a deep knowledge of the game.

"My mom is the number one fan and a coach as well. She always unofficially coached me and my sister. I say number one fan because she'd be at our middle school games ringing her cowbells. She was eventually told she couldn't bring them anymore, but they couldn't stop her from bringing her pom-poms."

A running theme throughout this narrative has been the sibling impact. So, too, has been the theme of strong mothers. "We wouldn't be where we are today without my mom. She was the first one in our family to graduate from college. She helped set up the wave of college students in our family. My sister graduated from college. My cousin graduated from college and is now a professor." I notice a slight crack his voice. "She always preached college to us, and it was always in the back of our heads. She kept us in extracurricular activities. Made sure we were good. She also worked full-time as a single-mom. It was tough, but she did it."

Ellis has not mentioned his father until I ask.

"I've only seen him twice in my lifetime. It's been rough growing up without a father and not having a male figure in my life. I saw him once when I was a young kid, and then once when my sister played a game in Seattle only because he lives there. But my mom made sure we were always involved with extracurricular activities. So many coaches throughout my life have become role models and helped me understand what it means to be a man and a better person."

Coach Gabriel and Ellis have a special relationship. "When I first met him, it was nothing but laughter. He's a funny man. He really helped me out academically. I struggled my redshirt year. I took, and still take, classes in the summer to get ahead. Coach Gabe has helped me become better organized and efficient when it comes to writing papers, and he taught me how to use library resources. He has helped my confidence grow and has always believed in my potential."

Ellis lives with Tanner Giddings. This couldn't have been better scripted, but like most things with this basketball team, it wasn't scripted but just kind of happened. What a seemingly unlikely match: A white kid from the country and a black kid from the city, both who are intrinsic and quiet, both who are competing for the same position, and both who are extremely talented.

"I heard that this guy was coming in from Fresno and might be taking my spot," Ellis says. "I saw some highlight videos of him playing at Fresno State. He was good." Ellis says that entering his sophomore year he didn't have a place to live. Giddings was also looking for a place to live. "Brett, the assistant women's basketball coach at the time," Ellis says, "had lost two of his baseball roommates over in Nord Gardens. The coaching staff contacted him and gave him my number and Tanner's number."

And that's how the friendship between the two big men was forged.

"The first night was a little awkward." Ellis says. "We lived upstairs and our rooms were literally across from each other. There was a little tension the first day, not bad tension, but I was just trying to feel this guy out, you know, who is Tanner? Who is this guy who wants to take my position? We were both quiet. It was hard to get a read on him. Brett's not quiet at all, so he got us talking. After that first night, we hit it off. It was nothing but smiles and laughter in the house from then on."

I only tell the following story not to steal the thunder from the young man who might become the greatest player (for sure defensive player) in Chico State history, but to add to his thunder because it reminds me of the unique friendship that Isaiah Ellis and Tanner Gidding have.

I grew up in Jackson, Mississippi, in the 1970s and 1980s when neighborhoods were still divided by where the white folks lived and where the black folks lived. White kids in Jackson—most of them—did not go to public schools.

I was a hotshot private school basketball player who found the white kids' pace of the game boring. I wanted to use the moves the black players used—the players I played with in the summers—but all the teams I played for in the winter made you pass the ball five times before you took a shot and cited *Hoosiers* as their favorite movie. I got bored and took my game to the church courts. I was the leading scorer in seven different church leagues. Basketball was literally my religion. I had to attend service to be eligible. I was Jewish, Catholic, Baptist, Methodist, Presbyterian, Lutheran, and Episcopalian. I was a gym rat. I'd been expelled from my ninth grade private Baptist Academy. The dean demanded that I cut my hair. I looked at the picture of Jesus behind him and said: "But he had long hair?" I didn't give a flip about school, anyway, and wanted to do nothing but play basketball. It was decided. I would go to the only school in Mississippi not that whites could attend but *did* attend:

Murrah High School.

Murrah was around 82% black.

It was also the biggest basketball powerhouse in the state. Maybe be the nation.

The year was 1986. Players still wore short shorts. Air Jordans were barely a year old. Run DMC and the Beastie Boys and Whodini and the Fat Boys were screaming from playgrounds and gyms across the nation. Basketball players were still skinny. The three-point shot was not around.

My plan was to play at Murrah for two years. Learn the black kids game. Transfer back to the private school. Dominate that league. Get a full-ride some place far from Mississippi—like Oregon or Maine.

Like I said, it was a plan.

I was bullied the moment I stepped foot on the Murrah campus. I was an outsider from the private schools, and the white kids who had been together in the public schools since kindergarten resented me. They threw me into trash cans. They would pick me up by the ankles and dunk me head first into the toilet and flush it. They would call my house and tell my mother to come down to the city morgue and identify my body, said I had been killed in a car crash.

When the white kids weren't terrorizing me, the black kids were. The white kids would tell the black kids I was calling them racially inflammatory names (N-word) behind their backs, or that I was trying to hook-up with their girlfriends. I would have never done something like that. I was always hiding. I got jumped a few times in the school parking lot, beaten to a pulp, and I knew better than to go into the bathroom. If I had to go, I'd hold it all day. I even urinated in my pants once to keep from going into the bathroom. I was not cool. I was not popular. I did not have any friends at the school. All I had was basketball. And I was good.

Everyone laughed at me—white kids and black kids—when I said I was going out for the basketball team. I would show them. Basketball had always been my refuge, the one place where *I* was the bully.

I went to the gym. First day of tryouts, I was wearing Chuck Taylor's, which had no traction because they were also my skateboarding shoes. I had to keep spitting on my palm and wiping the bottom of my shoes to keep from slipping. It was late September and hot. I wasn't wearing socks. My feet burned. I looked around. I was the only white person. The other 25 players were black.

I knew when I stepped on to that court that I was surrounded by greatness. I broke into a cold sweat when I saw the legendary and late Coach Jordan, who is now in the Mississippi Sports Hall of Fame. He looked like a bulldog. He never smiled. For a month after school and before tryouts, I'd been hanging around the gym watching a young man named Steve Galloway (the greatest high school basketball player in Mississippi history) drain jump shots. Sometimes I would catch his rebounds and pass him the ball. There wasn't much to rebound, though. It was usually me standing underneath the net and catching the shots he made.

Coach Jordan would let his players horse around the first few minutes of practice. It was the only time his players horsed around. I could not take my eyes off the kid with the toothpick in his mouth. I had him in a couple of classes, but he didn't like to talk much. He was introverted. But on the court he was an extrovert. He was doing windmill dunks, draining shots from half-court, dribbling between his legs as if the ball were a Yo-Yo. This was James "Hollywood" Robinson. 6-foot-2 shooting guard. He was my age, 15, and looked like a pro. In six years he would be. Although he had never played a high school game, his reputation preceded him. Everyone knew he was coming to Murrah. It was a big deal.

Robinson would eventually break all the school and state records. He was a Parade All-American, McDonald's All Star, and Mississippi Player of the Year. He would go on to star at Alabama. How good was he at Alabama? Put it this way: NBA greats Latrell Sprewell and Robert Horry played in his shadow.

Coach Jordan blew his whistle. Everyone lined up at the free throw line. We ran single file, jumped, and slapped the backboard glass. I could barely slap the foam that hung down four-inches from the glass. I was made fun of. I would show them when I got a chance to shoot.

I was slow. I couldn't jump. I couldn't defend. I couldn't dribble. But I could shoot the lights out. That was my thing.

The next drill had us dribbling in a zigzag pattern down the court and going in for a layup. It was more of a defensive drill than anything. Lindsey Hunter was guarding me. He was going half-speed. I was going full-throttle.

Instead of dribbling in for an easy layup, like I was supposed to, I pulled up at the elbow and let it fly. String music. The few who saw my shot gave Lindsey a hard time. I did a little trash-talking to some guys sitting in the bleachers. By the time I turned around, Lindsey had already blown by me with the ball and was headed toward the other basket. By the time I had taken three steps, he had already laid it up. There was no need for him to trash-talk. His smile said it all.

Lindsey Hunter would go on to have a 17-year NBA career. He won two NBA championships. His total earnings: $34,640,600. And he even became the interim head coach of the Phoenix Suns.

Coach Jordan told me I had a shot at making the team. If so, I would be the first white player on the team since desegregation. But I couldn't compete with these guys. I would rather score 40 points per game in the church league than sit on the bench for 40 games and never play a second. That's where my game belonged: in the church leagues. The only regret I have in my life is not sticking it out. I still have dreams about playing for Murrah. I never got beat up again, though. The black kids respected me and had my back. I had more black friends than white friends.

I only tell this story because it reminds me of the unique friendship that Isaiah Ellis and Tanner Giddings have. Were it not for basketball, would these two have become friends? Most likely not. But sports seem to be the great equalizer, a place where one's race or ethnicity doesn't matter. You can either play or you can't play. Look at Clink's roster, a gumbo of race and ethnicity: Armenian, African-American, Hispanic, Italian, Filipino, and Caucasian. Clink does not deliberately intend to create diversity—it just happens.

I like to run out on the track before the Wildcats begin practice at 1 p.m. My favorite sight is when Giddings and Ellis walk side by side and take a shortcut beneath the outdoor bleachers to enter Acker through the backdoor. I often stop in the middle of a sprint to watch this. Were this the Mississippi that I came of age in, this black basketball player and this white basketball player would have possibly chosen a backdoor entrance to keep their friendship concealed. Now the backdoor entrance is just because it's the shortest route to their destination. I love seeing them loafing and laughing, patting each other on the back, and flashing wide grins. I can't help but to think of how proud Dr. Martin Luther King Jr. would be if he were to see this black kid from the city and this white kid from the country walk through the Red Door together every day: "One day right there in Alabama little black boys and black girls will be able to join hands with little white boys and white girls as sisters and brothers." And it's taking place right here in Chico.

CHAPTER 23

Farmer Prodigy

TANNER GIDDINGS IS LATE. I'VE scheduled a 10 a.m. meeting with him. Clink's players are never late. At 10:01 my office phone rings. "Thesis Editor here," I say. "Mr. Medley, this is Tanner Giddings. I'm lost." If I didn't know that Tanner Giddings is an inch shy of being 7-feet-tall, I would assume from his soft and somewhat wavering phone voice that he might be a balding, middle-manager type in his mid-40s.

Tanner Giddings is lost and late.

A lot of Chico State fans consider Giddings the "X" factor." I don't. I think of him as the "? factor." Who is this kid? What is he capable of? Why won't he be more aggressive? Does he realize his potential? After talking to

Giddings for less than a minute, it becomes clear that Giddings is not the aggressive, rah-rah-wild beast on the court that so many people are waiting for him to become. That kind of personality is against his nature. One looks into the open yet searching face of Giddings, one peek into his deep, soft blue eyes, and you are invited into the soul of this young man. Many images flood my mind. I can see him years from now living out his existence in a cabin in the woods somewhere, having grown a long, flowing beard and long hair, yielding an axe and wearing work boots, jeans, and flannel shirt, hands hard and calloused from physical labor. I can see him carrying an arm load of freshly chopped wood, walking stooped through driving, blinding snow, throwing open the cabin door, and gently laying down the wood in front of the roaring fire place where his wife is breastfeeding his daughter and a pile of other children and dogs are sleeping by the warmth of the fire.

Giddings will never be the banger that fans want him to be. He is, though, a skilled surgeon of the game, a young man an inch-shy of 7 feet tall, who has a jump shot so soft and silky you just want to cuddle up in it and go to sleep. It's not surprising that Giddings learned to shoot that way from a 78-year-old man, Mike Farmer, who played alongside the great Bill Russell before Farmer was drafted as the third pick in the first round of the 1958 NBA draft, two spots back from Elgin Baylor.

"My high school basketball coach met Mike Farmer playing golf," Giddings says. He told him about me. Said he saw potential. Next thing you know, Mike is teaching me to shoot for the next three years."

Giddings is a Division I transfer. Clink rarely takes transfers. He likes to bring in young players, redshirt them, and let them get used to the system. Giddings is an exception. He comes to Chico State from the basketball powerhouse Fresno State Bulldogs. But Giddings doesn't have the personality of a bulldog. He doesn't have much bite. "I'm a finesse player," he proudly says. When asked is if he feels the pressure of having to become a bulldog—or a pit bull—he smiles: "That's what we have Isaiah for."

Giddings started playing basketball in the fourth grade. He hit a growth spurt in middle school. "Between sixth and eighth grade I reached 6-foot-4."

He says he didn't have any good coaching until he reached high school, and said he was a little behind despite his height. "It was always someone's dad coaching me." In high school he would meet Farmer who would pass on to young Giddings the skills he had picked up playing with Jerry West and Bill Russell. "Everybody wanted (and they still do) me to become a physical power forward. Farmer knew I was a finesse player. He worked with me a lot."

No one in Giddings's family played basketball. They were all clueless about the recruiting process. "Fresno State was on me. I took their offer a week before my senior season started." It was a senior year to remember. He set his high school record with the 1,307 points. He was also the only player on the team who went on to play college basketball. Clink and Coach Cobb recruited him in high school, but they knew it was a long shot. Coach Cobb had a feeling that Giddings would not fit in at Fresno State and find his way back to Chico State.

Giddings averaged 20 minutes a game his freshman season at Fresno State. During his sophomore year, he broke his shooting wrist. The recovery took longer than he expected, and he sat out for a long time. When he did play again, he wasn't the player he was the season prior. "Fresno State just wasn't the best place for me to be successful," Giddings says. He got back in touch with Clink and Coach Cobb. "I made an official visit to Chico. I committed that day." Giddings said the campus was certainly a selling point, but more than anything he came here because of Clink. "He's a player's coach. He doesn't yell. I don't like to be yelled at. Fresno State had a lot of yelling. I don't do well in that kind of environment."

Giddings has gone up against some of the best players and teams in the country.

Sophomore year at Fresno State he played UNLV, Pitt, and Florida when they were all ranked. He has also played against the University of New Mexico, Colorado State, and Boise State when they were ranked. He has played in some of the toughest gyms in the country. I asked him if he was nervous about playing at Arizona. "I've played in the The Pit." He's referring to the home venue of the University of New Mexico Lobos, one of the wildest basketball arenas in the country. "No, I'm not nervous." Giddings gets up for the big games. "I like the intensity of a big atmosphere. I like the noise. It helps me cancel things out." He scored the most points against rivals UC San Diego (16) and Humboldt State (16) last year. Giddings doesn't regret not coming to Chico State first. He realizes going to Fresno State made him a better player. "But I do wish I would've started here. I felt like I fit in here right away. I'm really grateful to be here."

Giddings admits that he's not the most outgoing person. He's also not a vocal leader on the court. He prefers to lead in other ways. "I lead by example. I want my play on the court to do the talking. I don't like to yell." He explains that when he starts to express his emotions on the court, his game unravels. "My dad's the same way. We're just not aggressive. But I am learning to flip the switch." I ask Giddings if he feels any pressure this year. "The only pressure I feel is that it's my last season. I need to be more of a threat. I'm going to score more points and get more rebounds. Things will be different this year. I'm going to have the mindset that I will—that I'm going to take the game over."

One thing I've noticed when watching Giddings play is that only he is capable of stopping Giddings. I've seen players of his caliber before, and I've seen these players "flip the switch," as Giddings calls it, and make the game theirs. "I never want to feel like a ball hog," he says. "That's kind of my problem. If I'm the only one scoring, I feel selfish." He finally admits that he knows he can take a game over. "This year I'll do it. I have to. It's my senior season." He says he also feels better taking a game over if he has to because he's no longer the new guy.

His living arrangement with Isaiah Ellis seems too perfect to be true. Both are quiet and gentle off the court. Both are nice, reserved guys. Both are such darn good basketball players. Giddings's freshman year at Fresno State had him rooming with Harris Johnson, who at the time of this book had just signed a two-year million-and-some-change contract with the Orlando Magic. Johnson's sister, Lauren, is (at the time of this interview) on the women's team here. He doesn't talk about Harris too much, but I get the sense that he believes that if Harris can make it, so can he. "I want to play in the NBA. I know I have the potential. I just have to make it happen.

I'm hungry," he says. I hear his stomach growl. He finally eats the cookie I gave him an hour ago. But his appetite is just a metaphor for the season that awaits him. "Last year was the year that Rob became a star." He takes another bite. He doesn't say it, but I can see in his eyes what he wants to say: "This year's it's my turn."

Giddings, now a senior, now in his prime, is no longer lost and late. He has found his way and is right on time.

CHAPTER 24

Cool Marvin

MARVIN TIMOTHY SHOWS UP WITH a bandage on his hand. He sees me looking at it.

"I was cooking. Got burned by the skillet."

Cool Marvin Timothy—a suave young man, a smooth dresser. A performer. Cool, smooth, Marvin. Coolness that only a nineteen-year-old sophomore and 6-foot-9 power forward can exude. His sister is an actress in Los Angeles. His brother is a model on his way to Miami. Cool Marvin is a basketball player. He and his siblings are entertainers. Cool Marvin is also a great student. He takes pride in academics and has a high GPA. This semester is particularly a busy academic semester for Cool Marvin. "I'm taking chemistry, sociology, psychology, philosophy, and yoga."

I detect a slight accent in Timothy's speech. "I'm Nigerian. My parents were born there." Timothy's parents are successful. He's following in his mother's footsteps. She is a nurse. Timothy—at the time of this book—is a nursing student. "She's been a nurse since 1994. I've been in and out of hospitals since I can remember." His father is a businessman who owns Medical Wear Outlet. Cool Marvin works on campus as a desk attendant in a dorm. It sounds important. He laughs. "I sit down the whole time. I literally get paid to sit down and greet people." Timothy says he's learning a lot from Tanner Giddings. "I watch him. I watch that shot of his." Timothy worked hard on his game during the summer. "Played ball all summer. Mainly at Sac State. Played with my cousins. One of my cousins is the starting point guard for Washington State. The other plays at Southern Idaho."

Timothy starts to relax the more we talk. He seems closed at first, speaking in clipped one or two sentence answers, as if responding to a reporter—the same kind of ubiquitous responses, sound bites, that appear nightly on ESPN. He looks up at the poster that hangs over my head, the one that was created for my first book, *Ain't Whistlin' Dixie No More.*

"What's it about?" he asks.

I point out the inscription on the tombstone: 1865-1994. He gets it. "Sports are a big deal there, right?" he asks. "In the South?"

I could teach a semester-long class on sports culture in Mississippi. I refer to him what I think is the best book ever written about the mixture of sports culture and racism in the South—*The Courting of Marcus Dupree* by Willie Morris. I tell him that we have two religions down South: SEC football is for Saturday, and Sunday is for church. Timothy leans back and relaxes. He starts to open up more and ask me questions, almost as if he has flipped the interview and I am the subject. Writers like to talk about their craft as much as basketball players like to talk about theirs.

"Were you always a really good writer?" he asks.

"No," I tell him. "I have always struggled with writing. I still do."

I explain to him that the difference between being an average writer and a good writer, and being an average basketball players and a good basketball player is the same: If you want to be good (and eventually great) you have to first master the fundamentals and basic skills. "It's all about deliberate practice," I say. "Exactly what Clink has you guys doing every day from 1 to 4." I tell him that just as I was an averagae street ballplayer, I was also an average street writer. In other words, I started trying to break the rules before I first knew, let alone had mastered, the rules. I tell him I had to work really hard when it came to writing, surrender my pride, and become "coachable." He gets it. I also tell him I've suffered from years of disappointment as a writer—one rejected manuscript after another, one rejected screenplay after another—but not once have I been discouraged. I have kept working every day to master the fundamentals.

We talk about music. "I listen to the same song before each game. I've been doing this for five years. It's called *I'm a King* by Game." He quickly follows this with a caveat. "I'm not a lyrics person. I just listen to it for the chorus and beat. It gets me fired up."

I exhale. I Google the lyrics as he talks. The insulting lyrics of the song do not match the sweet personality of this young man. But it's the beat he likes. I get it.

I see another teaching opportunity, a chance for me to share my love of jazz. I can't figure out why more basketball players don't listen to it.

I ask him if he likes jazz.

"I like jazz. It's smooth. I like to hear it when I'm in a restaurant or a grocery store or something. It calms my mind down."

I ask him if he has ever listened to John Coltrane. He shakes his head.

For a music fan, for a jazz fan, not having heard of John Coltrane is like being a basketball fan and never having heard of Dr. J or Michael Jordan. I tell him Coltrane died in 1967 from liver cancer, and that he was only 40. I also assure him that the music he hears in elevators and grocery stores has nothing to do with Coltrane. I start laughing. I think of the perfect analogy. Coltrane and smooth elevator jazz has about as much in common as the Chico State Men's Basketball team and the old dudes that play in Shurmer Gym twice a week.

I don't have the time to go into a lecture about Coltrane. That would be the quickest way to turn a potential jazz fan away. I compare Coltrane to the game of Jalen McFerren and Mike Rosaroso.

"You know how Mike was great at controlling a game? How he played conservative basketball.

How he didn't turn the ball over that much. How he was a distributor. How he wasn't flashy but consistently good. How he wasn't the most fun guy to watch— just like Pete Sampras in tennis or the German World Cup soccer team or Alex Smith when he played for the 49ers—but he got the job done." We then talk about McFerren and how he's flashy but also consistently good. How McFerren controls tempo. He can play fast and furious, or he can slow it down and be methodical. McFerren is more of a performer, I say, someone who gives the crowd goosebumps. I tell him that Coltrane was first and foremost a street player. But like all the Chico State players, he also knew how to conform to the rules, master the fundamentals, and save flash for a time when flash was needed. I tell him that Coltrane knew when to go between the legs, spin, and dunk. He also knew when to lay the ball up. Timothy's eyes light up. He's interested. If only I can get him to listen to Coltrane's *Blue Train*. I tell him to download the album, put on his headphones, get in the gym, and work on his footwork.

The sky is the limit for Cool Marvin. I wonder if he knows this. It's hard to believe this will be his first year playing. He redshirted last year. Still, though, he's young. He has a lot to learn. "Putting on the redshirt was hard, but I knew it would make me a better player," he says. "I'm smarter, stronger, better than I was last year." He pauses. "I was able to focus on my grades. My GPA should have been a lot higher, though. Got a lot of minuses that killed me." He pauses again. "Nursing is a good back up for when hen I get through playing in Europe." There it is again, that same stroke of youthful confidence that so many of Clink's players exude.

But who is Marvin Timothy?

"I'm funny and goofy off the court," he says. "Once I'm on the court, I look mad." He says he's not mad, just focused. "I don't talk or smile or anything. I just play." Timothy defines himself as a post-player with a mid-range game. "I can throw down a dunk. I love to get the crowd riled up. But blocking a shot gives me the same thrill."

Timothy's idol is Dwight Howard. I see the similarities. They even look alike. "I love him not so much for the way he plays but the way he acts. He always looks like he's having fun out there and smiling." He also likes the game of LaMarcus Aldridge. "He plays like Giddings." He keeps mentioning Giddings. This is a good sign. What a player to learn from. Timothy says he watches lots of videos on footwork. He also studies the game of the former Duke player (now in the NBA) Jahil Okafor. Okafor is also Nigerian.

Timothy tells me he will be going to visit the homeland of his mother and father next summer. He also shares with me that last November his grandmother passed away. "I found out not long before I went to practice that day. I remember there was this play where Keith missed a layup. I was trailing behind. I jumped higher than I've ever jumped before and slammed the ball down."

Timothy hands me his phone and shows me several pictures of him and his grandmother. In most of the pictures, she's wearing a colorful head wrap. A big smile stretches across her face. Her eyes shine brightly. The picture that really catches my eye is the one of Timothy crouching down next to his grandmother as she lies in a hospital bed. This photo, he tells me, was taken not long before she passed away. "She was the most loving person. On her birthday—*her* birthday—she gave *us* presents."

Timothy's eyes grow moist. He tells me he has dedicated this season to her.

CHAPTER 25

Dr. Rap

KEITH DATU, A SOFT-SPOKEN FRESHMAN who looks like a movie star with his African-American and Filipino roots, comes from Santa Maria, California. He will be the first male in his family to graduate from college, following in the footsteps of his two older sisters who were the first females in the family to graduate from college. Datu is also a rapper. He and Lee Litvin, another talented rapper and the team manager, write and record music together. Datu's voice is smooth and silky, the kind of voice you might expect to hear from a radio DJ on a jazz station—back in the day—in the small hours of the morning.

Datu was the man of his house early on. He grew up with two older sisters and a single mom. Not even twenty seconds into the interview, Datu says of his mother: "She means the world to me. I don't know how she does it, but she gets it done." Datu has shared his rap with me, and many of his songs are about both his mother and his religious faith. Datu attended a small Christian college from preschool until the eighth grade. Growing up he went to church twice on Sunday and once on Wednesday. Still, his mother is his favorite theme and rightfully so.

"There were times when we were financially unstable and she always pulled us through. I don't know how she did it with three kids under her belt all by herself. We even moved in with my grandmother and my grandmother's friend. We lived there for a couple of years." Growing up without a lot of money, Datu says, has "taught me to value the dollar 100 percent." Datu is quick to let me know, however, that he was never poor. "I don't like to use that word. My mom taught me that nothing is handed out to you. She always told me you have to go and get what you want for yourself."

Datu says hip-hop of the 1990s spoke to him. "Listening to Tupac, a great West Coast example, talking about people growing up without a lot reminded me of my own experiences. Tupac talks about how he grinds every day to make money, and he talks about how he did it all for his mom." I ask Datu if that, too, is his main motivation—for his mom. He smiles. "Yes, most of it. Every year when we post a bio on the men's basketball website, there's a question about who your favorite sports and non-sports hero is, and every time I say my mom."

Datu also raps about his father. "I'm in the process now of writing a song called *Father's Day*, and it talks about how he was never around. As much as I love him—I know he has a good heart—he just wasn't there." Datu is yet another young man whose childhood was stained by his father's own troubled childhood; his father never knew his father.

I mention briefly that along with sibling rivalries, another common theme with all the players I have talked with seems to be strong mothers and distant fathers. Datu, despite his warrior stature, thinks before he speaks—thoughtful to the bone. His words resonate with sincerity, and his thoughts and ideas come from a deep place. "I saw something on Twitter the other day that was meant to be funny but kind of true. This guy Tweeted 'If I knock up this girl, I'm gonna leave her for the benefit of the kid because single mothers seem to raise NBA stars.' I understand he was trying to be funny, but if you think about it, I don't know, it's kind of emotional. I didn't know how to react when I saw this. I think I was supposed to laugh, but I found it sadly true."

I think of what Freud once said—there is no such thing as a joke.

Datu says the absence of his father doesn't bother him now that he's older. "But," he says, "I had a really hard time with it when I was a kid." But like me, the middle-aged writer, and all these other young men I have spent time with, basketball has been their safe haven, the one constant steady in their lives. "There would be days when I wouldn't talk to anybody," Datu says. "I would just go and play by myself. When I was younger, the only place I had to go was the playground. I would literally sit out there all by myself."

Some people believe that animals are the best companions for kids with bad childhoods. I have always believed a basketball makes the best friend. "That's what I loved and still love about basketball," he continues. "I could go and play by myself. I didn't need anyone else. To me there's nothing better than an open gym with no one else around."

Datu says he doesn't know where he would be today if it were not for basketball. "I don't think I would be in to music if I were not into basketball. I love that it brought me to my teammates here and where I am today." Basketball has also provided him with a deep connection to his grandmother. Growing up, Datu watched every single Lakers game with his grandmother, who was an avid fan. "I wore the same Kobe number 8 jersey every time I watched the Lakers with her. I still have it."

Datu says that everything he does, everywhere he goes, he is always listening to music. Music is always playing in his head, even when he's not wearing head phones. He loves to take his speaker to the court and play along to music. "I listen to before-game music that's inspirational. What I listen to after a game all depends on whether we won or lost the game."

Datu, despite his many dreams, has a level head and has future goals grounded in reality. "After college I want to enter the medical field. I want to be a physical therapist. I have to go to graduate school no matter what. I will work toward my doctorate." His entire family has worked in the medical field and all at the same hospital. "My grandmother was the president of volunteer services in the hospital. My sister is an ultrasound tech in the hospital. And my mom is a senior executive coordinator in the hospital."

Datu almost didn't come to Chico. "It was the last school I visited. None of the other schools I visited came close to making me feel the way Chico State did. Sure, a few schools I visited told me they wanted me and made an offer, but they didn't make me feel wanted. I had a gut feeling and gut instinct about Chico State. My mom and my sisters all thought Chico State was a bad idea and didn't want me to go here. They were pushing for Point Loma Nazarene University, my second option. It's in San Diego, right on the beach. Even though I had been in a religious private school my entire life, and so had my sisters, even in college, I felt like God was shifting me here. I'm super happy I came here. I wouldn't change it for anything." Datu says he wanted to be somewhere that felt like home. "I'm so close to my family. They're all I had growing up, but I'm not homesick here. I don't feel like I need to drive home."

A lot of players with a background like Datu play with a chip on their shoulder. Datu, though, says he doesn't. It's just not in his nature. "Jalen tells me all the time that I'm being too humble or that I need to shoot more." He says he realizes he hasn't been as aggressive as he should, but says his humble attitude goes back to the way he was brought up. "Growing up in a Christian private school, a main focus was to be humble. Don't boast. When I got to high school I was told I needed to be cocky and show people who I am, but that's not me." He believes this attitude negatively affects his game. "I know that I'm good, but I'll admit that I can be emotional."

Datu's freshman year was tough. "I wanted to play so badly, and I knew I was better than I played in practice." He plays sparingly, if at all, in games. "What hurt the most was having people think I wasn't as good as I knew

I was, but I never admitted to anyone how good I thought I was. Maybe that's why they thought what they thought. I have to keep reminding myself that, yes, I need to be humble, but it's that humble attitude that has held me back. I need to show everyone that I'm not as quiet as they think I am." I ask Datu if he has it within him to ever get angry. He laughs. "Funny you say that, because every practice Corey comes up to me and tells me I need to get angry today. It's hard for me to get upset. From where I came from, it's hard not to be happy about where I am now. I need to work on this. The few times I have been angry on the court, I play so much better. When I'm angry I want to tear the rim off, but I don't know how to turn that anger on and off. I just don't know what makes me angry."

I think this is what makes Datu such an exceptional young man, such an excellent songwriter, and such a good basketball player. And who knows— he might just yet turn into one of Clink's pit bulls.

CHAPTER 26

The Fountainhead and the Priest

TYLER HARRIS NOT ONLY PLAYS basketball but he also writes poetry. He cites these as his two main passions in life. "Basketball is poetry in motion," he tells me. Harris says he started writing poetry because he was bored in class. I interviewed him an hour after he had taken the last of his five finals. After our interview, he will be on his way home (Bakersfield) for the summer. His thoughts, though, are already on next year. "We've tasted it now. We can win our league. We can with the CCAA championship. We have to be hungry. We have to be ready every day. That's what it will take."

Harris knew after a few months at the Air Force Prep Academy that it was not the right place for him. He came home to Bakersfield for a 12-day break and Christmas—his friends have a month off—and sent out mass emails to Division I and Division II schools. "I was just putting out feelers. It was a form letter. I would just cut and paste the school mascot. That's all I'd change." He said that Chico State wrote him back within 20 minutes. "They really wanted me." When he came out for a recruiting visit, Mike Rosaroso took him to one of his classes. "There were 31 girls and four guys." He would later find out that all classes were not like this. Rosaroso was a Child Development major. "I was sold," Harris says, laughing. "Okay, that was just part of it. But, seriously, the coaches and the team treated me like they needed me. The team was also really good. I could see myself fitting into the system and being a part of the team culture. They were professional. I could also see myself fitting into the community. I wanted to be a part of something big."

Harris loves the atmosphere in Acker. "What's great about home games here is that we're friends with everyone," he says. By friends with everyone, he means that the players tell the friends in their circle that exist outside of basketball to come to a game and they do. He explains that the guys on the team are not only friends with just each other, but their friendship expands beyond the basketball team.

Harris's mother was born and raised in Mexico. English is her second language. She got her BA from Cal State Bakersfield when Harris was in middle school. His father did not attend college. He works as a shift supervisor at General Electric. Basketball is not a tradition in his family. "My Mom knew nothing about basketball. It wasn't popular when she was growing up in Mexico." When Harris was about five, he caught an NCAA March Madness game on television. "That's when I fell in love with basketball. That's when I knew I wanted to play at that level someday. Playing Division I ball was my dream." Since he now plays for a Division II team, his perspectives have changed. "A lot of DII teams not only compete with a lot of DI teams but can beat them." He knows from experience. "We scrimmaged St. Mary's last year in a closed gym. We hung with them for twenty minutes." St. Mary's would go on to beat Gonzaga that year—the year that Coach Few fielded one of his best teams ever.

Clink has said before that Harris might be the most aggressive player on the team. "I'm hungry to stay on the floor." He admits that he has had to overcome playing with too much passion and anger. "I don't know how to play passively. My whole career I've been trying to find a way to do this properly. To harness my energy properly. That's my progression. I just want to win so badly."

Harris reminds me of Howard Roark, the antihero from Ayn Rand's *The Fountainhead*. I recognize in Tyler Harris the same streak of idealism and defiance and boldness that Howard Roark exhibited, and I worry that this attitude will not fit-in well with Clink's program. Howard Roark was not a team player—he was too fiercely independent, passionate, and cold. It was him against the world. Players like Howard Roark don't fit into Clink's system. While I know Harris puts his team first, I also see in him the kind of young man who will not tolerate sitting on the bench. It's just not in his DNA. He's too much a fighter.

Harris gets defensive when asked about the bad rap on Bakersfield. "Unless you're from Bakersfield, you don't know Bakersfield and can't say anything bad about it." He says that being from Bakersfield puts a chip on his shoulder. "We have to take up for our city. It might not be the best, but it's where we're from." When he says "we," Harris means all the great athletes that the city produces. "Cody Cussler, Tyrone Wallace, Derek Carr—there's a lot of us out there. It's Bakersfield versus everyone else."

Harris says his practice regimen will start the day he gets home, six hours from now when he pulls into the driveway. "All the good players. We find each other. Word of mouth gets out where people are playing." He expects to play against the hyped-up future NBA prospect Tyrone Wallace over the summer. "He'll be around." Harris is a gym rat. "That's another great thing about living in Bakersfield. There's nothing else to do but play sports. I'm in the gym all day. Plus, I'm close to L.A. I can go down there and look for competition." Harris is always looking for a fight. "Most of my friends back home don't really play ball, and if they do it's recreational. I have to find players that will make me better. See, I have a big chip on my shoulder. All throughout my career, people were always telling me I wasn't good enough. Said I didn't have the right skills. No notoriety or publications. No recognition."

Harris had a growth spurt his freshman year of high-school. "I went from 5-foot-8 to 6-foot-1. I also dunked for the first time that summer." The dunk, however, does not excite him as much as the jump shot. "That's my game." Passing, though, is his favorite part of the game. He talks about the chemistry he has with Isaiah Ellis, whom he calls a "freak." He shakes his head. "I've been playing ball for a long time, and played against some great players. And he might be the best ever. We have good chemistry. We connect."

That is good news for Clink in the next couple of years to follow.

"I also really connect with Rob Duncan." More great news. "I'd rather make a good pass than anything in basketball," he says. "I have this skill that's a curse and a blessing. I can see a play before it happens. Sometimes this causes me to overthink the play and I make a bad pass. Turn the ball over."

Harris says he didn't get enough playing time last year. He wanted more. He was waiting for his opportunity. "My opportunity came when Corey hurt his wrist and was out nine games. I was ready. It's all about the opportunity. Just be ready." Being ready is something Clink stresses. "That's Coach in two words: Get ready." He points out that Robert Duncan did not become an overnight success. "But he was ready." Harris admits that sitting on the bench gets to him. "It's the anxiousness. Coach Clink walks up and down the sideline. You're just hoping he taps you. If he doesn't you can't pout. You just have to be ready at all times. And we have a team full of killers that can and will all contribute." Harris is a killer. He loves it when another team comes into Acker and he sends them home with a loss. "It's a thrill when someone comes in here to test themselves and we beat them. They had to travel here. They have to take a bus or a plane. They prepared all week. I like them leaving our building with the feeling of being unsuccessful."

When Trevor Priest signed with Chico State, Luke Reid, the Sports Information Direction, wrote an article titled: *Coach Clink Gets Answer to His Prayer.*

Trevor Priest was Chico State's biggest prep recruit in decades. NorCalPreps.com had ranked Priest—a 6-foot-5 wing who averaged 15 points, 6.2 rebounds, and 2.4 rebounds a game his junior year—the sixth best player in in Northern California. He was coached by his father Mitch Priest at Santa Teresa High School. During the summers, longtime coach of the West Valley Basketball Club Bob Bramlett coached him. Priest chose Chico State over several other Division I schools. Priest, despite not starring and actually taking a role on the bench that has made him ascend rather than descend into grace, remains a big man on campus. He is wildly popular. He walks through the food court and can't get more than five steps before a student stops him to talk. He's always giving high-fives and fist bumps. His hair has gotten long and flips out from beneath his ball cap. He's handsome in a dashing British kind of way—imagine Michael Caine fifty years younger and if he were a tall basketball player. "I didn't know what to expect when I got here," Priest says. He certainly didn't expect to play 3.6 minutes a game and score 1.2 points a game. "Last year was a struggle. I had a lot of talks with Coach Clink. He made me feel better about things. He promised me that my time would come. He's never given me a reason to doubt him. Coach Clink has stood by everything he's ever said."

Priest is now a junior—an experienced junior. He was part of the Elite Eight team. He was also voted "Most Inspirational Player" that year. "I wasn't playing. I wanted to contribute somehow. That's how I found my niche. Encouraging the other players."

Priest started playing basketball when he was five. In yet another Wildcats twist of fate, he played in a youth league for Clink's high school coach. "Yeah, I've known Coach Green since I was five. He was my SCBA coach." Priest's father, just seven years older than Clink, also grew up in Morgan Hill. Priest spent his entire childhood and young adult years playing AAU basketball in the summer, and of course basketball during the regular season. He almost played against Robert Duncan in the high school state tournament. "Yeah, if we would have won one more game, we would have played against Rob in Arco Arena."

Priest says that playing for his father was different than most people would expect. "We've always kept our basketball relationship separate." He laughs. "Yeah, Dad cut me my freshman year on the JV team. He said I needed more time to develop. I wasn't happy, but he was right." By his sophomore year, Priest was coming off the bench as the sixth man. "I got my first start in a playoff game against Bellarmine." That's also where his father played high school basketball. "I was nervous, but once I got the nerves out, I've been confident ever since." By his senior year, he was a star. He came in second place for player of the year to the former University of Arizona star and NBA player Aaron Gordon.

Clink saw Priest play his junior year. Clink, however, had gone to watch a different player. "I walked away with Trevor's name written down," Clink says. "He was a junior and played great in the section championship game I was at." Coach Cobb soon got wind of Priest, too, and went down to Los Angeles to watch him play in AAU tournaments. "I wasn't too impressed with Chico State at first," Priest says. "But then I started getting all of these letters. Every day a new letter. A stack of letters. I saved every one of them." He says that Chico State became his first choice. "And then I visited the campus. My family and I loved the community and the people. I saw tremendous opportunity here."

I ask Priest—considering his lack of playing time—if he has any regrets about coming here. "None," he says. "I don't know what it is about this place." He shakes his head, thinking hard, trying to grasp the essence of this town, this Chico that has become his. "I love walking through town. Past *The Bear*. Past the fraternity houses." Priest has found a home, a place that makes the former star be able to cope with his current status of limited minutes.

Priest says he gets a lot of his positive attitude from his father. He says he's talked to him a lot these last two years as he has struggled with not playing. "My dad played at Bellarmine. They were dominant. His senior year, he played less than five minutes. But he was so happy just to be on the team." Priest says that his father gave him some invaluable advice: "Dad told me that my job is to help make each one of my teammates be the best player they can be. Always do the little things that make them better. One of his teammates went off and played ball at Stanford. Dad did something right." His father had a burning desire to stay around basketball, even though he was an average player. "He went to San Jose State and got a job as the team manager for the basketball team. The next year he walked on. He worked his tail off. He's always told me that you get out of something what you put into it."

A few days after the Wildcats were knocked out of the NCAA tournament by Cal Baptist, I was in Acker playing ball with the old dudes. Priest was also in the gym, alone, taking one jump shot after another. I ask him about that. He says he felt terrible after the loss. Guilty. There was no sweat on his jersey after that game. "That's the worst thing about being on the bench." He says that the second after that loss, all he has wanted to do was play. He felt bad for not being able to help his team on the court. "I didn't exert myself at all. So after that game, I told myself I was going to get in the gym and stay there. I pushed myself really hard in the off-season. I stayed here in Chico and worked out all summer."

Priest, despite looking at another year of being an observer rather than a participant (at least in games), says he's ready to lead. "I know I'm ready to lead. The guys that are with us now have been here for a while. And guys still listen to me even when I'm not playing a lot." Priest's teammates point out that he's probably the most fun guy on the team. "Yeah, I try and make it that way. I'm the guy who's in there trying to fire everyone up at 7 a.m. when we're in the weight room and we're tired and we'd all rather be in bed." He smiles. "I learned this from the best. I learned this from Rahsad. Every single day he'd run through the Red Door and start firing everybody up and getting them ready. We feed off of each other."

Priest lives with Drew Kitchens. I don't know how in the world these two stay academically eligible. I find it ironic that Trevor is a Priest. I say this because he reminds me of so many sons and daughters of men of the cloth back where I grew up in Mississippi who went wild in high school and college as they broke free from the Puritanical chains that had bound them for so long. I see in Priest a young man who has been tethered to the game of competitive basketball for at least the last ten years, and he has arrived at Chico State and begun to realize that there is life outside of basketball. I just hope that other life does not interfere with his basketball talent, but this *is* college. Three steps away live Duncan, Magz, and Harris. "We have a good time," Priest says. "A really good time."

Priest has a vision for his future. "I'm going to become a coach. I'd like to start my own AAU team." He's making the best of his time on the bench. But as Clink promised him, his time will come. One has the feeling that time will be soon.

I do worry about the Fountainhead and the Priest. The former, so desperately wanting to play basketball, the latter so desperately just wanting to play.

CHAPTER 27

Division II Pistol Pete

Faith consists in believing when it is beyond the power of reason to believe.

—Voltaire

IT'S THE LAST FRIDAY BEFORE school starts. The campus teems with excitement. Young men wander around campus with their shirts off, revealing a summer spent working out. Young women are wearing sundresses and walking in groups of five, bubbling, eager and ready to go wild after two months spent under their parent's roof. Everyone is headed over to the WREC center. Free hamburgers from The Madison Bear Garden—simply known as The Bear and home to the Jiffy Burger—which is one of the best college hangouts in the nation. The players are trickling back to campus. I'm crossing the street to head over and get a free hamburger myself. I stop at the intersection and wait for the light to turn green. "Mr. Medley," says a deep voice. "Sorry I never got in touch with you this summer. I don't check my email." I'd been on the phone with my young son. I look up. It's Robert Duncan. He's on a skateboard. He has put on a lot of muscle. I tell him he looks big. It makes me nervous, seeing him on a skateboard. I can only imagine how it would make Clink feel. Clink will later tell me he doesn't care. "If I could ride a skateboard to work, I would," he says. "College kids ride skateboards. I still ride a skateboard. Part of growing up is falling off the thing."

Duncan comes to my office the following day. He has a sweet and sincere countenance. He reminds me of a young man who might not have had the best childhood. I can spot this kind of troubled past in the eyes of a young man from a mile away. It's something that stays in our eyes forever. It's a scar that never go away. It comes from not being hugged enough by our mothers, and not being patted on the back enough by our fathers.

Maybe that is why, basketball skills aside, I was so drawn to Robert Duncan. That and he's the kind of basketball player I'd always wished I could be.

Basketball, same as it was for me, served as loyal and constant companion, the place where he could go to get away from it all, a place where he could have it all in a world that otherwise seemed cruel and cold and offered little for him. He's also one of the nicest young men in the world despite the challenges life has thrown at him.

Duncan is humble—quiet, even—off the court. On the court he is a cold blooded assassin. He is tough. He is a competitor. He hates to lose more than anything in the world.

"I had to be tough growing up," Duncan says. "I had three older stepbrothers. My dad married their mom. I was also the smallest and always getting picked on." Duncan moved around a lot. In a world that bounced young Duncan back and forth like a pinball, basketball was the one constant. "I grew up in Foothill, Antelope, Rocklin, and Loomis. Then we moved to Carmichael. And when I was in the sixth grade, we moved to Nashville, Tennessee."

When Duncan talks of "we," he must be referring to himself and his father. Not once does he mention his mother. I'm starting to understand. That countenance, that sweet disposition, reminds me of a nice pit bull who's had a rough run, and if you rub that pit bull the wrong way, he will attack. His jaw will clench and he'll not let go.

By the time Duncan moved to Nashville, he'd already been playing ball for three years. "When I was in the third grade, I came home from school with a flyer. It was for a basketball team. That was it." I had a similar experience. My father didn't like basketball. That's why I wanted to play. When I was in the third grade, I spent the night at my friend's house. He had a basketball game at the YMCA that morning. I went to watch. I immediately fell in love with the game—a 34-year love affair that grows stronger each year. Basketball has saved me time and time throughout the years. Basketball has been my salvation and my saving grace. I wonder, can only hope, that Duncan will someday look over his shoulder at the game from the same perspective as I.

I hand Duncan an old cut-out of Pistol Pete that I keep on my bulletin board. Pistol Pete's wearing an LSU jersey and throwing the ball over his shoulder to a man trailing behind. Duncan and the Pistol have the same physique save the three inches that separates them. Duncan looks at the picture and smiles. "Pistol Pete," he says. "My dad gave me the movie *The Pistol* not long after I started playing basketball. I must have watched it 100 times. You know that scene where he's bouncing the ball on the train tracks with the blindfold on?" He starts laughing. "I did that."

I think of all the moves, all the flashes of brilliance, from Duncan's sophomore campaign last season. He couldn't have learned those moves, he could not have honed those skills and nurtured those instincts, on the playgrounds and gyms in Granite Bay, California, where he played his senior season of basketball. He smiles.

"I learned all that in Nashville," he says. "I played in predominantly black neighborhoods." Like Duncan, I, too, had played in predominantly black neighborhoods and with black kids. Unlike Duncan, I had transferred from an all-white Baptist academy known for football rather than basketball to an 87% black high school that year in and year out sends players to Division I powerhouses and eventually the NBA. But unlike Duncan, I did not have the talent, the discipline, or the ability to take orders from a coach. I never acquired the humility and hubris required to be a student-athlete, which is yet another reason why Clink's players impress me so much. I shared with him my own personal struggle with authority—how in high school I spent three weeks in a Jackson, Mississippi detention center that was like a maximum security prison and the next two months in a shelter for runaway youth.

Basketball got me through that time.

"Oh, I struggle with authority, too," Duncan laughs. "I don't like people telling me what to do. A couple seasons ago I had a really bad attitude." That must account for his numbers during the 2013-2014 season. He only played sparingly in nine games.

In Duncan's team picture from that freshman year, his head is shaved. He's skinny. His shoulders are slumped. It almost looks like a mugshot, that lost look, the drawn mouth, the look of uncertainty intermingled with regret and remorse: How did I wind up here?

"Yeah," he says. "That was a tough year. There were times when I thought about leaving. I was down. I felt a lot of pressure when I would go into a game. I tried to make things happen too fast. I'd turn it over." Duncan said the hardest part was that he knew he could play. "That's what motivated me. There was a time during that season when coach put me in. I went coast to coast. I couldn't believe how easy it was." He laughs and shakes his head. "Then I turned it over."

Duncan's 2014-2015 team picture shows a different kind of young man. His hair is a little longer and he's smiling. His smile tells the world that he knows something that we don't yet know. He knows something that even Coach Clink doesn't know.

The kid can not only play, but he's a legitimate star.

This year Duncan has a mop of long, curly hair that he wears brushed back when he plays. He's a lot bigger. He's not resting on the laurels of his success last year: 30 games played; 30.1 minutes a game; 13.9 points per game; .548 FG percentage; 3.5 rebounds per game; 1.4 steals; 2.3 assists.

And one constant that plagues him. Turnovers: 2.3 per game.

Who would've known that Duncan would be fourth in the league in shooting that year and make the All-West Region team? Some might question whether Clink should have played Duncan more his freshman year—a year of eligibility gone for just nine games played. But Duncan had to watch from the bench just like Steve Young had to wait his turn, Aaron Rodgers had to wait his, and another young man by the name of Jeremy Lin had to wait his turn. Nothing builds character and resiliency like riding the bench. Nothing tests that character and resiliency like opportunity.

Nobody knows this more than Duncan's coach. Both coaches. Coach Gabriel and Coach Clink spent a considerable amount of their college basketball experience viewing the action from a folding metal chair rather than on the court. Clink got a lot of playing time when he was playing at Gavilan Community College. Things changed when he got to Chico State and started playing for Puck Smith. "I only played in 13 games during my Chico State career," Clink says. He played in only one game his junior year and 12 games his senior year. "I had a role during my senior year," Clink continues. "I learned a lot about myself during my time here. I learned about selflessness. I learned that if I wanted to be a part of the program, I had to give myself to it. I had to commit. I had to surrender my own selfish needs and just get caught up in the team's success and what I could do to add to it," he explains. "Once I did that I was able to enjoy it. Coming here and trying out for the team and struggling to find a role was the hardest thing I ever experienced in sports. I wouldn't go back and change it though. It taught me a lot about myself and what I was able to endure. It also helped me become a better coach. I know what the guys on the end of the bench are going through. I can relate to them. A lot of coaches that were great players don't get this, and they never get the most out of the guys that don't play or they don't have the compassion for those guys and they don't treat those guys right," says Clink.

Duncan needed that season of humility on the bench to become the leader, the player that he is today, same as his coach needed those years of riding the bench.

Duncan shakes his head. "I could have done so much more last year," he says. "So much more. I had a terrible game against Cal Baptist. We were better than them. I take the blame." That loss is a fresh, weeping wound that has not, and will not, scab. It festers. It pains him all the time. "See, last year I was just happy to be in the NCAA tournament. This year my attitude is different. It's that we *should* be there."

A shadow washes over Duncan's face. I've seen this happen in several of Clink's players when I ask them about next season. They're hungry. They lost the last two games of last season. That's a long time to walk around with a grudge. They're ready to hurl that burden off their backs. Duncan nods his head and smiles. He almost rocks back and forth in the chair. "It can happen this year. It *will* happen. We have chemistry." Duncan, despite moving furniture all summer, worked hard on his game.

"I worked on my handle. I also put up lots of shots." The smile goes away then returns. "It can happen this year. We have all the pieces. Everyone knows it. Jalen's a gym rat. He also worked hard all summer."

I ask him if there are any teams that worry him this season. He shakes his head again. "I don't think about other teams. I don't think about other players. I worry about what I have to do." He quotes Floyd Mayweather Jr. "I'm not worried about Manny. The only thing I can do is take it one day at a time. When the fight gets here, I'll go out there and do what I do best and that's go out and fight."

Duncan says that this season he will no longer dribble as much. He will also make sure not to turn the ball over. "The team knows each other so well know that we can anticipate what the other four guys are going to do. I said it earlier. We have chemistry. The other guys understand what I'm going to do. I understand what they're going to do. I'm going to find the open shots." His mind drifts. "And there's Isaiah. He's a freak. Defensively he's like Kawhi Leonard with the Spurs. He can jump out of the gym, too."

Duncan also says he loves the sound the net makes when Tanner Giddings hits a jumper. "It's so smooth. The ball just splashes in."

I ask Duncan about the biggest benefit of being a 22-year-old junior when this season starts. "Things have slowed down. I can see everything now." I show him a few clips of his from last season that made the Chico State highlight reel, moves that cannot be explained rationally, moves that cannot be intellectualized, moves that cannot be taught, moves that can only be in the moment. Duncan seems in awe of himself as he watches. "I've looked at these a couple of times, but I don't think about them." I show him another clip that impresses me and ask him what happened when he drove to the basket with a couple ticks left, almost turned the ball over by dribbling too much, recovered it, and hit the game winner with 1.3 seconds left.

"The only thing I was thinking was that if I turn this ball over, coach is going to be angry and lose confidence in me."

The ball went in.

If he would've missed that shot, perhaps Duncan would not have had the season that he had. Perhaps Clink would not have given Duncan the green light to improvise. Perhaps the leash would've been shortened. Perhaps there would be no leash but a shock collar.

"But it went in," he says.

I show him a few more clips of other moves where he does a couple crossover dribbles, splits the defenders, and sails in for a layup. He shrugs his shoulders. There's another great clip when Clink is squatting down next to Duncan, obvious he has to make a split-second decision. Clink has a paper rolled tightly in his hand. He taps Duncan on the knee with it, whispers something, and Duncan sprints into the game.

"He told me to just go in there and make a play."

Despite Duncan's talent and his high level of assuredness, Clink intimidates him. "He's so serious. He always has this really stern look on his face. I mean, sometimes he'll laugh and play around a little, but most of the time he's all business." I ask him about the season to come.

"I want next season to be a dream," he says. "We will win the league. We will win the tournament championship. We will win the NCAA tournament. We all have to believe. We just have to believe. We have to find a way within ourselves. Our chemistry has to remain. We have to stay positive. Everybody has to buy into their role. We can't get too amped." He pauses. "We all just have to believe," he says. "Believe."

PART III

Preseason

CHAPTER 28

Being Greg in Spring

The past is never dead. It's not even past.

—William Faulkner, Requiem for a Nun

THE SENIOR BANQUET MARKS THE official starting point to the 12-month cycle that involves my following of Coach Clink and the team. I am off on my first assignment. This is the start of the book that takes place in "real time." I feel fresh and eager, a Division II basketball tourist for a year on the first leg of his expedition. Clink—despite looking equally as fresh—must have been exhausted. His regular season had ended more than a month ago, yet here he was, again, having to work a different kind of floor. He seems to enjoy it though, and has the glow of a man who not only realizes that he has been blessed but is grateful for the blessing. He talks to parents and thanks them for their support. His neck must be sore from bending down so much as older women whisper into his ear. Acker Backers, the fans that are official season ticketholders and athletic boosters of Chico State basketball, ask about his next recruiting class. Clink tells them in a tone that sounds as if he's filling them in on a secret, giving them just enough information to make them feel like they know a little more than the average fan.

The great ones have their names spoken softly, in almost a whisper— a reverential tone filled with respect, love, and closeness. At the Senior Banquet, alumni and boosters speak softly of "Greg." The name "Greg" sounds like December snow falling on pine needles. Sports fans like to call their heroes by their first name. No, forget about like—they *need* to call them by their first name. They want to get close to the untouchable, and for many basketball fans, coaches are untouchable.

Most top Division II programs like Chico State reside in small town America. Since the teams do not get television exposure, the only way folks in the community ever see the coach or the players is if they go to the games. If they don't go to the games, then the folks in the community might be standing in line next to the coach while checking out at the grocery store and not even realize it. However, this same person might be standing in line next to the local weatherman and start gushing and gawking and panicking for some kind of way of saying hello but missing the moment because they were so star truck and the weatherman went on his way. The same happens for the basketball fan that sees the coach out and about in public. Clink says he does get recognized in public sometimes but not often. "People will recognize me from being interviewed on the news," he says "Sometimes I'll be at the store or something and see someone looking at me like they know me, but they can't figure out where they've seen me before." Clink has been in a series of local television commercials, too. He laughs. "Yeah, those silly Will Katz commercials. More people recognize me from those than the games."

Clink says that after the Wildcats won the West Regional in 2014, he noticed a lot more people watching him. "We were in the news so much that spring. People I'd never seen or met before were following us and would come up out of the blue and congratulate me."

The fan gets that same kind of excitement seeing a coach out and about in public as a school child gets upon seeing his or her teacher out in public. Fans and schoolchildren are a lot alike in this way; they find it hard to believe that someone whom they respect so much is subject to the same daily grind as they are. And that's the thrill that Division I basketball fans who fall upon their knees and wash the feet of a one-and-done freshman, those fans who call their big shot seven-figure coach by the first name when that coach has his eyes set on a bigger job in a bigger town, will never feel. The only time Clink's student-athletes are one-and-done is if they leave the team for personal or academic reasons. This rarely happens in his program.

About 90 parents and fans are in attendance. However, if a picture is worth 1,000 words, then one loyal fan, one loving parent, is worth 10,000 bandwagon Kentucky fans. There was love in that banquet room. A feeling of family and brotherhood. A feeling not unlike the kind that the Holy Spirit rouses in the souls of an intimate church gathering where the faithful have gathered to cleanse their souls from six-days of hard living, a Mississippi tent revival where the vanquished are given new life, bankrupt souls soon teeming with riches.

What a strange sensation it must have been for the Wildcat players as they arrived at the Canyon Country Oaks club, a glimpse into a life they might one day have, a reminder in the present of what little they have materially. But what they lack materially they've made up for with their physical gifts. A private golf club that on this one evening of the year is open to these young men who otherwise would be turned away for not being members. However, they are members of a club that money cannot buy: to join this club, character is the most important commodity for entrance. The players, dressed in their Sunday finest, or trying to veil their Sunday best in the fashion of the big dance that will happen later that night at The Graduate, a college bar in town, walk past men smoking cigars and reclining in golf carts, strut past pretty women in matching springtime pastels and putting on manicured greens.

The players walk up the stairs. They turn to look at the rolling green hills behind them—that verdant, vibrant green grass that is the promise of their future and the reminder of their present struggle. Carts are lined-up in front of the green as the players watch a foursome put. The players' jaws work, their eyes squint, and they crane their heads to watch the competition out on the course. This is how the moneyed compete when they can no longer jump and run and shoot: golf.

These young Chico State basketball players have plenty of time and days ahead to play golf, but only when their bodies are worn out from a life time of scrambling for loose balls on a hard floor, nerves tested and steely after a lifetime of whistles being blown in their ears and one coach after another screaming his head off and telling them they have to do to get better. What a sight—rows of corpulent, red nosed, middle-aged men dotted in pastel shirts—Easter Eggs on a telephone wire stooped and drinking cocktails while reliving their heroics of a birdy on hole six and improvement on the back nine and that one long tee shot that will get them through the long week of whatever hell it is they have to pay to afford a life (or lie) of golf. Some of these golfers cast bemused looks at the Division II ballplayers who have showed up on their sacred, hallowed grounds to celebrate a season of sport that's about as different from golf as Minnesota is from Arizona.

The irony here is that these young men going into the banquet have what these middle-aged golfers, here and around the country, want and covet most: youth, mobility, strength, and fandom. Surely these sun-drenched visor-wearing golf guys must have looked at these young men in wonder and thought back to their own youthful days when life really was just a game of sport and school. They might have even asked: What happened along the way? I certainly have.

I watch Clink from across the room. He pauses and stares out the big glass window looking out into that sloping sea of green lawn that washes upon the shore of the 19th hole. I imagine him thinking it was indeed an ocean, but an ocean far away from the landscape of college basketball, an ocean with real waves, the salty kind that smell of seaweed and ocean life, a salve to assuage the cuts and bruises and broken bones of a season on the grind, a season that began long before he wore a wedding ring, long before his three children arrived, a season that began when he was first introduced to the game of basketball in a California town called Morgan Hill. He will take a vacation soon, though. He will have a small sliver of time before mid-June and the month of July when he will kiss his wife and children goodbye and head back into stuffy summer gyms, back into airport hangars that have been converted into mega-gyms, back to looking for the best players that scholarship money mishmashed with federal student loans and grants can buy. But even then, when he is with his family on vacation, allegedly far away from the hustle of recruiting, and the responsibility of keeping 15 young men walking a straight line, the strain of keeping fans and alumni and boosters content and hopeful, he will have his phone with him. Someone will have his number. Someone will text him when he's out to dinner with his family. Someone will Tweet while he's walking on the beach with his wife at sunset. Clink might be out bodysurfing with his kids, but from the ocean he will be able to see his beach umbrella. He can see the brightly colored towel and his bag of beach gear. He can see his wife reclined and drinking something fruity and losing herself in a book. He can also see his phone.

He cannot help but think about the text or the voicemail message from that recruit he has sent a letter to every few days, the kid who is almost perfect yet flawed enough that he might choose a high-flying Division II program like Chico State rather than a down-in-the-gutter Division I school. It always occupies his mind. Basketball is in his blood, a coach with an insatiable hunger to win.

CHAPTER 29

The Booster

What matters most is how well you walk through the fire.

—CHARLES BUKOWSKI

IT'S HOT IN ACKER. ANOTHER 100-degree day in Chico. High school players hoping to become better, many hoping to get noticed and offered a Division II basketball scholarship, have showed up to Coach Clink's Elite Camp. Parents have also accompanied the young men. It's time for everyone to get serious. They want their kids to play basketball at the next level. They want their kids to play for Clink. Palpable tension fills the gym. All these players competing for what may only be one spot on the Chico State basketball roster. The players only have a few hours to show off their skills. What most of them don't realize, though, is that Clink is more interested in their character than their basketball skills.

Clink calls all the campers out into the center of the court. They fan out in a circle. More like a sea of players. Clink's voice has its usual blues singer scratchiness to it. He has to be especially loud today. His audience is not just the young men gathered at his feet, but the row of parents that line the back wall of Acker from one end of the court to the other.

I'm reminded of the Pentecostal tent revivals my grandmother would take me to when I was a young boy, a gathering of the Christian hopeful, the faithful, coming from all corners of the state to catch a glimpse of the preacher, the healer, the *coach* who might bring salvation—basketball salvation—to their sons. But Clink is not here to preach the Lord's gospel but a gospel of his own. He's no evangelist. He's a basketball coach, and he's here to preach the tenets of a different crusade.

"I want to coach people who want to get better," he tells the players. "I'm here to tell you about what we know is one of the best programs on the West Coast." The gym is midnight in the mountains quiet. It's so quiet and hot you can hear drops of sweat hitting the hardwood. A few parents look at each other and nod their heads in approval, their eyes glowing with the seriousness of the religious person who has driven hundreds of miles to the old Christian camp meeting, and in the earnest tone of the coach's cadence have suddenly felt in their tired souls the first stirring of the Holy Spirit. Only Clink is not speaking in tongues; he's speaking in a clear and concise manner that all can relate to. He is not here to sell snake oil, either, but a simple formula for winning: hard work and good character.

The best speakers are always aware of their audience. Clink knows the parents are his main target at this point. He looks at them in the back row. "For the parents, I want you to start thinking about any questions you have about our program or recruiting or about the university. Anything, okay." Clink takes a deep breath. He knows what the parents want to hear next, and what the players need to hear. He knows how to inspire, and he has a talent for inspiring at exactly the right moment.

"We've had six guys in the last four years that we've seen here and signed from right out of this camp." The players start to wiggle. They're fired up, ready to play.

More parents look at each other. Clink has issued a challenge. "This camp is about opportunity." He tells the players that being a good basketball player isn't enough. The body language of the players changes. The sea of players gets choppy. They know that right away half of them have been eliminated. "We pass up players, great players, all the time because they have bad attitudes or don't put in the effort needed. We're looking for players who want to get better."

Clink has now given hope to all the players in attendance who are used to getting passed over because of the way they look—maybe they're too small or too slow. Maybe they just don't look right, but if only they were given the chance. Clink will give them a chance today. "We're looking for guys who have positive body language. We aren't looking for guys who are too cool, don't want to listen. We don't teach coolness here." At least 15 more players have been eliminated, and the play of camp hasn't even started. "We want effort. Passion. Enthusiasm. Great attitudes." Not once has Clink talked about athletic skill.

Clink introduces the staff and then breaks the players into stations. I've been watching basketball players and playing the game for a long time and it only takes about ten seconds to pick out the players who have the skills to take their play to another level. There's a grace that a player exudes when he hustles over to get a rebound, a softness to his touch, nimble feet, long arms that work like rubber bands, and an instinct to know where the ball will bounce. The good players, and the ones who have the potential to become great, have innate skills similar to the skills of an expert magician: Like the magician, they have spent thousands of hours watching other "magicians"—basketball players they wanted to be like. They have watched the DVDs and read the basketball skill books and pestered their high school coaches and AAU coaches with a 1,001 questions; they understand the discipline that it takes to become a magician on the basketball court and master the tricks necessary. And, most importantly, they've realized that there really is no traditional basketball school. The good ones with the potential to be great latched on to an apprentice, a mentor, and were quiet and listened and watched and worked while everyone else was sleeping.

As the former Chicago Bulls player and past Utah Jazz coach Jerry Sloan said: "Just play defense and shut up."

I've only seen a few types of these players at the camp.

An old man who is pacing up and down the baseline sees one.

"That's the kid I came to see," he tells me. The old man reminds me of the legendary college football coach Lou Holtz, and for a split-second I think he is. His eyes scan the three courts and the six stations and the hundred-plus ball players. "I think his name is Michael White. He's from where Damario went to school. Bill Russell, too." The old man puts his chin in his hand, lowers his ball cap, and stands erect. He puts his hands on his hips. His gaze is fixed on the Oakland player named Michael White. I've seen the same countenance in this old man as I've seen in dozens of coaches over the years, mainly football coaches prowling the sidelines: Chuck Knoll, Bear Bryant, Tom Landry, and Bill Wash all come to mind. The old man sees me scribbling wildly in my legal pad. He thinks I might be someone. He bends down and extends his hand. "Gene. Gene Rideout."

I shake his hand and stand up. I've heard his name before, and I recognize him from the banquet in May. I also remember now that he's the same old man who wandered into the practice that Clink was giving with an Argentinian team that was visiting a few months ago. At the time I thought he was a birder who had gotten lost. Now it all makes sense why he's here now, and why he's anywhere where Chico State basketball is happening. He watches the current players who are helping out, and he watches the potential future players, with the heaviness of a man who has invested everything he has in the bank, a small fortune, into an enterprise. In a way he has. Gene is no spring chicken. At his age, every day is a gift worth a million dollars. In fact, there is no dollar amount, no price tag that can be put on a man's final days. He has chosen to spend his time, his old age, watching and rooting and supporting the Chico State Men's basketball team. He might not only be the team's biggest supporter, but also the man with a big investment.

"I fund a scholarship for Isaiah Ellis," he says proudly.

Gene has earned the right to exude his Bear Bryant presence from the baseline. He's obsessed with Chico State basketball. He points out to several potential Chico State players in attendance and tells me their backstory. He's been following the possible recruits closely, to the point where I wonder if he tailgates them out of the Acker parking lot. How does he know all of this? Where does he get the information?

"That kid's from Oakland," Gene continues. "He's got all the skills but one. He can't shoot," Gene says. Gene studies number 45 intently. The kid shoots from around the 3-point line. It clangs off the back rim. Gene looks at me. His lips flat line. He raises his eyebrows then grunts. He's made his point. I ask him about number 22, a kid I think has talent. "There's at least three players out there wearing number 22. Haven't you noticed that a lot of players are wearing the same number?" He's not impressed by my questions. His gaze is back on Magz on the other end of the court. I ask Gene if he thinks this will be the year Magz finally breaks out. The old man looks at me as if I'm the dumbest person on the planet. He grunts and holds up his hands. "He's got small hands." He spends the next five minutes talking about Cool Marvin Timothy who'll be playing this year after sitting out last season as a redshirt freshman. He's high on Cool Marvin.

Gene is a repository of Chico State basketball history. He's one of those guys who likes, who demands, to be in the know. He gives me a list longer than a child's wait for Christmas of men I should contact for my book. "I played here in the 50s," he says. "Then I went to work for J.C. Penny's. Spent my life there." Now he's part of another franchise that's starting to take off: Chico State basketball. "Isaiah Ellis is my kid," he says. He can tell by the look on my face that I'm confused. "The Rideout scholarship. Isaiah has it now. Before that it was Amir Caraway. Before that it was Jay Flores." Jesse Holmes is grabbing rebounds and feeding the ball to kids on the wing. "You know his story, right?" he says, pointing to Holmes with the casualness of someone pointing out the perfect peach they want at a farmers market produce stand. I tell him yes. "I bet George Maderos will get him for his scholarship. They both went to Chico High. What do you want to bet?"

A father walks in with his tall, gangly son. The father looks panicked. He sees me and my legal pad and approaches me. "We're late," he says, breathing hard. I can tell that he parked the car, probably skipped feeding the meter, and ran here with his boy as fast as possible. "We're late," he says again. "How can I get my son started?" Gene forgets I'm even there. He practically walks through me. "Come on," he says to the father and son, "follow me. I'll take you where you need to go."

Gene shuffles out the door of the gym and stops. "Just a sec," he tells the father. He comes back to me. He fishes out a card from his wallet and hands it to me. "Don't use the email. It doesn't work. Just ring me." He shuffles back to the father and son. I look at the tattered green card. It has a golf ball on it with two golf clubs in the background. The card reads: "Motivational Speaker, Gene Rideout."

I walk to the other side of the gym and lean up against the pushed in bleachers. The parents lining the walls have hungry eyes. They want the best for their kids, and right now this is the best. For some of them it might be the only thing. They're also watching me as I take notes on my legal pad. In fact, some of them are more interested in me than the play taking place in front of them. One parent comes and stands next to me. He's not discreet. He keeps glancing over my shoulder. I'm writing too fast to be evaluating talent, he probably figures, so he goes back and sits in his fold-up camping chair next to his wife. He whispers in her ear. They're no longer interested in me.

Gene shuffles over. His eyes are on a man who has arrived and is in the corner of the gym with a bike propped up against him. Gene beelines toward him. He passes by without acknowledging me. Now that Gene knows the direction he's headed in, he can start surveying the action on the court again. He pauses occasionally to watch. He finally reaches his destination. He and the man leaning up against the wall have a short conversation, a lot of hand gesturing. They watch Coach Gabriel working with some big men playing half-court offense for a while. Gene grows bored. He makes his way over to Clink's station. He stops and watches Clink for a few moments.

I can only imagine what it must be like to be 80 and still full of energy but with a body in decline, and watch Clink, half his age, move with such fury and force and precision. It's hard to imagine a man like Clink ever getting old, not unlike it's hard to imagine a man like Gene (who will later tell me he once played against the great Bill Russell) ever being young. Clink is just as physical with these high school players whom he's never met as he is with his own players. He leads by example, and he gets involved and mixes it up with them.

I'm the same age as Clink. At 44, I'm crippled for the weekend after playing noon ball with the old dudes on Tuesdays and Thursdays. I live on Ibuprofen and rely on my foam roller and the university pool to put my body back together. I often wonder if the pain from playing basketball two hours a week is worth the 96 hours of pain that it brings me. But for those two hours playing ball I am young again. I feel free and in control and get in touch with my animal instincts and intrinsic masculine urges. The physicality of basketball in such a confined space with bodies banging despite trying to be agile and graceful brings out a suppressed manhood in my person that working in an office keeps at bay. On the court I don't have to apologize for my aggressiveness for two hours a week. In fact, it's encouraged. I get to yell at my teammates, shame them, even, for not hustling to get a rebound or not lifting their eyes from the ball to make a pass to an open man or for not guarding a man or for insisting on a water break every fifteen minutes.

Playing basketball is not the real world to me. This is my fantasy world, but for Clink this is his reality. His profession is one based on winning or losing, an either/or world where the top pack of alpha dogs who can surrender their egos and work as a team will thrive, survive, and win. It's only natural that old men like Gene, and middle-aged men like me, and all the old dudes I play noon ball with, and all the young athletes on the 18-to-25-year-old spectrum, and all the working-stiff parents, are drawn to a man, a coach, like Clink. He's the Old Testament father-figure who rules by structure and discipline and hard work and rational punishment that young men and old men alike need, but there's just enough New Testament father-figure in him to know that as long as you tried your best he'll still love you.

Clink's reality is our fantasy.

Gene rubs his chin and smiles as Clink puts the cardboard recycling bins to good use on the court. He uses them as obstacles for a player to make a stutter step and then run around. I've seen him use the recycling bins in a number of ways. Orange cones, blue pads, and the recycling bins seem to be his go-to tools. Clink stops the action. "Okay, guys, we have three minutes to get in a perfect rep." He's always striving for perfection despite the inevitable imperfection that always follows. Gene shakes his head and meanders down the baseline to where Isaiah Ellis is working his station.

I amble over to Coach Gabriel's station. I'm interested in seeing more of the kid from Oakland whom Gene has advised can't shoot. I find out that the man sitting by the bike isn't just any man. He's Gaber—Coach Gabriel's father. "Hey," he says, "I've heard about you. You're the guy writing the book." Gaber (as I will later learn he is called) looks like an older version of Coach Gabriel. He has a sweet, trusting, welcoming, warm, and unpretentious disposition just like his son. He is wearing a beanie that fits like a swim cap, and he has the laid back demeanor of guy who came of age in the sixties. He reminds me a little of a retired stand-up comedian or maybe an activist who has learned to bite his tongue. A free spirit for sure. Not only that, but he was a Chico State basketball player in the sixties. He laughs. "It was a tennis shoe league back then." He watches his son coach players beneath the basket. "None of us were ever this good. I was in the program for five years. During that entire time, there were maybe two guys who had the talent to play for one of Clink's teams."

It only takes a few minutes talking with Gaber to discover how much he loves his son. He's proud of his boy who's now a grown man. "He's come a long way," he says. "He's worked for it all. None of it came easy. The thing about Lucas, you see, is that he's always been in the right place at the right time. Man, he's lucky like that."

Gaber is the one who planted the basketball seed in his son's head at an early age. "He was always around it. He'd come with me to the gym and watch me play. I built him a court in the backyard when he was little. I put up a small goal and gave him a little ball. I didn't want him to get any bad habits. I never, ever had to undo his shot. He got it, and he got it right the first time." When the family moved to Lawrence, Kansas, so Gaber's wife could pursue her doctorate degree at the University of Kansas, Gaber was in basketball nirvana. "I would take Lucas and his brother when they were, let's see, between the ages of five and eight, into the Alan Fieldhouse. We'd have the place to ourselves." He'd also take the young boys to watch the Jayhawks practice under Coach Larry Brown. "We were there when Danny Manning led the Jayhawks to the national championship. Lucas had Jayhawk blood running through him early on." Coach Gabriel would have the Jayhawks when he was little, and the University of Arizona Wildcats when he was in high school. "And when my wife was a professor at the University of Arizona, her office was in the gym," he says. "She worked with all the players. Lucas grew up around those two programs." Gaber beams with pride when he talks about the path his son has taken. He wants the best for him not unlike any good father. He also believes that Coach Clink is the real deal. "He's a much better coach than he was when he got here. Heck, he was already good then." He shakes his head in amazement. "But the kind of players he's getting now. Wow. He also started winning, fast. We went a long time without winning a league championship. He's already done it twice."

Gaber wishes that his son could stay here forever, but he understands that his boy has a family and must think about the future. "When I was at Kansas," he says, "I got to see firsthand the way that a top-notch basketball program does business. People put in. People give back. They knew how to fundraise. But there's no money here. That's what makes this program so special. He's doing this without any money. Coach Clink is doing more with less. This is a good fit for Lucas. He understands the struggle. He knows how to persevere. He's been doing it his whole life." Gaber is about to tell me more, but he remembers he's talking to a writer. He takes a deep breath. "If you'll excuse me, I've got to hit the bathroom."

As Gaber walks off to the bathroom, I look out at all these hopeful players. I watch Coach Gabriel and I watch Coach Clink. Men at work. Men using their bodies. Men using their brains. Men doing what their soul has told them to do. Coaching basketball is a gamble. It's a shot in the dark. It's not for the weak. The passion can't be faked. It's a furnace that never goes out and wants to burn faster and hotter and with more fury. I wonder how many of these kids will make it to the next level. Most of these kids at camp will never play a second of college ball. A few of them will play college ball, but they'll play ball in obscurity. They'll not be on ESPN. They'll not play professionally in Europe. They'll not play in the NBA. Most of them will graduate from college and go straight to work. A handful of them might wind up being 44 and lucky enough to still have the body and the stamina and the humility, the sense of humor, to lace up their high tops a couple of times a week and go out and play at lunch.

Gaber comes back and sits down. He leans back up against the wall. "Yeah, what we need to do this year is really handle the last 12-13 seconds." He wipes the sweat off his forehead. "You know one thing that bothers me?" he says. "It bothers me when coaches or the guys on ESPN or whatever are talking about how a player should follow his shot. That's ridiculous. You should never tell a great shooter to follow his shot. I learned that from John Wooden when he came speak at Butte College a long time ago. He said you don't want your shooters thinking about having to follow their shot when they're taking the shot because that allows doubt to enter." I feel pretty dumb. I've been following my shot for 34 years. I look up. Gene is headed back in our direction. He has seen something on the court that has ticked him off, and he's going to let Gaber know all about it.

CHAPTER 30

Rabbits

JULY 15

CLINK'S OFFICE IS PACKED. THE last day of summer camp for the group of 5-to 7-year-olds. Camp has only been out for five minutes, and Clink is already hovered over his laptop and viewing a spreadsheet, trying to tune out the chaos inside his office. There's a large box of water and chips leftover from camp. Ellis, his legs stretched out, takes up a big section of the room. He's filling out the paperwork so he can get paid for working the camp. His basketball shoes are ripped and old-looking. He notices me staring at them. "These were my shoes from last season," he says unapologetically. The shoes of a successful freshman campaign. Coach Blake walks in. He always has an urgent look on his face, always seems to be sweating a little bit, even when he laughs.

"Isaiah," he barks, "you ready?" Ellis looks up from his paperwork and nods. Clink, brow furrowed, still hunched over the laptop, his eyes fixed on the screen, yells from over his shoulder:

"Where are you taking Isaiah?"

"Get his paycheck," Coach Blake answers.

Clink likes to be in on everything. His voice is tired and strained, hoarse, from a month of commands directed toward 90 kids under 13. Clink's son, Tyler, and Amir Carraway, come in and sit down. Tyler turns 12 tomorrow. Meanwhile, Carraway is waiting to hear back from his agent.

"Yeah, I'm 65 percent sure that I'll be back in Germany," he tells me. Carraway has turned his Chico State career into a professional basketball career. He looks down at his phone, his thumbs working madly. "Or somewhere in Europe, hopefully," he says.

The phone rings. Clink answers it, his eyes still fixed on the laptop.

"Hey, bud," he says. He finally looks away from the computer. He leans back in his chair. "How many teeth did you chip?" It's his other son, Justin, Tyler's twin. He crashed into the side of the swimming pool, teeth first. "Three bottom teeth. Whoa." Clink says this calmly, as if it happens all the time. He's seen a lot of injuries. Teeth aren't a big deal. A basketball player doesn't need to chew when he's on the court. "Be brave. See you and mom here in a few."

Clink is a Northern Californian. He hails from San Martin, a town of around 7,027, in between Morgan Hill and Gilroy. San Martin is known for producing garlic, table mushrooms, and wine, not basketball coaches. The town is surrounded by the Santa Cruz Mountains to the west and the Diablo Range to the east. Clink grew up on 2.5 acres. "We had goats, chickens, peacocks."

He laughs. "And at one time, 350 rows of rabbits. My dad was into that for a while. I still get nightmares from it." He leaves me hanging as to why.

Clink's father, a dreamer from Ohio, grew up on a farm. Then, at 19, he hopped on a Greyhound bus and moved to Los Angeles. He eventually made his way up to Oakland. "He met my mother in a bar in Jack London Square." Clink's mother grew up in Gilroy, the Garlic Capital of the World. She was a teacher for 40 years. She, not his father, is the one who introduced Clink to sports. Turns out her brother had been an outstanding ball player at Humboldt State University. "Dad never had the opportunity to play," Clink says. "He was always working different jobs." Clink's face turns white. He shudders again. "The rabbits. He did it for the pelts to pay for his barn." He pauses and takes a sip of his water. "They looked like Easter bunnies." He pauses. "But it was a nice barn." I have suddenly become more interested in Clink's connections to these rabbits than how he built a basketball powerhouse.

Clink excelled at soccer. He was on a travelling team. But once he discovered basketball, he had found his athletic soul mate. "It was basketball year round. My dad laid down a slab of concrete and put up a hoop. I just played and played."

I often wonder what Clink does for fun. It's kind of hard to imagine Clink *having* fun. Fun often involves something corny. Wearing a silly hat or doing a silly dance or making a silly face. Fun is silly. But there doesn't seem to be a silly bone in Clink's body.

I think that maybe his job is fun. Is he following Aristotle's advice to make work play? Coaching, though, is not play for Clink. "What I do isn't fun," he says with a slight grimace (I wonder if he's thinking of the rabbits again). Only he's thinking of last season and next season and the seasons to come. "I mean, it's rewarding. It's satisfying. I wouldn't call it fun, though. It's work. I love it, but it's work," he says with a slight wince.

"Games are the worst part. The pressure of being great. The pressure of being prepared. If I wasn't like that, it would be more enjoyable." Like what, I ask? "So worried. So pessimistic. I'm terrible to be around on game day." He takes a deep breath.

I've seen Clink on the Tuesday before a Friday night game when he comes out to play ball with the old dudes. His mind is anywhere but on the lunch-hour game. His mind is on Friday night. Sure, he runs the floor, but he's not worried about hitting a jumper over Curtis to even the score of the elbow that ripped into his abdomen on the last trip down.

Out of the blue Clink says: "Coach Knight wrote a book on the power of negative thinking. I prepare for every bad scenario so we can avoid them." Clink is stonefaced on game day. "There's no giggling and running around on game day." I can tell that Clink is tortured by the inner demons that compel those who are driven to not be good or great, even, but the *best* at what they do.

"The pressure," he says. "It's self-imposed. I want to be great. I feel like I have an obligation to be great. The pressure to put a quality product on the floor night after night." Clink says he isolates himself on game day. "Courtney has finally learned not to come near me on game day." He smiles.

I can imagine Clink shaving before the game, scraping the hard angle of his jaw, wondering how the undersized McFerren, who'd been so productive lately, would guard the 6-foot-2 and 200-pound Barry Bell of Pomona, or should he start the equally sized 21-year-old freshman and former football star with the nagging injury, Jesse Holmes, and Courtney pops in to ask him a question about something happening next week at their sons' school. I can imagine the scowl Clink must cast at her when he nicks his chin with the razor, his reverie over the future point-guard play disrupted.

"I want to be the best coach in Chico State history," he says. "When this is all over, I want people to say that not only did he win, but look what he's done."

Clink wants to leave a legacy. He's well on his way. That kind of ambition and drive, though, does weigh heavily.

"Yeah, it'll be 3:43 a.m. here real soon," he says. "Just me and *Frasier*."

I'm amazed at what Clink has been able to do in such a short amount of time. Further, he has done it with such limited resources. He doesn't let that stop him, though. That's not the Clink way. I think Clink likes the challenge. "This place, Chico State, is built for winning," he says, "even though we're challenged with the infrastructure we have." Yet nobody in the CCAA or DII has done more with less. Is coaching basketball like writing—less is more? Clink has to fundraise to help pay the salary of his head assistant Coach Gabriel, while the other assistant Coach Blake works for free. Coach Blake makes some money from running Clink's summer camps, but his income is supplemented by bartending weeknights and weekends (offseason) at Round Table Pizza.

"And our facilities," he says with a wry smile, "our facilities need an overhaul." Clink thrives on this. I wonder if this motivates him. It must.

"Now that we're winning, though, it's become an expectation. Our fans want more and more."

I ask Clink if he plans to take a vacation this summer.

"I might go camping or something."

But Clink isn't going camping. The summer will be filled up with basketball clinics and recruiting trips and the return of his players to campus. Football season will be underway in August which means the first basketball practice is around the corner.

The only place Clink will be camping is in his mind. But even that is doubtful.

CHAPTER 31

Blood Moons

THE LAST DAY OF SEPTEMBER. Clink has already turned the calendar. Every day in October is busy. The offseason officially ends on Thursday, October 15. Tonight, my family and I are sprawled out in lawn chairs and looking up at the sky. The night air is still warm. Chico Indian summer. We watch as the blood moon rises. My wriggling son Holden—yes, named after the most misunderstood teenager in literary history—is pinned to my chest. It's past his bed time.

The mania that we call "Jack Sparrow Time" has set in, that point at the end of a three-year-old's day when he hasn't napped, a mood that moments ago was giddy like Captain Jack Sparrow after his first few nips from the rum bottle, a mood that turns with the quickness of lightening into that of a foul, cantankerous, edgy drunk, a teetering, muttering, ornery Jack Sparrow. I try and calm my boy, explain to him that the last time a blood moon appeared was when I was 11 (33 years ago). He only knows eleven if we're counting out cookies or moving his yellow piece forward on the *Sorry* game board.

The next time we view a blood moon together, Holden will be away at college. Blood moons don't come around often.

Neither do teams like the one Clink has assembled for the 2015-2016 season. And conference titles and championships are even rarer.

A blood moon, also called a super moon, occurs when the Moon is in the closest part of its orbit to Earth, making it appear larger in the sky. The eclipse has made the Moon appear red, visible in North America, South America, West Africa, and Western Europe.

This phenomenon was last observed in 1982. It will not be back before 2033.

The Bible makes two references to the blood moon. In Joel 2:31 it is written that "The sun shall be turned into darkness, and the moon into blood, before the great and terrible day of the Lord." Meanwhile, Acts 2:20 writes that "The sun shall be turned into darkness, and the moon into blood, before the great and *notable* day of the Lord."

The beauty of life is that we get to form our own perspectives and frame situations. Athletes are superstitious. So are fans. I see the blood moon as a symbol, an omen, of the season to come—a premonition that should put fear into the blood stream of all teams in the CCAA save Chico State, a sign that the Wildcats are coming.

Sure, the blood moon is apocryphal but for all the other teams.

I don't know if Clink saw the blood moon. If he did, I imagine he viewed it through a logical and rational lens. I doubt he was thinking the same thing as I. I am a fan. I have the luxury of dreaming about basketball.

I can look at a blood moon and make an abstract connection to sport. I imagine that Clink doesn't want to think about basketball if he doesn't have to.

The blood moon was a cosmic, scientific happening. Therein lies the difference between a writer and a coach. We see the same moon but through a different lens.

Yes, blood moons are a rare astronomical phenomenon. The moon "appears" slightly larger than usual. It has a reddish hue. It is a super blood moon. And in the super blood moon I see a basketball season that I've been itching for since last March.

The next time the blood moon appears Holden will be a junior in college. Beatrix (Baby Bee) will be a senior in high school. Clink's kids will have graduated college already. Clink and I will both be 60. How many championships will he have? How many bestsellers for me? What if the championships, the bestsellers, the success, never comes? Will it have all been in vain?

The players in this book will all be pushing 40 the next time the blood moon rolls around. They will most likely have families and careers. A lot of the other people in this book will have passed on. But for now, as I write this, they are all living and young and mortal yet on their way to becoming immortal. Such is the power of the written word in book form.

Blood moons get people interested in astronomy. The rare, beautiful occurrence gives parents an opportunity to take their children outside to see something special. So, too, does a team like the Chico State Wildcats—a team made up of good basketball players and even better young men.

I think back to what happened the last time there was a blood moon. My timeline in life has always been sports centered. I recall vividly being 11 years old and watching the North Carolina Tar Heels take on the Georgetown Hoyas. The last time there was a blood moon, basketball fans outside of Chapel Hill were just being introduced to the names Michael Jordan and Patrick Ewing. They were both 19-year-old freshmen. James Worthy and Sleepy Floyd were also on the team. Coach Dean Smith, only 51, was in his prime. John Thompson, 41, was just getting started.

Clink, like me, was even younger. Probably outside in the driveway of his Morgan Hill home dreaming of playing in an NCAA Championship someday. He was concerned about playing. Coaching probably never entered his mind. Clink's players would not be born for another 20 to 25 years. I thought I was going to be the next Larry Bird as I practiced his signature corner shot for hours after school every day. And if that didn't work out, I was going to be a famous writer of sports books.

How does time pass like that? Where does it go?

Blood moons, like National Championships, like great seasons, serve as bookends, repositories, for the past, the present, and the future of our lives.

My daughter Beatrix does not yet have teeth. She has only recently started to crawl. Holden has only recently learned of a reindeer named Rudolph. He does not yet know that I have a name other than Daddy.

Blood moons and championship seasons.

A couple days after the blood moon I'm standing outside of the Student Services Center at the university waiting for my wife and kids to pick me up. I'm depressed. It's the first Tuesday in almost a year that I've not gone to church—what I call playing ball with the old dudes at Shurmer. I'm depressed because I've been hampered by old man injuries for the last year, and my father-in-law, a physician, has told me that I have strained abductors and bursitis (at least I have an excuse for my play as of late). For a couple of years he's been trying to get me to quit running in long distance events and playing basketball. I thought it was just because he wanted me to start playing golf with him so he'd have an excuse for me to bring Holden along and introduce him to the game. I recall my father-in-law lowering his glasses and squinting those wise eyes that have seen a lot in 67 years, half of those years spent being a physician, saying: "Men past 40 have no business playing team sports." Maybe it is time to play golf. Normally on Tuesday afternoons I'm still high from the 50 minute run with the old dudes, but today there was no sweat, there was no trash-talk, there were no air balls. The only air ball is me, wounded, waiting in the drop zone for my wife. The pain in my hips and groin reminds that I'm 44. My father-in-law keeps echoing in my ears: "Men past 40 have no business playing team sports."

I feel physically broken and spiritually bankrupt. I don't want to merely be a basketball spectator. I think of poor Larry Bird at the end of his career, stretched out on his stomach at the hallowed grounds of the Boston Garden, watching the action by the scorer's table, knowing his days playing the game he'd loved since childhood were numbered, maybe over. I like to imagine I am Bird when out there playing with the old dudes. That's my fantasy. I love the thrill of diving for the ball. I love to show off my bruises a day later. I pop a handful of Ibuprofen at night before bed and embrace the pain. I ponder my retirement from the game, the spectacle, rather, of noon time ball. At night I curl up with my oversized Bill Bradley book of photographs and basketball and life wisdom, *Values of the Game*, and dream. I relive my childhood, take comfort in Bradley's closing that he, too, had to step away from the game in middle age. I put a pillow between my legs to stave off the pain of my knees touching and drift off to a heaven that is pain free and where basketball is played all day and all night. Would anyone other than myself care if I no longer played? Not one jot. What would I do? Run again? Where's the brotherhood? Tennis? Might as well play basketball. Swimming? Like driving to Fresno in a 76 Ford Pinto with no air conditioning and no radio. Golf? I don't have the money nor the time nor the patience.

Maybe I could keep playing noon ball, but what if I have to guard the former decathlete who's been showing up lately? What if I have to guard one of the 30-year-old soccer players who has joined the old dudes prematurely? What if I have to guard Curtis or Clink? The alternative: I can guard one of the old dudes who are even more banged up than me. Do I really want to join the wrinkle room that camps out in the paint or stands at half-court, bent over, burping up castor oil?

That old saying it's better to have loved and lost than to have never loved at all doesn't work for aging athletes who are in the decline yet still trying to keep pace. I can still shoot, but I can't do all the other things that made me a complete church ball player which is chiefly to hustle.

I look down the street to see if I can spot my wife's minivan, yet another reminder of my aging self. I see two tall young men crossing the street. My spirts lift. Trevor Priest and Tyler Harris walk in my direction. I consider shuffling away. I don't want these young men to see the wounded me, the depressed me. I suddenly snap out of it. I feel better. I am young again. They see me. I salute them. A glimmer of light.

"Mr. Medley," Priest says, his cheeks puffed from a mouthful of sunflowers seeds, "how's the book?"

I beam. The book. My hope. My portal back to youth. The promised land. Basketball has always saved me. If I can't play anymore then doggone it, I'll write about it.

"It's great. In fact, I was just thinking of you guys. Not you two specific guys, but, you know, the guys. The team."

"What page you on now?" Harris asks. He looks just as serious when he's wearing a backpack and drinking pop as he does when he's on the court.

"Just hit page 287," I say. Feels good to say that. Probably like the feeling they get when dunking. When you're a writer, mentioning page length impresses those who aren't writers. For me, though, the reality is that saying I'm on page 287 is like the middle of January in basketball season for Clink. The season has just gotten started, and there's a long way to go.

"Whoa," Harris says. "I remember when you interviewed me and were fired up because you'd written 40 pages."

"I just wrote Marvin Timothy's chapter," I tell him.

We talk for a while about the season. They're elated. Like kids a few weeks before Christmas break. Priest, despite knowing that it might be another season of waiting his turn, is enthusiastic. He takes a long pull from his orange pop. "The chemistry is great," he says. "It's going to be an awesome season."

I can't help but tell them about my basketball injuries.

"That's too bad, man," Harris says.

"We saw Coach playing today," Priest says.

"Well, I figured my injury would allow Coach Clink to shine a little," I say.

The leaves are starting to change. A wind whips up. A swirl of fallen leaves rains down. It's only 4:15 in the afternoon, but the sunlight is weaker, liquid sunshine, dappled sunshine. Although 80 degrees out, I shiver. It feels like fall. It *is* fall. Best time for a sports fan. Week five of football season (no more patsy games). Postseason baseball (finally); preseason NBA; preseason NHL; and Midnight Madness in campus gyms across the country.

Blood moons. Championships. October 15.

I'm a father, a husband, a writer, a state employee with four side jobs. I've not watched more than six complete innings of baseball this season. I've not yet seen one snap of football. But every night when I close my eyes, I play basketball. I dream it. I'm living it. Even if it's a team of Wildcats I'm living it through.

I see my wife's minivan careening in. So glad we bought the farm and got the 2015 Honda Odyssey rather than the used Subaru. Appearances matter. I couldn't let Priest and Harris see the man who is immortalizing them in the pages of a book get into a family clunker, could I?

And I laugh—like they'd care.

Families, jobs, mortgages, all that stuff will come later for them.

For now, all that matters for these two are the books in the packs on their backs and the season that is two weeks away.

"I want you guys to meet my family," I tell them.

They're genuinely excited. My wife pulls in. I show off by pressing the button on the door handle that makes the door slide open. In the world of parents, my car brings envy. In the world of student-athletes, only empathy.

Beatrix, my nine month old, smiles up at the players from her car seat. Holden, who has been a fan since the throwback days of Amir, Rashad, and Sean— and was there when the Wildcats won the CCAA in late February 2015—waves.

"Hey, buddy," Priest and Harris say in unison.

They're like twins, these two ball players, or an old married couple.

"Want to give me five?" they both say again at the same time.

My son gives them a fist pump. Before I can even introduce my wife to the guys, they reach into the van and extend their hands, introduce themselves not unlike the way they introduced themselves to me at that first practice that seemed so long ago, that day back in early April when Clink told the players there was a guy who wanted to write a book about them and their season next year, the next year that's almost here.

I'm glad that Priest and Harris get a glimpse into my world, even if that glimpse is a 30-second peek into a minivan. The people inside that van represent all that my heart contains, my will, my purpose, my motivation, and my reason for being. Without them I am nothing.

Priest and Harris, Coach Clink, and the entire team have allowed me privileged glimpses into their hearts. I find peace in knowing that I, in turn, have allowed these two young men to see my world.

Basketball is life.

Blood moons.

Championships.

"We're off to study hall," Harris says.

"You coming to the banquet tomorrow night?" Priest says.

"I'll be there."

I crawl beneath my son's car seat so I can sit in the middle of the $40,000 minivan seat, a suburban fantasy, a family limousine, that I never drive and can't even get into without shimmying in. The pain in my knees and groin makes me yell. It hurts, but I'm reminded that the dead feel no pain.

I am alive.

Then it hits me.

I will play out my fantasy for one more year. I will not quit basketball. I will heal until Thursday, October 15, and when the Wildcats start practicing, I, too, will make my triumphant return to Shurmer Gym. I will play through the season, and retire when the Wildcats retire from the 2015-2016 season. I will play through the pain and the shame and relish my own old-man fame. I'm going to eat well. Stretch. Lift weights. I'm going to keep a mental stat sheet in each game I play. I'm not going to turn the ball over. I'll have a win-loss column of all games played. I'll hustle. I'll continue to be Mississippi Flash—live out the Larry Bird basketball fantasy for one final year, my 45th year of life. And when the Wildcats' season ends, I, too, will hang up my high tops, trade them in for golf shoes. Sure, I'll still play HORSE, but the days of running and gunning are done.

I'll take Clink golfing that day. Yes, that'll be the day I accept my age, my physical state, and embark on a new sports journey. I will give up the ghost. I might even finally go and see a phsyician to find out why my hips and groin and legs are in chronic pain every day.

The guys wave goodbye and head off toward the library. Meanwhile, my wife pulls out in our chariot and takes me back to my world of soggy diapers and mushed yams and shiny things and Legos and Crayons and Picasso Tiles.

I only hope my children find something they love as much as I love basketball.

I don't love writing. I only do it to keep from going crazy. But basketball brings me pure joy.

CHAPTER 32

Fundraiser

"YOU LOOK LIKE YOU SHOULD be wearing a white apron smeared in ketchup and mustard stains and selling hot dogs," my wife barks.

I look in the mirror. She's right. I wanted to wear something with a Chico State insignia that looked nice. I bought the most expensive shirt on the rack from the campus bookstore. I want to fit in. Tonight is a fundraiser. Fundraisers are for the older set. The older set are particular in how the younger set dress, particularly when a member of the younger set—or the middling set (I am middle aged, after all) is writing a book on the program. I'm an outsider trying to break inside.

"I saved the tag," I tell her. "I'll return it tomorrow and get something that makes me look twenty years younger."

"You can't take a tag off of a shirt and return it."

I smile at her and turn so she can see my back. I pull the tag out from beneath the collar.

"You can if the tag is still attached."

She shakes her head. I know. Morally despicable for a man of my age—any age, really. But I really do want to look nice. I even put on a pair of real shoes, not my Five Fingers (the toe shoes) made from hemp. My real shoes have holes in the soles.

I had planned on taking my son. He loves Isaiah Ellis, even though he has only met Ellis once. When I told Holden we were going to the dinner with the Chico State Wildcats, he kept saying: "Dada, Isaiah gonna be deya?" I bought a ball to have the guys sign, but my son is throwing major fits. He's downright cranky. I had texted Clink the night before and asked if I could bring Holden. He immediately wrote back: "It's fine with me. He may be bored to death. We have a social hour, dinner, and an hour presentation. Your call."

Clink has mastered the art of the text message as a tool for straightforward communication. It reminds me of how Hemingway learned to write. He had to write messages for the wire as a reporter during the war. He learned to write succinctly. No wasted words. Never confuse movement for action. Get the point across and say no more.

I leave Holden with his mother and newborn sister Beatrix. It's the right call. I don't leave him behind because I think my boy will self-destruct. When he was barely two, he sat through an entire women's and men's basketball game. I leave him at home because most of my time will be spent wrangling him and the Sharpie ink from his signed ball will rub off on the new shirt that I have to return tomorrow to redeem my $60.

Once the cost-benefit analysis is over (leave the boy at home for the sake of the shirt), I say goodbye to the family and head down the street to Beatniks. A much different venue—more prone to conviviality, more relaxed, spacious—than the country club banquet. More my style. Golfers bring out the introvert in me.

The Beatniks parking lot is as crowded as I've ever seen it. Granted, I'm late. But not really. It's a social hour, and the way I understand a social hour is that if it's from 5:30 p.m. to 6:30 p.m. and a guest shows up at 6:25 p.m., well, technically the guest is not late. He just has less time to socialize.

Social events give me anxiety. Guess I'm not the only one. That's why most social hours serve alcohol. Besides, these are my people, basketball people. I do worry that if the word gets out about the book then I won't be able to be as much of a fly on the wall. I won't be able to kick back as freely and then watch and take notes on my legal pad. But then I worry that if I'm sitting by myself and not being social and scribbling like a madman than that is exactly how I will be perceived: a madman. Then, of course, there's the low self-esteem narcissistic part of me (all *real* writers have it—we want a little attention because so much of what we do is done in isolation and never seen and pats on the back rarely happen because books rarely get published).

I'm working myself up into a frenzy and starting to wonder why I even came. Right, back to the mission. I'm writing about the season. This is part of the season. I put my pens in my shirt pocket, grab my Moleskin, and shuffle in. I mill around outside and look for a friendly face. I pull out my cell phone and pretend to be talking to my wife so I don't look completely alone. I see an older, scholarly man walking by (ah, I start to relax. I always feel better, safe, in the presence of older men in cardigans and older women in flower-adorned sweaters because they won't judge me as much and be impressed, maybe, because I'm trying to engage them in conversation and actually interested in what they have to say). The man is wearing a name tag: Don Alger. Yes!

Don Alger is the author of an outstanding history that was recently published: *One Hundred Years of Basketball: A History of Men's Basketball at Chico State*. Alger's research is exhaustive. He left no stone of Chico State basketball history unturned. It's a wonderful compendium of Chico State men's basketball history, a must-have coffee table book for any Chico State fan. Alger is currently working on another book: *History of Women's Basketball at Chico State: 1896-2016*. His wife Barbara edits and proofs all his final drafts. Don is also more than an author. He taught in the Department of Chemistry and Biochemistry at Chico State for nearly 40 years—and, yes, even wrote a book titled *Chemistry at Chico State* that examines both student and faculty work in the department stretching from 1900 to 2014.

I approach Don. "Hi, Don. Carson Medley. Hey, great job on the book."

There's nothing a self-published author loves more (other than someone actually buying his book) than being recognized, appreciated, and patted on the back for this often unrequited, unread labor of love.

"Thank you," he says. He gives me a long look, trying hard to recall where he's heard my name. "Best Game in Town," he says. "You wrote that letter to the editor about the basketball team."

He has returned the pat on the back. I did write the letter. That little publication—along with my first sight of Robert Duncan cutting to the basket—is what inspired me to write this book. We talk for a while about

his book. I ask him how long it took him. "Six months. When I get started on something, it's hard to stop." For six months all he did was gather
the information.   His wife, Barbara, walks up. We meet and talk. Turns
out the she was good friends with the lady who was the previous thesis
editor and advisor at Chico State—the one who had previously held my
post for more than 30 years. I tell her the story about how my wife and I
moved here from San Luis Obispo once we found out a child was on the
way. How we wanted our child to be close to his grandparents. I tell her
how I looked for work for six months, could find nothing, and was filling
out my application to work at Safeway and/or Barnes and Noble. About
a month before my son was born, the thesis editor and advisor decided
to retire. I saw the job advertisement. It was the perfect fit. Applied.
Interviewed a couple of times. And was offered the position on the day
my boy was born.

Chico State has had a special magic for me. I believe in destiny and fate
and answered prayers.

I believe this Wildcats basketball team is one of destiny and fate and
answered prayers.

I have no reason to doubt this. After all the good things that have happened to me in Chico—my job, my house, the birth of my children—why
would I not think that meeting Coach Clink and writing this book would
not also be part of the destiny that lead me to this town?

The universe is kind, I believe, and rewards those who in turn are
kind and put good energy out into it. That's what I see with the young
basketball players Clink has handpicked to fulfill the cultural mission of
his program.

I spot Coach Gabriel. He looks thin. He has definitely lost weight.
Working 24/7 for small pay with a young family will do that to a man.

"Carson," he says. He gives me a high five. He introduces me to the
woman he is talking with. "This is Carson Medley. He works at the university. He's writing a book on the program." The mother is interested. Turns
out this is Justin Briggs's mother. I tell her a little bit about the book.

"Yes, Justin is going to be the player that will represent the redshirt
freshman experience in the book." I go back over my tracks several times to

make sure she understands the red shirt comment was just some basketball fan/writer's misunderstanding of basketball terminology. I don't know if Briggs will be redshirted, and I don't know if he knows that he might be, but still. "Yes, the freshman student-athlete experience will weave its way into several pages of this narrative."

"We had two verbal commitments today," Coach Gabriel says. He's really excited.

"Nice," I say. "By the way, we're at 295," I tell him. He gives me a confused look.

"295? Who's 295?" he says with a brief panic. "The book. We hit page 295."

Coach Gabriel thought I meant one of the players had gained that much weight. Briggs's mother and I laugh. Coach Gabriel's mind is on the season. I can see it in his eyes. I see Duncan over in the corner talking to whom I presume is a booster. Duncan looks cornered. I meander over. He's wearing his hair slicked back with a little bun on top. Only Robert Duncan can get away this look. We talk about the book for a while. The booster he's talking to gets interested. Everyone gets interested when they hear you're writing a book. I make the writer's social gaffe of trying to explain a chapter in the book that I'm working on to the booster. That's the worst thing in the world to do—talk your book away—and it's even worse if you're trying to explain it to someone who is a non-reader. "It's called *Blood Moons.* It's kind of a prophetic rendering of the season to come that takes place during the blood moon. A reflection piece on not only the season ahead but all those seasons...the book is using a basketball season, you know, as a metaphor for the seasons in a man's life." The booster's eyes glaze over. Poor guy. He just wanted to talk crossover dribbles with his favorite player. "Anyway, it's a prophecy for the season. Kind of like how the National Championship this year is in Frisco, Texas. Right, Frisco, and so many of our players are Northern California guys."

The booster is fired up again. He takes over the conversation. I let him. This night is about him. He says he's already marked the trip to the finals on his calendar and reserved a hotel room. He has studied the town of Frisco, Texas. Now I feel bad for Duncan. What fans don't realize is that the players, the student-athletes (most of them) are often not aware of who they play and when they play and where they will play until the time arises. In fact, the coaches don't even know this off the top of their heads. This was something that at first surprised me when I started writing the book, but after a while it all made sense. Fans have the luxury to study and obsess over this kind of information, but coaches and players don't. Their biggest focus is on getting better each day. They live in the moment.

"Oh, I was in Evansville back in 2014 when we made it to the Elite Eight. Let me tell you about Evansville…" the booster says.

I grow bored and politely excuse myself. McFerren is talking to a tall, balding man who looks important. The man talks in a low voice. I stand beside McFerren and try and eavesdrop. The man excuses himself. "I got your prayer into the book, Jalen," I tell him. I had asked McFerren about his program ritual, a prayer. He gives me a big grin. What a great young man. I can see him moving into politics eventually. Definitely running a company. We don't talk long. He has a big role to play here tonight, and a lot of people want to find out who is this young man that has replaced Mike Rosaroso. I talk to Nate Ambrosini. Ambrosini looks like a tall and skinny version of the actor Ryan Gosling. We talk about the book, too. I finally meet Justin Briggs. He reminds me of Kevin Durant. Clink announces that it's time to take a seat and get ready to eat.

I'm hungry. The last time I was able to eat a meal without my little ones tugging at me was at the April banquet. I'm not about to pass up this chance to eat. I get in the food line behind Cool Marvin. Salad is piled high on his plate. I would expect nothing less from him. Dr. Gabriel, Coach Gabriel's mother, is behind me. I introduce myself. We talk briefly about my doctoral program. She asks me about my research interests. "Getting that piece of corn that's bobbing in the butter there," I say, only half-joking. I explain to her that I'm a parent who has eaten his son's left over cheese quesadilla and milled over "blue dip and honey" (Greek yogurt with honey) for the last five days. I beeline into the backroom with my plate of food piled high. I have a flashback, an uncomfortable memory, back to my first day at a new school when I was in the sixth grade, and that lonely feeling I had when carrying my lunch tray into the cafeteria and scanning all the tables and open seats and looking for a friendly, familiar face. I know this is a good sign because the only familiar faces I see are those of the players. I spot Coach Blake, Tanner Giddings, and Isaiah Ellis down at the corner.

Basketball saves me again.

Coach Blake sits erect. He moves his head with the controlled rigidity of an owl. He watches with a close eye (almost like a father making sure his son easts all his meat and vegetables so he can grow up to be big and strong) while Ellis eats. I ask Ellis about his classes, and if there are any that interest him.

"I really like my psychology class," he says. "I'm writing a paper on how referees can influence a game by getting into a player's head by calling a technical on him." I no longer see Ellis as an incredibly gifted basketball player with a shy personality, but a young scholar who happens to be a really gifted basketball player. We talk for a solid five minutes about his research. Coach Blake continues to watch closely, speaking occasionally but through teeth that might seem on edge if I didn't already know that his personality is just intense. Coach Blake sways as he talks. "We try not to pay too much attention to the referee. Just go out and play our game. We don't like to start any problems with them. Just treat them with respect and be nice."

I ask Ellis about how he developed that jump shot over the summer. "Just practiced a lot." Coach Blake puts his fork down. "When he kicks his right leg out, he makes it. It's all about kicking out the right leg." Coach Blake asks me when I'm going to come around and watch film. "I'm always there," he continues. "Watching film. I'd much rather do that than be in class. Always watching film." I ask Giddings how school is going. He looks thoughtfully at the corn on the cob in his hand. Butter drips from it. He puts the corn down. "All A's and B's. I had one problem communicating with a professor. It had to do with technology. But I learned from it." I ask him if he can put me in touch with Mike Farmer. Again, a thoughtful response.

"I remember meeting Mike Farmer," Coach Blake says. "When I came to your house. Do you remember what he said when I asked about your shot?" Giddings smiles sheepishly and nods. I can tell he'd rather be anywhere, probably in the library studying or in the gym putting up shots, than here. He nods. Coach Blake continues. "He said, 'When Tanner shoots the ball over his head, it goes in. When he shoots the ball below his head, it doesn't.' Yep, that's what he said." Coach Blake likes to chew when he talks, a nervous habit. Kind of like Brad Pitt does in every movie he's in. Always eating, chewing, talking, one-liners packed with fortune cookie wisdom.

We start talking about basketball movies. Ellis says he likes *Coach Carter*. "Ever seen *Blue Chips*?" Coach Blake asks Ellis. Ellis shakes his head. "Oh, you got to see that one." Coach Blake is fired up. He talks about the movie in detail. I can tell he's seen it a hundred times, probably at a pivotal age in his life, at a time when his own dreams of becoming a great player were fading but the reality of being a great coach started to loom large. Maybe like the time when I read *A Season on the Brink* and knew that since I had failed as both a basketball player and basketball coach (Okay, I never really got the chance to coach because life got in the way), maybe I could fulfill these two dream by writing a book that combined the two. "Yeah, Shaq's in it," Coach Blake says, his mind still on *Blue Chips*.

I want to ask Ellis and Coach Blake if they remember the days of Shaq playing at LSU, the man-child, but it dawns on me that they might not have been born yet. "Penny Hardaway," Coach Blake says. "Penny's in it, too." Barbara Alger has been listening with pricked ears. "Now that's going way back," she says. Barbara knows basketball. She and Don are huge fans and supporters of the program. They are often the only Chico State fans at away games. The players frequently have supper at their house, and Isaiah Ellis once brought Barbara a bouquet of flowers. "Yes," she says again. "That's going way back." Not that far back, I think. Seems like yesterday. I remember meeting a guy when I was only 20 who worked as a basketball manager at the University of Memphis. He kept telling me about this kid named Penny and showed me a VHS of him. How have I gotten this old?

I ask Coach Blake about *Hoop Dreams*. "One of the best," he says. I tell him the story about how when it first came out, when I was an undergraduate at Cal, I went to see it in the theater seven times with seven different really smart girls who I thought would be impressed. "And they never went out with me again," I tell him. Sad but true. I was always trying to get smart people who didn't like or understand basketball to try and see it from the artistic and intellectual lens that I've always viewed it through. Maybe that's another reason I decided to write this book.

My back starts scratching the dickens out of me. It's the tag. I pull it out. Coach Blake sees it.

"Thinking about returning it?" he says.

I laugh. Might as well be honest. We're basketball family. "Yeah," I say.

"My kind of man," he grins and shovels food into his mouth. "Something I'd do."

Giddings pushes the meat around on his plate like he's jockeying for position on the block. He's quiet. I can easily see him feeling comfortable in the Midwest. He has that kind of quiet disposition, the kind of quietness that when he does speak at the table, everyone is in awe.

"It's cold out today." And everyone looks at each other, slackjawed, as if it were the wisest thing they'd ever heard.

Yes, Giddings only speaks when he has to.

I ask Coach Blake if he's ever read any of Bill Bradley's books. Coach Blake drops his corn. "Yes, he was one of the greatest, maybe the best, college basketball players of all time" Coach Blake turns very serious. He's dad at the dinner table again. Stern. "Yeah, he played at Princeton," Coach Blake adds. "He was one of the hardest workers. Like you." He looks directly at Ellis and takes a bite of corn. He makes the statement that he'll continue to make to Ellis throughout the supper. "Anybody can be an All-American if they're willing to put in three hours a day."

Every time Coach Blake says this, I can feel a little tension mounting with Giddings and Ellis. I can tell they want to get in the gym, right now. If anyone on the team has the potential to become All-Americans, it's these two.

I know the potential for greatness that flanks both sides of me. Coach Blake talks about Ryan Anderson, the former Cal player, and how he was one of the best players he had ever played against. He recalls Anderson's work ethic. I think back to the first time I ever saw Leon Powe play, who would star at Cal and then contribute greatly to the Celtics first championship in years, back when he was playing at Oakland Tech.

"Quentin Thomas was even better," Coach Blake says when I mention that Oakland Tech team. "I played against those guys." I forget that Coach Blake is a Bay Area guy young enough, the same age, to remember guys like that. Talking to Coach Blake is wonderful. He has such a vast basketball knowledge. I feel like I can go back into history and talk about players and he'll know exactly who I'm talking about and probably even be able to lecture me on the player or the era. He's a student of the game. Maybe not a communicator like Clink, but he's a basketball egg head—a basketball professor still under 30, still trying to finish his undergraduate degree, if only basketball would let him. He takes a bite of garlic bread and looks at the two big men. "Anybody can be an All-American if they can put in three hours a day." Ellis and Giddings look intently at their food. "Right, Isaiah?" he says.

"Right, Coach," Ellis replies.

Giddings has done a great job of moving his food around by not eating it. "Not hungry?" Coach Blake asks.

Giddings keeps rubbing his hands on his thighs. His foot is tapping, mind adrift. He's nervous.

"Ready to give your speech?" Coach Blake asks the big man.

Giddings's hands are moving up and down his thighs with such friction I worry that his pants will catch fire. That might be his intention.

Giddings mumbles a guttural yes.

"Don't worry," Coach Blake says. "We're going to march out through the café. When we get outside, all you have to do is walk up on the stage and stand by the mic. Make sure you speak clearly and look directly into the news camera."

Giddings gulps a few times. Coach Blake points at Giddings. He gnaws off a piece of bread. A crooked grin stretches across his face, one cheek puffed out with food. Giddings exhales. Coach Blake had me going, too.

Clink, dressed impeccably, not like a coach but more like a guy attending a relaxed wedding—the cool best man—gathers everyone's attention. He starts by thanking everyone who has helped him organize the meeting, and then thanks all of the people who work at Beatniks.

Clink certainly has charisma and charm. Too often charisma and charm are equated to salesmanship and the offering, the promise, of something phony to close a deal, to impress, the air of the charlatan cult leader. But Clink is not a phony. He is sincere. It would be very easy for him to become a Larry Brown or a John Calipari type. I guess that's why he's at Chico State running a clean program based on transparency. He's not a Slick Rick. The old people love him, the university's favorite son. The coach who can walk on water, a coach who believes in values and character and integrity. Old birds, these boosters, these Acker Backers, these parents eat that stuff up. They eat it up even more when it can be backed up. Not a hint of scandal in this program. When I think of Clink's program, I think of the following quote by Supreme Court Justice Louis Brandeis: "Sunlight is said to be the best of disinfectants."

Clink calls all of the players to come up and stand in front of the room. I would be terrified to stand in front of all these important community members who had just dropped $150 to eat from a buffet and socialize with their favorite players. The players are all dressed nicely.

They stand straight, some of the shyer ones hiding behind the others, their hands professionally folded and in front of them.

Clink is a natural. One might assume that the guy could've made millions in business by now hawking anything. He could sell cotton to Southerners, corn to Midwesterners, snow to Easterners, and sunshine to Westerners. But Clink believes in passion. What he's selling to players and families doesn't have a price tag: What he is selling, getting them to buy into, is a blueprint for success. "I believe in a culture built upon how we operate on a daily basis," he once told me. "We graduate guys. The most important thing is that these players leave here with a degree."

This is a big part of his vision. He talks about how he doesn't recruit a guy unless he feels the guy can become a role model. Clink has told me this before, that he will only recruit a guy that he would feel comfortable leaving alone with his sons. Clink says he's always asking his guys: "Who's on the bus? I'm looking for coachable guys who are tough, motivated, passionate, selfless, and honest." Every player I have interviewed fits this bill. If not, they're darn good actors. I've spent a lot of time in my life pulling the wool over people's eyes. That's what storytellers do. The good ones. The ones who get paid. I can sniff out the sincere from the insincere right away. That's what happens when one is exiled from their county of birth, thrown out by the ear, and forced to survive on their own at 18. I left Mississippi with a change of clothes, a notebook, some pens, and an Army duffle bag of books.

Ambrosini addresses the crowd. I can tell he's nervous. He's a basketball player, not a public speaker. But Clink wants these guys to feel uncomfortable, to get over this hump, to become better socially. Ambrosini thanks everyone from the heart. I can tell he's practiced this speech. I can also tell he's nervous. The serious ones, the earnest ones, always are.

This is all part of Ambrosini's education. Coach knows this, all part of his plan, get these young men used to addressing specific kinds of audiences. The crowd applauds after his speech. Clink then talks about the importance of culture when the team travels.

"What's the common perception of Chico State?" he asks.

Everyone says it: "Party school."

"When we travel," Clink continues, "I see it as a 72-hour opportunity to change that perception. We are polite and respectful to everyone we encounter: flight attendants, hotel staff, waiters, and waitresses."

Clink has mastered the art of tone and inflection. He pauses. "I get more compliments on how nice and respectful our guys are than I do about how they played."

The crowd loves it.

Clink talks about pride in the product. "Coach Puck Smith taught me that the harder you work, and the more you give, the more pride you get.

Our product, this basketball team, is special because we outwork every-body. No one knows it more than this guy."

McFerren steps in front of the crowd. So relaxed and calm. The coolness of a high-end Vegas lounge act. He talks to the audience in a personal tone, his voice low but confident, thoughtful, as if addressing each person individually, a person-centered approach that makes each participant feel special.

Clink takes over again, but not before telling the crowd a little more about McFerren. "He was already wearing Chico State socks before he even committed." Clink talks about the daily grind and the Red Door. "Our guys know not to walk through the Red Door if they're not ready to play and grind it out. We're a blue collar program. And no one's tougher than this guy."

The Red Door is the door near the locker room and training room where the Chico State players enter into the gym each day for practice and pass back through on their way to change and become students again. Players do not merely go through the Red Door. Players are expected to go through and *beyond* the Red Door. Clink's mission is for his young men to transcend basketball. Clink says, "I talk a lot to our guys about the mentality they need to have every day when they enter the Red Door. If they're not right in the head when they open that Red Door, they'll get exposed—exposed by their teammates and coaches. We talk about walking the line that borders on being composed and doing something crazy. I like it when our guys teeter on that line. I never want them to cross it and do something stupid, but I want them foaming at the mouth. I use the phrase being full of piss and vinegar. They know it means they need to be aggressive. Rashad Parker used to come through the Red Door every day and yell something as he ran in. He was always ready and he got other guys ready, too. Damario Sims would run in and yell 'Let's go!' That's our rallying cry. It fires people up. Jay Flores would walk through the Red Door before anyone else and be in a full sweat before practice started. Sean Park always walked through the Red Door ready to compete."

Robert Duncan steps up. He, too, looks uncomfortable, so out of place in formal clothes. His hair is growing on me. At first I thought it looked like he was wearing a hair net, but now it looks more like a French beret. I don't think this is the image he's going for. Hair is important to young people: a stamp of their identity, a way to be unique in a standardized world. If Duncan can repeat the season he had last year, let the kid wear a Burger King crown—who cares?

Duncan is kind of like a basketball Rorschach test. He's a basketball inkblot, a complex basketball algorithm. If I saw him at Costco picking out a chicken, I wouldn't think: "Here's a guy that might be the best basketball player in the CCAA." But he is.

Clink tells the story about after hauling couches and televisions all day (Duncan spent the summer working for a furniture moving company), how he'd be leaving his office at 5 p.m. and hear a ball bouncing. "I'd open up the door to the gym and there'd he be, putting up shots, after moving fridges all day." Duncan's speech is quick. Kind of like his drive to the basket. He looks pained. Kind of like when he turns the ball over. It amazes me how young men can stand at a free throw line for a one-on-one, down a point, clock down to a tick, with ice in their veins in front of 1,300 raucous fans, and sink the front end and the back end. Yet, standing in front of a crowd and speaking incites terror and makes them petrified.

Clink knows public speaking is all about getting reps. Put the guy in the situation a few times, turn the uncomfortable into the comfortable. Clink talks about guys relishing their roles. He shines the light on one of the team managers who wishes he could play on the team but knows he's not good enough. "Lee would much rather be playing instead of being on his hands and knees and mopping up the floor," Clink says. "But we thank him. Everyday."

Clink turns his attention to Magz, the Acker crowd favorite. "This next young man has never flinched, has never complained, despite being placed in a different role each year," Clink says. Magz has the presence of a rock star. I almost hope he moves to Los Angeles when the season is over, his freshly minted degree in hand, and takes acting lessons, goes to auditions. He'd make it. That's his presence. One gets the feeling they are in the midst of greatness around him. Heck, he's Roman. Even though a Magz speech pales in comparison to a Magz dunk, his words hit home. What a joy it must have been for these fans to watch him grow into a man, a senior now.

Clink reminds everyone that even those who walk on water are also prone to falling in. Clink talks about the program being a billboard, and how the players are advertisements for the university. His PowerPoint slide—meant as a visual to explain to the boosters how he has created this program—has a few corporate logos on it. He talks about the symbolism of the Apple logo and the Adidas logo. Then the Starbucks logo pops up. The players laugh. Clink is notorious for his love of Starbucks. Each player has remarked that his coffee addiction is one of his most hilarious idiosyncrasies. "I love Starbucks," he says. "Love everything about it. I love the consistency in the flavor, the service. The guys always laugh at me because whenever we're on the road or something, I've always got a Starbucks in my hand. I just love it." For the moment, Clink has forgotten that he's in a neighborhood café, the antithesis of the corporate coffee giant. Mike, the owner of Beatniks, also reputed for his bristly personality, walks into the room. "Hey, Coach, come on. What about Beatniks coffee? Starbucks? Come on!" Mike is smiling, trying to be funny, but, again, like Freud said: "There's no such thing as a joke."

Clink knows he's been caught in the snares. The guy in charge of doing the busting has been busted.

The crowd goes wild. It's a truly funny, truly human moment. "Okay, okay, but the point I was trying to make…" He clicks to the slide of the Chico State Wildcats logo. We all get it.

Clink talks about transparency. "We have real, honest talks," he says. "I call it constructive conflict. I like to confront the snowball before it turns into an avalanche. I'm always looking for problems in the program. I stay on my assistant coaches about this. He also talks about holding his guys accountable for their actions. Clinks says that when he looks around the program and he sees something that not's broken, he likes to "break it and make it better."

Finally, Giddings gets his chance to speak. He no longer looks scared but relieved. Cool Marvin is behind him. He has shared a joke with someone. It looks like he's holding back a sneeze but I can tell it's a laugh. If he laughs, it's going to have a ripple effect. Don't do it, Cool Marvin. This 6-foot-11 senior standing in front of the crowd has such a boyish, innocent demeanor, his face having the appearance of a little boy who has stepped into an old-time black and white photo booth at the fair and for a dollar gotten six pictures. "I came here from Fresno State, and the culture here is a lot more like a family," Giddings says. Behind him are his brothers, most of them his little brothers, and he is the quiet, somber big brother, just prime for practical jokes. Cool Marvin holds back his laughter. I know he wasn't laughing at Giddings, but it's the same kind of nervous, pent-up laughter that I used to release after sitting in the church pew for an hour and listening to yet another sermon. I get it. These young men are a band of brothers. There is no mother. Only a father.

Finally, Clink talks about relationships. It's inevitable that the name and person, the character and unimpeachable integrity of Damario Sims comes up. His name always surfaces when the bonds formed in the program are discussed.

"A couple of weeks ago, I drove down to San Jose to see Damario being sworn in as a Santa Clara County corrections officer," Clink says. "Coach Argenal met us at the courthouse and several of the other players that Damario played with."

Clink wraps up his presentation with an optimistic glimpse into the season ahead. "I really enjoyed coaching last season's team," he said, "but I got to tell you, I'm so much more excited about coaching this group of guys. Their chemistry, and the way they let us coach them, is dynamic."

I've gotten to know Clink pretty well—at least the coach side of him—in the last six months. I know he wouldn't say this if he were not serious.

I make a quick reach for my Moleskin so I can write down what he said. In my haste, I knock over what remains in Barbra Alger's wine glass.

Red wine splatters all over the $60 shirt I had planned on returning in the morning.

I can just hear Clink: "Accountability, Carson, accountability." I have indeed been held accountable.

I'll have to keep the shirt.

CHAPTER 33

October 15

ONLY THE MOST RABID COLLEGE basketball fans put October 15, the official start of the college basketball season, on their sports priority list for October. I've been waiting for October 15 since last March. This is Christmas Day for me, a Christmas day that stretches into early April.

I have printed one of my favorite "basketball as a metaphor for life" quotes and will give it to Clink, ask him to read it only when he's down, or maybe, even, as a reminder of when he's up higher than he's ever been. The quote is from Bill Bradley's *Life on the Run* (1976)—essential for not only basketball fans but for anyone seeking wisdom and inspiration:

Yet winning and losing is all around us. From the high school level on, athletes are prepared to win and they in turn convey to a larger public what it is to be a winner. Locker-room champagne, humility in victory, and irrefutable knowledge of a favorable, clear-cut resolution are what championships resemble from the outside. The winning team like the conquering army claims everything in its path and seems to say that only winning is important. Yet like getting into a college of your choice or winning an election or marrying a beautiful mate, victory is fraught with as much danger as glory. Victory has very narrow meanings and, if exaggerated or misused, can become a destructive force. The taste of defeat has a richness of experience all its own.

The Chico State basketball team has had the taste of defeat in their mouths since last March. Today, they get to finally spit it out and move on.

I don't know where Clink gets the stamina. He came out today and ran fullcourt with the old dudes. I got banged up by Adam Stoltz, the Director of Admissions, today. It's the first time I've ever been down on the court, eyes closed, foot tapping, and had to lay there for a couple of minutes to see if I could get up. The pain in my hips, each day, is getting worse. I hobble from Shurmer over to Acker in my basketball costume. Chico State basketball tank top. Chico State socks up to the knee caps. Fancy Nikes with a fluorescent hot pink stripe. Baggy shorts with neon green stripes. Nike sweat bands. The old man who can't give up the ghost. Clink sits me at the scorer's table. The players come up and say hello. I tell them Merry Christmas. I don' think they quite understand why I'm so excited. I've also just found out that the Wildcats are preseason ranked No. 14 in the country for Division II. Meanwhile, the University of Arizona is ranked No. 10 in Division I. This just adds more drama to the game. I know: Rankings are not supposed to matter, but they do.

The lights dim. All the players gather to watch film cast on a dirty old wall. Coach has a pointer with a red light. He talks to the players about defense. After he has fired them up, they shout and hustle on to the court. They run drills. Gaber is there. He has brought a friend. His buddy must be in his sixties, but he still has the wiry body of a young man. I'm dumbfounded by how complex the plays are. The players move so fast. No one stands. Constant movement, a blur. Two players impress me the most. I have only met Keith Datu a couple of times, and he was wearing street clothes. I did meet him on the court once, but he seemed to nice to be a monster on the boards—probably because he is so sincere and humble. But after watching him I see that he's a warrior. I know the team is good when Duncan is no longer the player I'm watching the most. Nate Ambrosini seems the most improved, faster and stronger. His shot is smooth. He is aggressive. His face is constantly straining. Jesse Holmes makes a few drives to the basket, up and over Justin Briggs the man-child (I don't know how Clink can turn down the temptation to not redshirt him). He finishes strong on a dunk. All the players look good. There are several moments when I drop my pen and shake my head. I can't believe what I'm seeing. Surely every team can't be this good, this organized. Kitchens also confuses me. I can't believe how smart, how fast, he is. One would never know from looking at him. He springs off the tips of his toes.

Coach runs practice like a classroom. He'll stop a play and call on a player. "What are the two ways we have learned to defend a ball screen?" One of the players says, "Soft edge." Clink says. "Good job." He then asks Holmes. He doesn't know. Another player answers. "I want Jesse to answer." I can tell Holmes wants to kick himself for not knowing. Clink doesn't give him a hard time, though. Giddings bails him out. "Yes," Clink says. "But I wanted Jesse to answer. The squeeze."

They practice the soft edge and the squeeze with such brute force, such speed, tons of contact, whistle blowing when the play is dead, that I forget that I'm watching basketball. I feel like I'm watching football practice and the game is bull in the ring. Graceful, yes, but also physical. Clink will tell me later that it's easier to back them off when it's time to play a game than to try and get them more aggressive and pose a risk for the referees to call a lot of fouls.

Another play that Clink runs is called Punch. McFerren has the ball. The two big men set screens. McFerren goes around them. They break to the basket. The wings scramble underneath. It happens too fast for my mind to make sense of it. Why is it so hard for me to understand the movements of only five men? I have two MA degrees. I'm in a doctorate program. The young men running the plays are all undergraduates. I just don't get it. There is a different kind of intelligence at play here. Arizona has no idea what's coming for them. Neither does the CCAA.

CHAPTER 34

ZPD

OCTOBER 16

I WALK INTO THE GYM a ten minutes before 1 p.m. The gym is packed with college students running around. Looks like a kinesiology class. An older man, the professor, walks over to me. "Are you the coach?" I pause, almost laughing. Am I the coach? I'm honored. Someone mistook me for a coach.

"No, sir," I say without thinking. "I'm just the writer." He gives me a puzzled look. "Oh, well, if you would please let the coach know we're wrapping up and will be out in a few minutes."

I take a seat at the clock table. Magz shuffles in. He carries a big jug of a brightly colored sports drink. He looks exhausted. I ask him how he is. "Sick," he says. "Sore throat. Allergies, maybe."

Clink comes in at 12:55 p.m. He sees me at the table and comes over. He knows I was confused by the plays from yesterday. He hands me a practice plan for the day. Turns it over. Takes my pen. Starts teaching.

"Right now we're only running three plays. Blast. Runner. Punch. By the end of the season, we'll have 15 more plays." He sketches the play that confused me yesterday. "Punch is just what we call it." After he draws the play, it makes sense. I feel like I'm a kid again, crafting plays in the dirt with a twig. "Ball screen. Squeeze. Hard hedge. Soft hedge. Switch. Trap monster." I love the language.

Coach Gabriel has been working feverishly in one corner of the gym. He's getting the projector ready as the players warm up. The chatter amongst the players gets louder. Sounds like the dugout of a little league game. The players storm through the Red Door. They're fired up and ready to go.

"One minute," Clink yells.

Clink has every second of the practice dialed in. He has a set curriculum and instruction (not intentional on Clink's part, but something I have observed when trying to apply an academic theory to the practical workings of his practice) based on what Vygotsky called "scaffolding" and the Zone of Proximal Development. Each day will be about improvement, the older players helping the younger players get better. Deliberate practice. The players never walk. They're always running. Clink starts putting out the orange cones. He pulls the trash can out that will be an imaginary player.

At one o'clock sharp, Clink runs over to the projector. The lights dim. The players sprint over. The film appears on the wall. The three-minute theme: unselfishness on defense.

"I want you to put yourself in a situation where you might be at risk," Clink says. "Get out of your comfort zone."

After the film session, the team stretches then runs sprints and takes a breather. Clink gets the blue pad out. He likes to smash the big guys. As the players go up for layups, he hits them with the pad. He smashes Holmes pretty good. Holmes likes it. This is the first time he's even been on a basketball court in October. Normally at this time of the year he's in the middle of football season. He thrives on the contact. I understand. I recall last April, when I'd watch practice, I couldn't take my eyes off Duncan. Even though he's still great—better, even—there are so many other great players to watch. The kid who impresses me most is Ambrosini. He's fierce. Looks like he inhales gasoline and exhales fire. He's built like barbed wire. Tough as nails.

Silverstrom exhibits sheer joy on the court. The ball is like a yo-yo in his hand. "Create space," Clink screams. "Space. Create it. Corey, use your imagination."

For a fierce five minutes, the players go one-on-one full court. It's like Clink has opened up the gates and let the stallions run wild. The pace is fast and filled with fury. Breakneck speed.

During the defensive drills, Clink yells: "Bluff and recover. Bluff and recover." Repetition. Over and over. Same drills.

In the corner, Kitchens, the senior, is teaching something to Holmes the freshman. Here is peer mentoring at its best.

"Don't turn the ball over."

"Skip, skip, skip. Baseline penetration."

The ball is turned over.

Rage. The whistle. The explosion.

"Careless. Just catch it and pass it and don't turn it over."

Clink crouches in a catcher's position against the wall. Whistle in mouth. Rage building.

"Ball screen."

"Slip."

"You have to know the difference between favorable matchups and unfavorable matchups."

"Bluff. Bluff. Bluff."

"Your energy is good. The effort is great. But you're not talking. Communicate!"

"Use your imagination. Create plays."

Clink explodes again. The offense keeps turning the ball over in the "Three Skips to Live" drill. Not long after, McFerren walks over to the water cooler. He looks at me with a business-as-usual smile.

"Coach is pretty intense, isn't he?" he says.

Clink's rage is a controlled rage—a rage that has surprised me here on only day two. I've never seen Clink lose his temper. He did warn me I would see a different side of him.

The guys are going at it hard with lots of communication. Ellis and Giddings collide and make a hard landing. Giddings is in excruciating pain. The gym goes silent.

The color is drained from several players' faces. I wonder what coach is thinking. Is he automatically thinking whether or not he will have to use a year of Justin Briggs's eligibility? He will later tell me that he approached the situation with logic. "Most of the time, when a player goes down, he's fine," Clinks says. "Some guys go down all the time. They want attention." If Giddings is gone, do the Wildcats have a chance to win the CCAA this year? The energy is zapped. "Is it your knee?" Clink asks.

Giddings shakes his head.

The trainer comes running out with ice. He helps Giddings off the court. Play resumes.

A few minutes later, the trainer come jogging out to Clink. Clink closely watches the team. The trainer whispers something in Clink's ear.

"What are you guys doing?" Clink roars. "What are you doing?" The trainer shuffles off.

I can only imagine the trainer has delivered bad news.

I phone coach later that day. "Is the season over?"

"What are you talking about?"

"Giddings. Is he okay?"

"He's fine. Banged knees with Isaiah and went down. Ankle, that's all. They heal fast."

"What was going through your mind?"

He doesn't respond.

"Were you thinking about no longer redshirting Justin Briggs?" He laughs a little.

"That thought never crossed my mind," he says.

Another difference between the coach and the writer.

"That's why we have such a deep team," he says. "We expect things like this to happen. It's just part of the game. We're always prepared. Someone gets hurt, we move on."

CHAPTER 35

Arizona Bound

NOVEMBER 7

Jojo was a man who thought he was a loner/
But he knew it couldn't last/
Jojo left his home in Tucson, Arizona/ For some California grass.

—THE BEATLES

THE TRIP IS ALREADY OFF to an ominous start. I had assumed there would be an abundance of shuttles to take me from the Tucson airport to the Comfort Suites Inn. I guess I could have done a little research. After all, I had been researching this game since July. Drawing out plays on cocktail napkins. Drawing out plays on the beach sand in Maui. Dreaming of ways we could beat Arizona, having nightmares of the ways we could lose. Why could I have not Googled the distance of the hotel from the Tucson airport? Probably for the same reason that I thought basketball players, on paper, who are the same size are automatically a fair matchup on the court.

I call the Comfort Inn Suites from the Sacramento airport. "Comfort Inn Suites," says the front desk voice on the other end. "This is Jeremy." His words are slurred. He chews while he talks. I can just see him there, slouched, a highlighter pen in his right hand, the phone tucked under his chin. His other hand searches for that last Cheeto (hot and spicy flavor), and a Cliff Notes version of *To Kill a Mockingbird* is in front of him. "Hi,

231

Jeremy," I say, "I'm meeting up with the Chico State Wildcats basketball team later tonight. I don't have a ride to the airport. Is there a shuttle?"

"No, there aren't any shuttles at the airport. You'll have to call a taxi," he says.

Jeremy's surfer cadence marks him as a Southern Californian transplant. He pauses. Chews. Swallows. "It's pretty far," he says.

"How far?" I ask.

"At least thirty minutes.'

Thirty minutes of cab fare. There goes the pair of basketball shoes I was saving up for. He hears me let out a sigh.

"I recommend the King Pin Cab Company. Tell them Jeremy from the front desk referred you." Now I know I'm in for it. "We worked out a deal with them," he adds.

Sure they did. Well, at least I called the hotel. Otherwise, I might have been stranded at the airport. "How much will this cost me?" I ask.

"I don't know," he says.

Double trouble. I know the cabbie will be able to charge me as much as he wants, Tokyo rates. I have a layover in Las Vegas and about three dollars in quarters. Maybe I can win enough to pay the fare. I take a seat by my gate. The Denver University swim team arrives. They *look* like swimmers—tall, blonde, white teeth, heads held high, hair unkempt, tan with goggle imprints still surrounding their eyes. I smell chlorine and sun screen. We finally board the plane. The swim coaches sit behind me. They talk incessantly of the rankings, who beat whom over the weekend. They are much more concerned with what other teams are doing rather than what their own teams seems to be doing. I think back to Clink not even knowing—or caring, even—that the preseason Division II rankings and Division II coaches preseason poll was out. I had texted him. "Thanks. Will look at that," he wrote back.

Taking off feels lonely. Sacramento is a lot prettier looking down on it from an airplane window. Ten minutes in the air and squares of drought-choked farmland turns to snowcapped mountains. I see Tahoe down below, the wide paths of ski slopes. Great to see snow when there has not been rain for three years. The flight attendant brings me some water and a pack of peanuts and pretzels. I start drawing out plays. The peanuts are Chico State. The pretzels are Arizona. Since July I have been confident that we can beat, or at least keep up with, Arizona.

Now I start to wonder. The word on star center Kaleb Tarczewski, who they call Zeus, is that he has a bad ankle sprain and might not play. Who will score first? Will we come out playing it safe with a "glad to be here" attitude? Or will we go for the jugular? What if they come out fast and get a big lead? How will we respond? Will the lights and the cameras intimidate our guys? I get butterflies thinking about it.

I eat my Chico State peanuts and Arizona pretzels, ask for a couple more packs. I open up the packs and arrange them on the fold out table. I hear, see, Clink screaming at my peanuts. I have McFerren the peanut racing by York the pretzel. Magz the peanut has just thrown Zeus the pretzel to the ground—now half a pretzel. Duncan and Kitchens, the other peanuts, are on the wings. Ellis trails behind. In another scenario, I have Ellis the peanut throwing the Beverly Hills freshman Comanche the peanut to the ground. Ellis the peanut puts his foot in Comanche's chest. Comanche the pretzel crumbles. Ellis the peanut says, "Should've red shirted." Ellis would never say something like that, but when you're a peanut playing ball on a cocktail napkin, you can do anything you want. I think for a moment about Justin Briggs, the redshirt freshman, back home. Clink could have let the young man play this year, and he would have contributed. No doubt. Nevertheless, Briggs will be a star someday, but I can't imagine the pain that he must feel having to stay behind.

Flying over Las Vegas looks like the inside of an electronic device with all the grids. I think back to my Lite Brite when I was a kid. It's so beautiful down below, a manmade beauty, a striking contrast to the snow covered Sierra Nevada mountain range from earlier. I think of all the losers down below, and wonder how many people are actually winning. Would the world be better off if the plug was pulled on the sprawling city down below? No, it wouldn't. Maybe Las Vegas makes the world better, a hyper-simulated reality that makes anyone flying over feel thankful they live in a boring town like Salina, Kansas.

We land. I enter the airport and start roaming. I'm starving, but not about to spend any money on airport food. Unless, of course, I can turn my two dollars of quarters into something big. I find what seems like a lucky slot machine. Dump in the quarters. Nothing. I will have to eat the stale trail mix and smashed banana that's leaving a slug trail in my backpack. I put in another call to Jeremy back at the Comfort Inn. Still feeling uneasy about the cab. I don't want to be murdered and found out in the desert amidst the cacti with a rattlesnake crawling over my body.

"Hi, Jeremy at the Comfort Inn," the voice says.

"Hi, Jeremy, just checking back about the cab guy. You sure he's legitimate?"

"Yes, he's legitimate. Tell him Jeremy from the front desk sent you."

"Right.

I call the King Pin cab company. "Yeah, King Pin here. This is Michael."

"Hi, Michael. I need a ride from the airport into Tucson," I say.

"Sorry, I don't do pickups from the airport," he says. The voice is Eastern. It smacks of Philly cheesesteak sandwiches and cold winters.

"Jeremy from the Comfort Inn told me to call you. He said you were the man."

"Oh, sure, I can pick you up. We'll have to be kind of quick, though. I'll have to pick you up out in the parking lot. The airline people don't like me taking away business from the airport taxis."

I'm a little worried. "How much is this going to cost?" I ask. "I got a few rates from some other cab companies." What a lie.

"I'm the best," he says. "I'll get you there for $50. Those airport cabs, a lot of those guys will charge you $80. Here's the deal. Text me when you land. I'll be there 15 minutes later. Green Cadillac."

I feel a little better. At least I won't be stranded in Tucson. I head over to my gate.

Several white headed men wearing U of A polo shirts talk with their well-dressed wives in the lounge area of Gate C-24. A few of them give me the stink eye when they see my Chico State ball cap. I FaceTime my family. Try again to explain the project to my father-in-law and mother-in-law who are at the house helping my wife take care of the children. Everyone thinks I'm crazy for writing a book about a Division II basketball team. And the thing about a book is that you have to just write it—can't talk about it or your story might disappear. Just have to do it. Like playing the game of basketball.

I board the plane and head toward the back row. I'm always the guy that gets stuck in the back by the toilet. I pass one Arizona fan after another, smug, white haired, tanned. There are several middleaged fans, too, meaning my age. Probably the same fans who used to heckle me and whom I used to heckle back when my California Golden Bears would play the University of Arizona back in the legendary year of 1996-1997, back when the University of Arizona had the talented freshmen Mike Bibby and A.J. Bramlett, the sophomore Jason Terry, juniors Michael Dickerson and Miles Simon. That 1996-1997 University of Arizona team reminds me a lot of Clink's 2015-2016 Chico State Wildcats. Still young, but experienced and not old enough to really have any mental stumbling blocks, still young enough to believe anything is possible.

I'm always weary of teams with too many seniors. Give me a bunch of young guys with a handful of seniors any day of the week. Oh, yes, I think as I walk down the aisle and these Arizona fans snicker at me, the same fans, now older, who during that National Championship season run would chant "U of A" with suntanned faces, white-washed teeth, sweaters folded over their shoulders (you live in the desert, remember?), now in the halftime of life, portly, moneyed, and still waiting for another National Championship, still wondering what happened last year when the expectations were so high, anxious about what kind of team Coach Miller will unveil this year. I find my seat and call my family one final time.

"I have my prediction," I tell my wife.

"What prediction?" she says.

"The game. We're going to win 69-65."

"I don't think we'll be able to get the game on TV, honey," she says.

"Listen to it on the radio," I tell her.

"We don't have a radio."

I lean back and try to catch some sleep. I'm exhausted, but my mind is noisy. I don't imagine I'll sleep well the next two nights, either. I'll be too excited. But tomorrow, Sunday, November 8, I will have to remain calm, stoic, and detached. I will have to pretend that I'm not a fan; I am the writer, the biographer. But that's assuming I make it from the airport to the team hotel alive.

I make it to the hotel in one piece. I dash up to the second floor of the hotel. The first person I see is Coach Gabriel. He has a clipboard in his hand. Coach Blake is behind him. They're surprised to see me.

"We're doing bed checks," Coach Gabriel says.

"Where's Clink?" I ask

"200."

Isaiah Ellis—Zay—shuffles out into the hallway. He looks like a little kid at a sleepover party, away from his parents for the first time. He raises his hands high in the air when he sees me. I salute him and head off to Clink's room. I knock on the door. He opens it.

Clink is wearing basketball shorts and a Chico State basketball T-shirt. The room is dark save the lights of the flickering television, quiet save the hum of the air conditioner and murmur of the TV voices.

"Your biographer is here," I say.

I walk in. Clink lies back down on the bed. Stretches out. "How much was your cab?"

"63 bones and worth every penny."

He scratches his head and turns his attention back to a rerun of *The Office.*

"This isn't what I expected," I tell him.

"What do you mean?"

"I thought I'd get here and see you and the other coaches drinking coffee, pacing, watching film, drawing up plays."

In my mind I had an image of the old black and white photographs of politicians in their hotel rooms, smoking, drinking coffee, trying to put the finishing touches on a bill or something.

"Like I said, this game doesn't matter to me," Clink says. "It'll be a great experience for the guys, but it's just a way for me to measure where we are. See where we need to get better."

I take a seat on the other bed. My throat is already hurting from the hotel air conditioner. Every hotel I've ever stayed in with an air conditioner gives me a sore throat. I scan the room. Really no sign of life here other than the leather toiletry bag on the bathroom counter.

"Yeah," he says, "if you were to see me next Friday when the season opens against Montana State, I'll be worked up. But this one doesn't matter."

Clink has been saying this game doesn't matter since July. I've tried and tried to get him to admit that it does. I finally believe him. He yawns. "You like this show?" he says.

I look at the television. "I like the British version better."

"Only seen one or two episodes of the British version. I love this show," he says, half-asleep. "Oh, you might want this."

Clink puts the Arizona scouting report on my bed. Insider information. A basketball geek's dream come true. Underneath the Chico State Men's basketball logo is a quote from John Wooden:

"It's the little details that are vital. Little things make big things happen."

I'm a kid at Christmas. There'll be no sleeping tonight. I look at the starting lineup. Arizona is big and deep. I'd also forgotten they have four seniors.

"Can we win tomorrow?" I ask Clink.

"We have to be perfect. Flawless. No turnovers." Clink turns off the television. "You can turn it back on if you like," he says.

"I'll just read in bed if that's okay," I say. "Good night."

I don't fall asleep until about 3 a.m. I stay up late playing tomorrow's game in my mind. Clink sleeps like a baby. He doesn't even move. Maybe this is his way of shutting things out. The last thought I have before finally falling asleep is of all the basketball posters I used to have on my wall: Larry

Bird, Dr. J., Ice Man, Chocolate Thunder, Magic, and Steve Alford—also one of Clink's favorite players. The happiest times of my life were those times when I first discovered basketball, being ten years old and playing for the YMCA, making a shot and running down the court with a smile capable of scorching the earth. Pure joy. At 44, I think how lucky I am to have rediscovered this long lost love.

I close my eyes and start thinking. We have to play perfectly. There'll be mismatches. We will have to shoot well. Take good shots. Not miss, really. No turnovers. Rebounds. Put backs. Ball screens. Switches. Slips. Fakes. Score early. Be calm. Sleep finally comes.

Clink wakes up.

"What are you doing over there?" he says. I'm sprawled out on the sofa in the executive portion of the hotel room. I've been writing for a long time.

"Taking some notes. Want me to open the curtains?"

"Sure."

I open the curtains. The view: car lot after car lot. The bright morning sun beats down on the shiny new roofs and casts a blinding glare into the room. Clink comes over and looks out the window. His gaze is distant. He doesn't like Arizona. He's a Californian. And he can't wait to get this game over with and move on.

"My high school coach is coming," Clink says. "And 20 friends I haven't seen since high school."

If only, I thought, his high school coach and 20 high school friends from Morgan Hill would be as excited about the Seattle Pacific University game, a real game and the first home opener, a couple days after Thanksgiving. Then they could really see what his program, what his league, is about and what kind of players he recruits. They could see that playing in front of 348 fans in a small gym straight out of *Hoosiers* that can barely fit 1,000 fans is more of a thrill than playing in front of 16,000 fans in a multi-million dollar arena. I imagine tonight's scene in the McKale Center will be a lightshow of bread and circuses for the Arizona faithful. But going to a game in Acker is like sitting at the table with the Emperor Claudius while the masses in the spectacle outside.

Arizona has chosen Chico State for their circus, a spectacle of extreme cruelty, an exhibition, for the purpose of preparing the team for their regular season home opener against Pacific. The Arizona gladiators are not expected to fight until the death, but I know that our gladiators will. I have seen them, day in and day out, in practice. The Wildcats will not go quietly into that night. And they will not be the Christians and criminals thrown to the wild Arizona fans to be devoured.

Clink would not lead our boys into such a slaughter. He thinks we have a viable chance. And if we lose, so what? The Wildcats come away with the experience of a lifetime.

Clink steps away from the window. "I'm going down for coffee."

"You going to get breakfast too?" I ask.

"I don't eat breakfast," he says. "And I never eat on the road. I'll have some peanuts on the plane or something. But I'm too anxious to eat."

I go to the sink and brush my teeth. Clink's leather travel kit is on the sink. Barbasol shaving cream. I'm a little disappointed to see the shaving cream and an actual razor. I had wanted the rumors to be true that Clink refuses to use shaving cream and uses a rusty plastic razor.

Clink moves slowly, almost methodically, on game day. A man deep in thought. He has been doing this for 22 years—a chess master. He was never the natural born chess prodigy (basketball player), but he knew that to compete he would have to study, to work, and always look for ways to improve. I used to think that Clink had some kind of magic that the rest of us didn't possess. How could he do in front of crowds, a balance of hostile and friendly crowds, on back-to-back nights? How does he know what calls to make in the heat of battle, under the pressure of a ticking clock? How does he anticipate every move the other coach, the other players, will make? Then it hits me: He doesn't have to anticipate this. I'd always thought he had picked up the skill of anticipation from all the seasons he had been coaching. But what has happened is that Clink's experience, not unlike other professions where experience lends to expertise, has taught him to recognize patterns on the court, and patterns stemming from those recognizable patterns. He has trained himself to become a specialist.

Clink comes back to the room with his coffee and sits back on his bed. He starts writing out plays. I'm dreaming of the handshake at center court between these two coaches whom I admire so much, two of the most important coaches in the NCAA but whose teams come from different sides of the train track.

CHAPTER 36

Shot Heard 'Round the World

I HEAD DOWNSTAIRS TO THE lobby. Players are waiting for the vans to pick us up for shoot around. Robert Duncan, the young man whom I hope will emerge as the Pistol Pete type of player that I have detected all along, is taking advantage of the free coffee. Duncan's passing skills are superior. He sees things, patterns, movements, that nobody else can. He is able to predict, too, almost as if he can see into the future and tell how the play will develop before it happens. I once took a class at Cal by the Sociologist Professor Harry Edwards, and longtime member of the San Francisco 49ers organization, comparing the genius of Albert Einstein, John Coltrane, and Jason Kidd. Duncan has the same kind of genius as Jason Kidd, an instinctual knee-jerk genius, the ability to see many things happening on the court at once, things blind to the fan in the stands, things that cannot be premediated but must happen in the quick of the moment. I pray someone outside of the CCAA will get to see the brilliance that I've seen—his vision.

"Let's go," Clink barks. "Vans are here."

Clink's van always run on time: 9:30 a.m. sharp. I get on the van with Coach Gabriel at the wheel. Less than five minutes away from the hotel, Coach Gabriel points to a run-down Salvation Army. He slows the van. "See that Salvation Army, Coach?" Coach Gabriel says. Clink looks out his window, a slight grimace on his face.

"What about it?"

"I played there every day after school," Gabriel says. "Fifty cents a game."

Coach Gabriel is reliving his growing up in Tucson.

The van stops at the next stop light. "See that torn down building?" Coach Gabriel says.

Clink slowly turns and looks. "Yeah," he says, "it looks like a torn down building." Clink goes back to reading again "That was my favorite sandwich place back in high school," Coach Gabriel says. Clink turns back and looks at me. "You got the CD?" he asks me.

Clink is referring to the John Coltrane CD *A Love Supreme* that I burned and gave to each player, the album I told them would inspire my writing about their season.

Clink turns it up loud to drown out any more tour guide sessions from Coach Gabriel. They remind me of an old married couple. They kind of are.

I think back to the day in early July when I was interviewing Clink and Coach Gabriel and found out Chico State would be playing the University of Arizona in a November exhibition game.

That game would fire my imagination for the next four months.

Coach Gabriel is usually clean shaven, but stubbles covered his face that day. Still black, the color of his hair. No signs of gray. He is still young, 31, and has not been coaching long enough for his hair to turn white.

"Tucson is nice," Coach Gabriel says.

He grew up in Tucson. Coach Gabriel's mother earned her doctorate in education from the University of Arizona. She is currently the number one learning specialist in the world for at-risk student-athletes. Her office was in the McKale Center. Coach Gabriel grew up shooting in the McKale Center. "My mom had a key to the gym."

Coach Gabriel's parents were strict and would not let him go out at night. He and his friends would play one-on-one until midnight in the McKale Center.

"You'd like Tucson, Coach," Gabriel says. "We have the Desert Museum. Tombstone.

Bunch of stuff."

Clink rolls his eyes. He scans his office looking for a piece of paper to wad up and throw at Coach Gabriel, only his office is paperless. He does everything on the computer.

"There's nothing in Tucson but rattlesnakes and tumbleweeds," Clink growls.

Clink is excited, but not for the same reasons as everyone else. I ask him about it. "I'm excited for the chance to play someone good and improve and excited for the money we'll receive for playing them," he says when I ask him about it. "I'm not excited because I think we can beat Arizona."

Coach Gabriel points out that Arizona has lost three starters to the NBA draft, and also the senior point guard, McConnell. He fails to mention they have reloaded with what many analysts have been calling the best recruiting class in the nation. "This is nothing but a fundraising event for me," Clink says. "But it'll be a great experience for the players."

Clink needs money for the program. He also needs the experience for his players. But getting demolished is not the kind of experience a coach wants for his players. What general willingly leads his men into slaughter? "I want to get in and out," he tells me.

Clink says he will prepare for Arizona like he does for every other team. He has fingernail clippers in his hand. He looks down at the nail he's cutting. His mind, though, for the moment is on Arizona. "Nothing but rattlesnakes and tumbleweeds in Tucson," he says.

It's not a matter of the haves versus the have nots. Chico State has most of what they need for their level in Division II, at least in the CCAA. Arizona has what they need for their level in Division I. It's just that Chico State has a lot fewer resources than Arizona does. And it's also a matter of about three inches and thirty-five pounds.

"You want to come?" Clink asks me.

And for the next four months, not more than an hour will pass when I'm not thinking about the game.

Excitement builds as the van approaches the university. We pull into the parking lot. The players' eyes are wide upon first sighting of the Richard Jefferson Practice Facility. I, too, am in awe—reminded of the first time I left Mississippi and saw the Chicago skyline—the first city I had ever seen in real life. A few steps into the practice facility (not to be confused with a gym), scrubbed and shining like a hospital operating room, reminds me of a quote by F. Scott Fitzgerald: "The rich are very different from you and me."

I watch Coach Gabriel as he walks on the court with his arms wrapped around the broad shoulders of Isaiah Ellis, and I think of all the times in the last month I have seen Coach Gabriel down on his hands and knees, exhaustion on his face not so much from basketball but the arrival of his new baby girl, wiping sweat off the Acker floor. I recall the story about how Coach Blake and Coach Gabriel take turns doing the teams laundry when they're on the road, and a story about the night Coach Gabriel drove around downtown Los Angeles looking for a coin-operated laundromat after a game against Cal State Los Angeles—which was played in front of 34 people.

Coach Clink has to fundraise to help pay Coach Gabriel's salary. The money Chico State receives from this game will go to him. He has recently gotten married and has a new born. He's barely making it. The other assistant coach doesn't receive any compensation for his work. He works as a bartender at Round Table to make ends meet, and he's a 28-year-old undergraduate. The program does not have much scholarship money to offer. Clink takes the money he has in the scholarship pool and spreads it out the best way he can to field a competitive team not unlike a general manager for a pro team does with a budget and salary cap. Clink doesn't have academic advisors. Coach Gabriel handles that. His team trainers are graduate students in the Kinesiology department. He has one strength coach who is also working toward his MA in kinesiology. He has a few unpaid student team managers. The coaches take turns driving vans to the games, and chartered buses are only allowed if the team advances to the Division II NCAA tournament. When they play their team rival, Humboldt State—which is four and a half hours away, but usually six because of the weather—with a

7:30 p.m. tip, they will drive back immediately after the game and not arrive home until 3 a.m.

Then there's the matter of attendance. The 2013-2014 Arizona basketball season brought 258,749 fans to their games: 12,982 a game. Acker gymnasium, where the Chico State Wildcats play, has a capacity of 1,997. Chico State, when they won the CCAA outright their first time, had 1,992 fans present. Their opening game last season against Dominican brought in 670 fans. Against their rival Humboldt State: 943. In the CCAA Tournament championship on a neutral court against Cal Poly Pomona: 446. In the first round game of the NCAA Division II tournament against California Baptist: 477.

Not once have I ever heard anyone associated with the team complain.

I get down to the basketball court. A long row of Arizona basketball jerseys hanging above beckons me forward like a siren calling sailors to a rock. I instantly think of the advertisements hanging on the walls of Acker gym back home: Les Schwab Tires, Carl's Jr., Chico Electric, and Madison Bear Garden.

My jaw drops as I look at names on the back of the storied jerseys that have filled my basketball narrative for the last thirty years: Iguodala, Frye, Walton, Jefferson, Arenas, Kerr, Stoudamire, Dickerson, Terry, Simon, Gardner, Bibby, and Elliot. I try to conceal my wonder, but why bother. At this very moment I have become an official Division II basketball tourist, no longer the detached, objective writer I'm pretending to be.

The only other time I've felt such awe was when I stood in front of the Elgin Marbles at the British Museum—the collection of classical Greek marble sculptures taken from the temple of Parthenon and the Acropolis of Athens that inspired my writing hero, the poet John Keats, to write his greatest works. I pull myself together and take a seat against the wall.

A handsome man with a camera walks in. He looks as if he might have gotten lost and ended up here rather than the golf course. He approaches Clink. They shake hands. I hear him tell Clink that Coach Lavin sends his apologies, but "he's about an hour out." My heart skips a beat. *The* Coach

Steve Lavin? He had always been one of my favorites, in the company of Gene Keady, Nolan Richardson, and Bobby Knight.

The handsome man with the camera takes a seat beside me.

"JB Long," he says and sticks out a hand. "I'm going to be calling the game tonight."

"Carson Medley," I respond. "Anything you want to know about the team?"

We spend the next half an hour talking about our players. We also talk about JB's road to becoming an announcer. Before leaving, he tells me to meet to up with him before the game, says he will introduce me to Coach Lavin.

I've been dying to take a shot on one of the goals so I can add it to my collection. For the last twenty-five years I've gone out of my way to take shots on goals and play on courts all across the country. I once drove across country with my camera and Larry Bird basketball taking shots with both ball and camera on outside goals all the way from San Francisco to New Orleans. I must take a shot here, but practice is wrapping up. All the players and the coaches meet at center court to take their pregame ritual half-court shot. Nobody comes close to making one. I'm pretending to write in my journal, praying, really, that I'll be invited to take a shot. Sure enough, I hear Clink's tires-on-gravel voice say: "Hey, Mississippi Flash, want to take a shot?"

I play it off cool and detached. I can see it written in the players' eyes. The writer? He'll be lucky if he can hit the backboard. Little do they know that I had earned the nickname Mississippi Flash for a reason—having played with Lindsey Hunter at one point—yes, almost thirty years ago.

I put down my notebook. Take off my glasses. I bounce the ball back and forth a few times between my legs. The players cheer me on. Several of them are filming me. I stand behind the "A" at center court and take a few more bounces, spin the ball in my hands, take a few steps forward, and let the ball fly.

I count "One Mississippi, Two Mississippi" followed by the sound of the ball dropping through the net. The team, the coaches, the trainer,

I, go wild. The shot is pure and true. So is the moment. Leo Tolstoy said, "Happiness is only real when shared." I am happy. We are all happy. I have been playing basketball for 34 years, almost every day of my life, and this is the sweetest shot, the best moment, I've ever shared on a court. I consider it an omen of what's to come tonight and what's to come this season. I think the players do, too. Who knew the writer could shoot?

I could not do that again in a million tries. Nor will I ever try.

CHAPTER 37

Man-Bun: University of Arizona Exhibition Game

SHARING A ROOM WITH CLINK moments before leaving for a game against the University of Arizona is the privileged glimpse into the personal space of a man preparing to do battle. Clink doesn't talk much. He talks even less when preparing for a game. He showers, shaves, puts on his suit, sits on the bed, and looks over his play sheet. After a few minutes he looks over at me: "Let's go."

We get on the vans and nobody says a word. Most of the players listen to music on their headphones and gaze out the window. The van is full of nerves. I'm nervous, and all I have to do is sit here, watch, and write. The two vans carrying the players pull into the McKale parking lot about two hours before tip-off. A line is already snaking around the ticket office.

"You see that line," Coach Gabriel says from behind the wheel. "All those fans in red are lined up to see you play."

Really, though, all those fans in red are lined up to see Coach Miller unveil his new mystery team. We slip into the McKale Center like it's no big deal, but we all know it's a big deal. The only person who doesn't think it's a big deal is Clink.

An older man dressed like an usher sees my press pass and shows me to the press table. I set up shop by Mike Baca, who does the radio play-by-play, and look around. I see the talked about Arizona freshman Allonzo Trier for the first time. I've seen and been around a lot of great basketball players in my life. As a writer, I've always found basketball players and, particularly, basketball coaches to be the most interesting human beings in any profession to study and write about. I can immediately see the star quality of Trier. This will be his college debut, but in the pregame shoot around he maneuvers like a veteran. I've studied his game all summer. One of my favorite players, Corey Silverstrom, will be guarding him. I've been giving him Trier trash-talk since July.

The student section seems to be equally in awe of Trier, and the entire team, actually. The student section is already rowdy and boisterous, teeming with energy, and tip-off is more than an hour away. I'm immediately swept away in a reverie that takes me back to the Ole Miss football tailgating climate of The Grove in Oxford, Mississippi, where I came of age. The kind of mood that's building here has that of an SEC football game. This game, in fact, will be the closest I've been to SEC football since leaving Mississippi twenty years.

I watch in wonder as the Chico State players come out to shoot around and warm up. Chico State has many young players, several of them having redshirted together and playing in their first official game since redshirting 13 months ago. This is also their first time to travel together with the team. Their eyes are filled with wonder. I catch them occasionally looking up into the bleachers, taking in the moment, realizing the rarity of the moment that comes to only a fortunate, small percentage of the populace. Our players steal glances at the Arizona players. The Arizona players, meanwhile, seem to be teasing the student section with their slow movements and sleepy eyes, the layups instead of dunks. The Arizona players have the swagger of young men who've just gotten out of a hot tub and are wearing bathrobes, a relaxed feeling of being comfortable at home.

I spot JB across court and go to see him. We shake hands. He asks me a few more questions with Coach Lavin—the man who was given the keys to the UCLA kingdom in 1997 when he was only 32 (after working his way up in seven different positions from 1991)—and tell him briefly about my project. He is interested. Coach Lavin himself had been a Division II basketball player at San Francisco State. In fact, Coach Lavin even played in Acker twice back in the 1983-1984 season, and even played in one of the great games in Chico State history when San Francisco State beat the Wildcats in double overtime.

Coach Lavin has the kind of personality that makes you feel as if he has immediately accepted you and taken you into his fold. He seems like the kind of adult who was loved and supported by a caring mother and father when he was growing up, the kind of parents who told him as a young boy that he could be and do anything he wanted to when he grew up—even coach basketball.

Our conversation turns to writing and inevitably his father, a Bay Area legend in the writing world. His father, Cap Lavin, wrote 19 books and was the co-founder of the Bay Area Writing Project at UC Berkeley, where I went to college. I recall reading an article in *Sports Illustrated* about Coach Lavin back in 1997, an article that was just as much about his father as it was the young coach. Coach Lavin gives me his phone number and asks that I text him throughout the game with information about our guys. I also ask him to come around after the game and meet our guys.

Coach Lavin is a part of the tapestry that makes up college basketball, too young yet to be a legend, but he has worked with the legends: John Wooden, Pete Newell, Gene Keady, Coach K, and Jerry Tarkanian—just to name a few. Coach Wooden and Coach Newell were always a phone call away to offer the young Coach Lavin advice when he was at UCLA. Coach Lavin, after being fired from UCLA despite five appearances in the Sweet Sixteen and putting more than a baker's dozen players into the NBA, would find his way into the broadcast booth. Not long after being fired from UCLA, he took a walk on Venice Beach with another basketball legend, Bill Walton, who pitched the idea to Coach Lavin that he enters the broadcast booth. After a successful stint with ABC and ESPN (and also being mentored by the John Wooden of broadcasting, Brent Musburger) Coach Lavin went 3,000 miles away from the West Coast to the Left Coast to try and bring the storied Big East St. John's program back to life. It didn't take him long to bring The Red Storm back into prominence, get them back into the top 25, and make the NCAA tournament twice. Along the way, Coach Lavin battled and defeated cancer, married the beautiful and talented actress Mary Ann Jarou, and would get fired despite going 81-55 in six seasons. But Coach Lavin always lands on his feet. Now he's broadcasting games for the Pac-12 Network and Fox Sports. Every season his name pops up in the college basketball rumor mill as a head coach candidate, but Coach Lavin has high standards: his third tour of duty will be someplace special. Yes, the Wildcats have to meet Coach Lavin. It's part of their education.

The visitor's locker room is much smaller than I expected. Nervous energy mixed with bad lighting makes the locker room feel even smaller. The bathroom stall is a revolving door, the toilet flushing on loop. Only one player, the senior Tanner Giddings who had transferred from Fresno State, has ever played in an environment like this. Giddings left Fresno State to get away from this kind of atmosphere. One of the other seniors, Christopher Magalotti, will be getting his first start. He will face the 6-foot-11 star Kaleb Tarczewski—nicknamed Zeus—who many thought would be playing in the NBA after this season. The other senior who will get the start, Drew Kitchens, has experience but not on a stage this large. Jalen McFerren, the true sophomore, will also get his first start. Robert Duncan, a junior, is the other starter. He has entered the season with great leadership expectations, and he's just as talented as anyone on the Arizona team. I believe he'll send the Arizona fans home thinking twice about the level of talent at the Division II level.

The coaches don't deliver a St. Crispin's Day speech. No need. The players are as fired up as they can get. The players jog down the long tunnel and stand outside the door leading to the floor. Outside the fans are screaming. The court feels like a spotlight is shining down on it. The players run out of the tunnel to a chorus of taunts from the student sections ("Chico's not a state!"). I take my seat at the cramped media table. I look up into the arena, a sea of white hair and red shirts. I'm enjoying my Division II moment of being a writer following a sports team, thinking of how proud Norman Mailer, George Plimpton, Willie Morris, and Hunter S. Thompson, and the man whose book inspired this book—John Feinstein—would be of me. I sit there, dazed. The lighting is mesmerizing, not the fluorescent lighting in so many gyms that makes the fan feel like he's in an interrogation room, but an LED light system that has a spotlight effect on the floor and make the upper decks darker. The upper deck seats are red and the lower level seats are blue. A red block "A" is stitched on all the padded seats.

I'm in such awe that the pen in my hand is frozen.

I can see Coach Lavin across the court. I send him a text: "Keep your eye on number 5 Robert Duncan. D II Pistol Pete." He writes me back: "Eyes on him." I will send him messages about our players, random facts that might make for interesting color commentary, throughout the night:

Magz's mother was a super model and his father was a professional soccer player and they met in a Rome disco. Giddings learned his jump shot from Mike Farmer, the third pick in the 1958 NBA draft right behind Oscar Robertson. Silverstrom was once the second ranked Call of Duty player in the world. Coach Clink used to break dance in junior high school. Coach Blake works at Round Table Pizza during the week and takes classes toward his BA in the day.

The starting lineups are announced beneath swirling lights. This feels more like the 1997 Bulls being announced at the United Center than an exhibition basketball game in early November. 14,268 fans (only about 30 Chico State fans) are going wild. Chico State will not play in front of this many fans combined throughout the entire season. The game is lopsided from the start. Arizona takes a quick 12-0 lead. At one point, Chico State cuts the lead 17-13 with 10:34 left in the half. The lead at the half is only 37-24. Chico State has a lot of confidence during the halftime break. They've played poorly yet the game is still in reach. Clink, though, true to his word, is not playing to simply win: he's playing to give all of his players experience. Nor is Clink playing to keep the game close and respectable.

Chico State comes out going for the jugular in the second half. I can tell by the way Robert Duncan was brooding during half-time that he was going to come out and make someone pay. It's at the 18:14 minute mark when all the messages I'd been texting to Coach Lavin (*Keep your eyes on Duncan. Any second now*) reach fruition.

A lazy pass is made to York, and Duncan extends his right arm and bats it away.

Duncan gets the first step on York. He pushes the ball down the court and, blinders on, drives into the paint and leaps from a couple feet past the free throw line. York goes up for the block. Duncan doesn't flinch. He throws down the dunk. The video goes viral. Not for the athleticism of the steal, the lightning speed, and the thunderous dunk. No, it goes viral because of Duncan's hair. Websites around the world pick up on it: "Posterized: Gabe York Dunked On By Man-Bun." Everyone at the media table looks at the person next to them, jaw hanging, eyes popped, with that dazed expression of "What just happened?" I'm not surprised. I've seen Duncan make plays like every day in practice. The 14,268 fans are shocked, too, emitting a collective "Ooh-ahh" like the kind crowds make on the Fourth of July upon seeing the first colorful explosion in the black sky.

Chico State will keep the game close until the 14:27 mark, 47-37.

Arizona, though, will put their pedal to the metal and put the game away on a 36-13 run. In the end, Gabe York, Ryan Anderson, Kaleb Tarczewski, Mark Tollefsen, Kadeem Allen, Parker Jackson-Cartwright, and Allonso Trier—all of whom would become Pac-12 household names as the regular season progressed and Arizona became viable contenders for the National Championship—proved too much. The final score was Arizona 90, Chico State 54. Every Chico State Wildcat played.

After the game, Coach Lavin came around. I introduce him to some of the players. Later, when we get into the van, I will have to tell the players the interesting coaching history and life of Coach Lavin. I have to remember: a lot of these young Wildcats weren't even born, and the others were still in diapers, when Coach Lavin was doing his thing down in Westwood. Despite the loss, the sprits in the van remain high. The only one who seems downtrodden is Duncan. He had not played poorly, but he had turned the ball over a lot. And Robert Duncan had become famous.

All the players are checking their phones. Their media sites are flooded with Duncan's—the Man Bun's—dunk. It will be the biggest attraction in sports that night. Duncan will be famous for the next week, but soon after nobody outside of the CCAA will know Robert Duncan from Dunkin' Donuts.

PART IV

The Season

CHAPTER 38

Regular Season: Friday the 13th

TONIGHT IS THE OPENING OF the regular season against Montana State University-Billings. It's also Friday the 13th. While I await the opening tip to start the regular season, it's announced that in Paris, 130 people have been massacred by ISIS. How could something like this happen in the City of Light? If it can happen there, it can happen anywhere. I love sports because the only massacre that occurs is when a team gets beaten badly, or when a team gets "whupped" as they say down in my neck of the woods. Only pride is hurt. A taste of humility is good for everyone.

Ironically, it was an injury in the first game of last year that made Rob Duncan a "star." It was less than a year ago when Duncan would make his first start (and then another) and earn MVP honors at the 14th Annual

Sonoma State Ron Logsdon Basketball Classic. Tonight, Friday the 13th, Silverstrom will get his chance to shine. Another Chico State star will be born. But here's the thing: Clink doesn't recruit stars. He recruits players that, if given the chance, will shine like stars. His players are always prepared and ready to go. Silverstrom gets his start and makes the best of it. McFerren, too. Both these young men are showing extreme confidence after hanging with Arizona's stars just five days prior.

Clink's bench is deep. How deep? In the pregame interview with Clink, Baca asked him about Marvin Timothy. "Timothy will get his opportunity. But he's playing behind three other posts." That's depth. Not many teams in the CCAA or Division II have such a long bench.

The game doesn't start as hoped for. Baca says it best: "Their defense was better against the University of Arizona."

All is coming undone. Where is the beauty of this team that I've witnessed for the last three weeks?

Ellis picks up a quick third foul. A ball strikes Magz on the head and rolls out of bounds.

McFerren keeps us alive with nine points and a string of defensive rebounds.

The Wildcats are down 31-19, fast, to a team who won five games the previous year, and who only have eight players dressed for the game. The Wildcats hit five quick points. Timothy blocks a shot. McFerren scoops up another rebound: "He's willing his team back into the game," Baca cries over the air waves.

Montana State University-Billings has Chico State pinned on a 12-4 run. Clink calls a timeout at the 31-19 mark. After the timeout, everything changes. The game, hopefully the season, will never be the same. The Wildcats have a 5-0 spurt, followed by a Silverstrom to Timothy feed.

The points kept coming. A 10-0 run.

Silverstrom hits consecutive threes. It's all over. Chico State goes wild. Giddings and McFerren score 10 straight, cut the lead to two, and Silverstrom gets his chance. He'll hit three three-pointers in the final four minutes. This starts a 37-4 run. Silverstrom will finish 6-of-8 from downtown. As the game progresses, and the lead keeps building, McFerren becomes a 5-foot-10 verb. He shakes. He stutters. He dives. He jumps. He gets the breakaway steal and rim-rocking dunk.

Chico State will do to Montana State University-Billings in the second half what Arizona had done to the Wildcats. But despite the big lead, Clink keeps screaming: "Keep guarding! Play with your feet! Be good defensively!"

The game is never over until it's over and even then tomorrow becomes today. The season has not really started because for Clink it never ended.

CHAPTER 39

Clink's Agony

WEDNESDAY, NOVEMBER 18

I HEAD OVER TO CLINK's office with my notebook under my arm and carrying two cups of coffee. When I get to his office, Coach Blake is just leaving. Clink and Coach Blake look like they've not slept in days. I hand Clink his coffee. I feel bad for not bringing Coach Blake any. I offer him mine. He furrows his brow. He seems tempted. "I don't drink coffee," he says. "I've never had it."

"What?" I say. I can't imagine a life without coffee. Maybe that's why he's struggling to complete his BA. I know I couldn't have earned my degree without coffee, right about the time my twenty-year addiction began.

"Well, I'll take a sip," he says. "Do you have a cup or something?" The last thing I want to do is share coffee.

"You know, never mind. Next time," he says. Coach Blake hands me a copy of the scouting report against Dominican—their next opponent—and leaves. Clink downs the coffee not seeming to notice that it's still piping hot. He exhales and steam comes out. Clink looks like a man in agony, certainly not the man I knew back in June. He looks a lot thinner than he did one month ago. Dark circles surround his red eyes. "I usually drop 8 to 12 pounds once the season starts," he tells me. "I can always tell when I put on one of my suits that I maybe wore to a wedding in the summer and then don't put it on again until we start games. It fits much looser in February than it does in July. Once practice and games start my metabolism speeds up. I don't eat very much from Thursday through Saturday nights during the season. Stress makes me lose my appetite."

I want to make the guy laugh rather than hound him about last week's game. I ask him the question that's been burning in my mind since last Friday: What did you tell the guys when you called the timeout after the Montana State run that put the Wildcats down 31-19?"

"I just told them we weren't playing with enough tenacity. We weren't able to come off ball screens. They did a great job defending them. I told them we weren't executing our game plan. They just came out and slapped us in our face."

Clink bends over and rubs his eyes again. "I told the players we lacked purpose, and we had to find purpose in everything we're doing." He starts to come alive. I think he realizes he scorched his tongue. He sits up straight, takes another sip of coffee, cautious this time. He scoots his chair over to me and relaxes into the conversation. "We can't take quick shots. We have to play with purpose.

We're young and we make mistakes. It might take losing some games to learn." He takes another sip of coffee. "We finally started playing the way I knew we were capable of playing. I'm asking a lot of these guys. Asking them to do mid-season kind of stuff. And we're playing good teams on the road. We have a lot of room for improvement."

I ask Clink how he deals with a super confident personality like Silverstrom's after coming off such a big game. His first start and he scores 23 points. "I actually had a talk with Corey today. I let him know that Drew and Rob were still going to start. That an injury should never take a guy out of the starting lineup."

Coach Gabriel slips into the office. Normally, he's smiling and friendly. Today he looks serious. He sits down at his laptop. He types feverishly. "Tomorrow's scouting report?" I ask.

"Academy of Art," he says. "Tuesday."

"What do you think of all the man-bun Robert Duncan publicity this week?" I ask Coach Clink.

"I don't care."

I ask Clink if he looks for patterns during a game. "What do you mean?" he says.

"Instead of trying to anticipate what the other teams or players are going to do, have you been around for so long that you can detect patterns?"

"I don't try and predict what the other team will do," he says. "I'm only concerned with us. I only care about the things that we do. What we need to work on. How we prepare. Basketball is so unpredictable. It's all about how we prepare."

"There's this great speech from Hamlet," I tell him. "God controls everything—even something as trivial as a sparrow's death. Everything will work out as it is destined. If something is supposed to happen now, it will. If it's supposed to happen later, it won't happen now. What's important is to be prepared. Since nobody knows anything about what he leaves behind, then what does it mean to leave early? Let it be."

Clink kicks back in his chair, hands folded behind his head. He looks out the window and ponders the Hamlet quote with the same look I've seen in his eyes when writing on the white board moments before a game. "There are so many things that we can't control, so I only worry about the things we can control," he says. "That's why during the off-season I never look at what players are going to other teams. If I were to care about what the other teams were doing and worried about them, I'd go crazy. I only worry about what we're doing. I only worry about what I can control. We can always control how prepared we are. I don't dive into another team until it's time to play them. Then I try and know everything about them. We prepare ourselves for how we play, and we prepare for what our opponent is going to do. This is something that was done at every program I've ever been in, but Bob Williams was the best at preparing for opponents. He wouldn't overdo it with the players. He would give them just enough information to get them ready for what type of defense, offense, player tendencies, that were coming. But in his mind he had a plan and knew what he was going to run or what defense he was going to use to win. Sometimes I think we give our players too much information on our opponents, but it's better to be over prepared than the opposite."

Clink looks pained.

"You doing okay, Coach?" I ask.

"I just wish I enjoyed this more," he says. "All I can think about is winning. I can't shut my brain off."

"If you lose, so what?" I ask.

"Yeah, easy for you to say."

And it is.

"I don't like to fail," he says

"Would the pressure, the fear of failure, be less if you had a bad team?" I ask.

He doesn't have a bad team, though.

"I want these guys to fulfill their potential. I get this awful fear and anxiety about not doing that, about not tapping into that potential. You know who has the best job in the world?"

I shake my head. Ironically, up until last March, I thought it was Clink.

"Steve Lavin. I asked him if he thought about getting back into coaching, and he said he might like to someday. He's nuts. He has the best job in the world. All he has to do is talk about basketball. Don't get me wrong. I love coaching. I love the relationships I have with the players and my assistants. I love practice. I love building teams." He pauses. "But I hate the games. I don't enjoy the games, and I don't enjoy the days leading up to the games. When I was an assistant coach, I would get excited before games." He shakes his head. "Not now. I put too much pressure on myself to win. I can't shut my brain off from playing out every little scenario. I'm a pessimist. The power of negative thinking. That's how I prepare. I prepare for the worst thing that can happen. I play out every scenario."

Clink stares out the window where outside students walk by, orange and red leaves falling. He gazes out the window like he gazed out the hotel window and into the ocean of automobile lots in Arizona. "We have Dominican tomorrow and then Academy of Art and then, bam, Seattle Pacific. Then I'm thinking about Simpson University the following night. It never ends."

"It's a lot of pressure to have a bullseye on your back," I say.

"What do you mean?" he asks.

"Being the team to beat."

"That's not where the pressure comes from. The pressure comes from me. I can't enjoy any of this. I battle with this every year. I enjoy traveling. I enjoy being around the team, the guys. All the self-imposed pressure. It's just not a healthy way to live. If only I could just turn my mind off and learn how to enjoy this. I always wonder how other people deal with this pressure. But here's the thing. If I were coaching at the University of Arizona, I wouldn't feel any more pressure than I do here. Look, it's not about the division level, job security, or the money—it's about wanting to be great at what you do. I put a lot of pressure on myself and us to be great."

Only one game into the regular season and I'm seeing the internal hell that Coach Clink warned me about, the prison he creates for himself, a prison that he has built. A prison where he is both the jailed and the jailor. The warden of his own hell.

"I don't know how I can do this for another twenty years," he says. Here is a side of Clink closed off to the public. For the first time I have known him, he seems vulnerable.

"You know what my ideal career is?" he asks. I shake my head.

"To be a musician who lives by the beach and never has to travel because everyone comes to me."

He laughs and looks at his watch. It's 12:56 p.m. Time for practice.

"I want to be great."

He takes a deep breath.

"Take Sean Miller for example. He has an enormous amount of pressure on him. He has thousands more critics than I do, but I guarantee that the pressure we feel is no different. He wants to be successful, and so do I. There's no difference in how badly we want to win. This is what people on the outside don't understand about coaching. Just because someone coaches high school basketball or Division II basketball or JC basketball or even in the NBA, it doesn't change the expectations we place on of ourselves. I'm talking about the coaches that live it. There are a lot of coaches at all levels that treat it like a job and can go home and sleep and be just fine after a loss. But I'm talking about the ones who make coaching their life. The pressure is felt just as much when you live to be great at what you do. It doesn't matter how much money you make or how many people come to your games. When you live to be great at something then you put a self-imposed pressure on yourself to see it through. And it hangs over me like a dark cloud. But that cloud is what drives me. One time after a game at Acker in the 2012-13 season, Jay Flores had just gotten done playing professionally in Mexico and he was back in Chico for a while hanging out and coming to games. We won a game that night, and he and I were walking out to the parking lot and talking. He said, 'Great win.' I said, 'Yeah, what a relief!' He looked at me and said, 'What an awful way of looking at it.' I put my arm around him as we walked and said, 'Someday you'll understand.'"

McFerren stands at the Red Door. He's lacing up his shoes. "I came up with your nickname,"

I tell him.

"What's that?" McFerren asks.

"The Verb. You're a man of action." I show him an excerpt from my book. "McFerren slashes. McFerren cuts. McFerren pushes. McFerren crashes." He smiles. McFerren might be young, and he might be great, but he's humble. He knows he must improve every day. He always reminds me of this. "Perfection, Jalen. You were 11-of-11 from the line."

He is the first player in the Clink era to do this. He shakes his head. "I got a lot to work on," he says, smiling. McFerren always seems serious, his face a little cloudy, but when he smiles it's like the sun breaking through a storm cloud that warms you to the bone. He has a lot of responsibility for a sophomore juggling school, work, and basketball.

I walk back into the gym and it feels like home. Justin Briggs, as usual, has a serious look on his face and is working hard. He seems to always be working. Ricky is already sweating, his shirt drenched, running around and retrieving loose balls. Duncan is spinning the ball in his hand, smiling as always. His eyes have a twinkle to them. Hard to believe this guy is an assassin. I have a feeling he's going to explode against the Penguins, their next opponent.

I go and take my usual seat at the scorer's table. Keith Datu is sulking. No wonder. He has two big ice packs taped to his knees.

"Wait until you're my age," I tell him.

CHAPTER 40

172 Fans: Dominican University

DOMINICAN UNIVERSITY, HOME OF THE Penguins, is a private institution founded in 1890 and located in San Rafael (birthplace of mountain biking), about 12 miles from San Francisco. Only 1,628 undergraduate students and 579 graduate students attend the university. Primarily a liberal arts school, the student to faculty ration is 10:1. Dominican is also the only school in the country (at the time of this book) that has a joint BFA dance program led by a master choreographer.

The Penguins are already battle tested. They've played Nevada (lost 52-82) in Reno and Fresno State (lost 55-77) in exhibition matches. They took Sonoma State to the ropes in a loss (63-68) and beat a good Cal State Monterey Bay team (83-73). In the last four years—years that include the Wildcats' four straight NCAA Championship Tournament bids and two CCAA titles, only 10 teams have beaten the Wildcats in Acker. One of those 10 was Dominican who beat the Wildcats last year. The Penguins have been picked to finish 9th in the 14-team PacWest Conference this season. Clink doesn't care whether they're picked to finish first or last.

Duncan and Kitchens, after sitting out the season opener, are back. Earlier in the Clink's Corner pregame radio show, Clink told Baca that "We haven't been practicing bad, but we have to work on our level of intensity." The Wildcats were definitely more intense, but they gave up a lot more points than Clink was comfortable with. The final score was 96-75, the most points Chico State has had against a Division II team since 2007, but the most important number to Clink was 75.

The game sounds good offensively from the start of Baca's call: "Giddings into the post to begin." Clink's goal was 35 post entry passes this game. "McFerren weaves in and out and through traffic…Duncan scores coast-to-coast…" Baca sings.

Duncan is indeed a coast-to-coast player (he will score a team-high 27 points, 5 assists, 1 blocked shot, and go 9-of-11 from the line). He's also emerging as the Pistol Pete type of player that I've detected all along. His passing skills are superior. He sees things, patterns, movements, that nobody else can. He's able to predict, too, almost as if he can see into the future and tell how the play will develop before it happens.

There's a moment in the game when Priest comes off a screen perfectly facing Duncan as he cuts and Duncan whips the ball to him. The pass is so fast that it catches Priest off guard despite that he was already anticipating and in position to catch the ball. There are other moments of brilliance, too, moments that, sadly, the rest of the fans in the basketball world will never see because ESPN doesn't care about Division II ball. Only 172 will get to see the brilliance on this evening. However, if the masses could see these plays, they would care.

Giddings makes a gorgeous pass to his roommate Ellis, and when Ellis gets knocked to the ground and slides back to the wall, Giddings sprints over to pick him up. Harris, the Howard Roark-bulldog-barbed wire player on the team, has a knack for getting into his opponent's head. I just hope that he doesn't try and get into Clink's head or there might be trouble. "How many love taps does he give a game?" Baca says. Harris quickly huddles the team together. Clink screams consistently throughout the game: "Corey, Corey, Corey." And when he's not yelling at Silverstrom, he's shouting: "Get in your stance. Don't let up."

Ellis reveals tonight what he's capable of doing. The Wildcats sixth man, a role he accepts, scores 20 points, going 7-of-10 from the field. Silverstrom continues his hot streak going 5-of-9 and 4-of-7 from three-point land.

Both he and Duncan combine for 7 turnovers, though, that put an asterisk by their performances.

In the postgame conference with Baca—Clink's Corner—Clink seems fine with his team's performance. Baca wonders if Clink would have felt more comfortable with a 76-55 win rather than 96-75. Clink laughs. "For the first six or seven minutes we played with purpose," Clink says. "Then we had a few hiccups and our defense unraveled. We had to grind defensively. We had to hang our hat on this and guard hard for 40 minutes."

I wonder how a team can do both? Can they? It seems that something has to give. How can a team be superior on both ends? What is more important: Scoring goals or keeping goals from being scored? Clink believes that keeping goals from being scored is more important. "I feel that you can always control your defense," he tells me. "You can't always control your offense.

Some nights, players aren't going to shoot it well, or the other team may take you out of what you're trying to do offensively, but you can always be good defensively. I think this goes back to myself as a player. I knew that certain games it would be hard for me to score, but I could be one of the best defenders."

CHAPTER 41

Office Hours

NOVEMBER 20

THE FOLLOWING MORNING, I GO down to Clink's office for an interview. I stop to look out the window that's frosted over and looks out to where the campus pool used to be. I hear Clink walking down the hall. The dark countenance on his face from last week seems to have lifted.

"Nice to see you smiling," I say.

I'm shocked by how much thinner he looks. The black circles around his eyes have deepened, as if he's wearing eye liner.

He stands next to me and looks out at what used to be the university pool. He shakes his head. "Look at those weeds," he says. "You know those apocalypse movies where everything's beautiful one moment, and then in a flash everything's been demolished and all you see is smoke and rubble?" I nod. "That's what this pool reminds me of. When I was a student here, the place was gorgeous. Students were always out sunning by the pool. People were having a blast jumping off the high dive."

I strain my eyes to see out the window that I imagine has been spray painted so recruits can't see through it. It's hard to believe that in this old, dilapidated, leaky-ceiling building one of the best basketball teams, cross-country teams, and baseball teams in the country reside. How can these programs do so much yet with so little? At least that's what I used to ask. Now I know.

We walk down to Clink's office. No clutter here. No paper. Just laptops, an eraser board, and a plasma television nailed to the wall. Coach Blake is hunched over his laptop, silent, scrutinizing last night's game. Clink takes a seat and resumes watching game film on his laptop. Coach Gabriel comes in with sandwiches. He gives Clink back a dime and some pennies.

"Keep it," Clink barks.

Coach Gabriel needs every extra dime he can get. Every bit counts when a coach must fundraise to pay his head assistant.

"I have to fundraise thousands of dollars so my head assistant can make a livable wage," Clink says. "Lots of teams in our league have two paid full-time assistants. We have one, and we have to piece it together. This is the biggest source of frustration for me. Sure, I want all of my assistants to learn here and then leave for a better coaching job. But I don't want them to have to leave here for a worse job just because it pays them more. That's why I fundraise and pump money into the position."

Coach Gabriel sits down and starts working on his Academy of Art scouting report. Clink is already halfway through his sandwich. Cool Marvin comes in and takes a seat. He flips open his laptop. A minute later Duncan comes in. "Coach, I think I hurt myself again," Duncan says. Clink leans back and listens. "My legs were cramping up really bad after halftime."

"You talk to the trainer?"

"Not yet."

Duncan, his long curls dangling (he only wears the bun during the game) beneath a ball cap, takes off his hat and sits next to Clink. "Here's what I want to show you, Rob," Clink says. Coach Blake can't help but make a comment. "No dribbling off your heel, Rob," he says, but his words are unheard. Coach Blake tries to be light, but he just can't do it well. He's a serious dude.

McFerren comes in. He wants to see his dunk. Coach Blake pulls it up on the big screen. McFerren watches it over and over again, holding his iPhone up to film it. When you're 5-foot-10 and dunk like that, it deserves to be seen in front of more than 172 people. And since the rim-rocker came with less than a minute left, and the beating had already melted Dominican's Igloo, there were only a handful of fans watching. I stand in the background and watch the teaching happening between Clink and his star student, and how Cool Marvin waits for his feedback from the professor. Clink's office has the feeling of a professor's office hour, and reminds me of my years teaching composition, only my students didn't really want to improve their writing. They were only concerned about improving their grades. These players are really concerned with improving.

Sure, their "high grades" result in playing time. There is a motivation and incentive, but whereas my students would do whatever it took to "improve" until the end of the semester, knowing they'd never see me again, Coach Clink's students will be with him for at least four years and most of them for five.

CHAPTER 42

Roller Derby: Academy of Art

I STARTED FEELING OLD WHEN the sons of my favorite childhood baseball players started retiring. Now I know I'm getting old when players I used to heckle when they were college players, and I was a college student, become head coaches. The Wildcats next opponent is Academy of Art, a good team led by fourth year coach Julius Barnes who was the third best player on the 2002 Stanford team. He was only third because the two best players ahead of him, Casey Jacobsen and Curtis Borchardt, were drafted into the NBA. Barnes's brother is the assistant coach.

Winning has not been a tradition for Academy of Art Urban Knights (who don't have a mascot, as far as I know) basketball, but Coach Barnes is trying to change that. Last season he coached Academy of Art to its best season ever. They went 5-20 on the year. The PacWest is one of the tougher conferences, consisting of preseason top 20 teams such as California Baptist and Azusa Pacific.

Academy of Art, located in San Francisco, has been around since 1929 and has per their website "always existed on the vanguard of innovation and creativity." It seems only fitting, then, that they would have a good basketball team, for basketball is just that: innovative and creative. Students have a wide option of majors here from Animation and Visual Effects to Game Development to Interior Design to Jewelry and Metal Arts. Most of the players for Academy of Art major in Advertising or Multimedia Communications. They play all their home games in the legendary Kezar Pavilion.

The Kezar Pavilion gym, located in the Haight-Ashbury district, was built in 1924 by Willis Polk and Company. Basketball is just one of many events that have taken place here. The longest tenant was the Bay Bombers of the original Roller Derby League. Back in the 1960s, Charlie O'Connell ("Mr. Roller Derby") and Joanie Weston ("Blonde Bomber/ Blonde Amazon") attracted more than 19 million television viewers a week with broadcasts to more than 1,200 stations worldwide. By the mid-1960s, Kezar Pavilion was one of the most famous sports venues in the world.

Back in the 80s, Clink used to spend Saturday mornings watching Roller Derby on TV. "The Bay Bombers were my team," he says. "When I was about 12 and my brother was 10, the Bombers started playing their games at the old San Jose Civic Auditorium. My parents started taking us to the roller derby on Saturday nights. It was some of the best memories of my child-hood—Joanie Weston, Bill Groll, and Frank Apadaca were my heroes. One time later in high school, after the roller derby was dying out, I went to a box-ing match in San Jose with some buddies. I saw Frank Apadaca in the crowd. I went up to him after and met him. It was like meeting a childhood hero."

Kezar Pavilion, like the game of basketball, is simple: a peaked roof with shingles on top. It has the feel of a high school gym, even though, from a distance, it has the look of art deco (fitting Academy of Art plays here). Upon entering, one immediately feels the pull and spirit of the sporting history that has taken place here over the years—everything from boxing to volleyball to indoor soccer tournaments to professional female wrestling matches to Summer Pro-Am Basketball League games. I hope the young Wildcats will embrace the moment and pause to drink deeply from the air of the past. Clink, who appreciates the history behind the game of basket-ball, and a Northern California boy, will no doubt revel in the past. I just hope he can take a second to enjoy the ride, to inhale the pure joy he still feels for the game despite his internal pressure.

The game has an auspicious beginning. Duncan has to leave the court moments before tipoff. He's only wearing his warm up jersey. Is this a new ritual to go along with the man-bun? If so, it works. Duncan has another close to perfect night save the turnovers. The Wildcats struggle throughout the night, playing not to lose rather than win. Duncan, whom Baca aptly dubs "The Bail Out," keeps the Wildcats in the game. "Duncan, through the legs, splits two defenders, spins, hangs in the air, shoots— in. Unbelievable," Baca will announce more than once.

The Wildcats, despite 23 turnovers, will hang on to win by a score of 81-67. How does a team still win by double-digits with 23 turnovers? Does their offense keep them in it? Is it their defense? How do you evaluate that? Throughout the game, Baca jokes several times that the Wildcats will be having their turkey dinner in Acker on Thursday. Baca has been doing this for a long time, and he knows Clink's coaching ethic pretty well. I think even Baca is surprised with Clink's postgame announcement. "For all those fans out there," Clink says, his voice sounding like steel boots sloshing through wet gravel, "we're not taking Thanksgiving off. We had planned to practice whether we won or lost. We'll be in Acker at 9 a.m."

The Macy's Day parade, it turns out, is not a must-see for Coach Clink. Clink says that practice the day before was awful. "Balls were flying all around Acker," he says. "You play how you practice." Clink is riled up (even though his rile is controlled) because the referees were not calling any hand-check fouls during the game, a new rule this season. "We practice with hand-checks in mind. It's frustrating that the crew, who by the way is a great crew, weren't calling them." It's a strange feeling to feel uncomfortable about winning by 15, but when you view the game through the head coach's eyes, there really are such things as good losses and bad wins. This is indeed a bad win for the Wildcats, and Clink will remind them of this at the next practice.

Clink will soon find out that CCAA conference rival UC San Diego, picked to finish third in the conference behind Chico State and Cal Poly Pomona, has just knocked off nationally ranked number 4

Cal Baptist 76-67. It will be a long year. A lot will happen between now and February 12 when Clink takes the Wildcats down to San Diego, the hometown of the lone Southern Californian on the team, Drew Kitchens, to play the Tritons.

CHAPTER 43

Pace

NOVEMBER 25

ACKER GYM HAS COME TO life. The home Chico State benches and the visiting Seattle Pacific benches are out. The scorer's table is out. The fancy cushioned seat bleachers where the Acker Backers root have been pushed out. The players are warming up. A quietness hangs in the gym, a stillness, a hum. I see Magz. "Don't worry about all the turnovers last night," I tell him. "Kezar is haunted." Kitchens comes over and gives me a high five. "Yeah, that locker room was like being in *Hoosiers.* Wooden bleachers and wooden lockers. The place was huge, and nobody was there. Cold, too."

Ellis ties his shoelaces. He has a terrible, crunchy cough—sounds like he's stepping on fallen November leaves. Colds must love lungs the size of his. "Think I'm coming down with something," he says to me. Clink calls the players to the circle at midcourt. He's not happy. "Overall you were good defensively. We made some improvements. But the offense was poor." Clink has the tone of a preacher. His voice comes in waves, builds, reaches crescendo, falls, and rises again. "But the turnovers. The *turnovers.*" The players can feel the tension rising. "23 turnovers. 23 turnovers and we still scored 81 points? Let that sink in for just a moment. Do you understand how dynamic you are offensively?"

The pause which means the swelling of his ire.

"The game before you had 18 turnovers and scored 96. 23 turnovers last night and you score 81. Today we're going to work on execution. We're going to work on valuing the ball." A longer pause. Crescendo. *"How tough can you be? You've got to get tougher with the ball. Value the ball."* Clink catches his breath. "Seattle Pacific is good. They are really good. They are disciplined. They are well-coached. One of the best teams in the country. But they are not better than you. They are not more talented than you."

The players walk through their offense slowly. One unit will go through it a few times, then the other unit comes in. Clink gradually speeds everything up until they're sprinting.

"Carson," Clink yells to me, "get your notebook thing out and tally each player's turnovers." I swallow hard. Other than moving a few folding chairs and rebounding for Cool Marvin, it's my first assignment, the closest I've ever come to coaching. Duncan, Kitchens, and Magz get quick tallies. Datu walks up, ice on his knees. He's still out. "I'll get that for you, Carson," he says, seeing my struggle. Datu takes my job away from me. I'm back to being the writer again. It's better to have tallied turnovers than to have never tallied turnovers at all.

Clink works on the players moving the ball with "pace." He shouts "pace" almost as frequently as "stance" throughout the games. "Wait for your screens," he yells. "Get the ball across the split line. Split line!"

I ask Coach Gabriel what Clink means by split line. He always takes the time to explain something to me. He takes out a pen and draws on a sheet of paper. "That's a split line," he says. "The imaginary line that divides the court." When they move the ball with pace, it gets the defenders moving, rotating. Do that enough times and daylight opens up. This is what happened during the Montana State-Billings game when after the eighth pass Duncan gives the ball to Silverstrom and he rips the three. Clink stops the drill. "It's about being tough with the ball. Two dribble limit. You have to set a good ball screen." After a few more plays, Clink stops practice again. He grabs the ball from Silverstrom's hands. "You can't just lean back with the ball and hold it up when the defender is putting pressure on you," he says. "When you catch the ball, and if your defender puts his hands on you, rip his forearms off. *Rip it at your shoelaces.*" Clink gets low and swings the ball down by his shoelaces, back and forth, elbows like knives, ball swinging like a scythe cutting wheat. *"Rip it at the shoelaces. Rip his forearms off. Be tough."*

Ambrosini continues to impress me. His rips are the fiercest. Any forearm that gets in the way of those elbows will be severed. "Rip the shoelaces to alleviate pressure," Clink screams. Several of Duncan's passes bounce off the players. It's not his fault. They're great passes. "I want the guys on the sidelines to rate the ball screens," Clink says. "If you hold the screens, I guarantee you'll get a post entry."

"Rebound at another level," Coach Gabriel whispers to Timothy.

Once Clink is satisfied with their efforts, he calls them over. They huddle. "There are thousands of great players in the world," he says. "You all have your favorite players in the NBA. But it's the 7th through the 12th guys in the NBA, the ones who get traded to one team after another, who have the big time NBA careers. Why? Because they play tough. They don't turn the ball over. The Derek Fisher-type of players in the league. Not stars, but they last. Make a lot of money doing it. Guys that know how to bring the ball up the floor. Handle a guy. Never allow pressure. Rarely turn the ball over. Boom, boom, boom. A clinic. Guys who made a career out of being tough with the ball. Find value in the ball, guys. Fend off your defenders. Wait on the 5 man to sprint up. Set a good screen. Now let's go! Pace!"

CHAPTER 44

Beaten by the Belgian: Seattle Pacific University

FRIDAY, NOVEMBER 27

THE FIRST NABC POLL IS out. The Wildcats have received their highest ranking (8th) in the program's history. Tonight they're going up against the No. 23 team in the country, the Seattle Pacific University Falcons, in the 56th Annual Mac Martin Invitational named after Mackay "Mac" Martin. Mac Martin bled cardinal, a Wildcat to the bone. He was the General Manager of the Associated Students, oversaw the student bookstore, food services, athletics, drama, and team transportation. He assisted in student extracurricular activities, helped rebuild the Alumni Association, started the first food service, and was the first advisor of the Associated Students. He served as the Chico State Alumni Association treasurer for more than three decades and received the *Distinguished Alumni Service Award* (2005). He was an avid supporter of Wildcats athletics, helping launch the Athletic Hall of Fame program. He served on this committee many years and was inducted into the Athletic Hall of Fame (1986) as an honorary member. He was assistant coach for men's basketball when Art Acker was head coach.

Mac Martin was Director of the Chico State Invitational Basketball Tournament originating in 1960 and later named the *Mac Martin Invitational Basketball Tournament*. The *Mac Martin Student Leadership Endowment* was established (2002) to develop student leaders. He was community oriented and volunteered for nonprofit organizations such as the Salvation Army, March of Dimes, Sons in Retirement (SIR), and the Bidwell Mansion Association.

The Seattle Pacific University Falcons seem to really like Chico. This will be the third time in the last four seasons that the Falcons have spent Thanksgiving here. The Falcons are 12-2 against the Wildcats. The Wildcats won 73-70 when they last met two years ago. The Falcons, led by sixth year Coach Ryan Looney, have made the postseason each year of his tenure. Coach Looney played ball at Eastern Oregon University from 1996-1998. He set and still holds the school's career free throw accuracy record at 89.5%.

Seattle Pacific University is a private university founded in 1891 by the Free Methodist Church of North America. Students and faculty represent more than 50 different Christian denominations. The university is one of many Christian Universities in Division II basketball. Their mission statement is that Seattle Pacific University is a Christian university fully committed to engaging the culture and changing the world by graduating people of competence and character, becoming people of wisdom, and modeling grace-filled community.

The campus is a world apart from Chico State, located in a quiet north Queen Anne residential neighborhood. Seattle Pacific University's 40-acre campus borders the Lake Washington Ship Canal and boasts majestic trees, open lawns, beautiful gardens, and views of the Cascade Mountains. The university's undergraduate enrollment is small: 3, 202.

The Falcons are one of the biggest teams the Wildcats will face. They have a 7-footer and prolific rebounder in Belgian senior center Giles Dierickx. Brendan Carroll is averaging 20.5 points a game. He recently went off making 9-of-12 3-pointers and finishing with 30 points against Dixie State down in St. George, Utah. The Falcons, like the Wildcats, have a deep bench. Reserve players scored 38 points in a recent victory against BYU-Hawaii. 6-foot-8 junior center, Joe Rasmussen (son of eight-year NBA veteran and first round 15th overall draft pick 7-foot- center Blair Rasmussen who played in Denver and Atlanta) hit 9-of 11-shots and scored and 20 points in 17 minutes. This is another great team that only a handful of basketball fans in the country will ever get to see.

I show up at 6:45 p.m.—nervous—and linger around outside the locker room. I see a few of the players coming and going from the training room where they've been getting taped. Coach Gabriel comes out of the locker room. He's wearing a new suit. "What's up, Carson?" he says and gives me a fist pump. "Go on in and take a look at the board." He's always so upbeat, so kind, a softness to him, the child in him always burning bright, clawing to get out. His warm welcoming boosts my confidence. After the tender moment I experienced with Coach Gabriel in Tucson when he returned to his roots (he took me to the neighborhood where he grew up, introduced me to his childhood friends, and we even had lunch at the country club where he worked in high school), even if he went 0-27 on the season, I'd still say he's one of the best coaches in Division II. He has shown me that you can be both cutthroat and kind. Every time I show up at practice, and if I'm sitting down on the court taking notes, he comes up to me and asks me if I want a chair. He just makes everyone he meets feel like an old friend.

I walk into the locker room. My initial reaction is shock. The first thing I see is a torn-up leather couch. Then the bad lighting, the old benches, the lockers that remind me of the rental lockers at the skating rank from 35 years ago when I was a kid. These lockers alone *should* make these kids play with a chip on their shoulders. My heart aches a little for the team. I imagine that for many of them, their high school locker rooms were nicer. This is the kind of locker room that should inspire toughness. It's raw. Tough. Cold. Calculated. The locker room has endured. It reminds me of a snapped bone protruding through leathery skin. An open wound. The exposed roots of a nerve from a fractured tooth. For how many years have fists banged these lockers in frustration? How many tears of joy and sadness have warmed these cold floors? How many young men have entered and exited? The souls of young men's dreams resonate in these walls. I peer into the shower. Bikes are stored. I see a long skateboard. It's hard to think that these guys ride bikes and skateboard, walk, to Acker. I poke my head down a row of lockers. Silverstrom is lacing up his shoes. Magz has just slammed his lockers and is ready to go.

"Magz, when this becomes a best seller next year, I promise to make a donation and get you guys new lockers," I tell him.

"What?" he says. "I won't be here." He's laughing. He's right. Magz will be gone. Someone else will step into his role, but there'll never be another Magz. He's one of a kind. If only he would have started playing basketball when he was 5 instead of 15. That's what makes him special, though. He is a flawless human specimen, a warrior, but on the basketball court he struggles. An intimidating presence. But he does continue to improve. If only he can turn it up a notch in these final few months of his basketball career.

The players take their seats in front of the white board. I sit in the back row on a split wooden bench with a rusty old chain tethering it to the ground. The locker room door opens. Sound of dress shoes clapping on the floor. The hall leading from the door to the lockers is lengthy, prolonging the wait. The silence of the room, the wait for the coaching staff to come in, reminds me of those moments before the commencement of Christmas Eve service at midnight mass when all is still and right yet teeming with anxiety and then finally the procession begins—the altar boys, the candles, the choir, the Father walking down the aisle. Coach Gabriel walks up to the board. Clink hangs back. Coach Gabriel goes through each point on the board, starting with a background of the players.

"McFerren, tell me about the 1." McFerren tells Coach Gabriel everything he knows about the player. "Rob, what about the 2?" Each player takes his turn reciting the biography of the player he has been assigned to guard. I'm amazed by the amount of intelligence and preparation, the quick study, needed to perform at this level. The players are prepared. The players exit the locker room and head out to the corridor beside the bleachers. Clink hangs back, stern faced, and erases the white board. He immediately starts writing again. This is his alone time, his pregame ritual. Same thing every time. Coach Gabriel and Coach Blake join the players for their warm up.

I feel silly running out behind the team with my bag filled with pens, legal pads, index cards, and blue notebook while the camera around my neck bangs against my chest. Yet at the same time it's a thrill. I find my seat at the scorer's table. I am wedged in between Luke Reid and a writer for the *Enterprise Recorder*. I need space to write. I find a seat behind the bench. That's when I meet Tommy Wigton. I've seen him around sporting events since I moved here three years ago, and I've seen him riding his blue Schwinn cruiser—he's always wearing a red Chico State shirt, a Chico State baseball cap, and sunglasses. I always thought he was a Chico State baseball coach.

Tommy talks with a slight slur. At first it's hard to hear him. "What capacity do you fill at the university?" he asks me. Nobody really ever knows what a thesis editor is or does. "I work in the Office of Graduate Studies. I'm writing a book on the team. But it has nothing to do with my job."

"Well I've got 21 years of stories if you ever want to talk," Tommy shouts.

It only takes a pregame warmup to find out that Tommy has been around long enough to have seen Clink play back when Clink wore a Chico State uniform and played for Puck Smith. Tommy's career at Chico State started when he approached Clink's coach at the time and future predecessor, Puck Smith, about volunteering as a team manager. The next fall Tommy became the manager for the Chico State football team, and that spring he began the team manager for the Chico State baseball team. "I've got two college world series rings," Tommy quickly tells me. "I'll bring them tomorrow and show you."

I've only known Tommy for five minutes (I've seen him around practices, but he intimidated me and we never interacted) and he has already spoken about his mother five times. "My mother always told me that you have to be humble and have humility," he says. "Coach Clink is teaching that to the boys. Some of these guys are wondering why they're not getting to play. My mother always told me to find that answer, look at yourself in the mirror. Just look at yourself."

I soon realize that Tommy is not a manager as in "coach," but he is the team manager. He works as a volunteer for the Chico State Athletics Department. Since 1989, Tommy has been a team manager, first for just the men's basketball team, then adding football (until the sport was dissolved in 1997) and baseball. His duties vary from sport to sport. He is also the manager for the Chico High football team; he's the helmet guy.

Tommy's start came from finding a subtle need and addressing it until he became part of the program. When the Chico Heat baseball club was still in town, Tommy saw the workers picking up cups after the game.

"So I got a bag and started helping them pick up trash," Tommy says.

Eventually the team started letting him into games for free in trade for his help. That's where it all started for Tommy.

Moments before the game I search for my son Holden over in the Acker Backer section. I see his tufts of blonde hair bouncing up and down. I wave to him. He's with his grandfather. He sees me. I blow him a kiss. The blown kiss is reciprocated. The players start to run off the floor. I jog behind them. We enter the locker room and all take our seats. There's a pause. Clink gathers his thoughts at the board. It looks like he's about to speak, but he pauses again.

"Alright, here we go," he says, turning to the board.

I've now been through nine months with Clink. Each month his demeanor has grown more intense. I imagine he's still a couple of months away from peaking, but he's getting close.

"Defensively, we're in 41," he says. "We're not gambling tonight. Tonight it's about being tough guys. I want four guys crashing the glass. Rebound. Outlet. Run. First five minutes we're going to just play. Share. Do the little things that make us great. Stick together. Rally around adversity."

I run out through the Red Door trailing behind the team. Acker is busier than I thought. I see Clink's wife Courtney come in at the buzzer. Clink looks pensive as he waits. Rightfully so. He knows how good SPU is. Clink paces the sideline. He finally takes a seat. There's the tip. Game on. The turnovers come. Duncan is often faster than the ball. He sees things way before they happen—sometimes his greatest flaw. The shot selection for the Wildcats is good, but they're not falling. It's as if the rims are like the rims from a carnival game, smaller than the ball or possibly capped. The 7-foot Belgian University of Washington transfer who reminds me of the Russian villain from Rocky IV—actually, all the SPU players—are having their way on the glass. The Washington State and University of Idaho transfer Bryce Leavitt is carving us up. He, too, is a magnet for rebounds. Chico State can't hit a thing. They have the moves. They have the looks. They have the shots. But they can't finish.

Harris and Ellis come in off the bench and give the Wildcats a spark. For a moment, it looks like the game is in the Wildcats hands. They're starting to play like the 8th best team in the country. Harris makes a layup that puts the Wildcats up 14-12. 683 clapping fans shake Acker. The only real clapping that will come the rest of the night is the clapping, the stomping, of Clink's dress shoes on the hardwood floor. His foot will stomp continuously as if he's in a blue grass band at a hoe down rather than coaching a basketball game.

The score at the half is SPU 28, Chico State 22. One gets the feeling, though, that the halftime pause has only temporarily stopped the bleeding. It feels as if the Wildcats are getting beat by a lot more than six points. The Belgian is almost perfect in the paint at 5-of-7. SPU is shooting 48.1%. SPU has 15 offensive rebounds to the Wildcats 9. This leads to 11 second chance points. Thankfully, the Wildcats bench has outscored SPU 29-3 with10 fast break points. Kitchens is 0-of-5. Duncan 1-of-4. Silverstrom is 2-of-7. Giddings and Magz are just taking up space. Ellis is the lone bright spot shooting 3-of-5.

The locker room at the half is quiet. The team seems stunned. Held to 22 points. I know the Wildcats are in trouble when I hear Kitchens, breathing hard, ask Harris: "What's the score?" Clink hangs out in the hall and talks with his coaches rather than hot-footing it into the locker room. I believe he wants them to talk and figure things out. Only this is a team that doesn't talk much. Game five and no vocal leader save Priest. Duncan, whom the team needs most, goes inward. He looks petulant, pouting almost, and as he sits in the corner—like he did at Arizona—I can't tell if he's sulking or angry. I don't know. He has the demeanor of a wounded animal that one dare not tamper with. Giddings sits slack-jawed. Ellis works to catch his breath. He is coughing hard. I can tell he feels terrible. Magz doesn't say much. Silverstrom says, "We have to play with each other. Use each other." Eventually, they start talking, but it's just talk. Someone needs to direct. I know it's early in the season, but so far there are no signs of a leader emerging. I get the feeling that the stain of the talented Jordan Semple, his ghost, is still lingering. Someone must step up.

Clink, earlier in the summer, had described team leadership as a bunch of alpha dogs in a dogfight, and eventually one will win and the others will follow. This is what's happening now. It's beautiful to watch this unfold, young men feeling each other out, going slowly, prodding almost, until finally one or two will emerge as the leader. Others will follow. Finally, after ten minutes, the coaches come in to break the silence.

"I don't know what else to say in regards to our offense," Clink says. "If we continue to burp up contested layups, we will not win." He pauses. "We will not win." His eyes scan the players. "Our offense has deviated." He is flummoxed. This kind of step backwards is not something that can be fixed in five minutes. "I'm not going to yell at you, but I will say this is Arizona all over again. What you're doing tonight will not get a win against a great team like this. Sure, it'll work tomorrow night against an inferior team, but it's not gonna work tonight. It's on you guys and whether you believe and whether you buy in or not. The way you're playing right now ain't gonna win championships. Do it our way, not your way. I want you to share the ball. Have fun with the ball. Penetrate. Jump stop. Kick. Penetrate. That's the recipe. You guys can do it. Pure aggression. Keep punching them in the teeth again and again and again. It's right there for us. Right there for us. Now get out there. Let's go!"

I thought for sure a different team would come out in the second half, but it was more of the same. There are some moments when Giddings plays aggressively. I think he's finally letting the pit bull out, but his bark is worse than his bite. His aggressive play seems more about frustration than competition. The Belgian is perfect in the second half: 5-of-5. He really is the evil boxer from the Soviet Union, and the Wildcats have no Rocky to defeat him. Kitchens's dismal shooting continues: 1-of-5. Duncan really never shows back up save his 3 assists. Silverstrom brightens up. He scores 12 points in 11 minutes. But SPU will shoot 48% to our 33.3%. Worse, they are tougher than the Wildcats tonight. They own the paint. They own the glass. They put a beating on the Wildcats in their own backyard. Walking back into the locker room, I feel bad, really bad, for our Saturday night opponent, Simpson University.

CHAPTER 45

Simpson University Scare

SATURDAY, NOVEMBER 28

SIMPSON UNIVERSITY IS JUST UP the road in Redding. It, too, is a private Christian university with a Christ-centered learning community that has pledged an enduring commitment to world service and faith-infused education in professional studies and liberal arts. One-third of the undergraduates are first-generation college students and come from diverse backgrounds.

The Simpson University Red Hawks have already played 11 games thus far to Chico State's four (counting our exhibition game at Arizona). They are 1-10. Their lone victory came against Claremont McKenna College in OT, 77-72. They have suffered bad losses this year: 63-103 in an exhibition against Sacramento State; 54-85 against Southern Oregon University; 61-87 against Oregon Institute of Technology; 69-94 against Corban University; and 58-102 against Lewis-Clark State College.

The Red Hawks are tough. They'll not back down against anyone. The Wildcats tower over the Redhawks. The Redhawks biggest man is 6-foot-8, and their next biggest man is 6-foot-5. Their leading scorer is 6-foot-4 Jacob Kaler from Beaverton, Oregon. The Redhawks are coached by Jim Holcomb, who is also the Assistant Director of Athletics. He served as an assistant at Simpson from 1999-2003. He was the head coach at Anderson High School from 2003-2008 before becoming an assistant at Shasta College in Redding from 2008-2013. Holcomb is a family man, married for 34 years with two daughters. He likes to hunt and spend time outdoors.

Unlike a lot of ambitious coaches, Coach Holcomb seems fine at home and lets his heart rather than his whistle serve as his compass.

The game lacks such suspense that Baca is not here to make the call. I predict the Wildcats will score 140 and limit Simpson to 40. I pray for Simpson the night before the game. I feel sorry for them, a victim of the Wildcats wrath, yet I have immense respect for them; they have less talent than all the teams they play, but they will not back down from anyone. And they don't just lose but get the dickens kicked out of them in every game they play. I am sure we will win by 100. Turns out I should have prayed for *our* guys.

Before the game the Wildcats players were watching the East Bay-SPU game with interest. Why? Because East Bay was giving SPU a run for their money. Plus, they were reliving the game from the night before—replaying all the "what if?" factors rather than focusing on the team before them. I understand the team was hurting. They will no doubt fall far in the polls. Rankings are a big deal for young men. Rather than being angry, though, they seemed embarrassed, prideful, and rather than embracing the humility, moving forward, and using Simpson as a catharsis for their pain and pity, they let Simpson come into their house, eat from their fridge, put their feet up on the table, then hop into bed and snuggle.

The game is not a blowout. There are moments when I think this Division II basketball book is going to turn into a Disney film, where the little Christian school who gets their tails kicked around every corner they turn rise up and spank the big, bad bully, the best team, in the CCAA.

Kitchens is having another bad first half: 1-of-5. Duncan goes cold: 3-of-9. Clink tells Giddings he's playing like a scarecrow. I think he looks more like the tin woodsman in search of a heart. Hardly a pulse there. Were it not for Isaiah Ellis, Simpson would have taken the lead into the half. Ellis, playing sick, keeps the Wildcats in it. Going into the locker room, the Wildcats are up 35-21—but it's a sloppy, guilty 14-point lead, kind of like being the worse batter and fielder on the Little League baseball team but making All Stars because your father is the coach. The Wildcats have 8 turnovers and are 13-of-33 from the field. I feel for Clink. There's nothing he can do. This effort is out of his hands. I imagine he feels let down. Day after day in practice, week after week, everything that he has been teaching his players is now being thrown out the window.

Clink hates to lose, but I get the feeling he'd rather have a good loss than a bad win. Simpson is not a great team, and the Wildcats are playing down to their level. I know there will be a pound of flesh to pay in the locker room. As I sit on the bench in the locker room waiting for the coaches to walk in, and trying to manage my own anger and confusion, I try to think of highlights from the first half. There were plenty, but they had nothing to do with the game. I got to talk to Clink's wife. She came up to me before the game. "You must know someone to get a seat like this?" she said. I showed her my index cards and the blue notebook. We talked about our kids for a while. "This is Justin's first night as a ball boy," she says, beaming. "The kids are usually running up down in the stands, and of course Greg can't worry about that while he's coaching. We figured this would be good for him."

I told Courtney about the scene in the tunnel when the team was get-ting ready to come out on the floor, how all the kids were talking to the players, and how Ryan said, "I love you, Dad" before Clink walked out on the court. Of course, I didn't share with her how I was worried about the team, thought they were being too cool and relaxed and comfortable before the game. There was no sense of urgency. I also got to spend a little time with Justin before his debut as a ball boy and show him the book. He was proud of his new glasses, and I showed him mine. There was also the World Series rings that Tommy brought for me to see. That was touching. I'm still trying to understand Tommy. He's like no one else I have ever met before.

Yes, the best moments came off the court. I look at the team. Just as flat in the locker room as they had been on the floor. Most of the guys who had been out there playing weren't even sweating. I'm angry. Angry for coach. Selfishly angry for the book that I've been working on night and day, obsessively, since last March, about this team I've been singing praises of from high on the mountain top. I don't recognize the team that showed up tonight.

The locker room is the same as it has been in every game I've witnessed since I began following the team. I wish the players were sitting in a circle rather than the standard rows of chairs. The guys who had been out there playing should have to look into the eyes of the guys who were sitting. The guys out there playing should not be allowed to hang their heads and divert eye contact. Duncan, whom before the season started I'd expected to be the vocal leader, sits quiet in the corner, brooding. He seems to go inward when the team most needs him to be outward. I imagine that becoming the leader of a team takes time, particularly since he's only a junior and the team has three seniors that start. Silverstrom, my favorite creative player on the team, seems to be replaying a highlight reel of his moves in his head. Where are the seniors? Magz looked bewildered. Kitchens dumbfounded. Giddings with his mouth agape. Only Priest and Harris speak up. McFerren is slowly coming more into his role as a leader, but he is still tentative, a young sophomore.

Clink storms into the locker room. He burns like Moses's bush.

"You are embarrassing," he screams. "You guys only get 27 shots at this and you're throwing this one away."

I had predicted that the Wildcats would come out mad after last night, angry bulls seeing red. But instead they come out with about as much energy and passion and toughness as wax paper. At the half, as the teams walked to the lockers, I heard a Simpson player trailing behind say to his teammate: "We've got these guys. Their ours. Totally overrated."

Clink's explosion continues. He lights into them. My pen freezes as Clink turns into God of the Old Testament and hurls lightning bolts and brings famine and swords and floods and pestilence to the team. For a moment, just a moment, I empathize with the guys on the bench. But they're just as much at fault. They had been without a heartbeat for most of the game, golf claps here and there, cheering occasionally, more out of protocol, more like spectators at bad community theater rather than role players on the No. 8 ranked team in the nation. Clink's words must have singed their hearts, yet I still think he treaded lightly. I hope the players respond. Clink works harder than anyone I know, and he also runs the tightest ship of anyone I know. He is a perfectionist who thrives on the control of practice, and day in, day out, he works on the basics with these guys. Their play and passion tonight is a slap in his face. Here I get the first real taste of a coach's frustration—getting young men to tap into their potential, ditch their egos, become humble, and go deep within themselves. If only those players knew the gut rot their performance will give him, the mood it will cast upon their Captain Ahab, a doom and gloom hell hath no fury demeanor that will trail, haunt, and curse him, keep him up at night, rouse him early in the morning, until they play William Jessup Tuesday night.

Outside I hear Acker roar. A lightness of being has been restored. I will later learn that the joy came from Clink's youngest son, Ryan, offering a respite to the frustration of playing down to the level of an inferior team. He was the half-time entertainment, but Clink was too busy drawing plays and trying to keep his team from further imploding. The crowd cheered wildly for Ryan as he shot two free throws to try and win a prize. Fun was still to be had in Acker, everywhere accept in the locker room. There is no joy to be had when playing so poorly. The beauty of sports, though, is that even in the darkest hour hope shimmers. Hope endures. You can see the light if you look at it right. The season is early.

"How much time we got left, Coach?" Clink asks Coach Gabriel. "Four minutes, 40 seconds," he responds.

"Get back out there," he growls to the team.

It's been a long time since I saw and felt fury like that, but Clink needed to release it. His team needed to hear and feel it. For Clink this is a job. It puts food on his table. Gas in his car. Insures his family. These players, most of them, are getting help through school (granted, at this level it's not a lot and many of these young men rely on financial aid and part-time jobs) to wear the Chico State jersey. This is no longer playground fun. This is about winning. This is about representation of the school and program. And for twenty minutes, the unimpeachable reputation of the Wildcats basketball team has been compromised. I'm amazed that Clink can come back out on the court and look composed, but that's part of his profession. A coach is always being scrutinized. Someone is always watching, judging, injecting opinion, most of it unfounded. As I take my seat behind the bench, I realize that I, too, am changing. I am starting to view college basketball through the eyes of a coach, no longer a fan. I am starting to see the difference between a positive and a negative 14-point lead. I am no longer merely a fan. I will never view the sport or any sport the same way. I have gone to the dark side, and now I understand why the games make Clink sick, but why he loves all the other aspects. Some people like to keep score when they play tennis. Others just like to hit. The latter is a lot more fun.

I don't even know if I'll last the entire season.

The second half is only slightly better. McFerren is not playing aggressively. His head hangs and shakes at times. He is young. Magz misses an easy dunk. Giddings is still being Giddings, playing like a scarecrow. Clink pulls him. As Giddings walks to the bench and looks at Clink, Clink just stares ahead, burning inside. He is so disappointed, maybe sick, with Giddings that he can't look at him. The freshman Ambrosini brings sunshine back into Acker and hangs a rainbow by knocking down a beautiful three. Luke Reid looks over at me from the scorer's table. "That's the first of many threes he'll hit wearing that uniform." Ellis records his first double-double. Holmes finally makes his debut as a Chico State Wildcat. His fan club cheers every time he touches the ball, and I can hear tears falling to the floor when he stands alone at the free throw line, his brother Casey standing by his side just like they were kids again playing out in the driveway. Holmes will miss. How could he not have? Surely he must have paused to take it all in, to reflect, to shake his head in wonder, at the journey that has brought him back home to Chico.

The Wildcats only play slightly better in the second half. Silverstrom, again, steals the show with his 3-pointers. Ellis is a monster on the boards. McFerren makes some great passes. And Justin Clink has completed his first night as a ball boy.

Chico State will win 68-55 despite being outscored in the second half. Thankfully, only 563 fans are here to see the debacle.

CHAPTER 46

Teaching Moments

MONDAY, NOVEMBER 30

THE GREAT TEACHERS ARE ALWAYS looking for teaching moments. The near disaster against Simpson University provided 40 minutes of teaching moments and a lesson plan for the next practice. Clink would have all weekend to stew about the game. By Monday, his rage has cooled, his disappointment turned into hope, and he walks through the Red Door ready to remedy the situation and immediately work on getting better. The players take their seats and prepare to review film. Class is in session.

"Let's talk about the good things," he says." I thought our execution against Seattle Pacific on Friday night was dialed in. We did a good job with the scouting report. Our shot selection was good. I can live with that loss. But we need to work on blocking out." He sighs. "But I can live with that loss." Clink's voice starts to rise. The players know the bad is coming. "But I can't live with what happened Saturday night. You disrespected the game. You disrespected your opponent. You thought we'd just do the tip and run them out of the gym. What you did was waste an opportunity to get better. You wasted it. Yeah. Friday night we lost, but we got better. That's what has been eating at me since 10 p.m. Saturday night. It's eating me up that we as a *group* were not dialed in and ready to compete. We have to say to ourselves that that will never happen again. Never again." He pauses.

"Here's the specifics we have to improve upon. Let's start with the shoot around. I know you'll be tired the morning after a game, but fatigue is not an excuse to not be ready. Next, the pregame locker room. I don't want you talking about anything but the game. Warm ups. You have to be better. If I come out with 4:45 left on the pregame clock and see six missed layups or dunks, or if I see you miss a windmill dunk and you're laughing, I'll go nuts! If you're a guy who misses a dunk during warm ups instead of layup, don't do it. Don't do it. Do we all agree?" A few guys mumble yes. "Do we all agree?" Everyone says yes.

"The bench. Our bench has to be more effective. Our bench is flat. When things go bad, the bench goes mute. Mute." He pauses. "If you're sitting there on the bench thinking when am I going to get to play? Don't do it. Stop thinking like that. Our bench has always been better than any other bench in the league. Every guy on this team has been through it." He scans the players.

Clink points to Giddings. "This guy right here. He knows what it's like to spend time on the bench. He spent a lot of time on the bench at Fresno State. Rob played nine games his freshman year." As I look at all the players, I realize he's right. Every guy on the team has had experience sitting on the bench. He points to Priest. "Priest's one of the best bench guys we've ever had. Watch him. Listen to him. Learn from him. When you're on the bench, I want you to ask yourselves what you can do to help the guys on the floor. Start talking. Be enthusiastic, especially when things are going bad. Any comments?" Clink paces, thinking, tapping his chin. He looks at the team. "We all want to win every game. I know. But this is about getting better. Always improving. After tomorrow's game, we come back Wednesday and we get better. San Francisco State on Friday night will be sold out. They're going to come out and get all over you. Let's flip the script, turn the page. Let's watch some film and approach practice today the right way. Let's approach everything we do the right way."

Clink starts the film. "We need to work on our attack," he says. "We had nine shots in the first half against Seattle that were really good. They just didn't go in. Some nights are like that. We need to do more running. We'll need to run it down William Jessup's throat tomorrow night. They're big, strong, and athletic. We have to work on our jump stops. If you don't have an uncontested layup, jump stop and throw it back. When we work together, we can effectively move the ball across the split line. We share the ball, and we get good shots. All things we have to work on improving. We have to use ball screens quicker and better. If you penetrate and the shots are contested, jump stop in the paint and kick it out. Can't come in and penetrate and cough it up." He shows a half-dozen examples where the players do this. He is teaching and modeling. Here is where Clink most thrives, as a teacher. "We need more stops in the paint!" The lessons continue. The players watch in rapt attention.

The players get up and sprint to the court to start practice. I'm inspired. If I learned a lot from the bad Simpson win, I can only imagine what the players have learned. It's almost like Clink scripted it this way, for the team to lay an egg in late November, days before the CCAA starts. But sports are unscripted. The fates adore Clink. This is a season with positive omens lingering in the air. A rainbow, if you just look close enough, is hanging over Acker. He will not let his players fail, and if they do fail, then Clink, once the emotions cool, will use failure as the fertilizer to grow success.

"Turns out the bad win turned into a great win," I say to Tommy.

Tommy has seen it all in his years spent working in football, basketball, and baseball. He's lived with Coach Puck Smith and now he's living with

Coach Clink. "My mother always told me," Tommy says, "and it's what I tell all the players, if you're not playing, go home and look at yourself in the mirror. That reflection will tell you why you're not playing."

CHAPTER 47

Keep Improving: William Jessup University

TUESDAY, DECEMBER 1

WILLIAM JESSUP UNIVERSITY WAS STARTED during the Great Depression of the 1930s. Hopefully, William Jessup will not start Chico State's Great Depression. Hopefully that Great Depression was only last weekend's great depression. William Jessup is the third straight Christian university the Wildcats will play. Their mission: In partnership with the Church, the purpose of William Jessup University is to educate transformational leaders for the glory of God. The Warriors are coached by Lance Von Vogt. He is in his third season as the head men's basketball coach. Coach Von Vogt is a Floridian. He hails from Daytona Beach Shores, Florida. He cut his teeth under the legendary coach Lefty Driesell.

The Wildcats show improvement in this game. Their efforts prove true the dead metaphor of "rebounding." The students listened to the teacher. They start off right. Kitchens awakens from his slump and hits a quick three; he will do this all throughout the night. Hopefully his awakening will quiet fan murmurs (there aren't many fans here, period: 250) about why the senior is still starting. He's in a slump, that's all. At least that's what I hope is going on, and that being a fun-loving senior and reaping the social and cultural capital thereof is not detracting from his 9-5 weekday job (being a student) and his weekend job (being an athlete). Kitchens might have off nights, but he's always on during practice.

This will be a night when the Wildcats will kill the Warriors with their threes. I hope to see an inside game (teams that live and die on the three always terrify me), but when a team goes 12-of-19 from downtown, let it fly. McFerren and Silverstrom will contribute to the barrage by combining for 7-of- 8. The first half goes great. The Wildcats take a 51-27 halftime lead into the locker room. The second half will pale in comparison—the Wildcats playing average ball. But average at this time of year is good. More teaching moments for the teacher. Clink's students are still alert and not worn down form the semester of both school and basketball. They will listen to what he says and keep improving. They're outscored in the second half 31-27. Ellis will again show his half-time prowess. Lynch will pick up valuable minutes in place of the seemingly invincible Harris sitting this one out with the flu. Lynch was a high school star in Redding, and had starred so many nights in Acker gym while playing at Liberty Christian.

Despite the second half malaise, the players undoubtedly listened to Clink in practice the day before. McFerren has a steal in the open court and could have slammed it home, but instead settles for a layup. Duncan, who had been such an explosive scorer last year, is now doing things besides scoring. The word is out. He can shoot, but he can also pass. He finishes with six assists. Many of his passes lead to turnovers because his teammates weren't expecting the pass, a nice problem to have at this early point in the season. Silverstrom has been stepping in and filling the void when Duncan struggles. Eventually, this will pose a big problem for all the CCAA teams.

There'll be no way to stop these two guys at once, and it might turn into a season of taking turns being the highest scorer. Clink is content with the lack of turnovers. His players received and acted on his message: take care of the ball. But they struggle with the boards. They lose the offensive rebound battle 26-25. The bench is stellar, outscoring William Jessup 34-16. As William Jessup gathers at center court for their postgame prayer, as most of the Christian schools do, Clink and his team join them. After the Amen, Clink ambles over to Baca's table. "We improved," he says during the radio interview. "We shared the ball. We have to work on not being complacent and satisfied."

The Wildcats so far have not been a second-half team, and his players realize this. "We have to learn how to extend the lead," Clink says. "We have got to get better at blocking out and rebounding."

CHAPTER 48

Do It Again

WEDNESDAY, DECEMBER 2

CLINK HAS WASTED NO TIME working on the next lesson plan. He starts off practice by putting Coach Gabriel with the big men and rebounding medicine balls. The players throw the ball off the glass (it weighs at least fifteen pounds), catch it, and then put it back in. Magz does it easily. He even dunks the heavy ball once. Briggs struggles. I now understand why Clink thought it would be best for him to redshirt and spend the year developing his body. I imagine this is a tough time of year for him. He will soon be taking his first college final exams. Ricky has the blue pad out. He swats the big men like flies. "Give me that thing," Coach Gabriel says. He snatches it from Ricky and starts pounding the players. Ricky slinks off with a smile, looking for pools of sweat to mop up. He's having the time of his life. Down on the other end of the court, Clink can be heard: "Do it again. Do it again. Do it again."

Clink brings all the players back together. As he talks to them, I realize, finally, the reason coaches scream. It's not so much that they're angry all the time (granted, many of them are), but it's the only way they can be heard amidst all the other noise. A whisper cannot be heard from one end of the court to the other. Clink continues to work with the players on their screens. The players go through some rotations. He blows his whistle. "We're not working hard enough on our rotations."

He jumps on the court and slowly shows them what he wants to see. "And then I want to see four guys going hard to the glass." I watch the court demeanor of Silverstrom and Duncan. Something has changed in each of them. I think these two stars are trying to figure how to play with each other. Silverstrom is so creatively gifted with both his moves and his size, whereas Duncan has will the size of Mt. Rushmore, and his physical talents, his acrobatics, are jaw-dropping. I automatically think of the Golden State Warriors and the Splash Brothers. Duncan and Silverstrom have the potential to become the Division II version, maybe the 530 brothers. "How are the block outs, Coach?" Clink barks to Coach Gabriel.

"Average at best," Coach Gabriel responds.

Silverstrom and Kitchens go at it. Every pause Silverstrom makes with the ball poses a threat to the man guarding him. Time stops. His eyes scan the court; his imagination opens up. He has less than a split-second to make up his mind. Clink sees something he likes. "The thing that was good about that…" he says after blowing his whistle. When he sees something he likes, he lets the players know right away. Say that enough time and it sticks, turns into a self-fulfilling prophecy.

Clink blows the whistle again. He's no longer happy. "Our spacing must be better!" Ricky continues to run up and down the sidelines wiping up sweat. Tommy says to him: "Good job, Ricky." Big smile. "You too, Tommy." Ricky is loving this. He has found his home at Chico State. Tommy frowns a little when he gets compliments, almost embarrassed. "I better be doing a good job," Tommy barks "Been doing this for 30 years!"

The whistle.

"One more time, please."

Coach Gabriel is working with players on the other end. He shoots the ball, the players have to run and touch the outside arc, then race to get the rebound. I have wondered for the last two months how he is so good at missing. He seems to have made an art out of it. At the break, I finally ask him. He smiles. "There's a cap on the rim," he says. "Otherwise, I'd make every one of them. I'm still the best shooter on the team. Have been for two years now." He winks and ambles off. Clink calls the guys over. Another drill begins.

"Here's where we're gonna get really good." He huddles five guys. Draws some plays on his clipboard. The act has the same innocence to it as kids playing football in a field, drawing plays in the dirt with a finger. "Take care of the ball. No turnovers. Quick decisions."

CHAPTER 49

Sixth Man Shines: San Francisco State University

FRIDAY, DECEMBER 4

THE LAST SIX GAMES HAVE been dress rehearsals, every opponent a crash test dummy.

Tonight the season really starts. Conference play. These are the games that determine a team's fate in March. Every game counts. The Wildcats will play 8 of their next 10 on the road, and 6 of those 8 are conference games. San Francisco State University (SFSU) is a big school. SFSU has students from nearly every state and around 100 countries. Like the game of basketball, SFSU is diverse. There are close to 30,000 students that attend SFSU.

The Gators are coached by Paul Trevor, another Bay Area product. Coach Trever and Clink have known each other since 1996. Clink was an assistant at UC Davis and Trevor was an assistant at Sonoma State. Sonoma and UC Davis were travel partners back in the old NCAC. Clink would go over to Sonoma on Friday nights and scout their opponent because Davis would be playing them the next night at UC Davis. He and Trevor became friends. "We would go out and eat after the games," Clink said. "He would come to Davis and scout, too. Trevor's one of my favorite coaches in the league. Great coach and an even better person." Trevor enters his sixth season as the head coach of the Gator men's basketball program. In his five years at the helm of the Gator men's basketball program, Trevor has guided SF State to 66 wins including 55 conference wins.

The Wildcats and the Gators are playing each other for the 200th time. The Swamp is a tough place to play. It's also "purple-out" night. The Swamp is packed. Hardly an empty seat in the house, the stands flooded with fans in purple T-shirts. The Gators punch the Wildcats early, knocking down 7 of their first 8 three-point shots. The fans in purple are going wild. The Gators take the lead 43-36 into the half despite that the Wildcats have a remarkable field goal percentage of 52%; however, they are 8-of-24 from three point land. They also have 10 turnovers. However, the second-half will change.

The Wildcats will cut their turnovers down by half, and only take 10 three-point shots. They pound the ball inside. Clink has said all along his teams are defensive teams, and the Wildcats shut the Gators down, holding them to 9-of-29 from the field. All week long in practice Clink had worked on the team getting better on the glass. The deliberate practice paid off as the Wildcats would outrebound the Gators 32-21. Giddings was no longer playing like a scarecrow. He had six rebounds. And Ellis—oh, the sixth man Ellis whose star was beginning to shine—came off the bench and scored 14.

Tomorrow night Clink would face his former player, assistant coach, and mentee.

CHAPTER 50

Armpit of California:
Stanislaus State University

DECEMBER 9

SAY THE WORD STANISLAUS TO most Californians outside of Stanislaus. Most wrinkle their nose and let out a grunt. "It's located in the armpit of California," many respond. But some people like the stench of the arm pit. A lot of the Chico State players come from the Central Valley.

Many of our most beloved and respected leaders cannot resist temptation and become deviant. How, then, can young student-athletes be faulted for doing the same? They are poor. They are overworked. They spend at least twenty hours a week at practice, and then there are the games and the travel. Time management—with the absence of academic advisors at this level—becomes an art: how to juggle 15 units a semester and 20-plus hours of athletics. Clink, though, does not have the added pressure of worrying about the corruption of his program, the eroding of the university's academic values, the deviance of his athletes. Basketball will not corrupt the academy. Only the academy will corrupt the academy. The world that he and his players live in is free from the leprosy of commercial entertainment business. The lure is spending four to five years at a great university in one of the last college towns in California, and being a star who does not have to compete with the adoration of football players.

The only illusion is the one that might come from getting a big head, an inflated ego, from being one of 15 players playing on a team with the best game in town from November to March. Certainly, Clink and his players would like to have the opportunity to appear on ESPN, or be seen on national television, but unless they make it to the Division II final game that is unlikely. The sport is pure here. There is nothing suspicious going on. His players refer to men as sir and women as ma'am. Off the court they are polite. Soft-spoken. Neatly groomed. Intelligent. They give eye contact and stand straight as a flagpole. They are respectful. They are what people over 40 call "good kids." And Clink's good kids come from some of the worst Central Valley towns in California.

The Central Valley refers to the geographical area that spans from Shasta to Kern. The length of the valley is about 450 miles, about the distance from Chicago to Pittsburgh. It takes about 7 hours to drive from Chico to the south end of Bakersfield. Fresno is the heart of the valley. Chico is about a 1.5-hour drive to Sacramento, and from Sacramento to Fresno it's about four hours and tack on another two to get to Bakersfield. This might be the most boring drive on the planet.

Clink drops his trot lines in theses parched places: Bakersfield, Fresno, Merced, Stockton, and Sacramento. And these cities are constantly ranked as the worst places to live not just in California but America.

No wonder the good kids of the Central Valley consider going to Chico as "getting out." If the town of Chico itself is the number one recruiting tool that Clink has, then the deplorable living conditions of the Central Valley must be a close second.

Cal State Stanislaus is located in the heart of the Central Valley (Turlock)— "the place beneath the armpit where you want to make sure the deodorant goes," someone once told me. This is farm country.

The Warriors, like most of the teams in the CCAA, play with a chip on their shoulder. They've heard every red neck/farmer joke around. Their coach, Larry Reynolds, though, took the straw out of his teeth a long time ago. Larry Reynolds, who has coached Division I and II championship teams at Long Beach State, Cal State San Bernardino and now at Cal State University, Stanislaus, became the head coach of the men's basketball program in June of 2009. Stanislaus gave Reynolds a second chance. When he was the head coach at Long Beach, shortly after going 24-8, winning the Big West Conference Championship and a spot in the NCAA tournament, he was fired for violating NCAA rules. In his time at Stanislaus, Reynolds has led the Warriors to an NCAA West Regional Final, two NCAA tournament wins, a CCAA conference tournament championship (2013-14), and four CCAA conference tournament appearances. Since Reynolds arrival in 2009, the Warriors are 89-79, including a school-record 23-win season in 2013-14. He has produced a program first NCAA Division II All-American and two players on the NCAA Division II All-West Region First Team.

Coach Reynolds is one of Clink's favorite guys in the league. "He's a good guy and an old school basketball coach. He has always been good to me. He won't remember this, but when I was a young assistant at UC Davis, and he was the head coach at Long Beach State, we were both at West Valley College one fall recruiting. After their practice we went to dinner with the West Valley Staff. Coach Reynolds bought my dinner. I thought it was a nice gesture. He didn't know who I was at the time."

The players gather for the shoot around at 1 p.m. I help rebound for Magz. His left wrist is taped. I ask him about it. "Dunk in the last game." I ask him how he wants me to pass him the ball. "Make some bad passes. That's how Rob always throws it to me," he says, half joking. The players have a reason to be particularly fired up today. ESPN has just announced they will be coming to Acker when the Wildcats take on rival Cal Poly Pomona. Magz shakes his head in disbelief. What a punctuation mark to his senior year.

"The only thing," Magz says, "is that I wish it were a different game. It's always a slow, low scoring game when we play each other. They play like us. All about the defense."

Clink runs the players through several plays. He stops. "They are going to try and get you to play at their pace—very slow. They will walk around. Their offense will be going at around 50-60 percent. We have to play our pace. 100 percent. No turnovers. Our offense is going to have to be as good as it's going to be all year. 100 percent. Play fast, and I..."

Clink stops. He sees something he doesn't like. "Marvin, go get your socks on." Cool Marvin nods and runs off the court. It's the little things that really get under Clink's skin. "Falcon 2. Let's go."

Many of the Wildcats have hair new haircuts today. Their heads are almost shaved.

Coach Gabriel and Coach Blake, too, are sporting almost shaved heads. Coach Gabriel teaches them the Stanislaus sets. They run this until Clink thinks it's perfect.

"Let's talk about some other things that could happen." He is always preparing for the worst. "We will dictate the pace of the game. Don't let them lull you to sleep."

I look around at the gym. ESPN will love this atmosphere. Nostalgia is inevitable here, a reminder of the day when players played (and they still do) for the name on the front of their jersey, not on the back. I finally get a chance to talk to Tom the graduate assistant trainer—not to be confused with Tommy the manager. I'm reminded of how little you really know about a person until you get to talking, yet how much you think you know just by looking. Tom has a soft brown beard, perfectly groomed. He always looks like he just took a warm soapy bath after having slept for ten hours. He is calm and relaxed, always leaning in, watching, waiting.

"So your job is to sit around and wait for someone to get hurt?" I ask. He laughs and nods. "Pretty much."

These are the first words I've ever heard him say. I wonder if he ever has the small town cop kind of boredom, not really wanting anything bad to happen but it sure would justify his existence if it did.

Tom is from Florida. Born and raised outside of Tampa. He attended University of South Florida. He had already been certified as a trainer, and was looking for a place to go to graduate school and get good experience. One of his professors said he had a friend he went to graduate school with at the University of Arizona and believed was still at Chico State. That friend was the head athletic trainer, Scott Barker, husband of Anita Barker, Athletic Director. What a couple they make. I would give anything to be a fly on the wall in their dining room and hear them talking sports.

"So here I am," Tom says. Tom travels with the team to all the games. "Once this season is over," he says, "I go straight to baseball." He has come to Chico State at the right time. All throughout practice, Clink's message is the same: "Don't fall into their trap. Pace, pace!"

Clink calls the players over to the corner of the gym. The folding chairs are out. Time for film on Stanislaus and the scouting reports. Silverstrom sits down. Duncan says that's where he sits. Like two brothers, they compete for the chair. Silverstrom ends up giving him his chair. I think the season will be like this. One night Silverstrom will be the man in the chair, and the next night Duncan will be that man.

"Do not let the three point shot beat you," Clinks says. After the scouting report is finished, Clink tells the players the vans are rolling out at 2:15. "It's 1:48. Don't be late."

The ride there should have taken three hours. Instead it took six. They get stuck in traffic. Three hours in a minivan for guys over 6-feet-tall is hard. Six hours is torture. Particularly when it's an important in-region non-conference road game against a rival and in Warrior Arena. The players arrive ten minutes before the tip. The game, scheduled to tip at 7:30 p.m., gets pushed back to 7:50 p.m. The players barely have time to get out of the van and get dressed and taped before the game. It's a good thing Clink prepares so much before the game. He always prepares for the worst. This is one of those times.

Although Kitchens will start the game with a three, the good will turn quickly into the bad and the ugly. The Wildcats are not blocking out. The Wildcats have no rhythm. Clink calls a time out when the Warriors take the lead 13-4. He calls another one when the Warriors go up 17-4. Things are getting out of hand, fast. They score on the backdoor Clink has practiced and warned against all week. Baca, almost chanting, keeps saying during the broadcast: "The Wildcats just need to stay within the vicinity. Stay within the vicinity." Magz fails to block out. McFerren throws a bad pass. Six quick turnovers. Ambrosini loses his dribble, has the ball picked clean for an easy Warriors layup. Will this be the tragedy of Highway 99? Hardly. Chico State does not shy away from adversity: adversity unites them.

Silverstrom crashes the boards. Ellis goes three-for-three. Duncan has two beautiful assists. He also blocks two shots. Kitchens nails two three-pointers. McFerren has three rebounds. The Wildcats storm back and take a 32-30 lead into the locker room. The team that comes out in the second-half, though, no longer has van legs. Something has happened to Duncan in the locker room, some switch has been turned on, and he will have one of the greatest nights of his career. He puts on his Chico State cape. He has been quiet the last couple of games, doing the little things that often go unnoticed to the fan's eye, but tonight he is invincible. There are 424 fans in the arena to see his performance, but for those lucky enough to see it, well, they will be talking about it for a long time. Duncan has the ability to score at will. His dribble-attack-crossover-spin-in-the-air-acrobatics, as Baca calls it, is a phenomenon that must be seen. For two and a half minutes, Robert Duncan will wear wings.

He enters what athletes call the zone. He scores ten points. He uses his anger, his imagination, his passion, his instincts, to not only create but to finish shots. Here is the Division II Pistol Pete that I knew was coming, and it appears when his teammates need him most. "He's the magician," Baca roars over and over again. Whatever happens to Duncan in the future, wherever he ends up, and whatever age he lives to be, as long as him memory endures, he will have these two and a half minutes of perfection. Most of us are lucky if we have thirty seconds of perfection in our entire lives, and this young man has two and a half minutes. His perfection, his showcasing of talent, is not meant to bolster his own ego but to lift up his teammates. And he lifts them high.

Duncan will go 7-of-9 in the second half (4-of-4 from the three-point line). He has three assists. He has a blocked shot. Three rebounds. The only weakness of the night comes defensively, but approached from a cost-benefit analysis, his defense can suffer slightly for his offensive genius. Giddings goes 5-of-6. McFerren is perfect 2-of-2 with a couple more dazzling assists. Silverstrom hits a big three when needed. Ambrosini begins to flower with hustle and a breathtaking finger roll. And Kitchens will have a career high 15 points. After the game, Clink sounds exhausted, exhilarated, and emotionally spent. A six hour road trip full of detours and side roads and random parking lots followed by a 14 point deficit followed by a 52-point second half (and almost three minutes of the greatest individual play from a player in Clink's eight years) will do that to a coach.

"We had weary bodies walking off those vans," Clink says in the postgame interview with Baca. "We persevered, though. The last three games have thrown a lot of adversity at us. We rallied around each other. We had multiple guys stepping up. Needed stops and got them. Took care of the ball. We learned great lessons. You get down. You keep fighting. Keep grinding, chipping away, and good things *will* happen."

Clink says that Duncan came up to him moments after the game and asked: "What happened to me out there, Coach?"

Clink says he didn't have an answer. "He is amazing," Clink continues. "He gets like that in practice every now and then. Where he just takes over and can't be stopped. In a game like that I just let him go. Not all the shots he took were great, but they were going in and I try to just let him ride it out. I might call a play for him, but more importantly just don't get in his way."

Baca interviews Duncan next. He asks him the same thing: "What was going through your head?"

"Nothing," Duncan says. "The game just slowed down." He pauses and laughs a little. "When we walked in, Magz pointed up at the blue banner.

He looked at me said: 'We still owe them for that one. It was ours and they took it.'"

The loss to SPU and the debacle against Simpson seem like seasons ago. Amazing how a team can change in ten days. The Wildcats are starting to find themselves, discover a theme for the season.

Leaders are emerging. Chairs are literally being swapped. Tonight the chair is Duncan's. Next game Silverstrom's. The game after that McFerren's. Enough chairs to go around, and if a chair is not available then a seat on the bench is. And a seat on the Wildcats bench is almost as good as playing.

CHAPTER 51

Miracle on 400 W. First Street: San Marcos

⁓

DECEMBER 14

Destiny is a good thing to accept when it's going your way.
When it isn't, don't call it destiny; call it injustice,
treachery, or simple bad luck.

—JOSEPH HELLER

A LOT OF AMAZING THINGS can happen in one second. Three Barbie dolls are sold a second. Sixty lipsticks are made around the world. A bullet travels

900m. A snail travels 1cm in the rain. Saliva travels 100m. 6 babies are born. 10,450 Coca Colas are consumed. Lightning will strike 6 times. Bees beat their wings 270 times. The United States throws away 216 pounds of food. And Giddings will inbounds the ball to McFerren in time for one dribble before he launches the basketball, the prayer, the miracle—the Wildcats down 82-80 in the second half.

Acker is filled to capacity. The student section is standing room only. Fans in Santa hats jump up and down. The band is back. It's a small, grass-roots looking band, but they make a lot of noise and have talent. The cheerleaders have also arrived. Willie the Wildcat prowls the sideline. Magic fills the air on this night. The student section has a lot of steam to blow off. They have been studying all week, all day. Finals start Monday. It's the last home game before Christmas break. Acker smells like sweat, popcorn, and anxiety. It's cold out. The team managers, usually donning baggy sweat, are dressed to the nines. They look like they're ready for Christmas Eve service rather than a basketball game. The team managers are fired up. It's their first home game. It has all the feelings of a "Welcome to the big time, boys" show. Ricky, a freshman, has been dreaming of this night. His glasses fog over as he walks into the tunnel, peers out to see the women's game still in progress. His jaw drops a little as he scans the crowd, soaks in the electricity.

The players, one by one, all come out to check out the crowd. There seems to be a small fan club for each player. The student fans all hang their hands down for him to slap them a high five. Silverstrom's back still ails him. He grimaces, walks stiffly, hand occasionally rubbing the small of his back. The band plays "Tequila." The opponents in blue mix with the Chico State players. They have entered the Wildcats space in the tunnel to stretch, to check the time on the clock of the women'game. Not that different from tennis matches where opponents must share lockers, the bench, in the same locker room. The Wildcats check out the other players. It's the first time they've seen each other. The first thing that comes to mind when I see the San Marcos players: fast. They are known for shooting the three. Clink has been warning the Wildcats about this all week. Tonight they have to defend that three. Their lives depend upon it. As the women's games comes to an end, the fans grow more excited. The players know the time is near. The excitement of the fans reminds the players why they chose Chico State.

A little before 7 p.m. and the players start to fill the locker room. They take their seats in front of the board. At first, chatter. Slowly, the chatter fades. Stillness. A restless muteness washes over the locker room. The pulsing of hearts, the coursing of nerves. Finally, right at 7 p.m. sharp, the door to the locker room is thrown open. The shuffling of six dress shoes. The coaches have entered. Clink folds his jacket and lays it down on the torn leather couch. It's like God has entered when he comes into the locker room. Everyone's blood pressure rises.

The pregame show is all Coach Gabriel's, the young professor in training. He talks about consistency and references the Kevin McHale quote that was the theme of the week. Coach Gabriel finishes and hands it over to Clink. This is when it gets serious. The moment just before the battle ensues. Rapid firing in bullet points, reminders, of everything they worked on during practice all week.

"We're staring out in 22-23," Clink says. "Defense sprint back. Block out. Constant communication. Pace." Ellis sways back and forth. It's like he's in church and slowly the Holy Spirit is building within. He likes to hang on to the metal lockers, shake them, punch them, and kick them. They are good for that. Beg for it, even. "I want you to use your voice," Clink continues. "Communicate. I want you to value the ball. Share it. Everybody touch it."

Ellis starts shaking the lockers now with more intensity. "It's all about the defense!" Ellis chants, the Holy Spirit bursting forth from beneath his jersey. "Now let's go!"

The team huddles, put their fists together in the air then run out into the tunnel and then through the Red Door into Acker ready to battle. A band of unlikely brothers who span the entire length of California from San Diego to Humboldt. The band plays a slightly recognizable version of *Eye of the Tiger* as the last of the team makes its way through the Red Door. I walk through the Red Door with Ricky. He turns to me and says: "There's no place I'd rather be." Ricky is also ready to go to war. Moments later, he and the other freshman, the redshirt sensation Justin Briggs, stand in the Wildcat at center court and take in the atmosphere.

All the familiar rituals that take place before the game, the order before the chaos. The head coaches shaking hands and engaging in small talk. The gathering of the team captains. The national anthem. The calling out of the starting lineup. Clink, just before the game starts, always grabs his chair and pulls it out. I can always tell the level of his intensity by the way he grabs the chair. It's rarely gentle. Often looks like he's picking up a puppy by the neck who has just soiled his really expensive carpet and must now learn a lesson—controlled rage.

The game begins. Duncan immediately goes into attack mode. A bad call starts the game. This will be 40 minutes of agony. A stream of consciousness rant. The bliss will only come after the game. Once the ball has finally descended from the air and exited through the hoop. Until then, until the final second, only agony. My pen does not lift from the paper. I enter into a stream of consciousness that James Joyce would envy.

The huddle is a fortress. A chain link fence. The student section behind me is the sixth man. Clink looks like he wants to get in there and start swinging. Kitchens misses two free throws. I have a bad feeling about this. My instincts tell me it will come to down to a free throw. Clink growls, stomps his foot, as Kitchens misses the second free throw. Priest gives some good minutes. Magz is using his body out there. Duncan is playing pickup ball. Every time he touches the ball, the crowd goes wild. Everyone wants him to do something special. How do the Wildcats stop the three? San Marcos keeps draining it. They won't miss. The Wildcats are in trouble. How will Clink stop the bleeding? San Marcos blood bath floods the Acker floor. McFerren is penetrating like he was told to and then executing the perfect jump stop then kicking it back out. He looks fierce out there. 510, baby, and finally looking the part. Kitchens, unassuming, uses every ounce of his body. He puts his shoulder down and drives. Brilliant. Uses every ounce of talent the good Lord gave him. Wildcats look fundamentally sound. Save the free throws. Down 12 at 4:38. Clink calls a time out. Rabbit still in his pocket. He's saving the fire. Must be. Harris shoots two free throws.

Misses them both. This doesn't happen. But he gets his own rebound. Something Clink said resonating in his ear. The massacre continues. Media time out. Clink pulls out the kerosene. What he tells them lights a fire. This is what the great ones do. From the huddle Clink screams: Light fires. "Just do what we go through every day..."Harris comes out on a rampage. He gets the fire going. The kid is barbed wire. Knew the comeback was coming. Even when this team seems out of it, I know they never are. There is always hope. Coach Blake looks calm, medicated. Coach Gabe doing the shouting. "Shooter. Shooter." Anywhere else in the country save a basketball gym and yelling "Shooter" is like screaming "Fire" in a crowded theater. Writing is stream of consciousness. So is basketball only the refs keep calling Mickey Mouse fouls. What? Do they need to check their text messages? Half time. Thank the good Lord only I think the good Lord is ashamed of us because a free throw is alms to the poor and we have rejected that which He deemeth charity. 8-17 from the line. You do the math. Yet still we go into the locker only down 1. Locker room at the half never more talkative, animated. Why tonight?

Kitchens gets it going: "We can't be selfish. We can't be selfish." Magz chimes in, the most vocal he's been all year. Says something funny. That's what seniors do. He calms everyone. Harris starts in. He has earned it. Old Barbed Wire: "Keep playing defense. They will start missing the three." Clink and Coach Gabriel and Coach Blake still out in the hall. "It's now a 20-minute game," Magz says. Glad to hear his voice. Leaders are emerging. Still no sign of the coaches. I can feel Clink's ire smoldering outside. Almost see smoke creeping in from beneaththe locker room door. More from Harris: "Let's get out there and take charges. Fire Coach up." Kitchens: "Trust your teammates." They run out of things to say. Three good minutes of talk, though. Finally, doors open. Coach throws down his coat. Walks straight to the board. "Same place we were in the second half at Stanislaus. We're in a great spot. The 3-point shot is killing us. Get up in their chest. Number 22 is killing us. Do a better job containing the penetrators. Keep them out of the paint. Anything else to talk about defensively? What about the offense? Selfish. Undisciplined. Trying to score off the first touch. We need you to buy in. Drive. Penetrate. Lift. Fake. Kick. Get to the free throw line. Knock them down. Every time a team pressures us, we revert back to week two. Lift, attack, kick. It's not gonna happen on the first one. Not gonna happen. Trust me. It's right there for us. Bench also has to be better. Have to run to bathroom. Been holding a piss for an hour. Clink comes in. Awkward. "Not the time for humor," I say, "but thank God I'm the writer and not the coach."

Clink forces a half smile. Peeing while studying his folded playbook. Back on the sidelines, Clink in his folding chair. Head down. Pensive. Looking at his plays. Searching. Ellis goes by and gives him a quick shoulder massage. Clink with a knee jerk reaction followed by a smile. The touch soothes him. Just a game, he thinks, but it's not. It's everything to him. 20 minutes of agony. Duncan's brilliance. Two steals. A perfectly timed pass to Ellis that leads to a dunk and gets the boozy crowd fired up. McFerren hits a jumper and puts his arms up in the air. Crowd erupts. Mt. St. Helens style. Giddings throws a guy to the ground and looks like he wants to apologize. Nature versus nurture. He's too kind to be the kind of pit bull the coaches want him to be. Ellis always so relaxed. Nothing can get him down. Reminds me of old man in a young man's body. He reminds me of the Eddie Murphy movie where Eddie played the old man. Ellis has that kind of wisdom (only a sophomore) about him, and he moves like a gazelle.

11:53. Time out. Magz is talking up the players. They listen. Can't hear Clink in the huddle. Don't need to. Vein in his neck like a cobra trying to break through. Wonder how many minutes of life that kind of intensity takes off the old ticker. Maybe it makes the ticker stronger. Takes a different breed to make it in this business. How many basketball games across this country are being played in small gyms, big fieldhouses, like this tonight? All the effort, the planning, that goes into it for both the team and the fan. The agony and the ecstasy. Someone has to lose. Someone will win. One man's heartbreak is another man's joy. Kitchens is a warrior. Keeps us in it. Nate the youngster is a textbook for what Clink teaches. Perfect jump stop. Obedient player and so coachable. So perfect that the lefty gets one of their hot hands to foul out. That is the kind of play Clink lives for, the kind of play that one will never see in a stat sheet.

Duncan has taken the game over. Always a threat. Our penetration is getting them into foul trouble, only we can't make a free throw. It will come down to that in the end. Who will make their free throws? Are we trying to miss?

There is certainly a time for that, but the time is not now. Clink gives up his chair for Isaiah. Clink will not sit the rest of the night. Kitchens fouls out. He leads the players in cheering on the bench. Nate steps in. Big shoes to fill for the young leftie. McFerren hits a big shot. Tied up at 1:21. Nothing rattles Ellis. He has a ferocious blocked shot. Duncan makes a layup to put us ahead with 33 seconds left. All comes down to the last shot. Duncan, playground mode, cat toying with the mouse, waits for the clock to wind down. He lets it fly prematurely. San Marcos bats it away. San Marcos picks it up close to half court with three seconds left. Duncan flies down to the other end. Don't know how he got there. Always Superman. Fouls a San Marcos player with only 1.2 on the clock. Makes the first one. They take the lead 81-80. All he has to do is miss the free throw. Game over. Clink calls a timeout. Keep checking score, time, as he talks to the team. How can they be so calm? Clink almost looks relieved. The pain is finally over. Even if it's a loss. Coach calls a play to try and inbound the ball up court on the run toward our basket. The ref comes over to Clink and tells him it's time to go. Seems like he feels sorry for Clink and gives him a few extra moments before saying: "Come on, coach, let's go again." Prayer. Hope. It all comes down to this.

Prayer.

Sports.

Prayer.

Backbone of the country…

And then it happens.

The San Marcos player banks in the free throw he is supposed to miss. Miracles can happen in less than 1.2 seconds.

McFerren takes the inbounds pass from Giddings in front of the San Marcos bench. He spins left. Dribbles once lets and lets it fly from the half-court line directly in front of the scorer's table.

All net.

A mob ensues.

The shot will be dubbed McFerren's Miracle. Miracles, though, are for those whom no longer have hope. Prayers are different. Most of them go unanswered. There were many praying in Acker on Saturday night. For the fans, the last second thrill is ecstasy, everything a fan wants to see. But for Clink it's like winning a game of pool by having your opponent scratch on the eight ball. The Wildcats should never have been in this situation to begin with. And the irony that what almost lost the game for us—poor free throw shooting—put the Wildcats in a situation to win the game: a made free throw when the intention was to miss.

McFerren's Miracle.

But the shot, although a surprising and welcomed event, is explicable to natural and scientific laws and therefore not to be considered the work of a divine agency. The shot is pure luck. Everything that led up to the shot was luck. The free throw the San Marcos player was supposed to miss. The inbounds play that Clink drew up that was abandoned. The dryness of the ball when it landed in McFerren's hands. Was it the fact that he had wiped off the bottom of his shoes when standing at the free throw line moments ago? Was it the extra few seconds that the referee, who surely must have felt a pang in his heart for Clink's defeated Wildcats, gave him?

The shot was also chance: something that happened by accident and without design. Even though Clink prepares his team for the worst case scenario, there was nothing he could do to prepare his team for this. The shot might have also been destiny. The team, after all, is a team of destiny—there is a hidden power that seems to be controlling the future of this young team.

McFerren's Miracle is San Marcos's bad luck.

Some words must be held in reservation. Miracles happen in March, not December.

McFerren did the unthinkable. He sunk the shot from beyond half-court. Even more unthinkable was the unshakable demeanor of the coaching staff, the guys on the bench, and, most importantly, the young men on the court. McFerren has become immortalized. One second is all it took. His shot, the chance, the luck of it all, had what is called a butterfly effect that is grounded in chaos theory, the sensitive dependence on initial conditions in which a small change in one state of a deterministic nonlinear system can result in large differences in a later state. I doubt that his life will ever be the same after hitting that shot. The effect rippled. It touched his peers, his family, the Chico community. For old time fans, it gave them a memory to take to their graves. The shot created an entire new legion of fans. The shot might have been the pivotal moment in the season.

The shot that brought the team, the fans, together. Yet the shot also reminded Clink that there's a lot the team needed to work on to not find themselves in a position like this again. For me, the biographer of the season, the coach, and the team, it awakened me to a thrill I have only felt a few times in life. There was the thrill of graduating from college. The thrill of my wedding. The thrill of my children being born—a real miracle when any child is born. But these are rites of passage. A Hail Mary to win a basketball game is not a rite of passage which gives the thrill that much more value. The miracle shot sent me storming the court with my blue book held high, a 44-year-old man returned to his youth. Clink, meanwhile, rubs his face and immediately heads over to shake the other coach's hand. Clink then embraces the young man who accidentally made the free throw while the Wildcats, the fans, celebrate on the court.

The locker room is festive. Clink lets the players have their moment. His three boys are in the locker room. The only thing missing is the champagne. Even Coach Blake is smiling. "All I will say is that it wasn't pretty," Clink says to the team. "This is one T-shirt I'll be glad to give you, Jalen," Clink says in reference to the T-shirt a player receives if he makes the traditional shoot-around half-court shot.

"This is a situation we can build on," he says. "I'll watch the film tonight. In three days we'll talk about it. For now, I want you to just enjoy the moment and get ready for finals."

Clink, though, will stew until the next practice. Winning on a prayer is not his style. Four days later, his team 9-1, 3-0 in the conference, No. 17 in the country, will have an intervention.

Sure, Clink will take miracles, just not in December.

CHAPTER 52

Intervention

DECEMBER 15

McFERREN'S SATURDAY NIGHT MIRACLE TURNS into Tuesday morning's intervention. When I arrive to practice the folding chairs are in a circle around the Wildcat emblem at center court. Coach Gabriel walks up to me, pensive, playing it off like he's relaxed. "Coach is the only coach in the country who at 9-1 overall, and 3-0 in the conference, is holding an intervention."

"Is that really what this is—an intervention?" I ask.

He nods. "It's an intervention."

The players enter the gym and sprint over to the chairs where Clink is already waiting for them. He sits with his head down, gathering his thoughts, for thirty seconds. The tension rises. The festivities from Saturday night are history.

"I've done a lot of soul searching the last couple of weeks," he says. "Where we were. Where we are. Where we need to go." He takes a deep breath, voice still flat. The players know his voice will soon rise. "I think we're in a great spot." Another pause. "But I'm not satisfied. Here's where I am with our evaluation. We need to stop trying to score off the first attack. Two or three attacks are just fine."

Clink takes a deep breath, teeth clenched and jaw set. "When I went home after the game Saturday night, and I looked over the stats, I was surprised. We were 42.9% from the field. That's good." The pause. "But here's the thing—and I want you to pay attention. Pay attention. We were 14-of-29 from the free throw line. We shot 48% from the free throw line and still scored 83 points and won. Let that sink in."

Silence for thirty seconds. "I looked at the box score." He shakes his head. A disgusted look comes over his face. "We burped it up all night. Missed half our free throws. Yet we still score 83 points. It's not our offense. Nope. Not the offense. The offense is positive. Here's the kicker." His voice rises, slows down, each syllable piercing the air. "We cannot give up 82 points. Not if we're going to get where we want to get. We have to work on our defense." He looks around the circle. Each player receives his eye contact.

"Magz," Clink says, "what do we want to accomplish this year?"

"Final Four," he says.

"What about you, Nate?"

"At least the Elite Eight."

"Isaiah?"

"Win league. Win West Regional."

Clink asks each player, and then stops with McFerren.

"What about you, Jalen? What do you want us to accomplish this year?"

"Complete games. Offense and defense."

"To accomplish this," Clink says, "we all must strive together to be the best defensive team in the country. We're not even close right now.

Our defense ranks 12th in the league. We're giving up 65.5 points a game. We're third in field goal percentage defense. 7th in giving up the 3. Teams are shooting 34.3% against us from the 3-point line. We're outrebounding teams. That's good. We're fifth in forcing turnovers. And 12th in fouls. We're fouling 21 times a game."

Clink stops talking to let the players chew on the stats.

"We're not 100% committed as a group to being the best defensive team in the country," he continues. "I've not been committed. I take the blame. I know we have the ability to be the best defensive team in the country. But we're not walking into practice or into games with that mindset. It's not you, though. It's me. I've not been demanding enough on the defensive end. This is on me. I need you to recommit. We have to reestablish the identity that has been Chico State basketball for the last four years. See, other teams, sure, they're talking about our offense. Everybody knows we can score. But what they're not talking about is our defense. Just our offense."

Every player is stone faced. They get the message.

"We as a team must be focused and committed. It's about walking through that Red Door and into this gym every day with the right mindset. Get better defensively. It's an everybody thing. I want to see you diving for balls. Taking charges. I want to see you taking pride in everything you do, individually and collectively. If you can commit to this and work at it every single day, the sky is the limit for you guys. But you must be committed."

Clink pulls out a stack of index cards. He passes one out to each player. "I want you to think long and hard about what you want to improve upon and commit to. Then I want you to write it out. It's time for me to put my money where my mouth is and make sure that I help us make these things happen."

Some of the players start writing immediately. Others get out of their chairs and stretch out on the ground and think. Most of the guys are scribbling wildly. Some use their chair as a desk. The players write without pause for fifteen minutes.

"Go ahead and put the chairs back where you got them," Clink says. Three minutes later, as I walk out of the gym, I hear Clink's voice trailing behind. "I want you jumping and bluffing. Be there on the catch. If you're going to be committed to being a great defender, you can't be comfortable. If you're comfortable, that means you're not working hard enough. Know who you're matched up against. Now find somebody and grab a ball. Let's go!"

The intervention doesn't work.

Sonoma State will ruin the Christmas break of the Wildcats coach and players. The luck of the Wildcats will run out in Rohnert Park on December 19 when they take on the Sonoma State Seawolves—actually when the Wildcats take on one player who will manhandle them. James Davis, not Robert Duncan, shows up as the Pistol Pete of the CCAA. Davis will score 30 points in the second half going 11-of-14—including 6-of-8 from 3-point land. Luke Reid sums it up like this: "Sonoma State's James Davis was so hot he could have been throwing in 3-pointers through the windows of The Wolves' Den." Duncan, though, is almost as hot as Davis. Duncan will finish with a season-high 12 rebounds to accompany his 25 points in the second half.

The ghost of Christmas past—James Davis—will haunt the chambers of Clink's mind during the long Christmas break.

CHAPTER 53

A Long December

DECEMBER 28

THE FIRST PRACTICE SINCE CHRISTMAS break. The Wildcats have had a long time to think about the last loss, the one where one man wearing a Sonoma State jersey, not five, beat them. The players are stretching. A train whistle blows outside the gym. The campus outside is dead. The faculty are all checked out. Only a few staff members linger, those, who like me, prefer this time of year. The quietness. The loneliness slaked by solitude. A time when work gets done. No interferences. No meetings. No chatting.

After the players finish stretching, they start warming up. The same drills as October 15. Coach Blake works with the big men. He throws them the ball in the post. They work on their footwork, pivots, head fakes, lifts, and layups. The guards and wings work on their outside shots. Coach Gabriel is fired up. He must be happy, like me, to no longer be cooped up in the house changing diapers. He just celebrated his first Christmas with his baby girl. I ask him what he got her.

"Some tissue paper. She won't remember."

Children, not mortgages and car payments, are the best things for a man's job security. Christmas break for a lot of men is just that—a clever pun the break that breaks a man. There is no break when small children are in the picture, particularly when the mother stays at home with them all day. Being a stay-at-home mother, I believe, is the hardest job in the world. Yes, even harder than what Clink is doing, and even harder than writing a book. My break consisted of the chaos stemming from piles and piles of dirty diapers, a day in the life of my wife. Kids with the croup and a midnight visit to the emergency room. Sick children and sleepless nights. Floors to be mopped, dirtied five minutes later. Presents to be wrapped. Strewn wrapping paper to collect. Boxes broken down, jammed into recycling bins. Staying up all night assembling toys. The heartbreak of not having batteries for the toys the next morning. Round after round of family visits.

Clink's basketball practice presents a break from the Christmas break. For an hour, order is restored. A reminder that hard work is good. An escape, even. I have not touched pen to paper since the Wildcat loss. The loss that made me sick. If it spoiled my Christmas, what kind of havoc must it have wreaked on the players, on Clink? I'll never forget the name James Davis. I imagine the players are able to quickly put it in the rear view mirror and move forward. That's what athletes do. It's the writers who live in the past, stir it over and over, sift it, strain it, freeze it, thaw it. The pen scratching the legal pad feels so good—good, I imagine, like Ellis feels when grabbing a rebound or McFerren feels dribbling behind his back or Silverstrom nailing a three. This is where we (the coaches, the players, me) all belong: in the gym. Players, writers, coaches never really sleep—at least the good ones who want to become great. How can we? There's always someone practicing, working, while we dream. But the obsessed don't dream.

"Let's go. Get your feet set," Clink shouts as he makes his post-Christmas entrance into the gym. "Hustle, Nate." He blows his whistle. It sounds like sleigh bells. Nothing but sleigh bells for 30 days. The whistle sounds great. The whistle sounds like work. The players spend 11 minutes taking shots to shake off the Christmas rust. The big stretch awaits Clink and his team. The next three months will be hard. The season might have started October 15th, but it really gets started in January. No, it really gets started in three days, on New Year's Eve, when the Wildcats play Cal State Los Angeles. The Wildcats are out of the polls. Probably a good thing. Now they get to play the role of underdog to Cal Poly Pomona and UC San Diego. Clink studies all the players. Santa's list might have told him who has been naughty or nice, but Clink's eyes are telling him who has gotten soft since the loss and sat around and ate grandmother's pie all day and played video games and watched television.

A few poinsettias still linger as a back drop for sports commentators. Boy Scouts have started driving around Chico and picking up Christmas trees curbside. Christmas lights are being taken down from the houses. Wreaths taken off the doors. The trees are bare. Jack Frost visits nightly. The NFL playoffs have arrived. College bowl games are underway. And even though the Super Bowl will not be until February 7, college basketball rules these two months. The baseball geeks are getting excited because pitchers and catchers will report in February, but for most sports fans all that matters is right before us: college basketball. Clink knows what awaits. January and February, the cruelest months.

Duncan has finally showed up to practice. The trainer is paying close attention to him. The Wildcats are deep, but without Duncan hope fades. The players line up for right handed layups. They pass me in a blur of speed. "Run harder, Marv," Coach Gabriel shouts. Clink's hawk eyes burn brightly. Same fundamentals. Catch. Pivot. Crisp passes. Never changes. Same dance. Same moves. Clink, crouching against the wall, watching. A human metaphor for how he must feel right now. The season has been confusing. Each game has showed a different strength, but the strength has been weakened by constant turnovers and an average defense. The players do one-on-one drills. Ellis chasing down a defender, watching his acceleration from the midcourt line, then the leap, the arms extended, the swat, is one of the most breathtaking moments of every practice, an athletic feat so full of light and grace that it knocks the wind out of me. If only I could write like that!

The players transition into their rebounding drills.

"Do it again," Clink says over and over.

Harris, who has been in an awful slump and seems to be losing his confidence by the minute, takes a bad three-point fade away shot. Clink springs off the wall. "That is not a good shot. Was than A-shot?" Harris shakes his head. "Get your feet set. Take a good shot." Harris trots off to get some water. Coach Gabriel talks to him. "I want you all working on jumping to the ball and getting your feet in the correct stance," Clink says. "I want you to always be thinking about where you need to be. What you need to do. You can't turn your head and stare at the ball. I want you dialed in. Deny the three. I don't want to see you jogging at the interchange. I want to see a sprint."

Silverstrom takes a wild shot. "If it ain't a nice shot, don't take it," Clink shouts. "Kick the ball back out to Coach Gabriel. I will not be angry if you don't take the shot. I'd much rather have you kick it back out. You hear me? If it's not an A-shot, jump stop and kick it back out."

Clink still doesn't like what he sees. "Here's where we are this week. Take away the three. Take away the three. Magz, what do you not understand about this?"

The frustration in Magz has been building. He's been listening to Clink for five years. Clink has been telling him the same things, over and over, for five years. They're stuck with each other for three more months. Then for life. This is what happens you play for Clink and graduate. "I want you to communicate at a really high level. Have a conversation. Stop the three. Does anybody disagree with me?" Pause. "Good. Now take away the 3-point line."

Harris takes another long shot, another bad miss. Giddings and Timothy spring for the ball. Timothy catches it first. Giddings reaches in and grabs it. They wrestle for it. The two big men crash to the floor and wrestle. Clink blows his whistle. I see a slight smile. This is the closest Clink has come to grinning since McFerren's 3-point bomb. The players, coaches, are lighthearted. The loss seems behind them now. McFerren's miracle is long forgotten in everyone's mind except maybe McFerren's.

CHAPTER 54

New Year's Eve: Cal State L. A. Golden Eagles

THE WILDCATS UNDERSTAND THE IMPORTANCE of maximizing space. They watch game film on the same dry eraser board in the locker room where they do all the pregame breakdowns. Clink told me yesterday the film session was at 9:30 a.m. I show up at 9:26 a.m. The team is already into scouting the third player in the lineup. Coach Gabriel is at his best when it comes to breaking down film. While he talks, Clink occasionally chimes in. Even though Coach Gabriel is piloting the ship right now, Clink is still the captain. "Always have a hand in that guy's chest," Clink interrupts. "Block him out. Communicate. Bluff and recover." They talk about Duce Zaid, the Los Angeles star. He has the potential to explode like James Davis from Sonoma State and take control of a game. Clink won't allow that happen again. "Duce is not looking to pass," Coach Gabriel says. "When you see guys crashing the boards, block them out right from the get. Be physical. Don't give them touches."

Kitchens is rubbing his lower back. It seems to be bothering him. Even though the players are engaged, several of them yawn. This is early for them. "Let's talk about their transition offense. We have to get back. Help. Sprint." Clink has been talking about this all week. "Their second shot, guys, is their best shot," Coach Gabriel says.

"How physical will we be to start the game?" Clink adds. His voice is rougher than usual. It sounds as if he's fighting a cold. No doubt he's been up since early morning. The basketball language, the verbs, never grow dull.

"Watch the hand-off. The flare. The ball screen. After that, they're just playing," Coach Gabriel says. If the Wildcats can get them to that point, they'll win the game. The shot clock will be in their favor. Tonight will reveal just how fast the Wildcats truly are. Los Angeles possesses blinding speed.

"Let's talk about the Chin," Coach Gabriel says of another one of their plays. "They'll catch. Pass and run. Then the UCLA screen." Clink breaks in: "Be alert." Back to Coach Gabriel. "Don't fall for the down pick and the curl action," Coach Gabriel says. "Jump to the ball," Clink growls. "Jump to the ball. Opposite guard has to take it away." He pauses. "Any questions?" None. "Let's go!"

Walking into Acker gym from the locker room and passing through the Red Door is like being a kid and walking into the living room on Christmas morning. I love the pregame shoot around.

The house is all clean. What just the night before looked like the same old room from the previous 364 days is suddenly fancy. New. Full of surprises. The fancy red seats where my son and his grandparents will soon be sitting look pristine and elegant. The wooden bleachers behind me look so timeless and elegant, full of Nirvana's teen-spirit. Virgin scoreboard. Like the first run of the day for the skier in fresh powder. Chico, 0. Visitor, 0. 20:00 minutes on the board. 30 seconds on the shot clock. And soon it will all be messy. Chaos will disrupt the order.

Duncan is hobbling from the ankle he sprained over the break. The players take shots with Clink and Coach Gabriel. The big men go and work the paint with Coach Blake. Same thing, over and over. Head fake, pump fake, spin, shoot, off the glass, in. A while later the players make layups from each side. They count out each one as if they're in the military. Teams might get creamed, but teams don't die. Clink looks at his play list. He runs all the offensive plays they'll run that evening. It seems like he's always incorporating something new. I look at the scouting report. Another John Wooden quote.

The players sprint to the other end of the court. They start running the Los Angeles plays, walking through them slowly, figuring out how to stop them. Coach Gabriel is also a master of the slow walk through. He's an excellent teacher. It's sad to think that he'll not be around for more seasons. He's rare. He'll make a great head coach. Other institutions will come calling—only a matter of time. As Coach Gabriel shows the players where to run and get position, I'm shocked, yet again, at the amount of intelligence these young men must have to comprehend all of this. Basketball players get such a hard time about not being smart, called dumb jocks. It's not that they don't have the potential to be book smart, but basketball is just so much more fun. And the kids that are book smart, I imagine, are not nearly as spatially intelligent as basketball players. Some of these Wildcats, all of them, are young geniuses in the spatial domain.

The last day of the year. It's been a good one. Maybe the best in Chico State men's basketball history. The Wildcats have a record of 10-2 overall,

4-1 in the CCAA. Cal State Los Angeles is headed to town for a 3 o'clock tip. The Golden Eagles are hot. The two styles of play seem worlds apart. Even though the Golden Eagles are just 2-8 overall and 1-2 in the conference, they have won two straight. Anything can happen in the CCAA. The Golden Eagles roster has a totally different feel than the Wildcats. Whereas the Wildcats only have one transfer in senior Tanner Giddings, the Golden Eagles have several transfers from the following: Saddleback College; University of Hawaii; Weber State; Mt. San Antonio College; Simon Fraser; Fullerton College; East Los Angeles College; Solano Community College; Coppin State; Tennessee Martin; Mira Costa Community College/ Northern Arizona; and George Washington.

The Golden Eagles look tough, like players who cut their teeth playing on the Los Angeles city playgrounds and somehow wound up playing inside a gym. They have talent. Individual talent. But as I have learned from following Clink and the Wildcats, this game is about teamwork first and talent second. Sure, occasionally one man will beat you, like James Davis for Sonoma State game, but it's rare.

The Golden Eagles head coach, Dieter Horton, has been around. Like his players, and like the ball of the sport he coaches, Horton has bounced around. He has coached at every level. This is his second season as the men's basketball head coach at Cal State L.A. Last season the Golden Eagles had an overall record of 10-16 overall and went 8-14 in the CCAA. Horton is known as much for his defensive mind as his recruiting. Last year Los Angeles was ranked 14th in the country in scoring defense after allowing opponents just 62.9 points per game. The Golden Eagles were also among the national leaders in field-goal percentage defense and allowed opponents to shoot just 41.7% from the floor. He has a 58-56 win over Cal Poly Pomona in the Eagles Nest on Jan. 17. Horton also led the Golden Eagles to a big road win over defending CCAA Tournament champion Cal State Stanislaus.

Horton came to Cal State Los Angeles in 2014 with an outstanding resume of success. He reached the post season in each of his 14 years as a community college head coach and spent four seasons as an assistant coach at

USC. Horton has coached a pair of players currently in the NBA: Dewayne Dedmon, while at Antelope Valley College and USC, and Nikola Vucevic, the 16th overall pick in the 2011 NBA Draft, while at USC. At the time this book was written, both players were with the Orlando Magic.

The Wildcats are restless and keep peeking out beneath the bleachers to check on the score of the women's game. The game is exciting, but certainly played at a different level. The slower pace of watching women's basketball reveals more of the fundamentals—something about it seems more pure. Ellis walks around like a child at a sleepover. His shoes are off, and he skates around the locker room in socks and baggy clothes. The young man is always loose. He knows this is just play. Each player has his own ritual and prepares in his own unique way. Toilets are always flushing during the pregame warmups. Fingers snapping. Jangled youthful nerves. Occasional whoops of anxiousness. Old lockers clanging open and closed. Duncan has his hair down, a mess of draping curls that touch the shoulder. The starting line-up is on the white board. When the coaches walk in, Coach Gabriel walks to the board. He looks exhausted, eyes squinting. "Jalen, talk to me about your man, "he says. Earlier during the film session, the players were reading from the scouting report that Coach Gabriel handed them. Now it's memorized. McFerren talks about his opponent as if he's his brother. The goal for the night is to take 40 A-shots. Clink reminds the players that he'd rather have the shot clock expire than for them to take a bad shot.

"We have to bounce back," Coach Gabriel says.

"We just got punched in the mouth by Sonoma," Clink adds.

"Listen, we gotta have blind faith in each other," Coach Gabriel continues. "Coach had blind faith when he gave me my first job out of college. When we recruited you, we had blind faith. When you chose to play here, you had blind faith. This carries over into the program. Blind faith. You must have blind faith that we've done a good job on the scouting report. It doesn't matter what role you play, whether it's the whole game or three, four minutes, you must blind faith."

Clink later tells me that blind faith goes back to his early years at Chico State. "We were building the program and had all these new guys and no one knew what direction we were going in except for me. I told them all they needed was to have blind faith in the program, blind faith in the guy next to them—blind faith in me and the coaching staff."

The team is fired up. Ready to erase the memory of James Davis from their minds. Turn a new page and enter the new year on a good note. They huddle and break. When the team runs through the Red Door, a trail of fire follows them. Now is the point where most of the fans have gone to get popcorn or spring a leak, check their cell phones, take some air. But they're missing the best part. Watching the teams get ready. Watching the players watch each other, make their assumptions, a process not unlike what we fans go through when issuing our own assessments and evaluations from the bleachers.

Los Angeles looks tough, fast. The teams are two stark contrasting images, the perfect Southern and Northern California matchup. Silverstrom shoots until it's time to head into the locker room for the final talk before the game. His ritual is to always be last, whether it's taking the half-court shot during the shoot around, leaving practice, leaving the locker room before the game, or heading over to the bench for the introduction of the starting lineup. Clink talks briefly. "It's a no-man's land game," he says. No-man's land is a game the players play in practice to keep the ball from being driven into the key. "Make sure you hit somebody," Clink continues. "Block out. We're going to track all the A-shots. It's about sharing the ball. Sprinting back. Getting your tails back to the basket. First play, if we win the tip... lifting, attacking, pace. No man's land, guys, getting good shots. Pace." The players head back to the court. Clink always stays back. He retreats into the bathroom. I have to go, but I'll hold it to avoid the awkwardness. Save it for half-time. The Wildcats head out to the court. I take my seat behind Clink and Baca. Baca, always talking to himself, laughing. Clink and Horton meet halfway. Clink immediately unwinds. Just like that. He gives Horton a wild, loose handshake. They hug each other followed by big smiles and pats on the backs as if they were old college pals. Horton looks tired. Maybe over basketball. What was once a passion has now become a job. They talk for a few minutes. Once they part, the boxer's scowl appears back on Clink's face.

Clink picks up his clipboard and scoots out his chair. The game is on. The first possession of the game looks exactly like what the Wildcats practiced all week: patience and A-shots. The game begins and McFerren gets the tip and scores right away. Practice is being emulated. What a thrill to see it then and now—deliberate practice in prime time. On the next possession, Kitchens hits a shot right as the shot clock expires. I'd seen this all week during practice. A time out is later called.

"Patience," Clink says in the huddle. "Get a good shot—A-shots. Work it."

Silverstrom checks back into the game. He plays with patience. He has listened to his coaches. He penetrates and kicks it to Ambrosini for a three. String music. Jump stops abound. Kicking the ball out to an open man and not taking the first shot. Most of the people in the stands really have no understanding of what they're watching. Pure entertainment to them. I, too, used to think that perfect play like this just happened. But the reality is that an entire week is boiled down to 40 minutes. But what started out as perfection soon comes undone. Los Angeles gets hot. The half ends with McFerren being thrown to the ground and no foul called. Clink explodes. The team, too, wants to explode with him. They know better and hustle off the court and into the locker room. That's the place to show their emotions.

The locker room is deflated. The players knew how perfectly they had played, and then how imperfectly. It can all come undone so quickly in basketball. They only have a four-point lead: 32-28. Waiting for the coaches to come in seems like eternity. When they do come in, Clink wastes no time. "Okay, guys, give me your thoughts." A few mutters. "We had 16 A-shots with five minutes left in the half. For fifteen minutes, we played great. Great. We need to continue to be tough with the ball. Rip it at your shoelaces. Use ball screens. Do the things we talked about in practice every day." He pauses. "15 beautiful minutes. Tanner, you had six rebounds. Great job. We only had six turnovers. We only get four more in the second half. A-shots. Work together." He pauses. "Anything else from you guys? It's a game of no-man's land. Let's go!"

Duncan is about to heat up. I see it in his eyes, the urgency in his movements on the court. Clink was so relaxed in the locker room despite the poor play of the last five minutes because he knew they were in a good spot. Experience. Magz has an open court dunk. He almost shatters the glass. He'll never be more alive. The crowd erupts. No matter if he is destined for a life of cubicle-confinement and computer screens and headsets after college, he will always have this moment. A smile stretches over his face. Duncan and Silverstrom seem to have again traded high scorer again for the night. Tonight is Duncan's turn. When a timeout is called a little later, Clink lightly grabs the chair and scoots it out. "Dig in," he tells them. Whenever the Wildcats have their biggest leads during a game, that's when Clink yells the loudest. The Wildcats have a 17-point lead with only one minute left. It's almost as if he doesn't feel comfortable whipping someone, and anxiously resorts to his mantras: "Stance, stance. Pace, Jalen, pace! No man's land! No man's land!"

Even though the Wildcats have a huge lead, Harris takes a bad shot— not an A-shot—with a few seconds left on the clock. Clink stomps his feet and throws his hands in the air. Pulls Harris from the game. Harris scowls. Even his hair looks angry. This will give Clink something to coach, teach, during the next practice—something for Harris to learn. Silverstrom will wind down the game with his last three-pointer of 2015. There's such a calmness that comes over him when he catches the ball behind the line, zeros in, takes aim, sets his feet, and lets it fly. Here he has the beginner's mind. The Wildcats will exit 2015 with a 73-55 win.

After the game, the locker room has the celebratory mood of a family ready to ring in the new year. "Good win, guys," Clink says. "Let's talk about our defense. We held them to 55. That's 11 points under their average. A major step forward. Overall, great defensive effort. And we had 39 A-shots." Everyone cheers. The goal had been 40. "We outrebounded them in the first half 41-26."

Duncan speaks up. "Coach, I'd like to give a shout out to Magz," he says. "He really cleared out space for us to drive and attack." Everyone claps. "Yes," Clink says, "I think that was one of the best games of your career, Magz." Clink takes a deep breath. The players know a "but" is coming. "But one of the areas we have to work on and get better at is not turning the ball over," Clink says. "We turned it over 15 times. When we get back here tomorrow, we'll work on that."

There's no break for this team. More deliberate practice on the first day of 2016.

"Listen, I know you're all going to go out and have fun tonight," Clink says, "but be smart. There will be a lot of people coming into town. I want you all to hang out with each other. Watch each other. Be someplace safe. And take care of your bodies. I want you back here tomorrow ready to go at 11:30 a.m. Have your bags packed. We're leaving for Dominguez Hills at 2 p.m."

CHAPTER 55

Chico State Reunion: Cal State Dominguez Hills

JANUARY 2

ONE HUNDRED SIXTY-ONE FANS HAVE come out to watch the game. Coach Blake is called to do the pregame interview with Baca. Coach Blake has gained a lot of confidence since I first met him last March. He talks with such certainty. "Our emphasis all week has been shot selection," Coach Blake says. "Tonight we are going up against maybe the best shooting team in the league." Coach Blake talks about each player on the opposing team. He knows everything about them. After Coach Blake's interview, Baca notes that Coach Blake is one of the Wildcats unsung heroes. "He's an important piece to this team." Two nights later he'll be serving beers to customers at Round Table pizza where he bartends to make ends meet. If only the rest of the word could see how hard he works and his loyalty to these players.

Clink is particularly proud tonight. Over on the Dominguez Hills bench it feels like a Chico State reunion. The Chico State and Greg Clink torch has been passed on to the foe. Justin Argenal, his former player and four-year player at Chico State, is working as an assistant coach for Dominguez Hills. He had been bouncing around teams, hoping to make it back to California. Here he is. Ryan Fraser, also on the Dominguez Hills bench, was an assistant coach under Clink during the 2010-2011 season.

The gym is so empty that spectators sitting in the highest row of bleachers can hear Clink talking to his team in the huddle. As the Wildcats stretch their league, Clink seems to grow more uncomfortable: "Motion. Execute. Stance, stance, stance! Pace, pace." Duncan, who has been quiet all night, almost as if he feels embarrassed for being the leading scorer on the team, gets hot and scores eight quick points before the clock winds down on the first game of 2016. Even though the game seems far out of reach for the opponent, Clink keeps shouting: "No threes, Jalen. No threes! Keep your hands up."

The Wildcats will win easily by a score of 78-64 and move into a four-way tie for first.

Something has clicked in Giddings since he made the half-court shoot around shot before the Los Angeles game. He has become aggressive, assertive, the kind of player everyone was expecting, hoping, he'd become. I can't help but think that Clink calling him a scarecrow must have woken him up. Clink is thrilled. On a night when his two most prolific scorers, Silverstrom and Duncan, hit only one shot in the game's first 34 minutes, it's nice to have a fall guy like Giddings—particularly when he hits 9-of-14 shots—to fall back on. Giddings will finish the night with career highs of 20 points, 12 rebounds, four blocked shots, and three assists. Giddings has always been the missing link. Only the second day in January and the Wildcats are starting to put the pieces together. McFerren also shines. He scores 13 points and grabs seven rebounds but most impressive: five assists and no turn overs. Kitchens finishes with nine and Ellis 11. Duncan and Silverstrom combine for only 12 points.

In the post-game interview, Clink speaks modestly about the win. "We took two steps forward, and one step back," he tells Baca. "We have to play hard for 40 minutes. Our weakness continues to be how we defend the three." He takes a breath. "I'm really pleased with Giddings. His aggression level is rising." Giddings will come on to the set and talk to Baca. He doesn't say much, other than: "I had a different mindset tonight."

This different mindset will hopefully become a permanent one.

CHAPTER 56

No Man's Land

MONDAY, JANUARY 4

THE WILDCATS HAVE THEIR TOUGHEST road games ahead of them and against two of the top teams: Cal Poly Pomona, and Humboldt State. Next up: rival Humboldt State on Thursday in bone-chilling Arcata. The Wildcats are 5-1 going into the weekend, a four-way tie at the top. They can come home next Sunday in sole possession of first. Humboldt State will pose a big challenge. Not many teams win there. Luke Reid, in lieu of my previous court storming after McFerren's Miracle, has told me not to "cheer at the table when I go to Humble State—things can get out of hand, fast. One year a fan came down and stole Coach Clink's clipboard." More Clink mythology. Truth: Clink threw his play sheet in the air after a bad call and it went up in the stands. Two plays later, Clink scanned the stands and saw a fan sitting in the front holding it. He snatched it back.

The team sits in the folding chairs. There's a lot of coughing, nose blowing in shirts and throat clearing. These guys share everything, even germs. Clink offers the following assessment in the film session before practice gets underway: "We made some strides on our defense, guys. We still need to block out better. Post players need to get better. Our biggest weakness, though, is still the three point shot. We're allowing people to dribble too deep on us. They can't go over the top. Can't do it. We have to make them go baseline." Clink pauses, paces. "We have to stop over the top penetration. I think back to our 2012 team. We only allowed 8.5 three point attempts a game. We made as many three point shots a game as we allowed the other team to make." His ire is rising. "We're allowing 18.5. If we get this down to 13, we're in business, guys. We're in business. We're the ones who have to dictate where the ball is dribbled. You guys understand that? This is day one stuff we're talking about."

Coach Gabriel jumps in. "Put your nose on the high shoulder. You have to work harder." He shows a clip from last game where the players get off a three with a few ticks left on the shot clock and sinks it. "If you would've played harder for three more seconds, we would've gotten the stop," Coach Gabriel says. "And we need to have conversations on the bluffs, guy," Clink says. "We have to bury the shooter in the corner. Do not let him dribble out. Use your footwork."

Clink shows another clip of Giddings blocking out. "Watch this. Tanner is consistently blocking out to get the rebound. When you get the defensive rebound, you can run! Now let's go work hard."

The team runs on to the court. There is only one chair at the scorer's table. I ask Coach Blake if he wants it. "I don't sit down in January, Carson," he says.

The team is fired up. "Get your aggression level up," Clink shouts. He comes on to the court and puts a body on Giddings. "I want you to clear guys out. Find a guy and hit him." Clink is animated today. I sigh at the beauty, the finesse, of Ellis getting a rebound. Effortless. Like watching a snake glide through the water. He has a way of putting his palm on the ball and pushing it up in the air, as if it's a beach ball he's trying to keep alive in the pool, so he can then leap into the air and grab it with both hands. Silverstrom makes a play Clink doesn't like. He stops practice. "Jump stop, Corey. Jump stop and pass it out. No turnovers. Do it again!" Play resumes. Again, he stops practice. "No stances. Footwork is awful. Do it again!"

Watching Silverstrom catch the ball, set his feet, zone in, and release the ball has the same nice and easy movement of a good, clean golf swing. "Now get a rebound," Clink screams. Nobody has to. The ball is all net. Ambrosini takes a shot in the next sequence. Giddings gets the rebound. "You know why he got the rebound? Because he's a tough guy, a tough guy that nobody blocked out. Do it again. Let's go!" During the next sequence,

Clink continues shouting: "We will take away the three. We will not let a man go over the top. Take a one-minute break and it's no-man's land. No-man's land. Let's go."

After a thirty-second water break, Clink and Coach Gabriel work on defense. Coach Gabriel is in teacher mode. "It might seem harder," he says, "but it's actually easier. If you don't bury him in the corner and make him drive baseline, then he goes over the top and everything opens up." Clink blows the whistle. "New game. Let's get better. Stance! You've got be ready. Ready! You can't get better if you're not in your stance when the ball is in the air."

A few minutes later, Harris and Duncan get into it. Harris pushes Duncan. Harris takes a few steps and Duncan pushes him back. Clink has the whistle in his mouth. He appreciates this intensity. The brief stare down. "Guys, can we get back to playing basketball now?" Silverstrom drives the ball to the lane. He carries the ball like it's a fanny pack and times his finger roll just right—the perfect tear drop. The best plays these guys make are the plays in practice, the plays that take place Monday through Thursday behind the closed Red Door. Herein lies integrity. What you do when no one else is watching. Duncan's team will lose the No-Man's land game. His team has to sprint. Duncan is determined to win the sprint. Moments later Priest makes a play that catches Clink's eye. He knows how to keep morale high, "Great job, Trevor. Great job. That's exactly how we do it."

CHAPTER 57

Wildcats Arctic Expedition: Humboldt State

JANUARY 7

THE WILDCAT ROAD TRIP TO the northern tip of California in Arcata and down to the south in Pomona has the feeling of Shackleton's Imperial Trans-Antarctic expedition. Although Clink and the Wildcats are unlikely to get trapped in ice and almost starve to death, they did get trapped in traffic on their last road trip to Stanislaus. The drive up to Arcata where they will play rival Humboldt will also throw several driving challenges at them as they go over 299. Driving rain. Coastal fog. White knuckled hairpin turns. Tom the trainer, who is from South Florida and has never driven in snow, will be driving a van. The vans (three in all) have to pull over and put on snow chains. Clink will put on snow chains for the first time in his life. They'll drive in chains for four miles. Coach Gabriel, who "lived" in snow for six years while he was a student at Northern Arizona, convinces Clink to take the chains off after driving four miles at six miles per hour. The Wildcats will arrive in tact.

The Chico State-Humboldt State rivalry has been going on for 83 years. Tonight is stuffed toy animal night. Not long after Kitchens scores the first bucket for the Wildcats, stuffed animals are thrown to the court. Time is delayed as the toys are picked up. Kitchens picks up a stuffed dog and hands it to a young Lumberjack fan. Ambrosini, who is from Fortuna—just down the road—will hit two consecutive 3-pointers. His entire family sits behind the Chico State bench.

The Wildcats will win easily. The Lumberjacks, despite one of the best offenses in the CCAA, also have the worst defense. Duncan will again work his magic. He will be one of four Wildcat scorers in double figures, scoring 22 points on 9-of-13 shooting with four-3-pointers. Giddings will continue to improve, scoring 17 points and grabbing 10 rebounds while Ellis will score 14 points and get six rebounds. Kitchens will also score 11. Duncan's brilliance is that he knows when to turn it on. His only flaw is that he picks the times when to turn it on. Clink will tell him time and time again to not be so kind. His two 3-pointers to start the second half get the Wildcats off to the start they need, and they'll never look back. At one point, he follows up his own missed three-pointer for an easy layup. A scary moment ensues when Duncan turns his ankle. Baca is breathless. The season hinges on Duncan. Silverstrom will hit a layup with 3:01 on the clock. "People are heading for the exits," Baca announces. The score in favor of Chico State 84-65. Clink screams at Silverstrom: "Secure it! Secure it." More time passes, and the gym that at one point had 1,701 raucous fans (many who came to cheer and jeer the hometown star Nate Ambrosini who chose to play for the enemy rather than stay at home) has the feel of a dive bar at last call. Clink can really be heard now over the air waves. "Keep playing, Jalen. 46 seconds left. I know you're tired, but suck it up! Let's go, Jalen." The young point guard has played 34 minutes. Immediately after Clink's commands, McFerren will dive for a loose ball, despite the game being long over.

In the postgame interview with Baca, Clink will give his team a lot of credit. "I'm really proud of our effort. We stopped the three. We held their best player Witzel to 11 points. We only let them score 26 points in the second half. It's our best win of the year, and we did it defensively. We've constantly been improving since our loss at Sonoma State. We did a great job working together and sharing. I am after the unselfish moments, and we had several of those tonight." He stops to catch his breath. "We had some pretty moments." Pretty is an adjective I didn't think Clink would ever use to describe his smash-mouth football approach to the game. "I'll go back and watch the film tonight and see what we need to do go get better."

Giddings and Ellis, in what has become one of the greatest friendships on the team, score 31 points combined. They've become brothers. They live together. They eat together. When I am out running the track before practice, I always see them coming into practice together, loafing, walking slowly under the bleachers, talking in their hushed, reserved tones, like two school children working their way through the neighborhood on their way to school. Baca interviews Ellis. He sounds so intelligent, verbally gifted on the radio. He feels so comfortable when talking about the things he knows best—winning, teamwork, and basketball. It's almost like the positive commentary, the chatter, that Coach Blake always chirps in his ear has been imprinted and become a part of him.

"Between me, Magz, and Giddings, we go after every ball," Ellis says. "It's what we do every day in practice. What we're taught to do. Take A-shots. Make the extra pass to the wide-open man. It's been working for us."

CHAPTER 58

Kamansky-D: Cal Poly Pomona

JANUARY 9

IT'S A CRUEL IRONY IN college basketball, where two games are played almost back to back, that one night a team plays the best offensive team and the worst defensive team, and the next night they play, well, the best defensive team with an offensive team that is almost as explosive. Not only is there irony but also injustice. While Cal Poly Pomona gets to scout the Wildcats, the Wildcats will be in a van on their way from Arcata down to Oakland and then board a packed plane for the long ride to the Inland Empire before getting on another van and heading for the hotel. Clink despises this part of the road trip: getting the rental car. The Wildcats are tired. They played 11 of their first 15 games on the road. They are 9-2 during this stretch. Not bad. But the basketball gods are not all Old Testament. They also reward teams for paying their dues. After Pomona, the Wildcats will play 8 of the remaining 12 games at home. Pomona is downright tough. They also have the CCAA First-Team player Jordan Faison. He will score 24 of Pomona's 69 on this night and get 10 rebounds.

Greg Kamansky, the Broncos head coach, has not only one of the best reputations in the CCAA but in Division II basketball. Clink thinks the world of Kamansky. "I have a tremendous amount of respect for Greg Kamansky," Clink says. "He consistently has one of the best defenses in the country and he does it with really good guys. His teams are extremely hard to prepare for, and he has set the bar high for everyone else in the CCAA. He's one of the best around." Kamansky has been named CCAA Coach of the Year four times in his fifteen year (at the time of this book) tenure. He led the Broncos to the 2010 NCAA Division II title and won Division II Coach of the Year. He's been to the NCAA tournament ten times, to the Elite Eight four times in the last ten years (more than any other coach in program in the country), and won four NCAA West Region titles. If Clink is *becoming* the man to beat in the CCAA, Kamansky *has been* the man to beat since Clink took over the Wildcats program. And if Kamansky can beat Clink tonight, Kamansky will notch his 330th win and become the men's basketball all-time leader in victories at Pomona.

The game starts off with Pomona punching the weary Wildcats smack dab in the nose. It's all Pomona Star Faison to start the game. He'll score a quick 8. Clink calls a timeout down 11-2 to try and figure out how to attack the dangerous Pomona zone—dangerous because of their length. There's no way to prepare against this in practice, not unless Clink gives the defensive players pretending to be Pomona brooms to stretch them out. It's really hard to make a shot when a hand is in your face, to make a move when a defender is chest to chest. Things get out of hand by the 8:25 mark. The Wildcats have just given up—"burped" as Clink calls it—their 10th turnover, his greatest fear. The Broncos will dominate the Wildcats all night. The Wildcats get close with 9:42 left in the game, 46-44, but the Broncos defense puts the Wildcats in a vice grip and will not let go.

The loss puts the Wildcats in a three-way tie for second place in the CCAA. The Wildcats, despite the loss, have played 11 of their first 15 games on the road, posting a road record of 9-2. Sunnier days are coming. 8 of their next 11 contests will be held in Acker.

CHAPTER 59

Deliberate Practice

TUESDAY, JANUARY 11

THE WILDCATS ARE BACK HOME. When I walk into the gym, it's like nothing has changed since the first day of practice on October 15. The only thing that has changed is that the players have improved. Everyone is shooting. The team managers, Ricky and Lee, are already out-sweating the players. Tommy is pacing and rubbing his head, muttering. He walks toward a ball that has just rolled across the court like tumbleweed. Tom the trainer is filling up water bottles. He disappears then comes back in rolling a rack of freshly pumped up balls. Clink is ready to go. "Sideline. Let's go." The players line up and start stretching. A train whistle blows outside. "Ricky, put a cap on the rim." Clink puts the whistle in his mouth. He pauses, hands on his hips, to watch them stretch. He doesn't like what he sees. "Follow Nate. Hey, we're not doing this for fun."

Coach Blake has a green shake he brings to practice every day. He looks at me and winks, beats his chest. After a few more minutes of stretching, Clink calls the players into a circle before they watch film. "Let's talk about what we have to do to have a good week. It's going to be about our defense on Friday and Saturday night. We need to have an outstanding effort just like we had in the second half against Humboldt."

Clink pauses and looks into the eyes of all the men to make sure the message has been conveyed. "I want you guys to tell me right now what's wrong with our offense." There are a few mumbles. "That's right. It's our turnovers. We're ninth in the league. Can you believe that? Ninth. We have to eliminate careless 50/50 passes. We have to get better at all these little things." The players go over and take seats. "We're going to watch some bad things and some good things. We'll start with shots that need to be eliminated, okay." He shows Silverstrom taking a contested three. "This weekend we'll see similar defenses. We've got to be ready."

The team heads over to view film. Clink never hesitates to critique his best players to get his point across. He shows a clip of Duncan. "Rob, you can't burp it up like that." He freezes the frame and steps into the screen. "Look at all these open possibilities if you just jump stop and kick it back out. We have wide-open stuff if we have just one more attack." He shows several more examples of poor shots, then finishes off the film session with A-shots. "We can't settle this weekend."

Clink and Coach Gabriel take the wings, and Coach Blake takes the big men. The point guards and wings are the brains behind the offense, the big men the brawn. What the latter does is more brutal harm done with the body whereas the smaller players rely more on their intelligence and speed. Their job is to feed the monsters. The guards and wings continue to work on head fakes, lift fakes, and attacking the zone. Constant deliberate practice. Duncan shoots free throws by himself. Coach Blake continues to rattle off his motivationals with the big men. Magz looks like a man about to break, a look of humor and frustration and determination all etched on his face. He's been through so many assistant coaches. Twenty-five minutes on the shot clock. Clink and Coach Gabriel will hustle and shoot with the wings and guards this entire time. I watch Silverstrom making his drives to the basket. He cradles the ball softly like a swaddled child, lowering it and raising it, the movement so quiet, the spring so light, dancing light- footed on a featherbed, and then it dawns on me: he carries the ball on his hip like it's a fanny pack. I'll later ask him if he knows what a fanny pack is, and he pauses, laughs. "Don't call me that." I promise Silverstrom I won't.

Joseph Lynch's release of the ball—both his arms out straight—reminds me of a marionette. The ball is his puppet on a string. Duncan's feet are never in the same place when he shoots. Sometimes he steps into the ball as if he's stomping his feet at a bluegrass festival. It's comical to watch him—he skips. No set shot in his game. McFerren's shot is textbook, the rotation perfect every time. Giddings takes the ball down low and releases it high with lots of arc (his free throws have the hang time of what feels like a long NFL punt and really throws off the guys trying to get the rebound). Ambrosini has the most unorthodox shot. He's a leftie. He catches, brings it down around his abdomen and brings it back up in perfect line over his right eye. When he lets if fly, his straight arm and bent hand form the perfect swan.

Watching the big men is like watching heavy weight prize fighters working out on the bag. Ellis's footwork dazzles. He moves so gracefully, the ball off his fingers so easy, like bubbles. Cool Marvin shakes the ball, shakes his head, wiggles his whole body, in a way that reminds of little kids roller skating and dancing back in the day to Michael Jackson's "I Want to Rock with You Whereas Ellis seems to find beauty in the perfect finger roll and the drop of the ball through the net without making the slightest sound, Magz prefers a thunderous dunk of each ball. Each dunk sounds like he's trying to rip off the rim and shatter the backboard. I imagine he wants to: five years of this. Frustration, anxiety, and fear resonate with each dunk. The gym feels like it's rattling. The heavyweight wants to knock the bag off the chain. Coach Blake chatters the entire 25 minutes: "Perfect. Beautiful.

Explosive. Drive. Love it, baby, love it. That's it. Oh, yeah. Let's go." And there's Clink, loudest of all: "Now go get a rebound. Let's go!"

WEDNESDAY, JANUARY 12

The players gather in a circle at half court. "Here are the things we must work on to be great," Clink says. "We have to get better defensively. We have to take care of the ball offensively. We can't burp it up. A-shots." Coach Gabriel jumps in. "We have to work on being more aggressive. We have to make them dribble the baseline." Clink's turn. "Lots of lift fakes. We're also going to keep working on our rebounds. Rebounding and A-shots. No turnovers. Now grab a partner," he says.

"Everybody's got to block out. We're jumping to the ball. Be in the right spot," continues Clink.

The players switch to No-Man's Land. Eight minutes on the clock. "Do not get beat over the top. Block out." Duncan never stops amazing me. He can make anything happen. But often his brilliance results in a turnover. He moves too fast sometimes. Clink pulls him over and drapes his arm around him. He talks to him about jump stops, slowing down, being patient, and reminds him to kick it back out. Duncan, hands on hips, chin slightly down, listens to everything coach says. He hears him. The perfect student. Coachable, Clink says time and time again. The professor sees the unlimited potential. Nothing will be wasted. Meanwhile, Ambrosini is ripping every shot he takes.

"Everyone on the baseline," Clink barks. Today is about getting ready for James Davis on Saturday night, even though it's SFSU they play first on Friday night. Davis and his 30-point outburst in the second half of that loss at Sonoma State has haunted the coaching staff. One man can't beat the Wildcats ever again. What's a no catch, Robert?" Clink asks. He doesn't wait for the answer. "If you're guarding Davis, I want you belly to belly with him." The players break into four on four.

One player pretends to be Davis, and that player will not touch the ball. "Here you have to listen," Clink says. "Otherwise you might miss something important. Do not turn the ball over. Make post entries. You have to take A-shots." Ambrosini takes his turn being James Davis. Silverstrom turns the ball over. Clink stops practice. He strips the ball from Ambrosini. "Corey, if you're going to drive, it has to be this." He models what he wants. "Drive hard. Lift fake. Nothing there kick it out." A play later, Silverstrom does exactly what Clink had modeled. "Good, Corey, good. Now do it again, but I want to see our executions with more pace and aggressiveness. Do it again!"

The next play has Duncan on a fast break. He hesitates when he drives into the middle and turns it over. Clink is about to lose it. "Rob, use your instincts. Don't be in slow motion. You're being too kind. I want a 100%." If anything, Duncan's greatest flaws on the court are his greatest strength in the real world: his unselfishness and kindness. He, like Giddings, does not feel comfortable stealing the show—but it *is* their show.

WEDNESDAY, JANUARY 13

Another repeat of the day before. Groundhog Day, baby, but this is what it takes to win. It's about being efficient with time and executing fundamentals. If you want to be great, you have to do it over and over again—the right way. The cost of perfection is repetitious boredom. No secret. No magic. Just practicing the right way. Deliberate practice. Duncan is bluegrass dancing again, hopping and skipping to get each ball he shoots. The horn blows. Tommy meanders over to me and starts telling war stories again. He tells me about a story he recently read about a dog that saved several lives during 9/11 by leading firemen to people trapped in a stairwell. He then transitions into a story about a Marine who was stranded and had to take off all his clothes, strip down naked, and run back to get help for his men. "He turned down the Silver Star," Tommy says. "He said he didn't do it to get a reward. He did it to save lives, not because he wanted to become famous."

Tommy claps his hands a few times to emphasize his point before walking off. Meanwhile, Clink can be heard: "Lift and attack. It's going to be a No-Man's Land game. No catch against James Davis."

Tommy is feeling it today. He comes storming back at me, finger waving.

"If you believe you can do something, you will do it. I never let my disability stop me," he says, spit flying. Clink comes over to look at the practice plan. Sweat pours off him. Tommy continues. "The counselors told me I couldn't go to college." He claps his hands and walks off then turns back. He points his finger at me, shakes it: "It pisses me off when somebody tells me I can't do something. What would happen if somebody told those Marines that stormed the beaches at Normandy that they couldn't do it?"

He shuffles away. Wipes his face. Hands on hips. Stomps his foot. Comes back over and waves his arms out like an umpire calling a guy out. "Can't isn't in my vocabulary!" Tommy storms off after a loose ball in a way I've seen old men storming off to scare a cat from their garden bed.

"Fours and fives with Coach Blake," Clink yells, "and everybody else with me." When the players come over, Clink tells them: "We're working on the zone attack. Lift fakes, guys." Coach Blake has the medicine ball out with the big men. They crash the boards with it. Tommy now talks to me about Patton. I've learned a lot about Patton from him. "He had guts. He wasn't ever going to be disgraced." Clink is working hard: "We want constant movement on the perimeter. Pace! Constant movement. If you're standing there for more than a second or two, that's too long."

Tommy paces. He stands by me and looks down at my blue book as I write. "When my dad passed away, I went back to Butte College," Tommy says. "Took me four years." He walks away, comes back. Finger in my face. He puts a hand on his hip, leans on the right leg, and looks back at me. Anger rising. Face red, on fire. "They told me I couldn't do it. Well I took every class I could and passed most of them." Tommy sees a wet spot and takes his towel to wipe it up.

"We're doing the same thing we did yesterday, guys," Clink says. "Same thing."

Tommy returns. "When I told my mom I wanted to go to college, she said 'Sweetie, I'll help you do anything you want.'" He shuffles away.

"Go get a rebound—get a rebound!" Clink screams. "Let's go!"

I watch McFerren make a long shot from the corner. The ball looks like a Yo-Yo on a string—it's his "Walking the Dog" shot. When it comes through the net, the ball spins back toward him. "What's the emphasis defensively?" Clink asks. "Don't let them shoot the three. Don't let them go over the top. Let's go!" Silverstrom turns the ball over. "Guys, I want you talking through the entire possession. Look, it's not always going to be perfect, but we have to do our best to get everybody on that side. You got it?" Clink hates silence on the court. "We're not talking. If you talk, your body will follow. If you're silent, mistakes will follow." Ambrosini drains a couple threes in a row.

"Communicate! Communicate!" Clink bellows.

A few more plays and Clink likes what he sees. The pit bull is coming out of Giddings. Giddings wrestles Silverstrom to the ground for a rebound. Clink blows his whistle. The guys clap and cheer. "Good effort, guys, good effort." But for every good effort a few poor efforts must follow. Coach Gabriel sees something he doesn't like. "Can't guard like that. Close your stance." He shows them what he wants.

I watch Cool Marvin springing for a rebound. He reminds me of a young deer.

Silverstrom shoots a long three and the ball flies toward the corner. Holmes, football mode, chases after it like the basketball is a fumbled football. He dives right before it goes out of bounds and flips it back in. Clink blows the whistle. "See what Jesse just did there?" he shouts. "See the way he dove on the ball for the rebound? Are you going to reward him on the next play? Are you going to reward him? Let's go, let's go!"

When Clink gets fired up, the rest of the team catches fire. It's genuine. Tommy shakes his head then turns to me. "I've been around high school football for thirty years," he says, "and Jesse has the best pair of hands I've ever seen. And I got to see him for all four years at Chico High." Tommy walks away then comes back. "Best there ever was." He emphatically sticks his arms out straight like the wings on an airplane, the most dramatic "You're out!" in the history of baseball. "Best hands ever!"

The joy soon ends. Duncan turns it over, again, in transition. "Rob, hold on to it. Don't be in such a hurry." Ambrosini misses a shot. Datu crashes the boards. I can't believe the transition Datu has made since October 15th. When I met him then, he seemed too kind. Now he is ferocious. His Mohawk, his grimace, makes him look like a member of the cast in *Last of the Mohicans*. On the next series, Cool Marvin scores over Giddings. Cool Marvin has this way of peacocking, kind of a "Uh-huh, told you so" demeanor. A wry grin comes over Giddings's face that I've never seen before. He's going to show the kid something. The next play, he steals the ball from Cool Marvin and takes it coast-to-coast for the slam dunk. Clink loves it.

"Pass. Interchange. Cut. Movement," Clink screams. Not long after, Duncan turns his ankle. He shuffles off to not bring attention to it. Last time he rolled his ankle there was a sickening silence in Acker. The players looked befuddled. He and Tom the trainer head off into the training room. Ellis comes in. He glides on to the court as if he's wearing house slippers. A few minutes later, Magz limps off the court. He's in immense pain. Nobody saw what happened. It's like he was hit by sniper fire. He, too, heads into the locker room. An older man wanders into the gym. He has the stature and demeanor of someone important. He stands erect, hands behind his back, watching with a slight smile on his face every move Clink makes. At the one-minute water break, Clink comes over and shakes his hand. They seem like old friends, but I am starting to realize that every coach that Clink shakes hands with seems like an old friend. But how many old friends can a 44-year-old coach have? Holmes comes over and shakes the new arrival's hand. Turns out this is a football coach. He already knows Holmes. Not soon after, Gene comes in. He makes a beeline to the football coach. For the next twenty minutes, he'll talk into the football coach's ear as the football coach occasionally nods politely and watches practice, enthralled by what he's seeing.

"Space, space, space," I hear Clink shout as I walk out of the gym, Gene still jawing into the football coach's ear. A lifetime salesman, he's proud of the product he both endorses and sells: Chico State basketball.

Thursday, January 14

Clink shows the team six clips of the things they must do Friday night to win the game. "We have to attack the zone inside and out," he says. Coach Blake hasn't slept. And it's not from staying up late studying for school. "Attack the paint multiple times with passes and dribble attacks." Clink keeps stepping into the film to show them what to do and what not to do. "Coach Gabriel, stop the film." He shows them an instance when Duncan has driven into the paint and taken an uncontested shot. "Look what's open. Kick it out and start another attack. Does that make sense?" He shows them another example. "Here's a great moment where we attack their zone, crack it, and look what we create from the outside and inside attack. If you attack and reattack, you'll have anything you want. Anything you want, guys. Now let's dial in and have a great day."

I take my seat at the scorer's table. Tommy comes over with a white trash bag still wet from the rain. He pulls out a book and shows me: *The Battle of the Bulge.* Clink, meanwhile, looks like he's preparing for his own Battle of the Bulge. Battle face on. He's not happy today. "I need you focused today," he says. "We'll be going over a lot of new concepts in the next eight minutes. Dial in and coach each other." The players seem disoriented. Clink explodes into the greatest fit of rage I've seen all season. "You guys are in La-la land today. You're playing scared. Is it because we've got Magz and Duncan sitting in the training room with injuries? There's no communication. You're going to miss a great opportunity tomorrow night."

CHAPTER 60

Back Home: San Francisco State

FRIDAY, JANUARY 15

A BIG WEEKEND. THE WILDCATS are in a three-way tie for first place. Right now is the quiet before the storm. The shoot around. Nothing in the gym but a hum. I'm sitting in the bleachers taking it all in. A man comes in and starts setting up the scorer's table. A little while later, the local sportscaster Ross Field comes in to get ready for his interview with Coach Clink. "Back home, baby," he shouts. Field graduated from Chico State in 2006 with a BA in communication design with an emphasis in media arts. He covered the rise of Chico native and former Butte College football Aaron Rodgers as he ascended into the ranks of football heaven as a Green Bay Packer.

"It's about time we're home. Baseball will be starting up soon," Field says to the man setting up the scorer's table. "Wonder how many games will get rained out this year?" Clink and the team come in.

Field interviews Clink, then Giddings and McFerren. Giddings seems uncomfortable, but McFerren embraces the attention. After the interviews, the players start with the layups, counting out loudly. "Have to play tough defense," Clink shouts. "On offense, we won't score out of the set but the motion after the set. Lift and attack." Duncan isn't on the court. I ask Tom the trainer. "Yeah," he says. "Bad sprain." He explains to me that the trainer's job is to limit the bleeding right away. "It'll swell for the next 48 hours." If he had sprained it on Monday, he explains, he could probably play tonight. But he didn't. The team will have to persist without their best player. Could be a blessing in disguise and create opportunities for other players. I ask Tom the trainer if at this level coaches keep injuries a secret from other coaches. Duncan's absence would be a great relief for any coach. "No. We're not hiding it from him. Then again, we're not going in and telling him."

I ask Clink how he's doing. "Tired," he says. I start to tell him about my recent health conversion and the Vitamix I got for Christmas. I show him a picture of all the healthy stuff I put into it.

"It gives you energy?" he asks.

I tell him I've never felt better. He considers it for a moment then grunts and walks off. Goes back to coaching. Bluffs. Flairs. Challenges. Slices. Curls. Lots of great verbs today. Coach Blake is in charge of walking the players through the SFSU offense. He knows it like the back of his hand. He has no problem analyzing and unpacking basketball information. If only school came that easy to him. There are probably thousands of high school and college students just like Coach Blake, students trapped in the quagmire, taking classes, failing classes that have absolutely no relevance in their lives.

"If you hear Utes, jump to the ball," Clink says. "And don't get beat on the UCLA screen."

Coach Blake takes over again. He stumbles on directing a play. The players stop, look confused. He puts his hand on his face and closes his eyes, trying to recall what it is he has forgotten. I see a moment of panic set in, the same look I myself have experienced in math classes, a frozen moment I have seen countless writing students experience when they are writing under the pressure of a clock. Coach Blake starts again. Once more he bungles the play. The players all look to him. This job means the world to Coach Blake. It's his life. Clink lets him struggle for a moment, and only jumps in to keep Coach Blake from further stumbling. Once again I have witnessed the praxis—the synthesis of theory and practice—of Vygotsky's Zone of Proximal Development: the distance between the actual developmental level as determined by independent problem solving and the level of potential development as determined through problem solving under adult guidance or in collaboration with more capable peers.

Clink does not chide or scold Coach Blake for this misstep but supports him. He helps Coach Blake and spares him from any shame. "That's alright," Clink says to Coach Blake and helps him with the play. How in the world do these young men, these coaches, learn not only their own new plays each week, but also all the plays of their opponents and in such short time? Coach Blake has regained his composure. "My bad, guys," he says, patting his chest. "If you hear 'up,' it means the lob is coming." Coach Blake walks them through a few more plays.

"Any questions on that that?" Clink asks. "You've just got to be alert."

Ellis continues to shuffle around as if he's at a pajama party and wearing socks, but when play commences he turns it on full-speed. His legs look like bowling pins. He's so strong, though. I ask Cool Marvin about the pink and purple shoes he wore at practice yesterday. He tells me they're the ones LeBron James wore in the 2013 All-Star game. Clink seems relaxed despite the news that Duncan is out. The team works on their free throws.

"Step up. Concentrate. Make these," he says.

Giddings is loose and playful. The whole team seems to be having fun. Lots of smiles. They know the half-court shot is coming. This is about as playful as Clink gets during the season. Lee Litvin, one of the team managers, is goofing around with the players. Litvin has a swagger about him. He's a short young man and handsome in a felonious way. Reminds me of a better looking, younger Joe Pesci. He looks like the guy that will be the best man in a dozen weddings, the last of all his friends to marry. He also looks like he has street smarts—the kind of guy who always has the best hand at poker, something always up his sleeve. The players love him. He loves them. In ten years, he'll be rich. He's already an accomplished rapper and wants to own his own record label one day. He and Datu often record songs together. Giddings will again make the half-court shot. So does Datu and Coach Blake.

After the shots, the team huddles at the center court Wildcat. "Keep your mentality on both ends of the floor for 40 minutes," Clink says. "There'll be lots of opportunities for guys to step up tonight."

Some of the best action of the night always takes place in the fourth quarter of the women's game as the players get loose, coming and going from the locker room and standing in the alley next to the bleachers. The back and forth beneath the Red Door. Clink's kids always seem to bring their entire Shasta Elementary school with them. They call out to the players. Clink's youngest son hangs down from the bleaches and pours *Skittles* into the large palms of Magz and Ellis. Clink comes out to survey the land. He looks at his kids, hanging down, and gives them a stern look. He always looks pensive, maybe on the verge of throwing up. Ellis is dancing around. I ask Giddings, his roommate, if Ellis is always this calm. He nods. "Dude, these guys are weird, aren't they?" says Magz. I ask Magz what he thought about Clink's explosion in practice yesterday. "You know, every time he does that, I want to crack up. He does it a few times a year. And I've been listening to it for five years." Coach Blake comes out and looks around. He will be a head coach soon. I can see him taking a high school team to state then getting a head coaching job at a community college. Who knows? Maybe he will stay here with Clink forever. It might take him that long to finish school.

A little before 7 p.m. and the players head into the locker room. The mood is at first upbeat as tension gets worked out then grows somber as they wait for the coaches to walk in. Once the sound of the sliding door opens and the sounds of the coaches echoes off the floor, the players are in full attention. Coach Blake has been the lead scout on SFSU, so he controls the white board. "Jalen tell me about your guy." He goes down the line.

The players know the ins and outs of the guy they will guard. Duncan comes in late. He's been getting treatment in the training room. He sits down and puts a black boot on his foot. His hair is down, long brown curls resting on his shoulders. He takes the hair and combs it with his fingers, straightens out the curls and puts it up in a bun. He has the most competitive spirit on the team. Sitting one out kills him. After Coach Blake quizzes each player on individuals of the other team, he shifts into the motivational speech. They are always riveting and well-rehearsed. I imagine Coach Blake has seen every sports movie ever made. "Tonight's game is the future of our team," he says. "We have to set the tone defensively. Tonight we will mark where we are. We've had the most difficult schedule in the conference. And you know what they're thinking? They're thinking you're tired. But they weren't here all week watching you in practice. They didn't see us sweating, bleeding, and sacrificing all week. If someone breaks into your house, you attack them with a shot gun, and they're breaking in, guys, they're breaking in."

As the players line up in hallway to make their final entrance through the Red Door, Mitch Cox, the assistant Athletic Director, has to ask the players to move against the wall so the women's teams can walk by. Cox—who has been the ringleader of the old dudes who play noon ball in Shurmer for many years—can often be seen in the bleachers with a broom in his hand, perhaps a metaphorical message for the visiting team, but nevertheless getting the area clean for the fans. Cox is also an author of two books, one a hilarious romp about his undergraduate days at Chico State. Tonight, Cox will have to corral a mess of loud, rambunctious kids making loud sounds with penny whistles.

Clink meets briefly with head coach Paul Trevor of San Francisco State. If Coach Trevor were to ever have been portrayed in a movie, the late Phillip Seymour Hoffman would've been perfect. He looks more like a community college English instructor than a head coach. His demeanor exudes humor and good nature, and I imagine that is what he uses to temper an intense job. Clink says of Trevor: "He's a great coach and a wonderful person." Trevor looks like the kind of guy you'd want to go and have a few beers with. It's strange to have five backs with the following numbers facing me: 11, 15, 33, 34, 44. Duncan and Magz are missing. Great Powerball numbers, I think, staring intently at them as the National Anthem takes place. What a strange custom? Awkward, really, and it must be terribly grueling for someone who is not patriotic, kind of like the atheist who must sit through a long prayer before diving into the turkey and stuffing on Thanksgiving Day. This will be the first start for both Ellis and Silverstrom.

"At guard from Fresno, number 33, Corey Silverstrom." He has a big smile. He's been waiting for this day. Every player dreams of hearing their hometown called out. Silverstrom, though, will start the game with a terrible shot, a far cry from the A-shots Clink has been pounding into their heads for the last two weeks. Less than twelve seconds into the game and Clink is already stomping his foot. It's a shaky start without Duncan and Magz on the court.

Silverstrom, after missing a wild three, turns it over. Ellis makes an incredible block but turns it over seconds later. Kitchens makes a sloppy pass and turns it over. Clink calls a timeout. Lynch looks maniacal tonight. He has a crazed look in his eye, almost out of place in uniform, as if he should be at Coachella or Burning Man rather than an elite basketball player playing a backup role on an elite team. Harris is biting his nails. Duncan is coaching the guys from the bench. He's not moping at all. His eyes burn with the same intensity, maybe more, than when he's playing. Harris and Magz go in. The Wildcats start to put points on the board. The defense holds SFSU to a shot clock violation. At another media timeout, Clink gently drags the chair out. That's a good sign for the players. Clink will not be so happy during the next timeout. The first half is still young, and the Wildcats already have seven turnovers.

In the timeout he tells them: "The only reason they're close is because of the turnovers. Keep attacking. And take care of the ball. Take care of it!" When play resumes, Silverstrom makes an unselfish pass. He has the wide open shot, but from the corner of his eye kicks it out to Kitchens, who has a cleaner shot, for the three. McFerren gets hurt in the next series. He wanders off, but Clink yells: "Huddle, Jalen, huddle." Silverstrom makes another long three. He's feeling it. During the next timeout, he walks to the bench shaking his head and muttering: "They can't stop me. They can't stop me." This is the same Silverstrom I first saw at Arizona when he lit up future NBA player Alonzo Trier. Clink tells the players in the timeout: "Keep executing...Jalen will be the guy that sells it...It's just about taking care of the ball...we're in a good place."

Moments later, Cool Marvin will finally get the chance to show Acker his special gifts that up until now only I and the coaches have seen in practice. Off a Giddings miss, Cool Marvin will fly in the air, grab the ball, and thrown down one of the nastiest dunks in the history of Acker. Baca scoots his chair back and raises his arms. The chair clips my toes. He only rolls back on special occasions, and this is one of those times. Cool Marvin will score on another amazing shot on the next play, a reverse layup. The fans now know who he is, and perhaps Clink will worry less about what to do when Giddings and Magz leave next year. At the next timeout, McFerren is told to hold the ball for the last shot. Duncan has his arms draped around Tom the trainer and Litvin. They are all brothers: Tom the Trainer and Litvin are just as much a part of the team as the men in uniform.

The Wildcats will take a comfortable 29-19 lead into the locker room at the half. Normally, Clink hangs outside with the coaches and talks for at least five minutes—usually much longer—before coming in. However, tonight he will come in sooner. Before he comes in, though, Duncan has been doing all the talking. He has not been this vocal all year. He has turned into the coach. He tells each player what they're doing well, and what they need to work on.

After Duncan talks, the players start to chat. They're more relaxed than I've seen them all year. Duncan doesn't like the laid back feel. "Come on, guys," Duncan says. "Keep it serious." They listen, turn quiet. Cool Marvin always turns introspective during halftime. He seems to be reliving his dunk.

Clink enters. "Okay, guys, I couldn't be more proud of your defensive. But we need to do a better job blocking out. Other than that, great. Now listen. They only have 19 points. But 10 of those points are off your turnovers. Think about that. We had three in the first three possessions. Ask yourself: Do you want to have to win in the last minute? Or do you want to win and be comfortable in the last five minutes? We had seven turnovers in the first half. That means we can only allow three more in the second half to keep it at or under the goal 10. Hang on to the ball. Squeeze it like it's the last possession of your life. Here are some things that will help. Make sure you get more movement early on. Keep up the lift and attack. This will open things up for you. And don't back off your aggression level. Anything else?"

Coach Blake responds. "Yes. As tough as you are offensively, we need to match this toughness defensively."

The second-half doesn't start the way Clink envisioned. The Wildcats come out soft. They're settling into their lead, playing not to win. Playing not to lose. Floyd Wormley starts to heat up. The Gators are not wasting any time going straight for the Wildcats jugular. McFerren makes a couple turnovers. The Gators respond with a couple of threes. Before you know it, the Gator are back in it, 33-37. The Wildcats call a time out. Clink's message is simple: "You're not executing. Let's get back to doing what we do well. Lift and attack. We need more pace. We need more attacks." The attacks come from the Gators on both ends. They quickly take the lead, 38-37. After Giddings takes a bad shot, then fails to block out, then turns the ball over, Clink has seen enough. He calls a timeout.

"Don't play scared. Everybody, and I mean everybody, has to find someone and block them out. Attack, attack. Don't look at the scoreboard."

McFerren gets the message. He nails a 3-pointer seven seconds later. Clink screams something and walks back down to the end of the bench and squats, puts his index finger over his lips. During the media timeout,

Clink's song remains the same: "Everybody block out! Just raise your aggression level up. And communicate. Communicate!"

The score remains close. At the next time out, the Wildcats lead 44-41. "It's about stops right now. We're right there. Let's go!" McFerren again scores out of the timeout. Duncan leads the bench in a cheer. The Wildcats start to run away with the game. Everyone is scoring. And McFerren's three-pointer at the four-minute mark puts the dagger in the Gators. In the last 6:19 minutes of the game, the Gators will only score two more times. It's the last basket with four seconds left (to make the score 50-61) that angers Clink more than any play all night. The Wildcats quit playing. A Gator lopes in for an easy layup. Ellis fouls him on the shot, and sends the Gator to the line.

Clink, despite the last second malaise, is in good spirits after the win. "That was a great win tonight, guys," he says in the locker room. "Couple of things, though. We need to work on not being complacent. That's one area we really need to focus on. We have to eliminate complacency. One other thing. I don't care how big our lead is at the end of the game. You don't quit playing. You guys quit playing with four seconds left. When the other team leaves, I want them to walk out of this building feeling demoralized. You gave them something to feel good about at the end of the game. I want them demoralized." He looks around the room. "We had 17 turnovers tonight. 17. That's our one glaring weakness." He shakes his head. "Get it down to 11, and Holy…" He pauses when he sees his three young boys on the couch in the locker room. "Holy Smokes." The players laugh. "Get it down to 11. Now I want you all to go home and take care of your bodies tonight and go to bed early. We got a big one tomorrow night."

CHAPTER 61

James Davis, Part II

JANUARY 16

THE PLAYERS KNOW THE IMPORTANCE of this game. The last time they met, one man, James Davis, beat them. For most of the players, James Davis ruined their Christmas break. All week long Ambrosini and Harris have played the decoy. The Wildcats will put Davis in a no-catch situation all night long. They also know Cal Poly Pomona lost last night. If the unthinkable happens, and both UC San Diego and Cal Poly Pomona lose tonight, and the Wildcats win, they will be back in first place.

The players are silent in the moments before the coaches enter. Clink comes running into the locker room, down low, shouting: "Let's go! Let's go! "Let's go!" He gives the players high fives and pumps his fist then disappears around the lockers. The players, startled at first, laugh. Duncan combs his hair and makes his man-bun. Coach Gabriel owns the white board tonight.

"We're on all their calls tonight. We're going to know their plays better than they do. And we're going to know their plays before they call them."

Duncan wrings out his hair like a wet rag. Coach Gabriel is at his best here. He lives for the pregame speech. "I want you all to close your eyes. I want you to go back to that game at Rohnert Park, the one that ruined your Christmas break. I want you to remember how sick you felt going back for the break. I want you to remember that first three that James Davis hit before he got hot. Can you see it? Can you feel it? I want you to remember how their fans rushed the court after beating you. Now I want you to imagine James Davis just standing there in the corner, pouting, quitting, because he can't even touch the ball let alone score. I want you to see yourself diving for every loose ball. Imagine our bench erupting after we get the loose ball, after we nail the three-pointer. I want you to imagine redeeming yourself. I want you to spit out that bad taste they left in your mouths, the one that's been in there for a month." He pauses. Clink steps in.

"Now go have a great warm up," Clink shouts. "Let's go!"

The players storm through the Red Door, all but McFerren. His pants are falling down. Coach Gabriel spends a few seconds helping tie the back of his pants to keep them up. Finally, McFerren is set free.

Clink's final talk to the players in the huddle before the tip is subdued. His voice is almost gone from screaming all week during practice and from yelling last night. "Use the corners tonight. Get great spacing. Apply constant pressure. We're hunting for 40 A-shots. The magic number for turnovers is 11. Do that and great things will happen. It's about defense. Get in a stance. Play hard for 40 minutes. No complacency. Now let's go!"

Clink knows how to put on a face. All the consummate professionals do. Complete self- awareness. Moments earlier he wore the face of a starved Puritan in the throes of winter. Now, when he steps out to shake the hand of head coach Pat Fuscaldo, Clink looks like he's meeting an old friend for drinks. What a strange ritual, the shaking of hands with the other coach. Coach Fuscaldo looks like a mix between a handsome, older vampire and a bandit from the wild, wild west who has just taken a bath, groomed himself, and stepped into town for a night at the table: he's either going to win or win. He has pistols on his hips and he plans on using them. He also looks like he's a Marty Robbins type of music cowboy who moonlights playing cowboy music in the Sonoma wineries. Fuscaldo has a bad reputation in the league for his sideline antics and temper. "But once you get to know him," Clink tells me, "he's one of the nicest guys around." Clink also shakes the hand of James Davis. Respect.

The Wildcats win the tip. Kitchens has the assignment of starting off against Davis in the no-catch. They start off aggressive on defense, but on offense the Wildcats can't core. By the first time out Clink calls at the 16:10 mark, the Wildcats haven't made a basket. Sonoma State is up 7-0. Duncan is holding the clipboard tonight. He talks privately to McFerren, teaches him. McFerren nods, hangs on every word. Clink grabs the chair lightly. He's not angry. Coach Blake and Coach Gabriel look up at the scoreboard equally confused. Dumbstruck, actually, like they'd been punched from behind. Cool Marvin makes a rare early appearance at the 15:43 mark. Clink has to change something. Silverstrom will finally hit a three. It's our first basket of the game after almost six minutes. The Wildcats never panic. McFerren makes a steal. The momentum shifts.

James Davis, for now, has been shut down. Silverstrom seems winded tonight. He takes a seat on the bench next to Duncan. Duncan talks to him. Silverstrom listens. A little later Giddings shoots free throws. Most big men shoot line drives, but Giddings's ball goes incredibly high. A true moon shot. It must go 14 feet high before falling through the net. Clink's playbook has gotten longer since the game against Arizona back in November. He makes note in the margins during action. Duncan continues to lead the team from the bench. He directs Giddings on the next timeout. Duncan sees things nobody else does.

"Defensively we're doing fine," Clink says, "but we need to be more aggressive on offense. We're going to run a drop..."

Clink stomps his feet all half, almost in chorus with Baca talking into his headset. Silverstrom is particularly frustrated. His shots are way off the mark. Harris is playing fast and furious and turning the ball over. He, too, is frustrated. Giddings is missing free throws. McFerren starts to turn the ball over. The best moment in the half comes when McFerren and Davis wrestle each other to the ground for a loose ball. They roll and fight for it. Heading into the second half, I get the feeling Sonoma State has the Wildcats number. The half ends with Silverstrom missing a jumper. He has daggers in his eyes. One gets the feeling the miss will inspire more in the second half than a make would have. Despite a D+ first half with the Wildcats shooting 8-of-25, their defense put forth an A- first half and holds Sonoma State to 11-of-30. More importantly, James Davis has been silenced. He is 0-of-2, but not unlike the last time the Wildcats played Sonoma State and he came back and scored 30 in the second half.

When the season first started, Duncan would go inward during half-time. Even if he was playing well, he wasn't vocal. However, as the season has progressed, he has become more and more of a leader. It's almost as if the basketball gods were smiling on the Wildcats and injured Duncan so he could assume a different role over the weekend—that of bench coach. He has never been more animated during practice as he has been this week in the coaching role.

While the coaches are outside talking, Duncan steps in front of the players, carrying his clipboard, and talks to them. He has a bright future in coaching. I can imagine him joining Clink's staff someday soon, after his playing career overseas is finished. The coaches are taking longer than usual tonight. I wonder if subconsciously Clink does this on purpose. The torture is prolonged. Memories of being sent to the principal's office and awaiting a choice of ten licks from the paddle or two-day suspension. "Get the step up screen," Duncan says. "We don't need a screen to drive. And remember we can't sleep on Davis in the next half."

The door finally opens. Clink gets right to it. "Alright," he says stepping to the board, "we're in a good spot. Just have some little things to clean up defensively. They've given us their best shot, guys. Their best shot. Here's the deal. We can't be complacent this half. We have to clean up the 50/50 balls. Anything else to talk about?" Silence. "Offensively we need to get deep in the zone," he says. "Get all the way to the corners. Attack. If they come at us, pull it back out and swing it. Any questions on attacking their press? Okay, you have to understand—have to understand—that it's not gonna happen in the first five minutes. Not gonna happen. You have to grind. Get the ball in the paint. Inside out, guys. Settle down on offense. If we get two or three shot clock violations, no problem. We have to keep a high aggression level, but remember to stay poised. High energy level, okay. They've given us their best shot. Let's go!"

Clink was wrong. Their best shot is coming with one tick left on the clock. And it will once again be the ghost of Christmas past.

Silverstrom must have been stewing over the missed shot to close the half. He hits a three on the first possession of the second half. A couple possessions later he makes a steal then drains another three to tie the ball-game. McFerren soon puts the Wildcats up three with another three-pointer. Magz comes out of the game. When he takes his seat at the end of the bench, a young woman holding up a black and white sign with his name on it shouts: "I love you, Magz. Will you marry me?"

Halftime is such a beautiful thing in sports. If only everything in life was like that, a break to regather and recollect and restructure and come out renewed. Baseball and tennis are so difficult because this pause in action does not exist. During the media timeout, Clink tells the team: "If you keep running your offense like this, don't worry, we'll score enough to win. Wear them down. Win it in the last four minutes. Everybody has to block out. Guys coming off the bench, do the little things. Let's go!"

Clink almost runs on to the court when Ellis gets mauled in the paint and there's no call. The ref pushes Clink back on to the sideline. "Huddle," Clink screams. During the next media timeout, Clink tells the team: "We need post entries. Get it to the post. Throw it back. When you get it in there, lift fake. Lift fake." Not long after the time out, the refs make another bad call on Magz. The crowd erupts. James Davis finally breaks free five minutes into the second half. He nails a three, then gets a steal and layup. Tommy moans and rubs his head and face. He's been watching basketball for thirty years. He knows what it means when a player gets hot.

The Wildcats sputter for the next three minutes until Kitchens hits a three to lift the spirits on the bench and bring life back into the Acker stands. Magz has to sit with his fourth foul. He looks like he wants to run back on the court and smack someone. He breathes deeply, casts his gaze, and takes a seat. During the time out with 7:34 left, Clink tells the team: "Just keep executing. Don't take a play off."

Four seconds after the timeout, James Davis hits another three. Before you know it with a little over five minutes left, Sonoma State is up by 8. Basketball, like life, can change so quickly. Clink is right. The game will be won (or lost) in the final minutes of the game. The defense will have to win the game, and the offense will just have to do what it always does. Ellis is starting to feel it down low. He gets nailed and goes to the line. Hits them both to pull the Wildcats within four. During the media timeout, Clink tells the team: "We're right there, fellas. Go inside. Lift fake. Attack. Nothing there then throw it back out." Dead air for the next minute before Fuscaldo calls a timeout. Clink's message is simple: "You have to rebound. Do not let them have another offensive rebound. Don't do it!"

Down 52-50 with a 1:19, Duncan loans Silverstrom the Superman cape. He grabs a rebound and goes coast-to-coast. He gets hammered and goes to the line. He hits them both. The score is tied 52-52. With three seconds left, Sonoma State has a chance to win. Giddings blocks the layup, McFerren gets the rebound. There's a tie up with the ball. The possession arrow goes to the Wildcats. Clink calls a 30-second timeout.

A thirty-second timeout to draw up a play that must happen in two seconds.

Clink scribbles madly on his clipboard: "Jalen, you're here. Tyler, you're here. We're setting back picks. Hit Jalen on the run."

It will be McFerren who shoots the ball at the buzzer. He's in the exact same spot he was a month ago when he hit his miracle shot. This one falls short. Overtime. Clink tells them before the start: "Our defense is great, but we cannot—we *cannot*—give up any offensive rebounds. Ball screens and throwbacks. Keep your aggression level up. The ball must get into the paint."

New game. New life.

Overtime is a seesaw, the two middle weights exchanging blows, saving their best for the final seconds. The Wildcats appear to have the game in the bag. With six seconds left and a 62-60 lead, they're up with McFerren on the line for two. 63-60. He makes the first one but misses the second one. It can all happen, change, so fast. Sonoma State gets the rebound. James Davis gets the ball.

"Foul him, Jalen, foul him," Clink shouts."

Davis is smart. He knows the score, and he knows Chico State wants to foul him before he can get a three point shot off. McFerren runs toward Davis for the foul, and Davis hurls up a three point shot. Fouled. McFerren did what he was ordered to do. Davis will go to the line for three. Davis smiles. He lives for this. Playground joy. He makes the first two. 63-62. Clink calls a time out. Everything gets lost in translation. There's nothing to say. If he makes it, double overtime. If he misses it, the Wildcats dodge another bullet.

Guys like James Davis don't panic. He nails it.

63-63.

Overtime number two.

Clink's message before the second overtime starts: "Go have some fun, guys."

Every man on the court has put his courage on the line. Ten men staggering like heavyweights at the end of fifteen rounds. Endurance conquers all. "These guys don't quit," Tommy says, "they just don't quit. It's just like D-Day. Those men at Iwo Jima didn't quit. They helped each other out." Silverstrom, pale and wobbling, gets a second wind. He hits a free throw to give the Wildcats the lead, and then a 3-pointer in the next possession. The Wildcats are rolling. Everyone gets a second wind. Ellis dances in the paint. He makes his shots from the free throw line. The defense is relentless. James Davis is a ghost. McFerren makes amends for the missed free throws to close regulation. The sophomore hits four in a row down the stretch to give the Wildcats the lead for good. Silverstrom will put the final penny in the dead man's eye with a free throw to end the game 75-70.

I sprint into the locker room expecting a celebration. The only people in the locker room are Lynch, Ambrosini, and Duncan. The rest of the team is out celebrating and will be for a long time.

"How do you like that?" Duncan says to me about the overtime heroics of the young McFerren. "A true sophomore on the line makes four straight free throws to close out the game."

Magz will soon come in. I ask him if this is the best win of his career. He smiles and shakes his head. He's been through so many of them in his career. "Not the best, but it's satisfying."

Satisfying indeed.

Slowly the players trickle in. Clink looks exhausted and exhilarated.

"Let's bring it in. Two minutes." He leans against the board. Exhales. Smiles. "Everybody here?"

"Our sophomore guard is still out signing autographs," Duncan says.

Clink catches his breath.

"Pomona lost tonight," he says. "So did San Diego. We're in a two-way tie for first."

The locker room erupts.

"We made a lot of mistakes tonight," he says. "But we were tough and had guts. I take the blame for sending Davis to the line. I told Jalen to foul him. But we had stop after stop. We'll practice Monday. Spend tomorrow putting good things in your body. And I'm so proud of you five or six guys who wore black jerseys all week. You guys deserve just as much credit."

The basketball gods must have known this would be senior Drew Kitchens's last game, his last 41 minutes and his last five points—as a Wildcat.

The gods granted him with an unforgettable win for his final game as a college basketball player.

CHAPTER 62

Academic Troubles

DUNCAN IS BACK AT PRACTICE. It's hard to believe he was even hurt. He looks great.

Kitchens and Priest, however, are not back. They are academically ineligible. The team conducted grade checks about two weeks prior to finals in the fall semester. "Drew's grades came back with nothing on it that would make us think we had anything to worry about," Clink tells me. "Once grades were posted, Brian Ceccon, our compliance officer, called me down to his office. He said that Drew was ineligible. I was shocked. He'd always done okay in school. Now he's going to miss the last half of his senior season. It was hard on me because I really love Drew. He was easy to coach and brought a lot of value to our team. He had worked his way up the ladder to become a starter. He never complained as an underclassman when he was wasn't playing much. He just grinded it out and got better. I'm disappointed. More than anything, though, I feel sorry for him. This will be an embarrassing deal for him."

Clink doesn't have time to dwell on the loss of Kitchens. It's back to business. He tells the guys they'll be introducing new plays, then he takes Magz over to the side and talks to him, a part of their relationship that will end in six weeks. A good five year run. "Bigs down on that end with Coach Blake," Clink says. "Wings and guards stay with me."

Coach Blake continues to work hard with the big men. The same thing every day. Magz finds it easier to dunk than lay it up. Cool Marvin gets better with each practice. He reminds me of Dennis Rodman when he was with the Pistons. If he gains twenty pounds next season, he'll be unstoppable. The guys in the black jerseys amaze me, the guys who don't get much, if any, playing time: Jesse Holmes, Joseph Lynch, Keith Datu, and Marvin Timothy. They make the starters better.

"Posts," Clink says, "set your ball screens above the three-point line." Magz goes through a screen and Datu gets him with his knee. Once more Magz has been hit by sniper fire. The senior's body has been through the meat grinder. Tommy is fired up today. "General Grant failed his entire life," he tells me. "That is until he got into the military." Tommy tells me he has finished the biography of Grant and moved on to General Patton's biography. "It's my own. Right from my bookshelf. I can take my time with it." Tommy paces up and down the sideline. He doesn't have as many balls to chase today. A month ago, balls were flying all over the place. Today, though, the players are taking care of the ball. They're finally catching on to Clink's persistent reminder not to be careless and keep the turnovers down to 11.

"You know what it takes to be a winner?" Tommy tells me. "You have to prioritize. You have to be willing to commit. You have to budget your time. You don't even have to be that smart. Just show up and do your job. See, when I'm here, it's all about me worrying about those guys out there. But the minute I leave and get on my bike and start to pedal away on my bike, that's when I worry about me. And that's the only time." He walks off. A ball has finally rolled on to the other court. He never misses a loose ball.

"Do it again!" Clink screams. "The screen was good, but the pace wasn't there." I watch Magz hit four hook shots in a row. Late in January of his senior year and he's starting to peak.

CHAPTER 63

Hi-Ho Silver: San Marcos

JANUARY 21

SONOMA STATE WAS A REVENGE game for the Wildcats. The San Marcos game is a revenge game against the Wildcats. Chico State's miracle was their curse. The Wildcats 60-foot miracle changed the course of both Chico State's and San Marcos's season.

The Wildcats will do their shoot around at the San Marcos Boys and Girls Club. They will play their game at a small venue away from campus. Only 97 people will be present to see the official arrival of Corey Silverstrom both defensively and offensively. On a night when Kitchens and Priest have been declared academically ineligible, the Wildcats will need a lot of guys to step up. For the last two weeks, the coaching staff has worked hard on getting the players to defend the three. Tonight the hard work pays off: San Marcos goes 2-of-20 from the three-point line. Ellis will get the start and the toughest assignment. He must stop their high flying Tarren Brown. Darnell Taylor is the next big assignment to stop. During the pre-game show, Clink tells Baca: "We will attack Taylor. Isaiah will get his shot tonight. He must limit Tarren Brown. I believe he's going to give him problems."

Silverstrom will continue to wear the Superman cape that Duncan loaned him last week. He has the game of his life. The Wildcats trail for most of the first half, but Ambrosini nails two three- pointers to tie it at the half, 30-30. Silverstrom comes out in the second half playing with urgency. His penetration frees up the other players, chiefly his sidekick Duncan. San Marcos will keep it close until the 3:47 mark, but Silverstrom will bury San

Marcos with back-to-back threes. McFerren closes the door on San Marcos with four straight free throws to end the game. Silverstrom will finish with 27 points—21 in the second half, making all five of his three point shots.

The Wildcats will have nine days off.

CHAPTER 64

Limping On and Off the Court

MONDAY, JANUARY 25

MONDAY WILL BE TORTURE. CLINK and Kitchens are talking at center court. I didn't know if he'd be back. It looks as if Kitchens is pleading his case. Clink pats him on the back. Clink runs back to join the other players who have gathered in their chairs to watch film. Kitchens goes the other way.

"Coach Cobb texted me after the game Thursday," Clink says. "You guys who know Coach Cobb know that he doesn't say something unless he really means it. He said, 'Coach, if you guys cut it down to 11 turnovers a game, you'll win the National Championship.' And I believe him. This is our one glaring weakness. We have to fix it. Today we're going to watch all 18 turnovers from last game."

Clink goes through each one of them, freezing them along the way and breaking down each one to pinpoint where the play failed. After the players stretch it's time for No Man's Land. They'll work and work on reducing turnovers. Gene has wandered in and taken a seat by the scorer's table. Not long after, Gaber comes in with his bike. The appearance of Gaber is kind of like the reappearance of daylight savings time. Spring is coming. As the season tiptoes into February, the players, the coaches—Gaber—all know that with the Wildcats ½ game back going into February, the money is on the line.

I will see Kitchens and Priest walking home down 4th street three hours and fifteen minutes later as I drive home. They're limping. Kitchens has ice bags covering both of his knees. Priest is saddled down with a gallon jug of chocolate milk. The two players look like they've been through both a physical and mental ringer. It's been a rough week for them. I pull up and say hello.

"Practice was brutal today," Kitchens says. He's so tired he can barely speak. "Practice for two hours and then weights." I ask them about their grades. They explain to me what happened. I get the feeling they've both learned a lesson that will improve them as young men transitioning into the real world. I also get the feeling that this will light a fire under them that will bode well for what remains of the season. I drive off and watch Kitchens limping, see Priest struggling to put the milk jug to his lips. I feel bad for not asking them if they'd like a ride home. Then I remember: these are Clink's players. Clink's players don't ask for rides. I hope I will get to see them wear a Chico State University jersey again, but I have a bad feeling about this one.

CHAPTER 65

Blowout: Stanislaus State University

JANUARY 30

GAME DAY. THE PLAYERS HAVE been restless. Nine days waiting for a game. It's here. Kitchens is dressed in warmups. He looks heartbroken. Silverstrom, on the other hand, doesn't. He will get the start in place of Kitchens. The song tonight remains the same. Before the game, Clink tells them: "Stay aggressive. Take A-shots." Ellis has a new haircut tonight. A fade. The crowd is boisterous tonight. Chico State President Paul Zingg is being honored by both the men's and women's basketball teams. He and his wife are given Chico State jerseys with their names on the back and a ball signed by each player and coach.

The Wildcats start out slowly. The game swings back and forth in the opening minutes. Silverstrom starts the momentum by nailing a three. By the media time out at 11:49, things are looking good. "Do not deviate from our defensive game plan," Clink shouts in the huddle. Ellis is feeling it early. Must be the hair. Silverstrom is at his best in transition. He weaves in and out of traffic and hits a layup.

"Stance, stance," Clink shouts.

I follow the coaches into their private meeting at the half. They meet in a small room where four stationary bikes are housed and a rack of weights. One wall is mirrored. Some discarded tables and boxes line the others sides of the wall. The room has the feeling of being in a closet where athletic equipment goes to die, not where the coaching staff of the best team in the CCAA meets to discuss second half strategy. Clink sits in a folding chair and looks at the stat sheet from the first half. Coach Gabriel leans against a stationary bike and studies his stat sheet while Coach Blake mulls over his and starts writing on a chalkboard.

The Wildcats have a commanding lead: 42-24. Only four turnovers. Three by Giddings. Doesn't matter. His offensive streak continues as he goes 4-of-5.

"We can't lose our sense of urgency," Coach Gabriel says. They talk on. Clink takes notes.

"Where are we on the time?" he asks.

"We got ten," says Coach Gabriel.

"We have to be aware of Christian Bayne," Coach Blake warns. Bayne is their three-point specialist. So far they've done a good job containing him." He is 0-of-4. The ghost of James Davis, though, and what he did to the Wildcats in the second half still lingers in the mind of the coaching staff.

That night Davis was 1-of-8 in the first half. He went 11-of-14 in the second half.

"Anything else, coaches?" Clink says.

They shake their heads. Head back into the locker room. Silence. He comes out and gets right to it.

"Guys, we were right here just before Christmas," Clink says. The players know he's not talking about the score. Chico State and Sonoma State were gridlocked at 16 when they entered the locker room at the half. They know he's referring to the Ghost of Christmas past, Mr. James Davis. They know Bayne also has the potential to light up like a Christmas tree.

"Now is the time in the season when we have to develop our killer instinct," Clink says. "Don't deviate from anything we've done in the first half. It's about our urgency right now."

The Wildcats will put their feet to the pedal in the second half and only look back once when Clink calls a timeout. "Listen, stop trading baskets. Bust your tails. I want you to play these last 12 minutes with urgency. Urgency! Don't gamble out there. You don't have to. Get in your stances and play. Now let's go!"

From that point on the night becomes relaxed. While the players respond with urgency and build a lead comfortable enough for Clink to clear the bench, the spectators share moments of tenderness. Luke Reid's son comes and joins him on his lap. Behind him a young girl cheers with the Wildcats cheerleaders. The two children flash one smile after another, both having the time of their lives. Blowouts—and there aren't many in the CCAA—invite this kind of behavior from those whom are issuing the blow.

At 2:36, the black jerseys enter the game. They play with the sense of urgency Clink demands, just like they do every day in practice. After the game (85-50) the locker room feels lighthearted. Clink takes a deep breath. "The most complete game you've played all year. The last ten minutes of the second half you had that killer instinct. Let's build on that. You guys who came in at the end, great job." He lets the players revel in their victory just long enough to catch their breath. "Now, next Friday we have a really talented team coming in here. Let's not forget the dogfight East Bay gave us last time we played them, okay. Let's build on tonight. We need to have a great week of practice. Walk through that Red Door on Monday ready to go."

The basketball team picked a good night to honor the president. The win has put the Wildcats on track for an historic season. They've won 16 of their first 19 for the first time since 1941 and the third time in the

101-season history of the program. The Wildcats are now alone in second place behind UC San Diego, and a game and a half in front of Cal Poly Pomona, a team who would love nothing more than to knock their rival Chico State off the pedestal.

The Wildcats are close to peaking.

If they can only keep the magic going.

And for how long?

CHAPTER 66

Business as Usual

MONDAY, FEBRUARY 1

IT'S THE WEEK CLINK DREADS most. The game against East Bay where he has to explain again and again, yes, it's hard to play my best friend, even harder to beat him, but it's just like any other game.

Business as usual.

"We're not going long today," Clink says, players gathered at the circle. "But I want it to be productive. We want to a lot of enthusiasm today." Clink puts the orange cones out. I haven't seen these since October and early November. Clink runs the players through dribbling drills on the cones. Coach Gabriel and Coach Blake work with the big men on the end. They rebound with the medicine ball. Coach Gabriel works the blue pad. The backboard seems like it will shatter when Magz crushes his hands against the glass. He comes down with the ball. Coach Gabriel smacks him in the head with the blue pad. Who else, I wonder, is working on rebounding with a medicine ball in February? What other team is working on summertime ball handling drills around cones in February? Who else other than a team whose head coach called a team intervention after rattling off a string of consecutive victories—most coming from the road—and a nice spot in second place with their eyes on first.

"Very good, fellas," Clink says. "Very good."

The big men work on a different drill. Coach Blake puts a basketball in the folding chair. The players run up, pick the ball up, turn around, and shoot. Giddings picks it up lightly, as if a father caring for an infant, and places the ball through the hoop like the father gently laying the infant back down on the changing table. Magz works on his right-hand hook. Cool Marvin, too, will grab the ball gently off the chair, but he likes to dunk violently and kick out his legs like a frog swimming. Everything Cool Marvin does has his own signature style. That's why he's Cool Marvin. It's hard to think, as I watch redshirt freshman Justin Briggs's large hands grab the ball off the chair, that when he's a senior, Magz will have already been out in the world for four years, probably having started a career, maybe even settled down with a wife and child. I have no doubt that Magz will be a family man. God has such a wonderful sense of ironic humor, to have endowed a young man with so much physical prowess yet made his disposition so sweet, so sincere and childlike in a grown man's body.

Silverstrom and Duncan take shots down on the other end, a hard sprint to get each rebound. Duncan, again, looks like he's doing a blue grass dance act, his feet always dancing, never in the same spot when he shoots. Silverstrom is the opposite. His windup is always the same. His feet always in the same spot. Kitchens hangs around on the periphery, offering encouragement as he can, but not as confident. I go and lean against the pushed in bleachers. Here we are. Second place in February. A nice place to be. The American flag always hangs. I look at the small banner that says 2013-2014 CCAA Western Region champions. I imagine the beauty of a 2015-2016 banner. It's within reach, or, as Clink says: "It's right there."

Coach is watching the players work on more cone drills. I ask him how he's feeling.

"Tired," he says. "Right now things are kind of dragging. Happens every time around this year."

He explains that's why the cones are out. Try and mix things up. It's hard to believe 22 games have already passed. I look up at the banner section.

"What's missing up there, Coach?" Wrong question to ask.

He clinches his jaw and walks away. I think I hear him growl.

Tuesday, February 2

I arrive at 1 p.m. The players are already in their chairs, rapt, watching game film. "I thought we played some of our best basketball last week," Clink says. "But there's still a lot of room for improvement. Our approach has to be the same Friday night against East Bay. And Saturday night against Monterey Bay. We have to be ready to compete. One of these teams, East Bay, is in desperation mode." He paces. "Ever see one of those National Geographic TV shows and there's always that hungry animal? He's cornered, maybe corralled, and he's baring his teeth, his mouth foaming. You see the urgency in his eyes. He'll kill you if he gets the chance. That's East Bay. They'll be coming in here baring their teeth. They'll have the same look in their eyes. They'll come in here with razor sharp fangs and claws. They'll be going straight for our jugulars. We're going to need a playoff mentality. This will have to be about our defense. They have a lot of offensive weapons. Now fast forward to Saturday night. We'll be playing a team that's playing the best offense in the conference right now. Start it, Coach."

Coach Gabriel runs the film. "Magz and Giddings," Clink says, "9 out of 10 times you're putting a body on someone and doing a good job blocking out. We're going to show you some good ones, and some where we need to work on getting better. One thing, too, about offensive rebounds." He shows a clip of McFerren grabbing a rebound and kicking it out to Silverstrom. "It takes a real unselfish guy to do that," Clink says. "To kick it out to an open guy. Okay, here we go. Seven or eight clips of things we need to get better at." He shows a clip of Silverstrom taking a shot with guys all over him. "See how contested you are? This is a good time for a lift-fake attack." He shows a few more. "I thought your pace was good on all these, but you'll have to be better Friday night. Have to be better." A few more. "Rewind. Everyone who plays the five, dial in. Watch the timing of that second ball screen. This is something we'll work on all day tomorrow. Keep it in your head for now. Keep going. Watch your pace on this one." He pauses. "Stop the film. Jalen came into the office last week and we showed him five or six similar clips where he could have jump stopped here and got an easy assist. Now there was only one moment in this game where he did that, but that's okay. That's progress. You're getting better."

Coach Gabriel forwards to a clip where Duncan has taken too many dribbles. "Keep the ball moving across the split line," Coach Gabriel says. "Coach is right," Clink says. "Keep that ball moving and I promise good things will happen. Good movement, guys, good movement. Now here's one where the movement is really good. We have patience. Nothing is forced. Wait until the man is open. See." He pauses. "Now watch. The whole thing starts with penetration. Jump stop. The kick." The film commences. McFerren dashes into the middle. The defense collapses on him. He kicks it out to Harris. He nails the three. "We just need to keep getting better at the pace." The clips roll again. "Instead of uncontested shots, attack the edges. Good jump stops. Lift fakes. Attacks. Throwbacks. Inside out."

Every player is watching intently. If only all students could be this interested in their subjects, workers as interested in their jobs.

Wednesday, February 3

Long before the Wildcats will gather in a circle at center court, a crowd has gathered early in the cold morning (22 degrees) in Punxsutawney, Pennsylvania, at Gobbler's Knob. The crowd is awaiting the emergence of the official groundhog, Punxsutawney Phil. A cane taps Phil's tree-trunk cage. His door is opened. Out lumbers Phil. Even the crowd cheers his arrival. Phil's only response is a sleepy blink. He is placed on top of the trunk. He tries to run away. Then the emcee of the Groundhog Club screams out: "There is no shadow to be cast. An early spring is my forecast!" Across the country, groundhogs have similar responses. In Canada, groundhog Shubenacadie Sam also sees no shadow. Staten Island Chuck in New York and General Beau Lee in Georgia also agree with Phil.

It's always Groundhog Day when you don a Chico State basketball jersey.

The orange cones come out again. Clink will scream the same things today: "Do not turn it over. Go get a rebound. Block out. Do it again A-shots." The team engages in a vigorous game of No-Man's Land. "You got to communicate. Nobody's talking." He pauses, stops play. "Listen, you're playing two teams this weekend that will jam it down our throat. You're running as hard as you possibly can on these drills. Make sense?" A few more minutes and play stops again. "Pace, pace. What's wrong here? What's wrong here? Here's what we're doing today. I need five guys sprinting. Not jogging. No running. Full-on sprint!"

A few moments later.

"Listen, if you screen well, you'll get whatever you want this weekend. Let's finish up and circle."

The team will soon practice a no-catch session with Silverstrom and then Duncan. "Let's do it again!" A few more times. "That was good. That was good." Clink is happy for three minutes until Cool Marvin tries a fancy dunk and misses. Cool Marvin makes the mistake of laughing. "Is that funny?" Clink says. "I don't see anything funny about that. Does anybody else think that's funny? Maybe there's something wrong with my sense of humor. I don't know, but that's just not funny to me."

A few minutes later Clink will be riding a different train of thought. "Jump stop, please. Jump stop!" Magz will soon be next when he makes a bad pass. "You can't eye the pass. You have to do something to distract the defense."

Tommy walks over to me and starts talking about his mother. He tells me how much he misses her. "I look at her picture first thing when I wake up in the morning. Her picture is the last thing I look at before I go to bed. I miss her so much. When I got into the Hall of Fame, she would've been up there waving and saying 'That's my son—that's my son.' But I know she was looking down on me."

Clink has Tommy put 11 seconds on the clock. "Make the score 68-66, Tommy," Clink says. Tommy sets the clock. "Be aware of the situation.

Only thing beats us is a three." Duncan makes a mistake. The only thing— the three—does beat them. "Rob, they caught you sleeping. The penetration layup doesn't beat you. The three does. Pay attention. Listen to me, Rob. Stay glued—*glued!*—to your man."

Tommy puts four seconds on the clock and they run the same simulation again. Four seconds in basketball is a long time. Tommy sets the clock, turns to me. "You know where newspapers come from, Carson. Let me tell you a story."

Thursday, February 4

The team meets at the Wildcat.. "Think back to last Thursday's practice," Clink says. "It was an hour and fifteen minutes. Short but efficient. Be good at everything today. We gotta fly through this. We got to be great." Clink brings out the trashcan for drills. I ask Magz how he's feeling. Is he burned out? He smiles and points to his feet. "I got new shoes." He jogs off and practices free throws.

Lee Litvin sits next to me. Litvin transferred to Chico State from Diablo Community College. He has been going to Frank Alloco (Bay Area coaching legend) basketball camps since he was a little kid. "A couple of years ago I asked Frank if he might be able to get me a manager position at Chico State," Litvin says. "I interviewed with Coach Clink. Coach Clink said, 'I respect Frank Alloco, and you're here because of him.'" Litvin is also a rap artist. He frequently raps with Datu. "I paint pictures with words," Litvin says.

Litvin has the skinny on all the players. "It's what these guys do off the court," he says. "Rob is a great example. He works just as hard in study hall as he does out here. He has a lot of humility, too. Really humble guy." He tells me that McFerren, Cool Marvin, and Datu have just gotten a puppy. "Yeah, Jalen went home for a weekend and found the dog on a street corner. Brought him back to Chico." He confirms that Ellis is a class clown. "It's rubbed off on Giddings." He tells me that Lynch's father passed away when Lynch was eight. This gives me a clearer insight into his character. Lynch, out of all the guys on the team, is the one I would pick to be by my side in a bar fight. He tells me there's a You Tube video where Lynch talks about the death of his father. He tells me that Silverstrom is Armenian. His thoughts turn back to McFerren. "He's funny and likes to fool around, but on the court he's all business. Off the court he's super nice. The girls love him." He tells me that only Giddings, Magz, and Datu have serious girlfriends. That doesn't surprise me. However, what does surprise me is the insight on Clink. "He loves rap. I guess back in the day he would break dance, spin on his head and all. I heard he was known for doing the Worm Dance or something like that. Yeah, he's really into older hip hop. Gabe, too." Coach Blake remains a mystery. "I don't know much about him. I know he likes to take his shirt off in the weight room."

I watch Briggs and Ellis, the redshirt freshman versus the sophomore (who not long ago was also a redshirt freshman) go at it in the paint. Here I see the bright future of this team. Briggs will soon swat Silverstrom's shot. He will next block Ellis's shot.

"No turnovers," Clink screams. "Keep that ball moving. Everybody at 100 percent."

Tommy walks up to me. "See, fans only see the finished product. They don't see what I see every day at practice."

CHAPTER 67

Muskrat Love: Cal State East Bay

FEBRUARY 5

THE PLAYERS GATHER UPSTAIRS IN a classroom before the shoot around. They all sit dressed in their practice gear and sit in school desks. Coach Gabriel is playing a video at the front of the room and grilling Silverstrom with questions. "What are we doing offensively here? What are we doing here defensively?" Silverstrom seems flustered. Coach Clink walks in. The mood switches from playful to serious.

"Let's dial in," Coach Clink continues. "Tonight will be like a CCAA playoff game. We have to be perfect with all the things we've been working on in practice this week. We have to execute. Share the ball. All about sharing. Be as unselfish with the ball as you can."

Clink sits down. He turns the show over to Coach Gabriel.

"Your bluffs have to be good," Coach Gabriel says. "Stay in front of your man. They have a lot of dangerous players. Don't let them get loose."

Clink points out how much East Bay resembles Chico State. "Rob, this will be a big assignment for you. We have to communicate out there. We all have to talk," Clink finishes. Coach Gabriel resumes.

"If any play breaks down, be ready for a one-on-one situation."

He shows examples, one in particular where Duncan flies at a guy and flails his arms when he shoots. "Rob, this guy's not a good shooter. Just put a hand in his face. All you got to do. Okay, only three more clips, guys,"

Coach Gabriel says, the intrinsic teacher raised by two teachers who can sense when students are losing their concentration.

In the pregame speech, Clink reminds the players that East Bay is fighting for their basketball lives. How they are trying to get into the playoffs and will be prepared and ready to give everything they have. Earlier he had compared East Bay to a cornered animal and talked about how that animal is never going to give up. After the final warms up before the game, Clink lights into a rare pregame sermon, the first one I've heard all year.

"I want to tell you guys a story about a vivid memory I have from when I was a kid. This is a true story. When I was about 12-years-old we lived out in the country. Our house sat on the top of a slope. At the bottom of our driveway was a small irrigation ditch that ran alongside the road. Down in this irrigation ditch there lived a muskrat. If you've never seen a muskrat, it looks like a cross between a raccoon and a beaver. Well, one day this muskrat wandered up our driveway into our property. We had a Great Dane. This dog was tall, stood up to my chest and weighed about 170 pounds. Big, strong, powerful, and loyal. Beautiful, too. So when this muskrat came up to our house, our Great Dane attacked it. These two animals went at it. The dog would go at the muskrat and the muskrat would fight back. So this went on for a few minutes and the whole time I'm sitting on the couch watching TV. All of a sudden my dad comes in from the garage and sprints to the back of the house to his room. I sat there thinking: That's weird. Then about a minute later he comes running back down the hall loading a shot gun. So I get up and run outside behind him. When I got outside I see that our dog has this muskrat pinned up with its back against a fence. The muskrat had its fangs showing and his teeth were red with blood. It was vicious, fighting for its life. I looked at our dog who was barking and there was a stream of blood coming out of its face from where the muskrat had ripped part of his lip off. The blood was streaming. This muskrat would not give up. It was going to kill or be killed. My dad yells at me to grab the dog. So I grab our dog by the collar and try to hold him back. The dog weighs more than I do. The dog is going wild, the muskrat is hissing and lunging at the dog. And then all of a sudden my dad points the shotgun and BOOM! Game over. He blew the muskrat into about eight pieces. The moral of the story? East Bay is the muskrat, and our defense is the shotgun. Now go unload it on them."

The players are as fired up as they've been all year. They jump up and go wild, almost bust through the Red Door. They will unload on East Bay: 65-56. Ellis will play angry with seven dunks and finish the night with 24 points, a career high. Luke Reid says of Ellis: "His massive smile and monstrous dunks gave Acker Gym the feel of a tent revival. In perhaps the most impressive aerial display that Acker Gym has ever seen, he made the crowd believers and brought Cal State East Bay to its knees." Duncan continues to be an all-around team player with 10 points, seven rebounds, three assists, two blocks, and a steal.

No. 14 Chico State will go into Saturday night's game against Monterey Bay 17-3 overall and 11-2 in CCAA. They are now only a half-game behind first place UC San Diego.

CHAPTER 68

Full Parking Lot:
Cal State Monterey Bay

SATURDAY, FEBRUARY 6

THE HEART OF THE WILDCATS will be tested tonight. Ellis, who grew up right before the fans' eyes only 24 hours ago against East Bay, will have the tough assignment of stopping the Otters star and conference scoring leader Ryan Nitz who is averaging 20 points a game.

The Wildcats go down 12 points early. They'll be down most of the night but keep battling back. The sole of Clink's shoe will be worn down from all the foot stomping by the time they make it into the locker room at halftime down 34-32.

"The last ten minutes were great," he tells the team. "We kicked their butts. Let's talk about defense. You've got to do a better job blocking out. Secondly, they are 6-of-12 shooting from the three. We have to stop that. Now, you've done a good job in transition for the most part. I won't get mad at you for getting beat off the dribble. We'll help you on that. But you can't get beat by having number 11, 3, or 5 hitting a three. Three guys have been hitting the threes." He catches his breath. "Believe in it. Buy into it," he continues. "On offense, once we started using our ball screens, things were good. We need to have possessions where we get two ball screens. Remember to wait for the screen, too. Okay? Wait for it. Think about all the Cut-Throat we've played in practice. All the things we've done in practice. Just keep doing it. I'm not going to get frustrated. It's on you, guys. It's on

395

you. Here we go. Got four minutes left so get out there and have a good warm-up."

Journey blasts through the gym as the players get ready to go back through the Red Door. The crowd is going wild, singing: "Don't stop, believing..." Clink sits in his chair, alone, holding his clipboard. Silverstrom will finally get going in the second half and score a three then soon after hit a big layup. Duncan feeds off of Silverstrom's emotions and puts the Wildcats up with a three. At the next timeout, Clink demands hustle. "Keep sprinting back in transition. They've only scored four points in five minutes."

McFerren is moving through the paint like a salmon spawning upstream. The crowd starts chanting: "Jalen, Jalen." He soon makes a bad shot. Clink walks up and down the sideline, thinking. "Giddings," he yells at the big man on the bench. Giddings runs to the scorer's table. The Otters bang another three. Clink is livid. Time out. "Listen, get back in transition. Take away the three and we'll win this thing. Come on. We've got 13 minutes left. Take away the three, and we'll get whatever we want."

The Wildcats are getting crushed in transition despite Clink's pressure. The Otters are starting to run away with the game. They go up 55-43. No signs of panic on Clink's face. At the next 10:57 time out: "We can easily get back in this if we get back to our game plan. Get back to the game plan! Take away the three. Don't take bad shots. Keep getting A-shots. It's gotta happen now, though. Now!" Clink has turned on the players' switch.

Silverstrom comes out fired up and gets a quick bucket to get the lead down to 10. The number 10 seems to be the magic do-or-die comeback number in basketball. It's when the lead gets down to seven that kills the team with the lead, or when the lead goes back up to 13 that kills the losing team. Silverstrom makes a pass to Ellis that sends Baca's chair flying back and his hands up in the air. Wildcats only down seven. Duncan dunks and cuts it to five at the media time out. At the timeout Clink tells the team: "Next play is a drop. If we have to slip, run it for Corey. Get the ball in the paint and you'll get whatever you want."

Out of the huddle Duncan gets a quick layup in the paint: anything the Wildcats want. Next play down Duncan attacks the paint and gets a layup. Wildcats down two. Tommy is fired up. "Now is the time to believe," he says. Duncan's layup forces the Otters to call a timeout. "Do not change the recipe," Clink says. "Keep stopping the three. Dribble attacks. Post entry. Don't settle. You hear me? Do not settle. Keep attacking."

The way Clink keeps urging them on during the timeouts reminds me of the doula we had when my son was born, how she kept pushing my wife to stay with it. Victory, the crowning of the head, is in sight. A couple of plays later, Duncan will miss his shot then grab his own rebound and put it back in, a play of sheer brute strength and will that I imagine came from a summer of moving grand pianos. The team is more connected than I've seen all year. They huddle like brothers. The media timeout at 2:57 has the Otters up one. "Be strong with the ball," Clink says. "Get the ball in the paint. Go down and pound it inside. The game is in the paint."

A minute and a half will pass before Duncan scores on a fast break instigated from McFerren's offensive rebound. The Wildcats go up, 65-64. The Otters call a time out. "Don't change anything we're doing," Clink says. "Keep taking away the three. It all comes down to defense. Let's go!"

Silverstrom and Duncan stand at center court, talking, waiting for the Otters to come back out. Whatever they are plotting will work. The Otters will miss a quick three. Silverstrom scoops up the rebound and gets it to Duncan for another fast break. The Wildcats never look back.

This is the fifth time this season the Wildcats have come from 10-plus points down to win. McFerren finishes with a career high 22 points on 6-of-7 shooting and Duncan sinks six of the Wildcats last seven baskets, scoring 12 of his 19 points in the final 8:03 as the Wildcats improve to 18-3 overall and 12-2 in the California Collegiate Athletic Association (CCAA).

The 1940-41 Chico State basketball team, which finished the season 20-3, is the only other team in those 101 years to boast 18 wins in its first 21 games. The 14th ranked Wildcats have now won 16 straight conference games in Acker Gym and 32 of their last 36 regular-season games overall. Duncan's stock continues to rise: 10 rebounds, five assists, and a pair of blocks. He has 17 points and seven rebounds in the second half alone on the way to his third double-double of the season. He is playing like a CCAA MVP. Only time will tell.

Clink is thrilled after the game. He tells his players in the locker room: "It took a lot of toughness to sustain three different big-time blows they handed us. We had to gut it out. But here's my critique. We deviated from the game plan. We didn't get the ball in the paint enough. We didn't take A-shots. There's a lesson to be learned from this. We beat the hottest team in the conference. Now, next Friday night, we have an opportunity to take first place. If we stick to our game plan for 40 minutes, we'll win. Come in here Monday dialed and ready to get at it. Tuesday we'll have a game plan."

As I left that night, I marveled that it's the first time there's been a line of cars waiting to get out of the parking lot.

CHAPTER 69

Chico Snow

MONDAY, FEBRUARY 8

THE CHICO SNOW HAS ARRIVED even though it's 75 degrees outside. The Almond trees are in full blossom. Clink spends the first twenty minutes of practice talking about the ways they are going to beat UC San Diego. The game plan, turns out, comes a day early. I speak briefly with Clink while the players stretch. "A couple of the guys are sick. Giddings's been battling it all week. Corey's out sick today." I ask Clink if the warm weather throws him off. "I don't like the rain." I ask him if he'd like to be out playing golf. "That's nowhere near my mind."

Tommy walks up and starts recommending movies to me. *"Casualties of War* and *Platoon.* Now those are two good movies. I watch *Platoon* whenever I can."

The players finish stretching. Clink runs a drill. He takes the ball from Lynch. "The deeper I get on this dribble," Clink says, "the more things will open up. Make sense?" Kitchens watches on. His new role since becoming academically ineligible is one of wearing a Chico State T-shirt and being the decoy who sets screens. Clink is in teaching mode today. The look on Tommy's face as he takes a seat and gets ready to set the clock sums up what it feels like to be in the fourth and next to last month of basketball season.

"You've got to pay attention here," Clink says. "We're going to tweak a few things. We want to get this more up to the top of the flat screen. Get as deep as you can and catch it at the top. Got it?" He goes through the drill. "Any questions?" Kitchens runs the clock. I ask him how many plays they have. He shakes his head. "We have a lot. And we don't even use them all. I just know what I'm supposed to do when I'm out there. Not too worried about what the other guys will do. See, that's the great thing about the red shirt year. You spend that first year learning all the plays. Eventually it's just muscle memory. And motion offense means freedom." Clink runs a few more plays.

"Any questions on that?" he asks.

Coach Blake yells out: "Drew, come on. We need you." I sigh. Moments ago Kitchens told me that not playing is killing him. Shame and embarrassment is written all over his face. Not playing has eaten this young man up. "The worst part," Kitchens says, "is that I can't even sit on the bench." He shakes his head. "Can't even sit on the bench."

"Drew, come on. We need you. Now!" Coach Blake says again. Kitchens sprints over.

Kitchens is needed for different reasons now.

Wednesday, February 10

When I walk into the gym, the players are already watching game film. "Corey, I know you fish," Clink says. "You know what it's like to hook the fish. The minute you stop fighting the fish, he's gone. Same thing here. Constant attack. You can't let the line go slack. Keep that line tight." He nods for Coach Gabriel to keep the game fill rolling. "Stop. Okay, here, good angle against the ice. See how his butt is facing the Wildcat's nose. Now that's a good angle." A few more clips. "See those throw backs? Throw it inside. Now here's three examples of how we turn down the screen like we did yesterday. Here it is—freeze!" Film resumes. "See how he's wide open in the corner? That's what we're looking for." Clink, animated, steps into the screen. He points. "See that action on the down screen? That's what we're looking for. Now let's go have a good practice."

The players stretch. Clink watches them with stern eyes. Once they start to practice, Litvin shuffles over. He has the walk of a confident young man, not so much a strut as a glide, kind of penguin-like, and the smile of a young man who always has a chicken boiling in the pot. I pegged Litvin from the moment I saw him as a guy who was interested in making money someday. Sure enough, he's a business administration major with a focus in entrepreneurship.

Clink shouts at Datu to hustle more. Gene has walked in. Silverstrom walks by and Gene can't resist his usual greeting: "Hi-ho, Silver!" Silverstrom smiles. Tommy walks up and rants about Patton. "I watched the movie last night. Oh, boy." McFerren and Magz go at it for a loose ball. The Chico snow continues to fall outside. Spring is near. Clink's intensity is rising, and he must have lost ten to fifteen pounds since October. The Chico snow continues to fall outside while 592 miles down south the palm trees are swaying from the ocean breeze and the Tritons are preparing to crush the Wildcats season.

CHAPTER 70

Three Inches and 35 Pounds: UC San Diego

FEBRUARY 11

THE TEAM IS FLYING OUT to UC San Diego today. They'll play tomorrow night for first place. I saw this coming last June when I was comparing teams in the conference. A lot has happened since then. Three Chryslers, the rentals that will take them to Sacramento International Airport, are in a line. Clink is already sitting in the passenger seat of one. He's reading a magazine on Team USA basketball. Coach Gabriel is in the driver's seat talking on the phone. "This guy's the best player in the CIF," Coach Gabriel says, talking animatedly. Basketball is always on his mind. Clink nods and wolfs down a banana. He puts down the basketball magazine he was reading and steps out of the car to say hello as I approach. He's wearing his Chico State sweat suit. "You ready, Coach?" I ask. "Ask these guys," he says. "They're the ones who have to play."

One by one the players straggle out, their eyes squinting as they adjust to the bright morning sunshine. These players spend most of their time inside perfecting a game that spans three seasons (fall, winter, and spring), all chilly seasons. Ellis struts by, dancing, head phones on his ears. He's always playing the class clown, always, that is, until he steps on the court. Then it all changes. One by one the players get in the cars. Tom the trainer, Coach Gabriel, and Coach Blake will each be driving a car to the airport.

I watch the faces of the players as they drive off. They're leaving for their biggest road game of the year in a game that might decide who wins the CCAA. There are no fans here to see them off. Most of the students on campus probably don't even know who the team is playing. Many probably don't even know it's basketball season. The cars pull out. It's just me standing there, the sunlight also burning my eyes. I, too, am a gym rat—have been for longer than these players have been alive. I will have to listen to the game on the radio.

February 12: Game Day

Clink's Corner has Clink sounding fired up. "This is fun," Clinks tells Baca. "We're excited. We're ready."

My son Holden wants to watch the game.

"Daddy, I'm tired of listening to the games on the radio. I want to *see* Isaiah," he pleads.

We pull up the game on the computer. We'll get to watch the game but hear it from the perspective of the UCSD broadcasters. Magz walks out to the center court, laughing. He's having the time of his life. "San Diego will have a challenge with the senior listed at 6-foot-10 and 250 pounds," the UCSD announcer says. "Never fun going up against someone that's three inches taller and 35 pounds heavier." For the first time all year it dawns on me that Chico State is to most teams in Division II what most teams in Division I are to Chico State: Three inches taller and 35 pounds heavier.

The game begins. In response to a quick three made by Silverstrom, the announcer says: "Wow. You can tell how much this game means to these Wildcats just from looking at that reaction from the bench." On a Duncan steal: "Wow. More good defense from Chico State. They're really good at stripping the ball from the other guy's hand."

The Chico State bench looks like such a lonely corner. No fans behind them. The defense, though, is the best I've seen all year. Magz is walking around with his chest puffed out, nostrils flaring. After he blocks a shot, the announcer says: "That's what happens when the guy on the other side of the ball is 250 pounds. Not to mention the Wildcats have one of the best defenses, third or fourth, in the country." The Wildcats keep getting the ball in the paint.

"They're pounding the ball in the middle," one announcer says. "Going inside and out. Watch for the throwback."

"Yes," the other announcer says, "every possession in this game matters. That's what happens when two of the hottest teams in the country match up. Both teams are riding win streaks. Best defenses in the country."

"Chico State," the announcer says, "is not a team that will light up the scoreboard, but they will do it defensively."

"Silverstrom wanted to pull-up on that one," the announcer says. "But he kicked it out and made the right decision."

The Wildcats enter the locker room tied at 29 despite having turned the ball over nine times. The big men are playing well. Giddings, despite poor shooting, has compensated with eight rebounds. Harris has broken out of a slump by hitting two threes. More importantly, the Wildcats have stopped Klie and Dyer, the two Tritons' stars, from going off: Klie is 2-of-10 and Dyer 2-of-4. Dyer didn't even shoot a 3-pointer.

The game, as expected, turns out to be a heavyweight match. The announcers express it best:

"Coast to coast by Silverstrom. Where did that one come from?"
"Isaiah Ellis with a big time block. It's little plays like that that make a difference."

After Ambrosini drills a three: *"The winner of this game is in the driver's seat for the conference title."*

On Duncan's hesitation: *"If you're the leading scorer and have to think about the open shot, then something is going on inside your head. You have to be more aggressive if you're Chico State."*

On Ellis making a steal and going coast to coast: *"What a game this sophomore has had. If Chico State wins this game, he's definitely the player of the game."*

On Duncan's turnovers: *"Duncan looks all out of sorts. Chico State has turned it over 15 times. And they're on the road. We've only turned it over four times. How do they still have the lead? I mean, really—how do they still have the lead?"*

On Ellis's defense: *"We're losing the battle down low. Ellis has five inches on Dyer. He's getting Dyer in foul trouble."*

On Ellis's game: *"What a great game Isaiah Ellis has had. Can't give a great team like Chico State second opportunities. This kid is having the game of his life."*

On the long ball: *"They're making all their threes. Hopefully that won't be the difference."*

On Ellis stealing the ball and going coast to coast for a dunk. *"The story has been Isaiah Ellis. It's the third leading scorer on this Chico State team that's beating us."*

On Duncan's turnovers: *"I think Duncan feels like he has to start scoring now and is feeling the pressure."*

On Silverstrom's three that puts the Wildcats up 68-62: *"That five-minute stretch there might have cost San Diego the game."*

On the Wildcats' defense: *"A team that plays the kind of defense that Chico State plays is going to make a comeback really, really hard for the Tritons."*

On all the clutch free throws the Wildcats make down the stretch: *"If you're going to be the kind of team that takes the driver's seat in the conference, you have to make your free throws."*

On the UCSD crowd: *"The fans are deflated and beginning to exit the stands."*

On the win: *"Well, Chico State has taken sole possession of the conference, and they did it on the road."*

Clink's postgame interview with Baca sums it up: "Our guys did a phenomenal job buying into the game plan. We were dialed in."

Clink leaves quickly so Ellis can have this moment. Ellis sounds so poised on the radio, so intelligent. He really has blossomed in the last two weeks. "We set a goal to get 20 post entries," Ellis says. "We got 17. Tonight was about being unselfish. Rob only shot the ball five times, scored seven or something, but he's the happiest guy in the locker room. That says a lot about his character. At the shoot around today, Coach Clink talked to me a lot about free throws. It gave me confidence. We also talked about selfless basketball. We don't care who's scoring as long as we win and everyone's having fun. Tanner and I also remembered how Dyer lit us up last year. We weren't about to let that happen again."

Outside a van engine warms up. The Wildcats will change then immediately get in the van and drive three hours to San Bernardino—yes, after the biggest win of the season. This is life in the CCAA. A grind.

Robert Duncan had good reason to be the happiest player in the locker room, and his greatest achievement of the night is the one that will never appear in the box score. He had stopped Dyer, who coming into the game had made 65 threes and was shooting 53% from that range. The Wildcats held Dyer to 13 points on 3-of-7 shooting, including 0-of-2 from beyond the arc. The Tritons made just 5-of-17 from beyond the arc as a team.

First place with only five games remaining in the regular season.

Anything, though, could happen.

And everything would.

A lot can happen in two weeks.

CHAPTER 71

St. Valentine's Eve Overtime Massacre: Cal State San Bernadino

FEBRUARY 13

COACH CLINK AND THE WILDCATS are a couple of hours away from making history. If the Wildcats win tonight, they'll be just the second team in the program's 101-year history to win 20 of its first 23 games. It will not be easy. Nothing in the CCAA ever is.

In the pregame show, Baca asks Coach Gabriel how the win against UC San Diego felt last night. "We didn't revel in the victory," he says. "Coach reminded us that we have one more to get. He said we need to be a little greedy." Cal State San Bernardino is notorious for their trap style of play. "We've been preparing for this all fall. We bring the same effort every day." Coach Gabriel is asked about Duncan's performance. "Rob told the team to go out and do it offensively. He said he would handle the defensive end." On Ellis's recent performances: "His attitude is infectious with the rest of the guys. He's a good basketball player. But what makes him so special is that he's a great person." The Wildcats come out playing against Cal State San Bernardino the way one who studies basketball expects a team to play less than 24 hours after winning their most anticipated game of the season: flat. Not only that, but recall they had to immediately pack into a small van (imagine the tightening of the muscles) and drive until past midnight to their next destination and check-in to a low-budget hotel. Wake up and do it all over again.

Silverstrom and Harris will put the team on their back tonight and carry them.

They will hit 4-of-7 threes in the first half. The Wildcats play so sluggishly that the always candid Baca remarks: "This is the worst offense I've seen all night." But when the Wildcats get down, he reminds fans: "But when the game gets chaotic, that's when Chico State's breathing starts to slow down." Harris has been waiting for a night like this. He provides the energy the Wildcats need and keeps them alive. At one point in the second half, the Coyotes go up 41-34. The Wildcats will regain their rhythm thanks to a 16-8 run punctuated by Silverstrom and Harris hitting threes to take the lead at 57-54. The Wildcats have a two-point lead with five seconds left. Ellis commits a foul. The Coyotes hit both free throws to tie the game at 73. McFerren hurls a 3-pointer at the buzzer.

Although there will not be another McFerren Miracle, there will be a St. Valentine's Eve Massacre. The Wildcats start overtime like they should have started every game of the year. They punch the Coyotes square in the nose, draw first blood, and never quit landing punches for the next five minutes. Harris dons the urgency cap and hits three shots. Ellis hits two. McFerren one. The Wildcats are a perfect 6-of-6 in overtime. Silverstrom has five assists. The Wildcats get two steals and only commit two turnovers. They outscore the Coyotes 18-6. They play with the most urgency yet, not about to surrender first place.

In the postgame show, Clink explains how he went with a smaller lineup to match the Coyotes. He also talks about putting Datu in for a four-minute stretch in the second half to try and light a fire. Datu played outstanding, ripping down two boards. "He gave us the energy we needed," Clink says. All season long Clink has warned his players not to let opportunities slip away. "You can't take a night off in this league. Playing back to back like this, particularly on the road, creates mental fatigue. It's not conscious, you know, but in the subconscious. A team can't just show up and think they're going to walk away with a win because they have the better record. That might work in a city league, but not in the CCAA."

Clink always tells his players to be ready. They will be called.

Good things await the Wildcats. Lights, cameras, and microphones are coming. The big time.

ESPN will be at Chico State on Friday night.

CHAPTER 72

ESPN Week

TUESDAY, FEBRUARY 16

THE PLAYERS GATHER AT THE Wildcat. Coach Clink is in beat Pomona mode. The players are in humiliate Pomona on ESPN mode. "We'll start with the way to beat Pomona by giving you your stat for the week," Clink says. "They're 16-0 when they out rebound opponents. They're 3-5 when their opponents out rebounded them. The offensive key is the dribble attack. OK, here's what we're doing today."

Practice is intense for a Tuesday, particularly after the rough weekend they just had. "Do it again! Do it again!" Clink is agitated because the players aren't passing the ball with enough energy and pace. They're also sluggish today. "Sprint, sprint. Do it again!" Clink blows his whistle. "What are we doing? What are we doing? Turnovers led to points last weekend. We can't have turnovers. Protect the ball." The team doesn't chase down a rebound. "Keep playing, keep playing." Ellis takes a hard elbow from Magz on the next play. Everyone is fighting for loose balls. Litvin is up above filming. "If I'm the 4 man, I've got to be hanging out looking for opportunities," Clink says. "Let's go! Ball screen. Post entry. Throw back. Execute. Execute! Got to know what we're doing Friday night."

I can tell by the players' body language that they can't wait to get back to playing open gym basketball, hitting their favorite playgrounds in the summer. Their games at this point have been confined. Their individual talents have been restrained for the collective good of the team. Five fingers on the left hand. Five fingers on the right hand. Two arms.

"Isaiah Ellis, you look confused," Clink snaps. "Do you have a question?" Clink is trying to keep his young star focused. Ambrosini takes a wide open shot from the corner. His release always reminds me of a prayer thrown to the heavens. A season of endurance. I'm exhausted and all I do is write about *their* exhaustion. I'm watching one of the best teams in the country practice on a Tuesday in the sweet spot of the season. What a privilege. Clink sends them off to shoot free throws.

"Don't walk!" What was this team before Arizona and the Pac-12 Network and before ESPN 3 caught wind? They were the same team of integrity, their character developed by doing the right thing at all times behind closed doors. I've been the only outsider. Day after day. The consistent integrity of 15 young men. One Red Door. I pray being on television will not get into their heads. They have worked hard for what will come Friday. I just wish ESPN chose to cover a practice rather than a real game. That's where the real action devoid of the drama takes place. Play resumes.

"If I flash here, look opposite," Clink says. "Take care of the ball. Don't turn it over whatever you do!"

He could not care less about ESPN.

WEDNESDAY, FEBRUARY 17

The team is seated and ready for the film session from yesterday's practice. Clink stands in front of the projector, players paused in transition, young men frozen in time on a pockmarked Acker wall.

"We're gonna talk about things that were good," he says. "Then we're gonna talk about things that need improvement. A little tweaking." He shows a clip. Duncan immediately asks a question. Clink walks into the screen and points and explains. "Does that answer your question? Make sense? Here's one that's pretty good. I know we're really picking things apart here. But you did a great job on this one. You worked your tail off. Your efforts are great. Here's another good one. Not that the other ones weren't. These are just better. Excellent."

Clink's red laser pointer is all over the place today.

"Now let's talk about some areas where we need improvement."

Coach Blake takes over. "Always attack those two-on-ones. Always make that zone move side to side. Keep swinging it across that split line. Side to side." A clip is shown that illustrates this. The defense swings like a pendulum. Clink takes over. "Really good possessions here. We need more like these today. Three attacks will break down the zone. One, two, and by the third a man is wide open. One more, Coach Gabriel." McFerren stops on a dime and makes a jump stop. "Great jump stop. Now watch the attacks. One, two, three, and there it is the fourth time. Good job. More of the same today. Let's go!"

The players stretch. Litvin and Ricky watch, awaiting a loose ball or large body collapsing to the ground so they can mop up the pond of sweat. Ricky's back is already covered in sweat—an outline of a large heart on his gray T-shirt. As usual, Silverstrom goes to his corner and stretches alone. Play soon resumes. Something Clink sees annoys him. "Pace, pace. Keep it moving for two minutes. Here we go." Clink steps on the court. He receives a pass at the high post. On the other end of the court, Coach Blake continues his work with the big men. Clink says over and over: "Take your time. You'll get good shots."

Coach Gabriel, whistle in mouth, fires balls at the capped rim. Magz and Briggs go at it down low. Looking back on Magz's season, and looking forward to Briggs's season next year, and if people marvel at Briggs's talent, it didn't just happen overnight. Magz has groomed him for his success day after day in practice. Herein lies the genius behind Clink's patience to redshirt players who could become instant contributors. This is how he gets guys to buy into the culture.

The team gets together again. Clink talks about the cuts they will see from Pomona's star and All-League player Jordan Faison on Friday night. Silverstrom makes a steal. Clink storms the court.

"Let's go! Let's go!" He does that occasionally. He comes out of nowhere with this burst of energy. The players love it. A few minutes later,

Ellis yawns. Stars are allowed to do that as long as Clink doesn't see it. "No, Corey, don't do that. Work on your jump stop. You don't have to do anything special."

Briggs hits the deck on the next play. Ricky immediately sprints to where Briggs has fallen and drops to his knees, starts wiping up the sweat. He reminds me of the basketball version of a ball boy at Wimbledon. The players in black continue to make the guys who get all the minutes better and better. Only Clink sings their praises. "Do that one more time. Do it again."

If only the administrators, faculty, and staff on campus, all the fans in the stands, could see the sacrifices these unheralded players make. All they have to do is ask, and one of the players—probably even Clink—will escort them through the Red Door and into the gym and offer them a seat.

"Same play, Coach?" Coach Gabriel asks.

"Sure," Clink says.

"It's about anticipation, guys," Coach Gabriel says. "Anticipation."

"One more time," Clink says.

Duncan stops to ask a question.

"Does everybody understand what Rob just asked?" Clink says. "That's a great point, Rob. Now do it again." A few minutes later, Clink shouts: "Five and record. Run, run." The players go and silently shoot their free throws. Tommy comes over. He always has a basketball tucked under his arm. Like Linus and his blanket.

"Friday night will be a chance for everyone to see basketball played at a smaller level," Tommy says. "People will realize it's played the same way at this level as it is at the DI level. It's like a Great Dane versus a Poodle. You know what I mean? Same game. Just different dogs." He walks away then storms back. "It's gonna be like a gunfight in the movie *OK Corral*," Tommy says. "Shoot out in the end. I watch a Western every Thursday night to get my head right for Friday's game. I watch the *OK Corral* over and over. The one with Burt Lancaster. Seen it seventeen times and it never gets old."

Tommy's conversation has given time for several loose balls to find homes at different corners of the gym. He goes off to gather them. "Eyes,"

Clink says. "Do not waste dribbles standing in one spot. Do not waste dribbles being cute and going between the legs. Interchange, interchange, interchange. Chest passes. Two hands. Squeeze it." Play resumes. Harris passes up a wide open shot. Clink blows his whistle. "That was an A-shot. As good as you're shooting, Tyler, you gotta take that."

A few possessions later comes the whistle again. "What's the problem, guys? Pass and catch. Catch and pass. And why can't you get the ball in the post?"

ESPN is coming.

Thursday, February 18

I pass Coach Blake coming out of his office on my way to the gym. "It's the secret workouts," he says. "You have to see the secret workouts. Jalen and Rob are in here every day at different times. Secret workouts late at night. That's the secret." He runs off. Outside the Red Door Ellis is lacing up his shoes. I ask him if he feels any pressure with ESPN coming. He confesses he gets butterflies before a game whether he's playing on ESPN or in front of 142 down in Los Angeles. I would have never known. "Oh, yeah," he says. "I get 'em."

The players circle at the Wildcat. "Nothing special today," Clink says. "Another condensed practice." The gym has an excitement mixed with a calm that I've not felt all season. I walk down to Luke's office and get my media pass. "I never thought I'd be burned out from basketball," I tell him, "particularly this early. Maybe it's life that has burned me out. I don't know." Luke has a warm, kind presence that makes him the perfect confessor. He hands me the pass. I put it around my neck. It's official. ESPN is coming. And I will be there.

Giddings is the only player who has had this kind of big game experience from his days at Fresno State. At 44, I have the breadth of life, the long vision, the learned perspective, to realize what these young men can't comprehend: Moments like the ones they will share Friday night don't happen to many people. The chance to play on ESPN. The chance to see a dream reach fruition. Sure, winning the league, the West Regional, and a National Championship are the ultimate goals, but just about every ballplayer in any sport dreams about showcasing his skills to a wider—to a national—audience. I selfishly feel justified for taking on this book because ESPN has validated what I have always felt about this program.

Back in Acker, the players go through plays. They are moving at half-speed and making mistakes.

"How careless are we going to be tomorrow night?" Clink yells. "How careless? Come on! Do it again." Duncan and McFerren get into a scuff. There seems to be a breakdown in communication today. Tomorrow will be a real test of this team's character. How will they compose themselves under the bright lights? The black team—Briggs, Cool Marvin, Datu, Lynch, and Holmes—are more fired up than the starters. Ellis makes a great pass to Duncan, but he fumbles the ball. "Come on, Rob," Ellis says, kind of joking. Duncan's mind seems elsewhere.

Win 21 for Clink will be bigger than win 20. Greed. And if they win tomorrow night, it will also mark Clink's 150th victory. "We're just standing around on the perimeter," Clink yells. "You have to do something extra to beat the Pomona zone." On the next play, Duncan does exactly what Clink has told him not to do. He stands at the perimeter with the ball above his head. "Rob, everyone in the gym knows what you're going to do. You can't just stand there and fake an overhead pass."

Coach Gabriel joins in. "Listen, you can't start a possession against the Pomona zone with penetration." They continue. Clink doesn't like the pace. The black team is giving them a hard time. The Wildcats could never compete without these guys in black. They get the starters ready every day. Make them better.

"Tomorrow night the defense has to be just as good, if not better, than the offense," Clink says. "Here we go." A few plays later. "Postmen, don't waste your dribble." He calls out Tyler Harris, the only player on the team who he almost always calls out by his full name. "Tyler Harris, please shoot the open three. Come on, man. You're shooting too well. Please, okay?"

I've never heard Clink beg a player to shoot until now. On the last play of the series, sure enough, Harris hits an NBA three from the top of the key. Clink likes it.

"Five and record," he says.

CHAPTER 73

Sold Out

SAN MARCOS DID CHICO STATE a favor. They beat UC San Diego last night. The Wildcats are now two games in front of first place. Sophomore sensation Isaiah Ellis has been named the CCAA Player of the Week. Clink—if the season continues to play out this way—is on his way to a second straight CCAA conference title and second straight CCAA Coach of the Year. Not only that but Clink is standing on the precipice of history. His team is ranked higher than any Wildcats team in history. ESPN is coming to Acker for the first time. This will be the first time Acker has sold out since 2000. And Clink is one win away from number 150. He accomplished this in only eight years, the fastest coach to reach this milestone in school history. I want to ask him what it's like to be making history, but I dare not. It will only annoy him. How, though, can he not be aware of this? What kind of pressure does he feel? Is he aware of the legacy he is creating, one that will follow him and his children around for the rest of his life and long after he is gone? People die. Records get broken. History, though, is etched in stone. Our lives, yes, are writ in water, but legacies are the indelible and unshakable sandcastles of time.

Although I have only been on this campus for three years, I've never seen it filled with such electricity. Excitement floods the air. Staff workers are making appointments at hair salons in case they get "air time" on ESPN (at least that's a conversation I overheard while waiting in line to get coffee). Downtown businesses are bringing in extra employees for the weekend as record crowds are expected. Sorority girls are arguing over who the "cutest" Wildcat player is while fraternity boys are arguing over who's the best player. President Zingg, an avid sports fan, will be retiring in May. But before he sails off into the sunset, he will proudly be able to present his university on national television. All of this because of an underfunded basketball team whose coaches and players and managers and trainer do their best work behind closed doors five days a week.

I recall when ESPN first came out (that along with the first MTV video). I remember how excited I was—just 10. One of the first commercials for the network was of a kid dribbling the ball, fast and furiously, between his legs. I grew up on ESPN. For 15 years, before there were more commercials than sport highlights on the network, I couldn't go to sleep if ESPN was not on the television.

Today, like millions of other sports fan, the ESPN song, way more than the Monday Night Football song, gets me fired up. The only thing that gets me more excited is the sound of the bugles at the Kentucky Derby, the sound of the gates going up. I think of all the people, the sports junkies like me, particularly on the East Coast, who can't sleep, who are hanging out in the bars, flipping through channels, looking for a game, and might land on this one.

There was not a lot that needed to be talked about during the film session. The Wildcats had already faced Pomona before. There's no secret about what Pomona does defensively with the zone. When I enter the class-room where the players meet to discuss the scouting report, only Coach Gabriel and Silverstrom are inside. They are talking about the Duke player Grayson Allen. "You really think he's good?" Silverstrom asks Coach Gabe. Coach Gabriel nods. "Rob hates when people compare him to Grayson," Silverstrom says.

The rest of the players trickle in. Clink comes in takes a seat. Coach Gabriel can begin.

"Nothing special to be done tonight. Keep playing like we have all month. Sprinting back on defense. A-shots and rebounds. Also, when we go out for the shoot around, stay focused. There'll be a lot of people out there setting up cameras and lights. Stay focused. Laser sharp."

Reading the scouting report, looking at the game film, I'm startled by how much bigger we are than Pomona. Their biggest guy is Faison at 6-foot-7. "We're always up the line on him," Coach Gabriel says. "A three-quarter front. Only doubling him on post catches. Only when he enters with his back to the basket. That's his game." He shows a few clips of the senior All-American. "There are only nine players on this scout, guys," Coach Gabriel says. "That's all they dress. And only eight will play. About transition offense. When you take a long three, they're already in transition. Sprint back."

Clink sits up. "Can't be a jog," he says. "Has to be a full sprint. If we sprint and communicate, we're gonna be fine. Think about that individually and collectively. Sprint and communicate."

Coach Gabriel moves forward with the game film. "We have to be the ones to initiate contact. We can't give them a second chance. Remember that once we get them in half-court, we can stop them." Clink pops his neck and watches the film intently while squeezing his freshly shaven head with both hands. He does this during every game film, writhing in pain, almost, surely thinking of all the things that might, could—will—go wrong. The power of negative thinking.

"Looking at all these plays again," Coach Gabriel says, "I know we can guard all these. We've been doing it all week."

Clink sits up again. "Just guard," Clink says. "All you have do is just guard. And remember.

No distractions. Dial in. Now let's go!"

Acker has never looked like this before. Cameras, cords, lights, are everywhere. A TV van is getting set up outside. These young Wildcats who have grown up in the ubiquitous world of social media are soaking it up. All these cameras here to photograph them. Justin Briggs's eyes are big as saucers. Surely, when Clink tried to woo him to Chico State, this was not part of his pitch and probably not on the young future star's mind. I must admit that I, too, am in awe by the cinematic production going on around me. But as I look out at these young men, I am reminded that they are much bigger than the cameras. All of their hard work cannot be depicted in two hours of television, win or lose.

Familiar faces show up at the shoot around. Damario Sims and Terrence Pellum, two players who helped build the program, arrive. Many of the players come up and give the two young men a hug. The newer players watch with interest. They know of Damario. He is a legend, the student-athlete that Clink hopes all his players will emulate. The players practice hard in front of Damario. Clink comes over and hugs him.

It's cold and raining outside. Cables are being pulled in from the TV van. Men with cameras are up in the bleachers focusing their lenses. A cold, damp wind crashes through the open door. Late February. Basketball weather. Ricky, just a freshman, stands next to me, his jaw slack, eyes wider than anyone else's. "It's hard to believe," he says, a ball wedged beneath each arm, a towel wrapped around his neck, his glasses fogged, head wagging. "It's hard to believe, isn't it?" He looks around. "All these seats are reserved. People are thinking about us. Crazy hard to believe." He walks out to the Wildcat. Tom the trainer and Kitchens join him. The players move into free throw mode. One by one, they gravitate to the Wildcat and partake in a series of handshakes and fist pumps and high fives that are impossible for a 44-year-old man-to keep up with. They get ready for the half-court shot.

Four guys make it tonight. Even Coach Blake. When the excitement has worn off, Clink gathers them at the circle.

"Just visualize everything we've done and talked about all week," Clink says. "It's a down and back game. Lift attacks. Jump stops. Got be extremely disciplined. We've had great practices this week. Oh, and don't forget that you have to come in the front door tonight."

Silverstrom winces as if he has bitten into foil with a tooth that has a filling. He's superstitious.

What must he be thinking?

His eyes have a look of doubt and this worries me.

CHAPTER 74

ESPN Dirge: Cal Poly Pomona

~

FRIDAY, FEBRUARY 19

I'VE NEVER HAD TO WAIT in line to get a parking pass in the Acker parking lot until tonight. I wait for 20 minutes. I walk in with Courtney and her boys. She tells me that her husband really doesn't care about ESPN. "He just wants to win." I walk into Acker and slide through the rusty gate, the dividing line between the public and private space of Chico State athletics. The first person I see is Barry Bell. The battle-tested Pomona senior who has Chico State's number skips and sings a song. He seems to know something about tonight that I don't. Duncan pops out of the training room and walks toward me. "Hey, how much is coffee?" Duncan asks me.

"You want coffee. Now?" My shock leads me to ignore his question. "I don't have any money." I still don't answer his question. I reach into my pockets to show him I don't have any cash. I laugh. With my luck, I would buy Duncan a cup of coffee and ruin his career and the team's season for some kind of NCAA violation. If that happened, Clink might have it arranged that my body is found floating in Lake Oroville. Each player has his own unique way in the locker of preparing for the game. Silverstrom bounces a baseball out in the hallway. The players wait for Clink to enter and lay his jacket down on the ripped leather couch. There's always great speculation about where he is. "I heard he's been sitting up in the press booth watching the women's game," I hear one player say. The constant sound of toilet paper being rolled off and ripped away. Flushing of toilets. The sound of young nerves preparing to do battle. McFerren comes in and sits next to me on the leather sofa.

"Let's play tic-tac-toe," he says.

He takes my pen and draws the box. He makes the first move. He beats me within ten seconds. He smiles and gets up. Coach Blake walks in. Things get a little quieter. Flashes of Nate Ambrosini in the hallway running back and forth getting loose. A few of the guys groom their hair in the bathroom mirror. Litvin has been talking about rap. He's always smiling and loose. He reminds me of the owner of a popular nightclub. He's the guy you want to know. But Litvin's demeanor changes the moment Clink enters the locker room. He stands at attention. Everyone straightens up. The sound of the sliding door is the starting gun. "We have to win the glass, guys," he says. "Remember. 16-0 when they outrebound their opponents. 3-5 when they don't. Don't give up any transition points. They kicked our teeth in last time on this. Anything else, Coach Gabriel?"

"The press. You guys know what to do," Coach Gabriel says. "One other thing. After the shoot-around today, I saw Barry Bell and a bunch of their other guys out in the parking lot. They were singing songs. Dancing around. Feeling good. Feeling confident. See, they think they own us. Coach is right. They kicked our teeth in six weeks ago. Are you mentally tough enough, disciplined enough, to sprint back every time? If we play our way, we're the better team. Don't forget how they were laughing and smirking when they beat you last time."

Ambrosini's eyes burn. The players are released for the warm up. They have to wait in the hall for the women's game to finish. Duncan is wired and jumpy from the coffee. Tom the trainer gives him a jump rope. Duncan goes outside the gym and jumps like mad. Tom the trainer keeps a hawk eye on him. Although Tom the trainer is not that much older than Duncan, he has wisdom in his soft brown eyes, and the soft beard that makes him seem much older, much smarter, much kinder. He has become a big brother to many of the players.

The team walks through the Red Door and circles in the tunnel by the stands. I look beneath the bleachers to gauge the trash level. I get really fired up when it's deep in trash. Means a big game. It's usually pretty clean, though, but tonight it's trashed. Someone has dropped a cell phone. Mitch Cox, the assistant Athletic Director, crawls beneath, popcorn falling on his head like snow, and retrieves the phone. Chaos swirls. Everyone pitches in at this level. I'm still shaking my head over walking in with Courtney and her three boys. "Greg doesn't care about ESPN and the cameras. He just wants to win." And in the very next sentence she's telling her son to put down the stick he's sword fighting a tree with.

The Chico State women's assistant coach walks through the Red Door into the hall and stands against the wall. Her eyes are wide. She, too, has just been on ESPN. Even though the women lost, surely she sees the future. She has the look in her eyes of the runner who has just crossed the finish line and has a runner's high. The defeated and the victorious together walk through the narrow Red Door that leads from the world of Acker to the locker room. So many emotions have passed beneath this door that separates these two worlds that both winners and losers share. No one ever ties. Outside the noise decibel rises. I am 18 again and at an Ole Miss-Alabama football game in mid-October. Acker has the same feeling. For the first time I've been in California—for the first time in 27 years, I feel like I am back home in the South again, back home in a place where sports and religion matter and the two are inseparable. The experience at the University of Arizona has become a distant second to this experience.

Out on the court during warmups, the players have rock star status. A camera within two feet of Duncan follows him through most of his shoot around. Back in the locker room, Clink wastes no time.

"Okay, dial in. First play is Falcon 2." He goes through the plays then gets down to the other side of things. "Big crowd here tonight. Go out there and have fun. Enjoy the warm up. Let's go."

Clink hunts down Coach Kamansky. They talk for a while. The crowd is raucous, boozy. Fans are dressed up. From the student section is the chant: "Let's go, Clink. Let's go, Clink." He smiles and gives a little wave to recognize them. The fans love him. He is their Dean Smith. The national anthem is the most beautiful rendition I've ever heard or seen. It's a recorded broadcast. Sometimes I can hear people singing in a low tone or humming. But tonight the entire student section sings. It's beautiful. The police who have been assigned the job of watching the student section sing along with the students; they are having a ball. Misty eyes are all around.

Moments like these make the college experience.

Before the game, McFerren inspects the ball the referees have handed him. He doesn't like it. He goes over and picks out a different ball. The superstitious Silverstrom watches with slightly anxious eyes. First, they had to walk in through the front door and now the changing of the game ball.

Clink tells the team in the huddle before the game: "The timeouts are going to be long." The extended pause. Good for television. Magz looking around, taking it all in. The culmination of his career. The ball in the air. The tip. Silverstrom clanks his first shot. Not a good omen for one who is superstitious. Duncan travels on the next possession. Magz gets a quick foul. Duncan travels again. Must be the coffee. Duncan floats a high one off the glass, another shot he has willed in. The Wildcats are down early. McFerren hits a three to bring them closer. In the huddle, I can't hear Clink clearly. All I can see is the vein popping in his head, see him scribbling on the clipboard, jaw working, eyes roaming every player as if looking into their souls.

Clink is going at it early with the refs. The foot stomping starts early tonight. The Wildcats off to yet another slow start. Duncan makes a gorgeous pass to Ellis on a backdoor cut. Pomona comes at the Wildcats in waves. I feel like I'm in the boxer's corner at a professional fight. Pomona holds up signs to call plays. The game is fast. At the 11:22 timeout, Clink says: "Nine turnovers. That's the game right there. Once we stop turning it over, the game's ours. We can't keep giving them the ball. Settle down. Settle down! Our defense is good. Keep attacking, okay. Attack!"

Clink is erratic. Never seen his foot tap this much. The players keep turning it over.

Television jitters. The television presence eventually leaves their minds. Now they're back to just playing basketball. Ellis misses an easy dunk. Silverstrom misses an easier layup. Pomona scores. Time out at 8:32. "Settle down, guys," Clink tells them. Silverstrom misses a long three out of the time out. Duncan grabs it and puts it back. Time out at 7:13. The Wildcats are only down five, but they've already turned the ball over ten times. How is that possible? Faison and Ellis, two heavyweights, go at it. At the next time out, Clink says: "The last six minutes have been great."

The college women in the stands act like groupies and call out to their favorite players. These are the coolest guys on campus. Maybe the planet. Lead cut to 21-17 in favor of Pomona. The senior Barry Bell remains calm. "Move, Corey, move. Don't stand there with the ball," Clink yells. Duncan has now taken the game over. He rolls off 14 quick points, eventually outscoring the entire Broncos team 18-17. He pulls down seven rebounds. He also has five turnovers—probably the pregame coffee. The Wildcats go on a 19-2 run to end the first half. They go into the locker room up 29-17.

At the half, I consider following the coaches into their conference, but Clink does something I rarely see him do. He sticks his head into the locker room. "You stifled them defensively. 20 more minutes of that. Great job." He disappears. I watch Silverstrom. More concern in his eyes. I wonder if this, too—Clink breaking his patterns—has made the superstitious Silverstrom anxious. The players are fired up in the locker room. They know the game is theirs. Duncan is feeling it. "Rob could score 40 tonight," I tell Priest. "But that's now how Chico State plays," Priest, in street clothes, quickly responds. "It's about winning, not who scores the most." Clink comes back into the locker room faster than usual. "Okay, the defense is great. If we defend like that for another 20 minutes, we're in business. They only have one offensive rebound. We have ten. Just keep tipping the balls. Offensively we need to settle down. Stop gambling. We had ten turnovers in the first ten minutes. Only two in the last ten. Just settle down and share the ball. They've been stuck on 17 for a long time. Take care of the ball. Visualize yourself sprinting back, blocking out on every possession."

Silverstrom's struggles deepen in the second half. Frustration creeps into his face. He can't hit a shot. But everyone else on the Wildcats' roster is filling in for him. At the 10:26 mark, the game has gotten out of hand. The Wildcats take a 52-34 lead. They are humiliating Pomona on a national stage. By the 9:35 mark, it looks like the game is over: the Wildcats are up 17. But things change fast in basketball. Duncan turns the ball over by bouncing it off his foot, then later fouls his man on the three point shot. The Pomona player makes all three from the line. Giddings will soon air ball a free throw, not much worse a player can do on national television. Things turn. Fast. Pomona puts the pedal to the metal. I look over at Tommy. He's sweating bullets, knows the Pomona worm has turned. Faison, the senior star, only scored two points in the first. In the second half, though, he owns the paint as if he's the CEO of Sherwin Williams. The freshman Ogundiran can't miss. He starts a Pomona 13-0 run. They press. They mug McFerren. He coughs it up. They score. Pomona cuts it to 52-45 with 7:35 to play. This is exactly what ESPN wants. The Wildcats open the lead back up to seven, but Pomona comes right back and ties the game at 59 with 1:56 remaining. The body language of the Wildcats, the look in their eyes, reveal timidity for the first time all season. They need to get out of their heads, but how can they—blowing a lead like this on national television? Silverstrom has the body language of a tin can that has been stepped on and flattened.

Faison shows the country why he's the challenger to Robert Duncan for CCAA Player of the Year. He grabs an offensive rebound with 1:07 to go and puts it back in. Cal Poly Pomona takes the lead. Silverstrom and McFerren have wide-open looks for the three. No luck. Faison hits two key free throws with 11 ticks on the clock, and punctuates the comeback win by blocking McFerren's layup and grabbing the rebound to put the nail in the coffin.

All the life has been drained out of the players, the coaches, and the fans. Acker has the feeling of a funeral: 2,057 heartbroken fans. Inside the locker room is even worse. Someone, something, has indeed died. The players sit in silence for ten minutes.

Outside the Cal Poly Pomona players rejoice. They make that evil, sinister laughing sound that coyotes make in the small hours of the morning, a devilish glee that wakes you up with a start and rapid heartbeat. Clink comes in. "I'm not here to tell you anything you don't already know. We stopped playing in the last eight minutes of the game. We stopped blocking out. We turned it over. We stopped moving. We just gave it away. Gave it away. I'm not at mad you. Not mad, but I am disappointed. Really disappointed. I'm disappointed in myself. If you guys want to make a deep run in the NCAA tournament, if we get there, you're gonna face teams like this. Better than this. I'm disappointed. There was a moment when Isaiah dove for a ball and the bench was lifeless. Coach Gabriel had to yell at you to get up. We puckered up and got soft. Here's the deal. We have another great, ranked team coming in here in less than 24 hours. Another hungry team who wants into the NCAA tournament. You better walk in here tomorrow morning with an edge. It's going to be a war tomorrow. Everyone, and I mean everyone, has to be ready to step up. We are too good to be complacent and give another team a game. You have to play for 40! Step up."

Clink looks to Coach Gabriel.

"We didn't handle the pressure. The TV, the crowd, a lot of pressure," Coach Gabriel says. "We just didn't handle it well. But here's the thing and what makes basketball so beautiful, and why I love it so much. We get to play again tomorrow. We get to do it all over again. Tomorrow's game is just as important as the game we played tonight. The only difference is that ESPN won't be here. I want you to go home tonight and look at yourselves in the mirror. Take a long look. Look at yourself and ask yourself how you could have handled tonight differently. How you could have handled the pressure better. Come in here tomorrow and just keep doing all the things we've been doing that has made us successful." Coach Gabriel looks back at Clink.

"I'm not mad," Clink says. "Just disappointed. We gave it to them. Played great, terrific, for 32 minutes. Then we got soft. We got complacent. Go home. Do whatever it is you need to do tonight to get your head straight. Walk back in here tomorrow at 12:20 p.m. and walk through that Red Door with an edge. An edge! Learn from this. Let's have a great shoot around tomorrow. We have to respond tomorrow night. We have to play defense for a full 40 minutes. Walk in here tomorrow and make up for tonight. Keep your heads up and be ready to battle."

CHAPTER 75

Rebounding on Senior Night
Save One: Humboldt State

SATURDAY, FEBRUARY 20

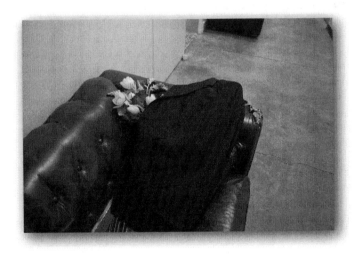

THE PLAYERS ARRIVE READY TO play Saturday night. Not only are the Wildcats playing Humboldt State, a rivalry game 24 hours after a loss on ESPN, but it's also senior night. Kitchens sits next to me on the ripped leather couch. Pain, shame, and humiliation are etched on his face. Tonight should be the night his fans and family and teammates celebrate his hard work—hard work that began five years ago when he began his Chico State career as a redshirt freshman. Academically ineligible athletes, however, do not receive such honors. Instead he will be a spectator in the press box and watch Magz give his mother—whom he redshirted with so long ago—the traditional bouquet of flowers to the adoration and applause of the fans.

Kitchens shakes his ashen face, shocked, confused, and a little guilty for what had happened less than 24 hours before. "We wanted the clock to run out," he says. We just stopped playing." He rubs the stubble on his face. "I could feel it slipping away. It was so painful to watch. I wanted to leave. I couldn't, though."

I ask Kitchens how he's handling everything. He's looked pretty upbeat considering his tragic circumstances. "What you see isn't what I'm feeling or thinking at all. I don't know what to do. I'm lost." He shakes his head. He's not yet ready to cry. "Last semester I lost the thing I love to do more than anything in the world. I've always played basketball. It's who I am." He sighs, head shaking still, staring off into space. "Basketball has always been my identity. I've been trying to find other outlets. I need to graduate. I've been going to the library a lot." I ask him what happened.

"I screwed up. I missed a couple of midterms. My teachers wouldn't let me make them up. The one that did me in was Estate Planning and Investment Planning. I tried talking to my professor. Said I'd do anything. I was emailing, going to office hours, calling. It's rough. I did it to myself, though. I could easily not come around anymore. I don't really want to come around, but it's still my team. What I did has affected everyone in my camp. My team. My support group. My family. I'm not even allowed to watch the game from the bench. I have to sit in the stands. Like a fan. Yeah, so right now I'm focusing on my school work. That's my number one priority right now."

His leg starts bouncing. His jaw clenches a little. "My favorite time of year has turned into the worst. If it happened last year, when I was a junior, I could have handled it a little better. But my senior year. And tonight. Senior Night. I can't even participate. I've been here for five years. I came in with Magz as a redshirt. All the fruits of my labor, gone. I had 15 family members that had to cancel flights and hotel rooms for tonight. My mom still came. She couldn't get the money back for her flight. She's sitting with Trevor's mom."

Kitchens says when he first found out he was off the team, he didn't tell anyone. "It was too embarrassing. So embarrassing. I was a dog with his tail between his legs."

Here is the player Clink had told me last May has the highest basketball IQ on the team. And tonight he's sitting in street clothes on the cracked leather couch talking to the writer who is supposed to be chronicling his magical senior year. I didn't see this coming. No one did. Clink enters the locker room. As customary, he takes off his jacket and lays it on the ripped leather couch. There is a bouquet of flowers. There should have been two. Silverstrom looks angry tonight, almost apologetic. Coach Blake stands in front of the board.

Clink stands next to Kitchens and puts his hand on the young man's shoulders. Kitchens lowers his head and sobs. Clink is in pain. This is one of his sons. Sure, Kitchens let Clink down and disappointed him, but fathers always want the best for their sons. He keeps patting Kitchens's back. This is the tender moment I was hoping would emerge from my experience following the team. I just wish it wouldn't have been under these circumstances. The last 24 hours, the loss on national television and now the heartbreak of Kitchens, has been emotionally draining. Herein lies the unscripted drama that only sports provide. I break down. My heart hurts so much for this young man, and what a price he has had to pay.

After the players huddle and break, the team takes a left and makes the short walk—ten steps—to the Red Door that will lead them into Acker. Kitchens, wiping the tears from his eyes, a hoodie pulled over his head, takes a right and makes the long walk to the press box where he will be a spectator. He has gone through the Red Door and beyond prematurely.

Most people say that Kitchens deserves this because they feel that's the right thing to say. I also find it honorable that the athletic department did not make any exceptions but stood steadfast to the decision not to let Kitchens participate in Senior Night. Sadly, Drew Kitchens will serve as the warning to all the other student-athletes who will come after him. A rule is a rule and Kitchens violated that rule. But here is a young man who has been disgraced and humiliated—a winner who has suffered the ultimate defeat, an unbearable loss, something that goes much deeper than a game. This is something that will dog him for the rest of his life.

But he is one of Clink's chosen players. You don't play for Clink if you can't handle adversity. Kitchens will be alright. He will learn from this. Become a better man. Make sure his sons or daughters don't make the same mistake someday. This is one of those moments that create character, the kind of character that a classroom can never teach. The kind of character that higher education seeks to mold, and the kind of character that in this case Chico State has successfully molded.

The student section tonight is only half-full. The Friday night hangover weighs heavily in the air. No cameras tonight. Only mirrors. The ones the players must look into after the game.

Acker still fills up. 1,356 fans in the house.

Clink grabs the chair with authority, more aggressive tonight, than he's ever grabbed the chair to start a game. Silverstrom comes out firing. He wastes no time hitting a three. Clink doesn't land his first foot stomp until the 17:05 mark. Silverstrom's rage continues. During the first time out, Clink's message is clear: "You have to sprint back. Sprint!" Silverstrom gets a rebound and goes coast to coast. That's his game. Clink soon benches three starters because they aren't sprinting back. More of the same in the next time out. "Listen, we can get anything you want offensively if you just sprint back. Got that? It's an absolute sprint back. Get back. Put it on them defensively. They have 10 points in five minutes. Wear them down."

Coach Gabriel gets up and walks down the bench. He unleashes a tirade on the bench players. "Get your butts up and cheer." It's one of the few times I've seen him get truly mad. His face is red. The players follow his orders. They stand up and clap, yell, about everything. Magz makes a monster block and sprints back. The bench is into it. During the media timeout,

Clink keeps telling them to attack the zone. "Inside out. Look at me! Inside out. Lift and attack. Don't settle. Just keep attacking. Lift and attack."

Silverstrom and Giddings go cold. Still, at the 7:31 media timeout, the Wildcats have a nice eight-point edge, 25-17. "We need to get more lifts and attacks. Listen, I'm all about shooting the three. But play inside out. It's gotta happen on the defensive end. Take them out of what they're doing. Everybody rebound."

Silverstrom comes out and hits a deep three. He then makes a steal and a few possessions later gives up a slightly contested three and makes the unselfish pass to a wide-open Ambrosini who drills it. "Big-time pass, Corey," Coach Gabriel yells three times. The bench erupts.

The next trip down Ambrosini misses a shot from the corner. Ellis keeps the ball alive with his palms, pushing the ball up like it's a beach ball being bounced back and forth at a crowded outdoor music festival. The Wildcats are up 10 at the next time out with 5 minutes left in the first half. "We do not let up defensively," Clink barks. The last eight minutes have been great. Don't settle for anything. Don't settle."

With fifteen seconds left and the Wildcats up 37-27, Clink puts in a couple of the black shirts, Cool Marvin and Holmes. Humboldt State scores an easy layup in the paint as time expires. Those are the kind of shots that come back to haunt a team. The Wildcats go into the locker room at the half up eight. I follow the coaches into their conference room. "We're getting any shot we want," Coach Gabriel says.

Coach Clink stares at the stat sheet. "Is there anything we need to do different defensively?" he asks.

"We've got to stay on number five," Coach Blake says. "He went 4-of-7 in the first half. Most of his points were off dump-offs."

"We hardly had any turnovers, Coach," Coach Gabriel adds. "We need to tell the guys to step on their necks."

Clink steps back into the locker room and translates to the players the analysis that his assistant coaches just provided. That's the half-time process. During the first time out of the second half, Clink says: "Put the lock down on them. Take some pride in your defense. The Wildcats have a

15-point lead when Humboldt State calls a timeout at 8:31. "We cannot go to sleep right now," Clink says. "We have to dial in. It's right there for us. Make them quit. Make them quit!"

Ellis continues to dominate the paint. At the 7:16 media time out, Clink says: "Don't let up. You've got to be dialed off the ball. You're doing great on the ball—but dial in off the ball. Let's go!"

The lead dwindles. A feeling of last night creeps in. Silverstrom misses a jumper then turns it over. He makes a quick foul. His body language is reminiscent of last night, a tin can being crushed. Clink takes him out and puts Harris in. He lets Silverstrom gather himself for a couple of minutes, then puts him back in to finish out the game. The Wildcats are up 10 at the 3:28 media timeout. Clink says: "Keep attacking down low. It's attack mode. Got that. Attack. Killer instinct, killer instinct. Three stops and we got them. Let's take it from them right here and now." The Wildcats falter after the time out. Humboldt State cuts it to seven. Ellis, though, saves the day. He hits his free throws and follows Clink's orders and attacks in the paint.

The Wildcats have proven themselves winners. They could have easily shut down after last night, but they came out and responded. They get the victory, 82-74. Coach Gabriel pats Clink on the back as time expires. They both breathe out sighs of relief. The weekend is over. In the locker room, Clink tells the players: "That was a great response. We were in a similar situation as last night. The big lead slipped but we kept control." Coach Gabriel cuts in: "Anytime you beat a desperate team, that's a great win." Clink nods. "I know you guys are fatigued. Get a lot of rest tonight. I want you to understand the opportunity we have next Thursday night. We have another muskrat coming in. Time to load those guns again." He pauses. "And I don't even think we've peaked yet." Clink had just won his 150th game. And he didn't even know...or care.

CHAPTER 76

Championship Week: Cal State Dominguez Hills

THE WORD OF THE WEEK is urgency. If the Wildcats can beat—and they should, although nothing is guaranteed in this conference—Cal State Dominguez Hills, then they will win the CCAA. That has been Clink's goal all along. The worst that will happen is the Wildcats will share the title with UC San Diego about the only time in this game when there's ever a tie. Clink will say the same thing all week at practice: "Do not settle. Play with great pace." Kitchens has a new position. He works the scoreboard during practice. Briggs rips down three consecutive rebounds. Kitchens shakes his head.

"Justin is going to be unbelievable," Kitchens says. "Look at the size of his hands."

Clink rides Duncan hard this week. "Rob, quit trying to be cute. Do you really have to go behind the back and between the legs?" And a few minutes later: "Lift and attack. Lift and attack. Rebound, who's going to go and get a rebound?"

It's Tuesday, February 23, and Clink witnesses something for the first time in his long career. Cool Marvin walks in (actually, Cool Marvin never walks in—he *glides*). He gingerly puts down a Kleenex box on the scorer's table. Clink, grouchy today, looks at Cool Marvin and shakes his head. He turns to me. "I've been coaching for 18 years, and that's the first time—the first time—any player of mine has ever brought a tissue box to practice."

I bust out laughing, the first time, really, I have laughed around the team. The atmosphere is always that tense.

Duncan comes in and looks ready to play. Ten minutes earlier I saw him speeding by to Acker on his bike. He was sending someone a text as he pedaled. A couple of men are working on the doors beneath one of the baskets. It's almost 1 p.m. Clink's practices never start a minute before or after. Clink keeps looking at his watch. He walks over and hovers around the men as they work. Clink is always polite, a definite friend of the working man, but this makes him angry. This is Championship Week, and here are three men interrupting his practice so they can put one screw in a door. Clink comes back over. His jaw is locked. "Would those guys walk into someone's class room and start doing this at the beginning of class? Can you imagine the uproar?"

Clink's right. This is a classroom. Cool Marvin comes over and grabs a few tissues. He blows his nose with style. Everything he does seems to be done with style. He's coughing and sneezing. He might have allergies, but a bad case of the flu has been circulating. I've seen all of the players have it at one time or another this season. Outside, Chico is experiencing an early spring. Everything is blooming. The men finally secure the door. It's 1:25 p.m. The players meet at the Wildcat.

"We have to practice with purpose and we have to play with purpose," Clink says "We have to work on three things. Offensive rebounds. Dribble attacks. And we have to throw the ball into the post. Every time down we have to play with purpose." A few minutes later, he will check-in with Duncan to see if he recalls the three things. Duncan thoughtfully rattles them off. Clink is pleased.

Thursday, February 23, finally arrives. It's a strange feeling to be playing on a Thursday night, and even stranger when it's for the CCAA (at least a tie) Championship. And even stranger still because the Wildcats have to fly out the next day to Los Angeles to play a team that's playing their best basketball of the year.

The locker room doesn't have the energy of a title game. They gym certainly doesn't with only 840 fans in the stands. Everything feels anticlimactic. The night's mission is simple: beat the worst team in the league for a guaranteed share of the CCAA title. The energy, though, is missing. Coach Blake gives yet another riveting and inspirational speech. "Tonight you guys have a chance to create a legacy. The game will be hard tonight just like it's been hard travelling up and down the state of California for the last four months. Just like all the years you've spent alone in a gym working hard for a moment like this. We've gotten here together. All you have to do is go out there and do the same things you've been doing all year long. You guys have a chance to do something really special tonight."

The locker room is fired up. Outside, though, Acker doesn't feel like a party. The student section is depleted. The players are loose tonight. They dunk with more ferocity during their warm ups than I've seen all year long. Back in the locker room for Clink's pregame talk, he says: "If we only give them 12 three-point attempts tonight, they can't beat us. We have to be in attack mode all night. We have to go inside 40 times. Dribble attacks. If you know you can't get the offensive rebound, sprint back. It's all about our energy tonight. How much passion can you play with? Can you play with passion for 40 minutes?"

The first half is a seesaw. Giddings, McFerren, and Silverstrom can't hit a shot. Clink tells the team during a timeout at the 11:40 mark, the score tied at 8: "I could feel something with you guys all week. I don't know what to tell you guys other than you've gotta communicate more and play with more aggression. Whatever's going on inside you guys, you've gotta pick it up. You've gotta go out there and play." At the next timeout at 7:19, things are looking really bad for the Wildcats.

"You guys need to loosen up. Have fun out there and play with passion. We can't keep getting beat over the top. Have some fun, okay."

The Wildcats, though, despite a chance to make history, to win another championship, are lifeless.

Dominguez Hills will take 26 3-pointers—14 more than the number Clink had given his team—in the first half. They only make eight of them, but that's enough to give them, the worst team in a great league, the lead going into the half at 32-31. The only bright spot in the first half is the five assists by Duncan and Harris's 5-of-5 shooting which keeps the Wildcats in the game.

In the locker room, Ellis speaks out for the first time all year. The sophomore finally has become the vocal leader the team needs. "This is embarrassing," he yells. "Embarrassing. There's no way they should be beating us." I have never seen Ellis angry until now. "If our defense was good, this wouldn't be happening."

Silverstrom says it's about the offense.

"No, we are a defensive team," Ellis says. Ellis has a rag in his hand that he's about to tear into pieces. He's tugging at it. His jaw is set. His eyes are burning. "Those guys are just out there having fun," McFerren says. "They've got nothing to lose. Let's take the fun out of their game. Lock them up and they'll fold." Kitchens can't believe it, either. "Grind it out, guys, grind it out," he says. Briggs watches, listens, patiently waiting his turn. Next year will be big for him.

Clink throws open the door. "Everyone in their chairs," he says, storming to the board. "Here's the basketball stuff first. We're back to just going in there and burping up the ball. You have to jump stop. You have to take A-shots. We only had 16." He takes a deep breath. "Here's the deal. I don't know if it's that we're scared of the moment. I don't know what it is. I'm searching for answers. There's no urgency. We need to talk out there. We need to open our mouths. I just don't get it. We don't have any urgency. What's the deal, guys? Is going out there and winning a championship not urgent? This is what you've all been working for since September. You want to talk about a feeling of regret? Forget about how you felt after the Pomona game. If you play another half like the one you just played, trust me, that's not the kind of regret you want to live with. You're letting the worst defensive team in the league control you. What's the deal? What is it? Wake up!"

Clink looks like he's on the verge of putting his fist through a wall.

Magz stands up. "The bench is scared," he says. "I've been here for five years and this is the worst bench we've ever had."

"We need some urgency," Clink screams. "A go-to-hell attitude or we're gonna be back in this locker room in 20 minutes crying like babies. We need urgency on both ends. If not, well, we'll just have to get lucky. I don't know what else to say. If you're not feeling it, fake it. Fake it! We need toughness. Toughness! Now let's go!"

Silverstrom comes out in the second half with vengeance. He makes a quick 3-pointer. On the next possession he gets a steal. He has the look in his eyes I've seen several times this year, the same swagger, the head shaking, mouthing: "They can't stop me. Can't stop me. Can't stop me." The only person who has been able to stop Silverstrom all year has been Silverstrom. A couple minutes later, right when it looks like he will take over the game, Silverstrom lands hard out of bounds. He hears a pop. He goes down. Tom the trainer has not seen much action all year. He stands there watching while Silverstrom writhes on the other end. "Go, go, go!" Clink yells at him. Tom the trainer sprints toward him. Silverstrom is carried off. He can't put any weight on his foot. Ambrosini runs in for him. Things aren't looking good. The Wildcats are down 36-34, and one of their best players has been carried off on this of all nights—Championship night. The game is slipping away. At the 14:20 mark, Dominguez Hills is up 44-36. But then Clink puts Harris back in and everything changes.

Harris, an unsung hero of the season (whose volatility often concerns me, a little too much Howard Roark as I have always said) who has done the little things (in practice) that most fans never see, will again step up, a young man whose unwavering toughness always shines through when it counts most. He passes well, plays great defense, grabs rebounds, and hits the big threes. The youngster, Ambrosini, will also provide a spark. And Duncan is just Duncan.

When the Wildcats are playing their style of ball, things happen fast.

Duncan makes consecutive baskets, a layup then a three-point play. Dominguez Hills takes a time out to pause and catch their breath. Harris senses the weakness and punches them in the gut with a layup. Then, on the next play down, smacks them again with a 3-pointer that puts the Wildcats up, 46-44. Ambrosini goes to work making his free throws, and right when it looks like Dominguez Hills is trying to get up off the mat, Ambrosini throws the definitive punch, landing another three. The Wildcats will keep pushing the lead by making their free throws. For the second year in a row, the ladder and the scissors will come out in Acker. The Wildcats bench will outscore the Dominguez Hills bench, 34-13.

The Wildcats have guaranteed a share of the title, but first they have business to care of in Los Angeles. If they can win one—just one— on the road there, the title will be there's outright.

Who wants to share a title?

CHAPTER 77

All's Well That Ends Well: Cal State L.A.

SATURDAY, FEBRUARY 27

IT ALL COMES DOWN TO this. If the Wildcats can beat Cal State Los Angeles in the Eagles Nest in front of 530 fans (call it fate or call it coincidence, but that's number in attendance), another number that should have the superstitious Silverstrom (out for the night because of last game's ankle sprain) shaking in his high tops since this is the area code for Chico, the Wildcats will clinch the CCAA title outright. But Los Angeles is tough. Their talent is peaking at the right time. The Eagles have not been playing like a team that is 9-11 in the CCAA. UC San Diego is playing Sonoma State. If the Wildcats lose, and the Tritons win, then they share the CCAA title. If the Tritons lose, then the Wildcats win the CCAA title outright. However, San Diego getting beat by Sonoma State is about as unlikely as Chico State getting beat by Los Angeles.

Anything, though, can happen in the CCAA.

And everything does.

Yes, the truth is indeed stranger than fiction.

Clink has told me time and time again that a lot in basketball comes down to plain old luck. I've seen this several times over the season, no example better than the McFerren Miracle. From the tip-off nothing will go right for the Wildcats. The Wildcats can't buy a shot, and the Golden Eagles sizzle from the field. Duncan only gets off seven shots—all missed but one.

Tonight, the absence of Kitchens and Silverstrom is felt. Magz doesn't even take a shot in the first half. His shooting frustration is revealed in three quick fouls. The Wildcats are blowing their biggest opportunity of the season. At the half, they enter the locker room down, 32-27. They are playing without passion. The 3-point shot is killing them: 1-of-9. Duncan has gone 0-of-4 from the 3-point line. He has also turned it over three times. Ellis keeps the Wildcats alive shooting 4-of-6. The Wildcats have a hard time handling Los Angeles stars Duce Zaid and Joshua Munzon. Los Angeles also turns the ball over just once. The Wildcats, meanwhile, cough the ball up eight times.

The second half doesn't get any better. The Wildcats trail by five with 41 seconds left to play. Ellis, playing one of his best games of the year, gets the Wildcats back within a point with a pair of consecutive rebounds and put backs. Ellis's bucket with five seconds leaves Chico State only trailing by one, 65-64. Duncan, wearing his Superman cape, flies down the court, plenty of time on the clock. He has a good look at the basket. He lets it fly. If the ball goes in, Chico State wins the CCAA title outright. If the ball goes out, they share the CCAA title with UC San Diego. I've seen Duncan make this shot at least 1,000 times since October 15. It's looking like string music.

But it falls off the rim as the buzzer sounds.

The Wildcats walk off the court with their heads hung low. They came all the way down to Los Angeles to share a title. As the Wildcats enter the tunnel, a Chico State player's grandmother leans over the railing and shouts: "San Diego lost! San Diego lost!" Sure enough, while the Wildcats were fighting for their lives with a minute left—surely the thoughts of what they were about to lose swimming in their minds—they had already clinched the CCAA title outright. The Tritons were the ones hanging their heads first.

It was a strange ending to an even stranger season and certainly served as a punctuation mark as to why I had decided to write this book in the first place. I had remarked all along that who knows what'll happen. The only thing I knew was that something *would* happen, but I could not have scripted any of this. The final regular game of this 2015-2016 Chico State season was symbolic of why I had decided to write this book. What had happened here in this last minute represented what I love most about sports—particularly sports that involve teams where nobody really cares about whether they win or lose (let alone knows they even have a game) other than the young men playing the game, the loyal fans, and the family members who love the players.

What agony the Wildcats had felt walking off the court seconds ago, and now what ecstasy they must feel upon hearing the grandmother shout: San Diego lost! How much different that long ride back from Los Angeles will be. And God bless those poor Tritons who had really blown it.

Nobody will remember how the Wildcats won the CCAA Championship in 2015-2016. Record books don't go into that kind of detail. All that will remain is that the Wildcats won the CCAA outright. No asterisk. No confusion over the shared title. It was the Wildcats and no other team that could lay claim to the title. Banners do not have footnotes. The regular season was over.

Clink and his Wildcats had just accomplished what they set out to do last March after the buzzer sounded and they went home vanquished after round one of the Division II NCAA tournament. There was no real luck in the events of tonight. It was all the little things, the three hour practices every day going back to October, the victories in December and January, all the comebacks, that put the Wildcats in this situation. Luck really is the residual of hard work. And the basketball gods rewarded these Wildcats for the heroic feats performed behind the Red Door. Yes, the basketball gods smiled upon the Wildcats periodically throughout the year. The players and the coaches and the trainer and the managers and the writer, it turns out, were not the only ones who knew how hard the Wildcats worked behind that closed Red Door Monday through Thursday.

It was one hell of a season. Ebbs and flows. Waxing and waning. Pace and stillness. A blood moon. Unscripted drama despite the relentless practice and preparation and choreography. Agony and ecstasy and the thrill of victory and the desolation of defeat. Miracles. Fortune. Misfortune. Laughter and tears. Shoves and hugs. Jazz, rap, and country music. Organic. Unedited. Pure spur of the moment-dang-good-old fashioned fun.

PART V

Postseason

Postseason

THE 2015-2016 WILDCATS PEAKED A month early in February when they beat UC San Diego on the homecourt of the Tritons. The Wildcats never seemed to recover from the loss to Cal Poly Pomona on ESPN 3. They went on a slide after beating Cal State Dominguez Hills at home for the CCAA championship. Cal State L.A. would beat them once more in Chico in the first round of the CCAA tournament, after beating them a few days prior down in Los Angeles, giving the Wildcats a scare before learning that UC San Diego had lost and given Chico State sole claim to the CCAA title. However, UC San Diego would get revenge and finish off the Wildcats' dream season on Friday, March 11, 2016, by bouncing them from the first round of the NCAA West Regional Championship tournament, 76-74. This would be the last time Christopher Magalotti and Tanner Giddings would lace-up for the Wildcats. Drew Kitchens, meanwhile, watched from home.

Despite losing the last three games of the season, the Wildcats not only won the CCAA title outright, but Coach Greg Clink would be awarded Conference Coach of the Year for the second straight year (three-time recipient in the last five years), and junior Robert Duncan would become the CCAA Player of the Year. He would also become only the second player in Wildcats' history to earn consecutive First Team All-CCAA honors and the first player to be named All-West Region in consecutive seasons. Duncan was also named Fourth-Team All-America—one of twenty players—out of more than 300 NCAA Division II college basketball programs.

Clink will wake up at 3:43 a.m. on March 12, 2016, less than 12 hours after his (still) young Wildcats were bounced from the NCAA Division II tournament. *Frasier* will not calm his thoughts: *What will I do next year without Magz, Giddings, and Kitchens? Wait—I don't have to worry about that. All my guys but these three are coming back. I have every starting position covered including back-ups who could start for any other team in the CCAA. And Robert Duncan will be a senior. No, that's not what worries me. It's the expectations that worry me. If we can have the kind of year we just had with all these young guys, and they're all coming back, we'll have the expectations of being great, and can we live up to those expectations?*

The 2016-2017 season nearly started with what many considered the impossible. Whereas the Chico State Wildcats were crushed by the University of Arizona Wildcats the previous year 90-54, they would almost knock off the highly ranked Division I powerhouse this time around. At one point, Chico State was up by 12 points and would go into the half behind, 40-37. Chico State would give the University of Arizona the scare of a lifetime. Ellis would hit back to back jumpers in the paint as the clock was winding down to cut the Arizona lead to 69-68 with 1:03. The McKale Center was not filled with the "Bear Down" chants from fans, but the sound of pace maker alarms going off—a one-possession game with less than a minute to play. In the end, the University of Arizona would prevail, 78-70. Redshirt freshman Justin Briggs did not feel timid on the big stage as he finished with 8 points, 3 rebounds, and a block in 16 minutes. Preseason All-American Robert Duncan, no longer sporting the man-bun, would finish with 16 points, 4 rebounds, and 2 assists. Jalen McFerren snatched 9 rebounds to accompany his four assists and zero turnovers in 29 minutes. Ellis and Silverstrom picked up where they left off last season. The Wildcats seemed poised to run the table in the CCAA. But this is the CCAA, and anything—as you know from just having taken this journey with the team—can happen in this league.

The Wildcats had many bright spots in the 2016-2017 season—winning ten straight from December 3 until January 21 when their nemesis, Cal Poly Pomona, broke the streak. After two more wins, the Wildcats got derailed from what was looking like a straight path to their third consecutive CCAA title. While one year ago the Wildcats had reached their season apex with a road win against UC San Diego, this February the Wildcats would reach the nadir of the season with three straight losses. The Wildcats would pick themselves up from the ground and finish strong by winning four straight, but their disappointing third place finish in the CCAA left many wondering if the Wildcats would even make the NCAA tournament. There was even talk that the Wildcats might need to win the CCAA tournament to guarantee their sixth consecutive entrance into the NCAA tournament. UC San Diego would beat the Wildcats in the semifinals of the CCAA tournament, 65-53. The Wildcats would have a tense week wondering about their fate, hoping for a chance to make up for not fulfilling their regular season expectations by exceeding their postseason expectations.

The Wildcats' dream at a run in the NCAA tournaments was fading. The team gathered at Mom's Restaurant on Sunday night to watch the NCAA Championship Selection Show, only to hear 63 teams called that were not Chico State. Finally, when all hope seemed lost, the 64th team was announced: The Chico State Wildcats would represent the No. 6 seed out of eight in the West. And the committee did the Wildcats no favor by pitting them against one of the best teams in the country, third-seeded and the No. 12 ranked Western Washington Vikings, who had the best offense in the West Region.

The Wildcats blew the Vikings away, 96-83. Isaiah Ellis, no longer the sixth man from the season before, was becoming a full-blown starting star with 20 points and 10 rebounds. Cool Marvin, who played sparingly the season prior, had 12 points. Nate Ambrosini no longer exhibited his freshman timidity from the year prior and scored 11 off the bench, as did Michael Bethea, Jr.—the senior transfer from Grambling State who didn't even play basketball in high school. Jalen McFerren was flawless with 16 points while Robert Duncan and Corey Silverstrom each had nine points. And the redshirt freshman man-child Justin Briggs gobbled up seven rebounds and had eight points.

The Wildcats next faced the No. 4 ranked team in the country and No. 2 seed Hawai'i Pacific Sharks, one of the most dangerous teams in the nation having won eight straight. Robert Duncan, though, was not about to let this be his last game wearing a Wildcats jersey. Neither was Michael Bethea, Jr. who was taking every advantage of the second-chance Clink had offered him. Silverstrom, McFerren, Duncan, and Ellis also had big games. But it was the senior transfer Bethea, Jr. that came up big. He scored eight points in two minutes, knocking down clutch-free throws and sealing the win with a steal. The Wildcats would now have a chance to avenge top-seeded UC San Diego to become the NCAA Championship Tournament West Region Champions, and do it on the Tritons home court in front of their fans and end the illustrious career of a Tritons star. The winner would punch their ticket to the Elite Eight in Sioux Falls, South Dakota.

This would be the night that Isaiah Ellis, the young man who would not be here were it not for Chris Cobb, would become a star—the struggles of the shy kid who redshirted his freshman year, the young man who cited Tim Duncan, not LeBron James, as his hero—and reach the full potential Clink now knew was within him. Ellis could not miss on this night. He scored an incredible 34 points and had 14 rebounds. Clink would later say it was one of the best performances he had ever seen from someone wearing a Chico State uniform. But despite the heroics of Ellis, it was a complete and total team effort. Silverstrom would score 18 points in the final 9:56. He willed the Wildcats to victory. Briggs, no longer playing like the redshirt freshman I had watched for a year do battle with Giddings and Magz, had become his own man scoring 10 points on 5-of-6 shooting.

Cool Marvin, Ambrosini, McFerren, and Duncan (quiet performance with eight points and three big steals) all stepped into their roles and got the big win: 95-86. Ellis was named the Tournament's Most Outstanding Player and Silverstrom was named to the All-Tournament team. The Wildcats had done the unthinkable—unthinkable to all but those who wore the Chico State jersey. In a span of four days, the Wildcats had knocked off three of the best teams in the country. Just like that, the unmet expectations of the 2016-2017 had been erased.

March 22, 2017, would be the last time Robert Duncan would ever wear number 5 for the Chico State Wildcats. Lincoln Memorial University out of Tennessee was just too much for the Wildcats to handle on this night; they would win, 74-61. Duncan would walk off the floor of the Sanford Pentagon in Sioux Falls, South Dakota, with the final statistics of his collegiate basketball career: 18 points, six assists, and five rebounds. Duncan finished his overall collegiate career with 1,237 points (8th in school history), 289 assists (5th), and 152 steals (3rd). Duncan—who had been so troubled as a freshman—had grown into a truly accountable young man who had become one of two players in Chico State history to score more than 1,000 points and have 200 assists and 100 steals. He also became the 16th Wildcat in history to hit 100 career 3-pointers. All this and he only played in nine games his freshman year.

Robert Duncan had not only lived up to the Pistol Pete potential I had pinned on him back in his freshman year, but transcended that potential. He unselfishly reigned in his own talent for the good of the team; he bought into the role Clink had assigned him and made everyone around him better. Duncan graduated not long after his last game. He is currently living in Sacramento and working out with long-time training legend Gus Armstead. Duncan is hoping to play professionally.

Christopher Magalotti graduated after the 2015-2016 season and is working in San Francisco as a skilled trade recruiter for Aerotek.

Tanner Giddings graduated after the 2015-2016 season and hung out in Chico for a spell, working with the Wildcats and coaching the Bidwell Junior High seventh graders to a local championship. He recently signed a professional contract with the Vaerlose basketball club in Denmark.

Drew Kitchens, after having his heart ripped out that spring semester of 2016, came back in the fall semester 2016, finished up his coursework, and graduated. He moved back to San Diego. He is working for Mulligan Funding as a business lending consultant.

Coach Lucas Gabriel took an assistant coach position with the Metropolitan State University of Denver Roadrunners.

Coach Justin Blake is no longer serving as Clink's assistant. He received a promotion to become a manager at Round Table Pizza, and he will also focus on finishing his undergraduate degree.

And for Clink, well, the Division I offer finally arrived.

Not long after Clink led his Wildcats to the Elite Eight, a story came out from *The Oregonian* that the Wildcats nation knew would eventually come—just not so soon and before they had won a National Championship: "Portland State Vikings Zero in on Basketball Coach Hire, Target Greg Clink." The news spread quickly. Yes, Clink had been pegged as the head coach to take over the Division I Big Sky Conference Portland State Vikings where he would have the job of filling the stands of the upcoming $50 million Viking Pavilion that was being built and would seat 5,000 fans. Rumors also began to circulate that Clink might take his former mentor's position, Bob Williams, as the head coach at UC Santa Barbara, who was calling it a day after 19 seasons. Clink's likely departure was all over the news and social media.

For two weeks, the Chico State players and all the Chico State family and fans were on the edge of their seats. I thought for sure Clink would leave. How could he turn down this offer? More money. Division I. One of the best cities in the country. But like so many people I had gotten wrong throughout the process of writing this book, it turned out that I had misjudged the very man I spent a year shadowing. Clink—without any drawn-out drama on his end—withdrew his name from the Portland

State University head coaching position. His four starters who would all be returning, three of them seniors (McFerren, Ellis, and Silverstrom) were overjoyed. So, too, was the rest of his team and the Chico community as a whole. In the end, as it always is with Clink, his decision to stay and coach at his alma mater came down to family—both his own and his basketball family. Clink's wife Courtney has a thriving business here. His three sons are happy in school and have great friends. And Clink is returning every one of his players next year except Robert Duncan and Bethea, Jr.

As the last lines of this book are being written, the news of the day is that ten Division I college basketball assistant coaches have been or will soon be arrested—including Book Richardson of the University of Arizona, the 2017-2018 preseason number one ranked team in the country, and who the Wildcats will again play this year—and indicted by federal authorities for allegedly accepting bribes to push players toward potential moneymakers such as Adidas and financial advisers. The great Rick Pitino of Louisville has just been fired. How could these head coaches not have known what was going on? Had I not followed Clink and his Wildcats for a year, I might have wondered—even given a head coach a pass per reasonable doubt—that perhaps they didn't know. But I know from watching Clink day in and day out that a head coach is in on everything.

I once thought that ESPN coming to watch the Wildcats validated why I put so much work into this project. After that magical season ended with three straight losses, and I searched for an ending to the book—one that I would receive a year later during the Wildcats' magical run to the Elite Eight—I again felt justified for taking up this project that occupied so much of my mind, body, and soul, particularly when the Division I offer came for Clink, and when he pulled an Atticus Finch and spurned the offer for loyalty to family over pay. But as these latest reports come out about the cheating and corruption and mendacity of these Division I powerhouses start to surface and the truth is revealed, I feel more legitimate than ever about spending what has now turned into three years of my life to tell the story of this coach, the program he built, and the honorable student-athletes that day after day, year after year, walk through that Red Door and go beyond.

Oh, and if you were wondering about me, remember all that pain I kept complaining about after playing ball with the old dudes in Shurmer Gym? Well, that pain, too, was justified. I finally went and visited an orthopedic surgeon. He put me on the table, went through fifteen seconds of range of motion movements, pulled up my X-rays and pronounced: "You need two hip replacements, son."

Ah, life. Just like the game of basketball, so unpredictable—unscripted drama that is whole and complete and of a certain magnitude, a truth that will always be stranger than fiction.

The End

67877047R00281

Made in the USA
San Bernardino, CA
27 January 2018